LOGIC® 7 IGNITE!

By Orren Merton
and Don Gunn

THOMSON
COURSE TECHNOLOGY
Professional ■ Trade ■ Reference

A Thomson Course Technology Professional, Trade, Reference Publication

LOGIC® 7 IGNITE!

Publisher and General Manager of Course PTR: Stacy L. Hiquet
Associate Director of Marketing: Sarah O'Donnell
Marketing Manager: Kristin Eisenzopf
Manager of Editorial Services: Heather Talbot
Senior Acquisitions Editor: Todd Jensen
Marketing Coordinator: Jordan Casey
Project Editor/Copy Editor: Rodney Wilson
Technical Reviewer: Len Sasso
PTR Editorial Services Coordinator: Elizabeth Furbish
Interior Layout Tech: Danielle Foster, Scribe Tribe
Cover Designer: Mike Tanamachi
Indexer: Kelly Talbot
Proofreader: Dan Foster, Scribe Tribe

ISBN: 1-59200-542-X

Library of Congress Catalog Card Number: 2004117709

Printed in the United States of America

05 06 07 08 09 BH 10 9 8 7 6 5 4 3 2 1

THOMSON
COURSE TECHNOLOGY
Professional ■ Trade ■ Reference

Course Technology PTR,
a division of
Thomson Course Technology
25 Thomson Place
Boston, MA 02210
http://www.courseptr.com

Acknowledgments

Orren Merton wishes to Acknowledge:

First of all, there's no way I would have been able to undertake *Logic 7 Ignite!* right on the heels of *Logic Pro 7 Power!* if it were not for the hard work, dedication, skill, and good nature of my friend and co-author Don Gunn. There is also no way I could have found the strength to finish this project without the grace, love, and support of Michelle, my mother, and my always faithful Shadow and Luna.

Don Gunn wishes to Acknowledge:

I must thank Orren for asking me to join him on this publishing journey and giving me some excellent guidance along the way. He's a consummate professional and a great friend. I also must extend my most humble gratitude and love to my wife, Kirsten, for putting up with the late nights and early mornings, and being my anchor through it all.

Both Orren and Don wish to Acknowledge:

We wish to thank Dr. Gerhard Lengeling, Thorsten Adam, Sascha Kujawa, and everyone at Emagic GmbH, both for their part in creating and developing this amazing program, and for their part in including us in the process! Further, we would like to thank the Emagic Betatest Community and Logic Users Group for their insight and support.

No book is produced alone. We'd like to thank Mark Garvey and the entire Course Technology crew for their support with this book. We would also like to give special thanks to the editors who were by our side for the entire journey: Todd Jensen and Rodney Wilson, our Acquisitions and Project Editors respectively; and Len Sasso, for his friendship, knowledge, and for keeping us honest!

Dedication and About the Authors

To Michelle

To Kirsten

Orren Merton, author of *Logic 6 Power!* (Muska & Lipman, 2003), *GarageBand Ignite!* (Muska & Lipman, 2004), and *Logic Pro 7 Power!* (Course Technology PTR, 2004) has been a musician and Macintosh user since his days at U.C. Berkeley in 1988. He has been writing in the professional audio field for more than five years, for numerous American and British pro audio magazines, such as *Electronic Musician*, *Computer Music*, and *MIX*. He has a master's degree in English from California State University, Long Beach. Orren is involved with many companies in the pro audio field, writing manuals and testing hardware and software. He also helps moderate the Logic User Group, an online community of more than 15,000 Logic users.

Don Gunn is a recording engineer and Mac fanatic based in Seattle. He contributed Expert Tips to *Logic 7 Power!*, but this is his first foray into (co)authorship. He is a founding member and moderator of The Mix Posse, an online gathering place of engineers and producers. When not trapped behind his computer mixing, testing various software, or consulting on all matters Mac and Logic, Don gets in touch with his analog side by playing drums, cycling, and spending time with his wife.

Contents

As mentioned on the cover, you can find the following bonus chapter and two appendixes on the companion Web site at http://www.courseptr.com/downloads.

Introduction

Apple Computer's digital audio sequencer, Logic, has a long and storied history. From its humble beginnings as a MIDI-only application called Notator Logic, to its ascendance to the heights of professional respect as Logic Audio on the Macintosh and Windows platform, to its current incarnation as Logic Express and Logic Pro, Logic has been one of the most dynamic and exciting programs in the rise of computer music. Countless songs, albums, and film soundtracks have been written and/or recorded using Logic, and the program just keeps getting better!

In many ways, Logic 7 is the most profound update to Logic in many years. It's the first version developed entirely since Apple Computer bought Emagic, Logic's producers, and it has much of the cutting edge look and feel of Apple Computer's Professional Application Suite. In a way, you can think of Logic 7 as the first version of the "new, improved Logic." Same amazing power and flexibility, but now with more "Apple Computer" style elegance. By the time you finish this book, you will hopefully agree!

Who Should Read This Book?

This book is for anyone who wants to learn how to use Logic. If you are upgrading from GarageBand to Logic Express, upgrading from Logic Express to Logic Pro, or are completely new to digital audio sequencing, this book will help you understand how Logic works. This book doesn't presuppose you have any knowledge of music theory or digital audio conventions. But if you do have knowledge of music theory or digital audio software, you will find it even easier to follow the exercises in this book. Logic has a reputation for being very complicated, but, as you will discover as you read this book, once you understand how Logic does things, it's simple...and you'll never look back!

1 Installation and Basic Configuration

Before you can start making music with Logic 7, you'll need to install and do some basic hardware and software configuration. You'll find installing Logic similar to installing any other Macintosh application, with the possible difference of there being so many files that get installed! You will also need to have your audio and MIDI hardware connected properly to your computer, and you'll have to configure Logic to access them.

If you are updating to Logic Express or Logic Pro from GarageBand, keep in mind that while GarageBand didn't require you to set up your workspace, Logic does. With GarageBand, the Default Song is the same no matter what. Since Logic offers you so many more options, you need to instruct Logic what your default song should look like. Don't worry if that sounds complicated—it's easy once you get to it, and Logic gives you a setup wizard, the Logic Setup Assistant, to make it even easier. In this chapter, you will learn to:

- Confirm your OS version
- Check your system RAM
- Install Logic 7
- Install the Logic 7 demo songs
- Install the Logic 7 manuals
- Put an alias of Logic 7 in your dock
- Run the Logic Setup Assistant

Checking System Requirements

Logic 7 requires a fast and capable machine to run. Apple Computer's minimum requirements for Logic Express and Logic Pro are a Macintosh with a G4 or G5 CPU and 512MB of RAM, although a dual G4 or G5 is recommended. All current models of Macintosh computers have at least a G4 chip, although they don't necessarily have enough RAM. Logic 7 also requires Mac OS X 10.3 (also called "Panther") or newer. Mac OS X 10.3 ships with all current models of Macintosh.

If you are not sure if you have the minimum system you need, this first section will explain how you can check. Conveniently, the About This Mac window offers all of this information.

1. Click on the Apple icon at the top left of the menu bar. The Apple menu will appear.
2. Click on About This Mac. The About This Mac dialog window will open.

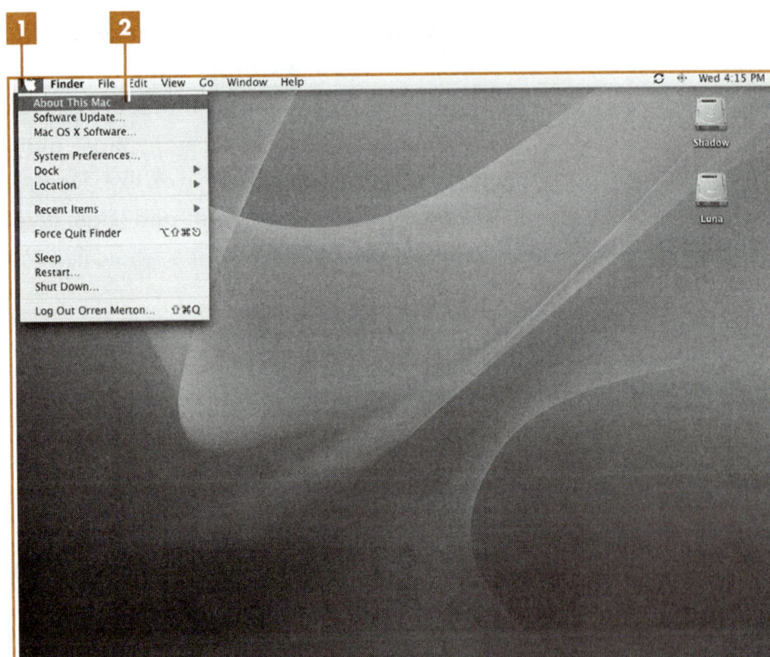

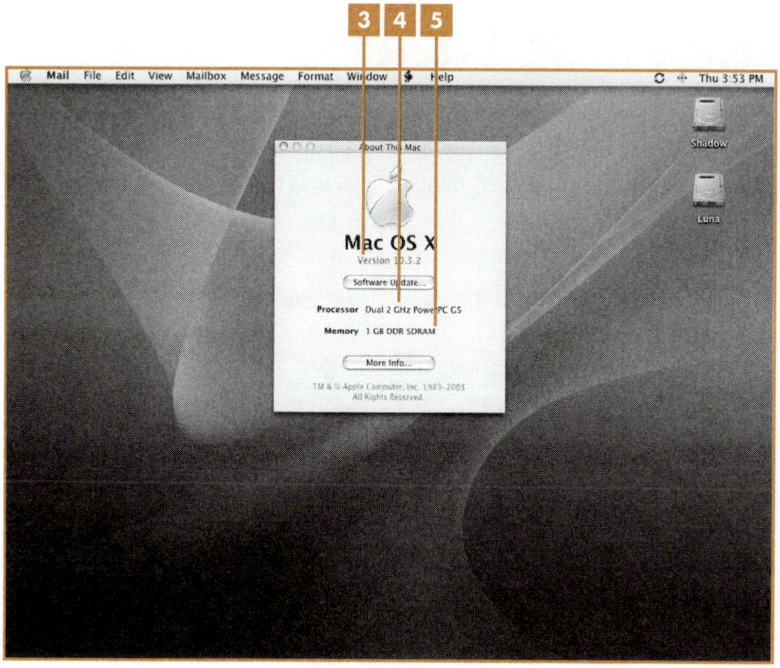

3 **Confirm** that your version of OS X is 10.3 or later.

4 **Confirm** that your Macintosh has at least a G4 CPU.

5 **Confirm** that you have at least 512MB of RAM in your computer.

More power, Scotty!

What happens if your system doesn't meet the minimum requirements? Logic might still operate, but not well. Many software instruments will not work if your CPU is not at least a G4, and if your system does not have enough RAM, you might find that your computer can't keep up with the demands Logic 7 places on it. We highly recommend that you upgrade to a faster Macintosh if you don't have a G4, and that you add RAM to your system if you have less than 512MB RAM.

And speaking of RAM, keep in mind that the listed minimum requirements are just that—the bare minimum. To get the best possible performance out of Logic, you should have as much RAM in your machine as possible. I have 1GB of RAM in my G5, and many other Logic users prefer to have 1.5GB or even 2GB of RAM, if possible. RAM isn't that expensive these days, and you won't regret having lots of it!

Installing Logic 7

Apple works diligently at making its software installation process as simple as possible, and installing Logic Express or Logic Pro is a relatively straightforward procedure. Just following the onscreen instructions will guide you through installing Logic and its helper files. However, it will not install the demo songs or documentation, which will be explained in subsections below.

Installing Logic Express 7/Logic Pro 7 Install DVD

The easiest way to install Logic Express 7 and Logic Pro 7 is to choose the Easy Install options. This will make sure that you have all the Instruments, Samples, and Apple Loops that come with Logic. If you already have GarageBand installed, Logic will not need to install those Instruments, Samples, and Apple Loops already installed with GarageBand.

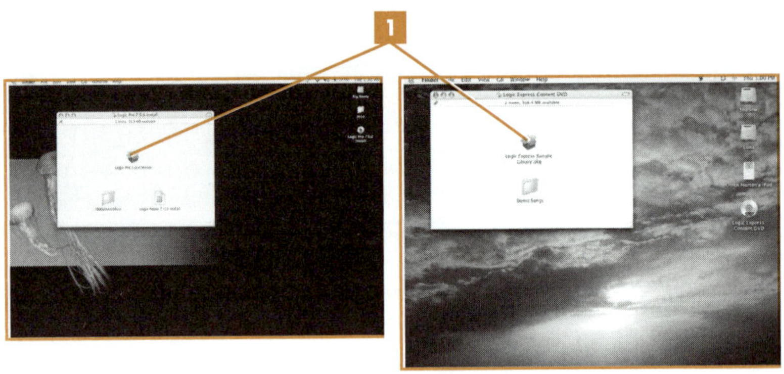

1. Insert the Logic Pro 7 Install DVD (or Logic Express 7 Install DVD) into the DVD drive. The Install DVD icon will appear on the desktop and the Install DVD dialog box will open to show you its contents. Double-click on the Logic Pro 7.0.0 Install (or Logic Express 7.0.0 Install) icon to open the installer.

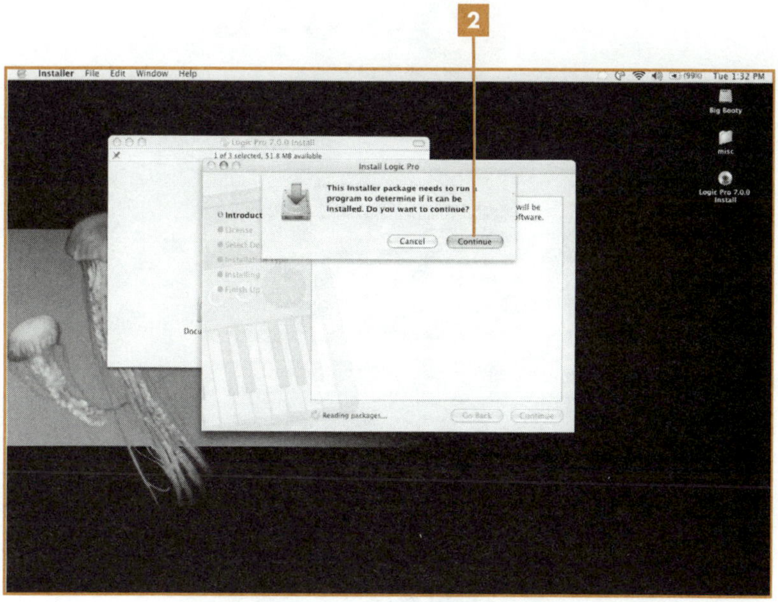

2 Click on Continue in the small window that descends from the main installer window. The system will run a program to determine if Logic 7 can be installed, and the small window will close.

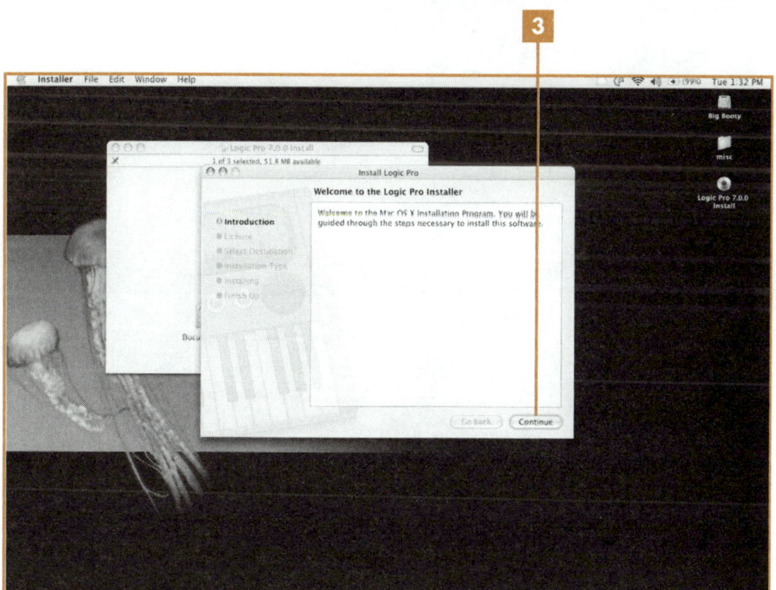

3 Once the system confirms that Logic 7 can be installed, click Continue.

4 Read through the License Agreement. Click Continue.

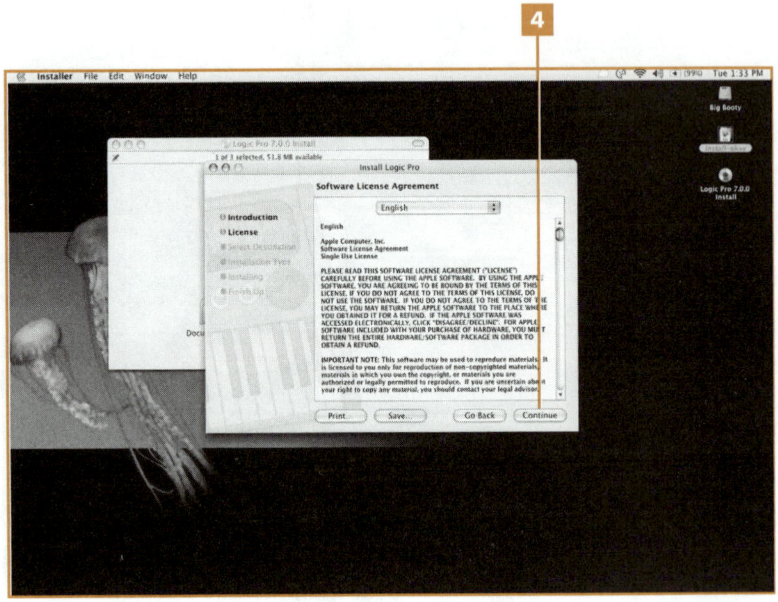

5 Click Agree to consent to the License Agreement.

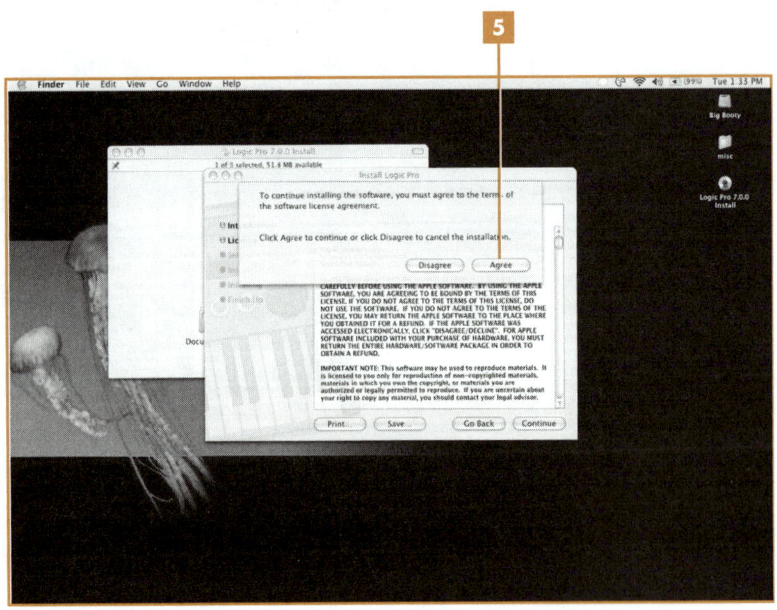

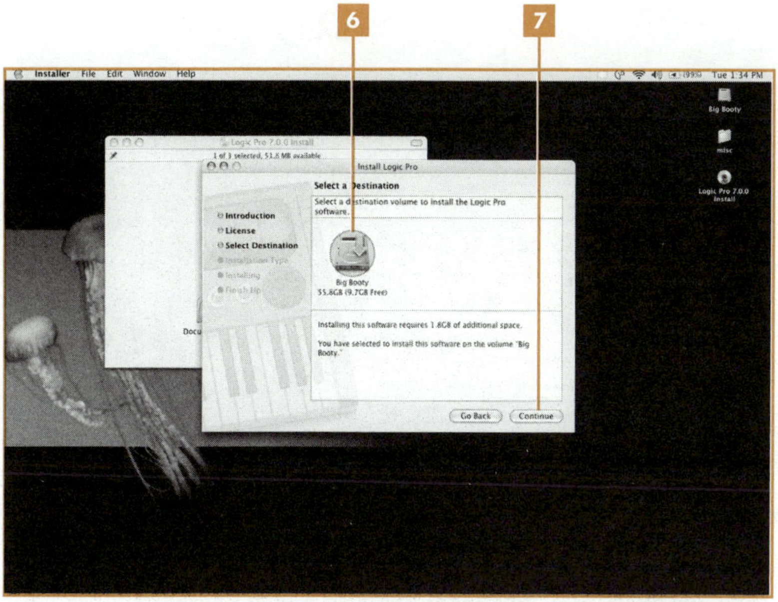

6. **Select** the appropriate **drive** on your computer for installation.
7. **Click Continue.**

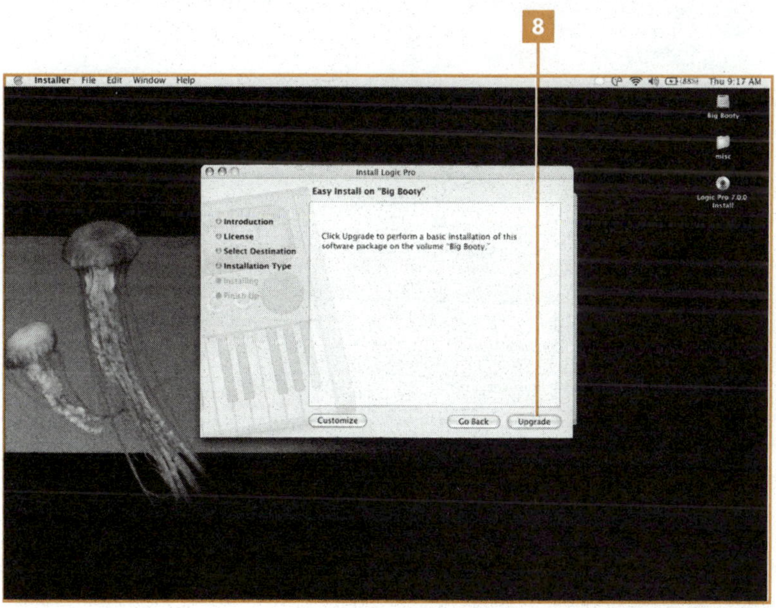

8. **Click Upgrade** (if you are upgrading from an earlier version of Logic) or **Install** (if this is the first time you have installed the application).

Do I Want to Do a "Custom Install" of Logic Pro?

Logic Pro gives you the option to do a "Custom Install" of specific components from the complete Logic Pro 7 contents. We *highly* recommend that you do not choose this option unless you are an experienced Logic user upgrading from a previous version of Logic, or you know exactly which components you are missing.

9 Enter **your** password.

10 Click OK.

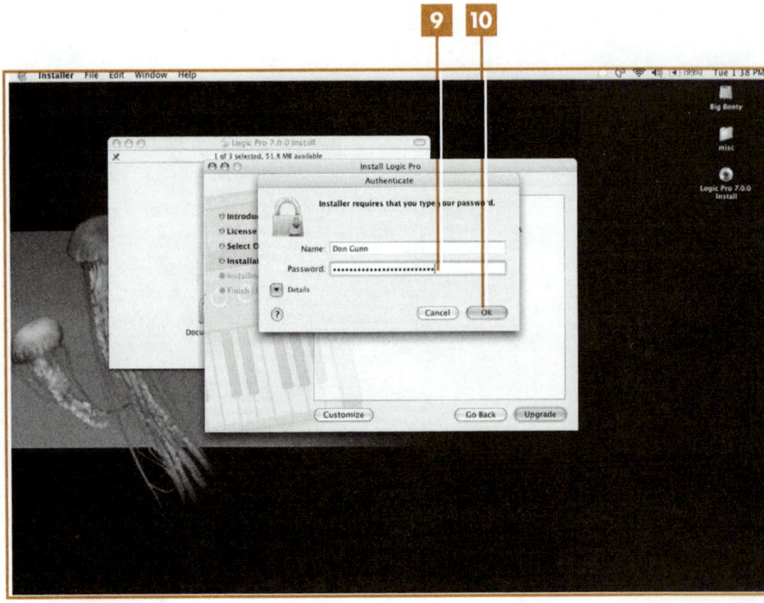

Why Do I Need to Enter My Password to Install Logic?

As with all Mac OS X applications, the installer acts as a "surrogate administrator," placing files where they need to go. As part of Macintosh OS's security system, no application or installer is allowed to act as a surrogate administrator until a user with administrative privileges gives it permission to do so. So in order for the installer to be sure you have administrative privileges, it asks you to authenticate your password before it actually does any installing.

If you do not have administrative rights on the Macintosh onto which you wish to install Logic 7, you will not be allowed to continue with the installation. In this case, either find a user with administrative privileges to install Logic or ask an administrator to set up your user account with administrative privileges.

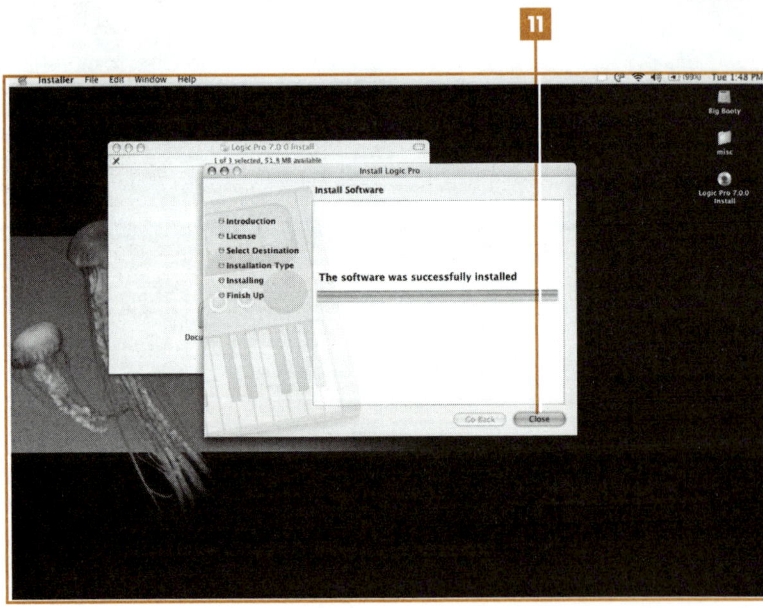

11 Click Close **once the software is successfully installed.**

Installing the Logic Express/Logic Pro 7 Content DVD

Apple includes an entire DVD filled with high quality supplemental content that you'll want to install to get the most out of Logic. These extra Instruments, Samples, and Apple Loops install as easily as any GarageBand Jam Pack. If you don't have GarageBand installed, the DVD will install both the Logic 7 Sampler Instruments and Apple Loops, and the GarageBand set of Software Instruments and Apple Loops. If you already have GarageBand installed, Apple will not re-install the GarageBand instruments and loops, and your install will take less time.

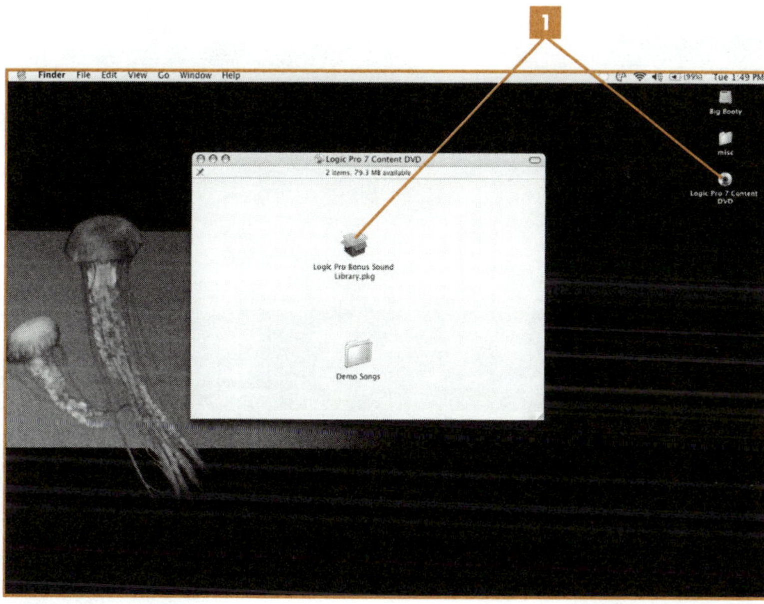

1 Insert the Logic Express or Logic Pro 7 Content DVD. The DVD icon will appear on the desktop and the Install DVD dialog box will open to show you its contents. Double-click the Logic Pro Bonus Sound Library icon or Logic Express Bonus Sound Library icon to open the installer.

2 Read the Introduction and click Continue.

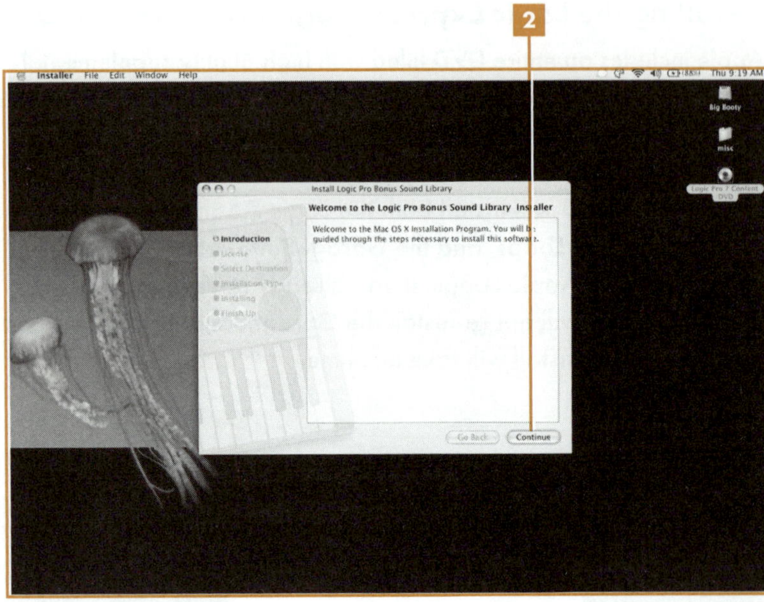

3 Read through the License Agreement. Click Continue.

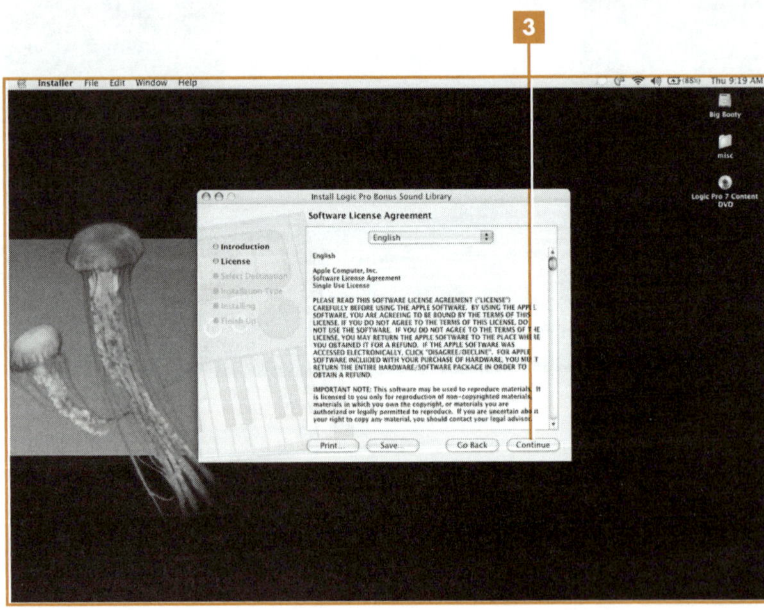

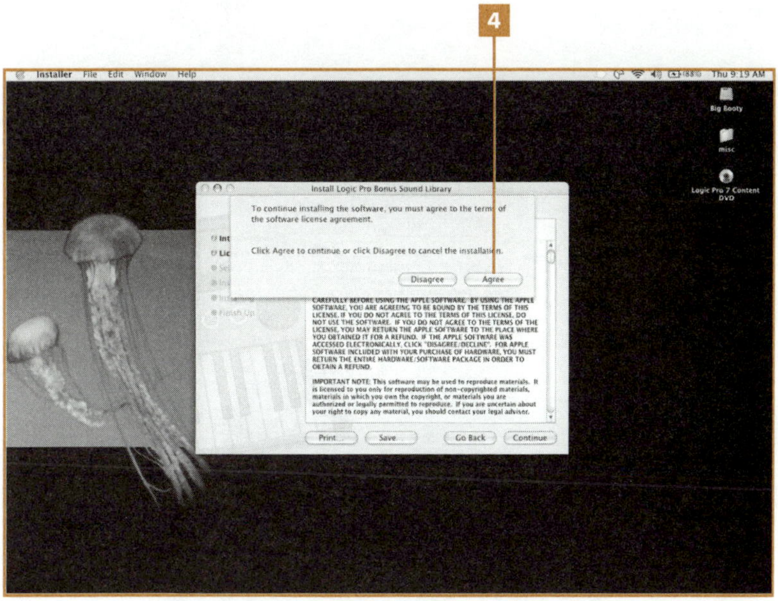

4 Click Agree to consent to the License Agreement.

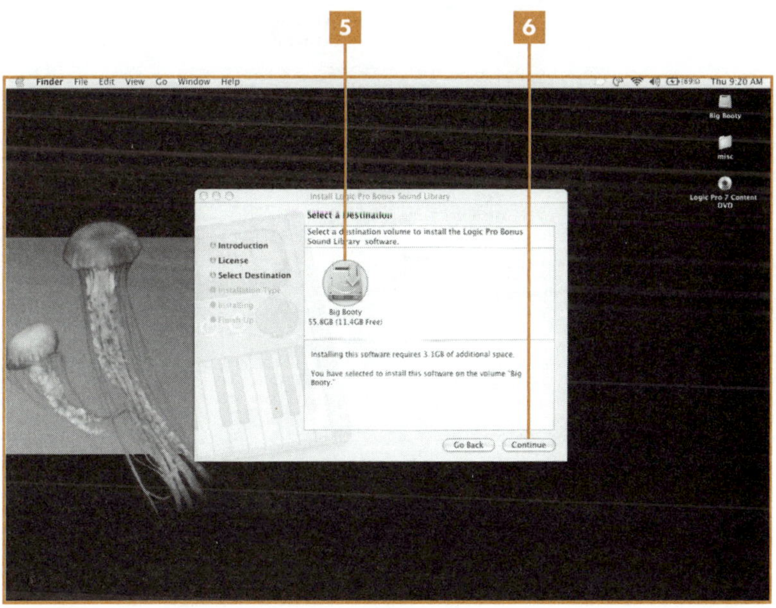

5 Select the appropriate drive on your computer for installation.

6 Click Continue.

7 Click Install (if a new installation) or Upgrade (if upgrading a previous installation) to install the Bonus content.

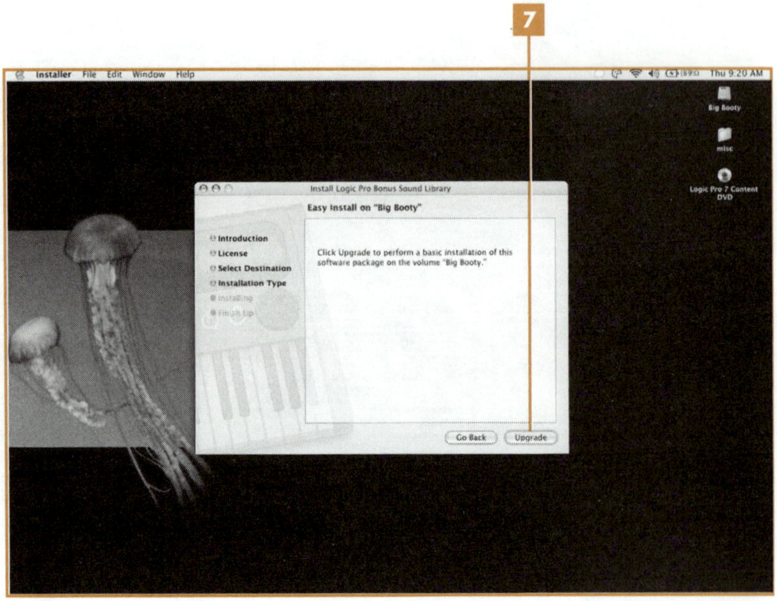

8 Enter your password.

9 Click OK.

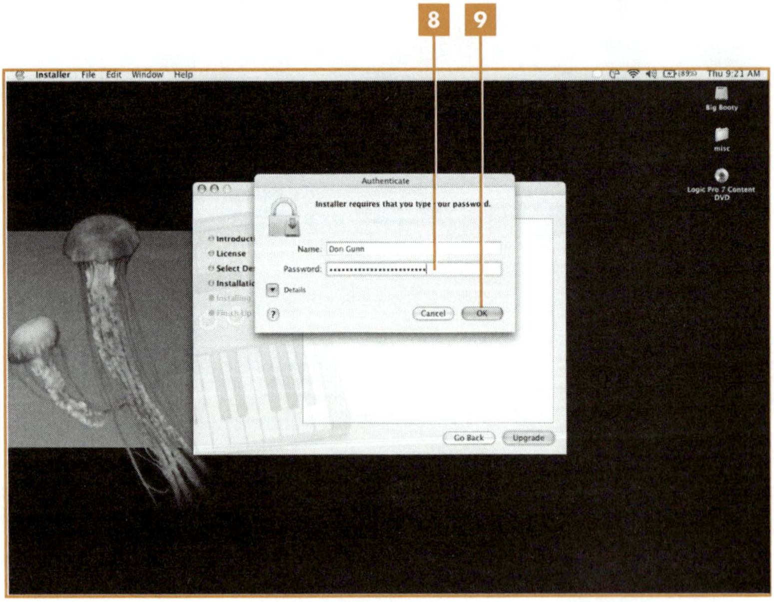

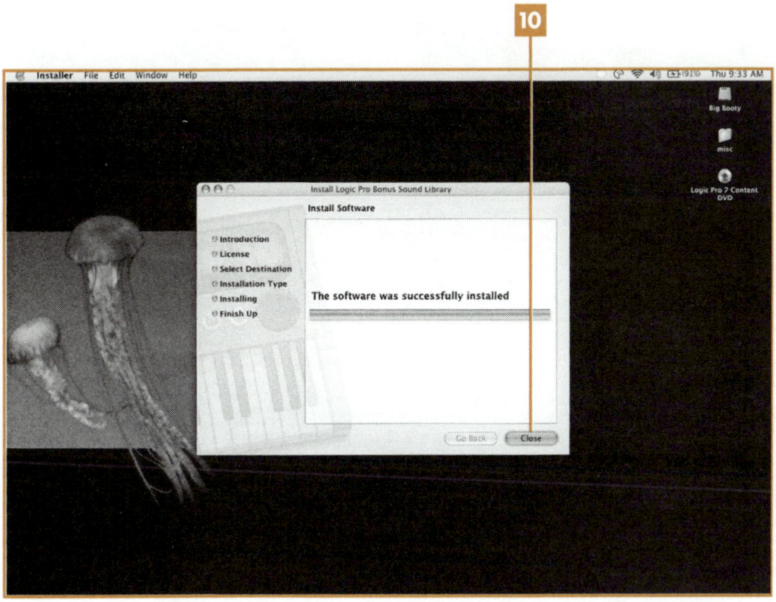

10 Click Close once the software is successfully installed.

Why Would Logic Install GarageBand Instruments, Samples, and Apple Loops?

One of Logic 7's features is that it will automatically open any GarageBand song. This allows you to use GarageBand as a simple, intuitive sketchpad, and then open your song in Logic 7 for more serious editing and production. To ensure this works, Logic 7 includes all the support files that come with GarageBand. Keep in mind that if you try to open a song created in GarageBand that utilizes some of the additional content from the GarageBand Jam Packs, you'll want to have those Jam Packs installed on your Logic computer as well.

Installing the Logic 7 Demo Songs

The Logic installer does not automatically install the Logic 7 demo songs. If you want to install the Logic demo songs yourself—*which we highly recommend you do*—you will need to copy the folder onto your hard drive.

1 **Move** the **Demo Songs** folder to your hard drive. Click it once to select.

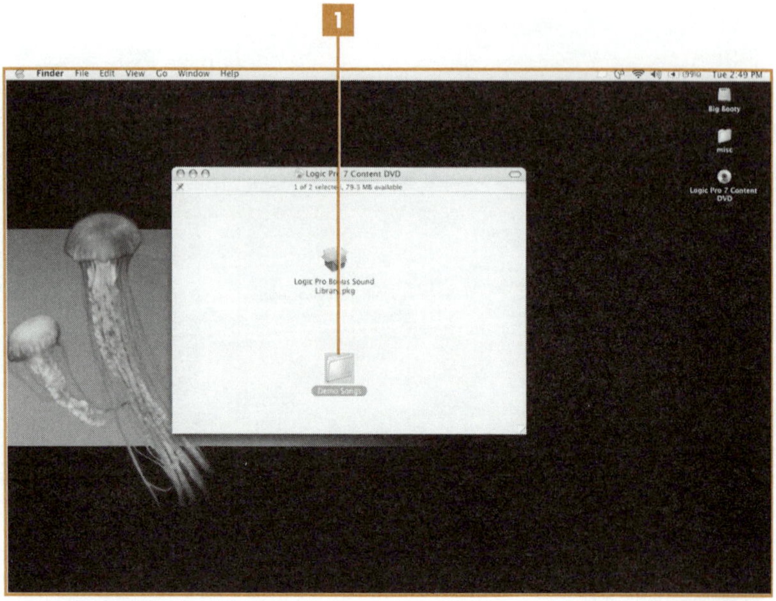

2 **Drag** the **folder** and drop it on your drive.

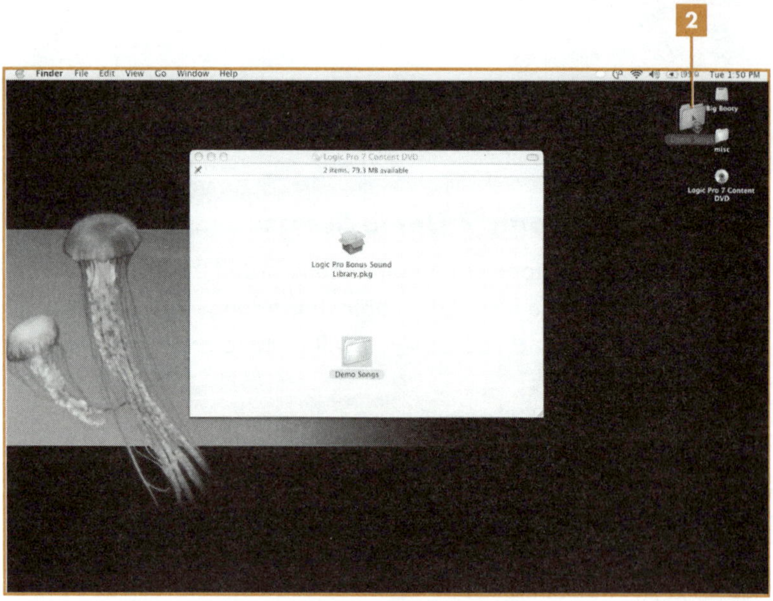

Installing the Logic 7 Documentation

While you can access the Logic manuals from Logic's Help menu, the Logic installer does not install the stand-alone version of the Logic 7 documentation. Again, we highly recommend that you manually add the documentation yourself, so you can access the Logic 7 documentation at any time, not just when Logic is running. To do this, you simply drag the Logic Documentation folder from the Install DVD to your hard drive.

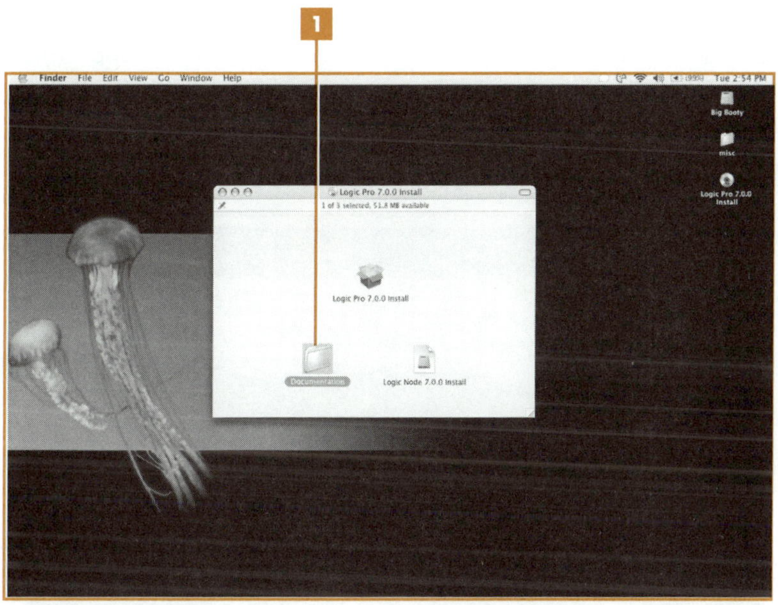

1 Drag the Logic Documentation folder to your hard drive.

Putting an Alias of Logic 7 in Your Dock

The Logic 7 installer will place the Logic Express 7 or Logic Pro 7 application icon inside your Applications folder in your hard drive. Personally, we find it a little tedious to always have to open a Finder window and navigate to the icon inside the Applications folder every time we want to use Logic. Instead, we put an alias of Logic in the Dock, so that it's always just a single click away. You can do this by dragging the Logic Pro or Logic Express application icon to the Dock.

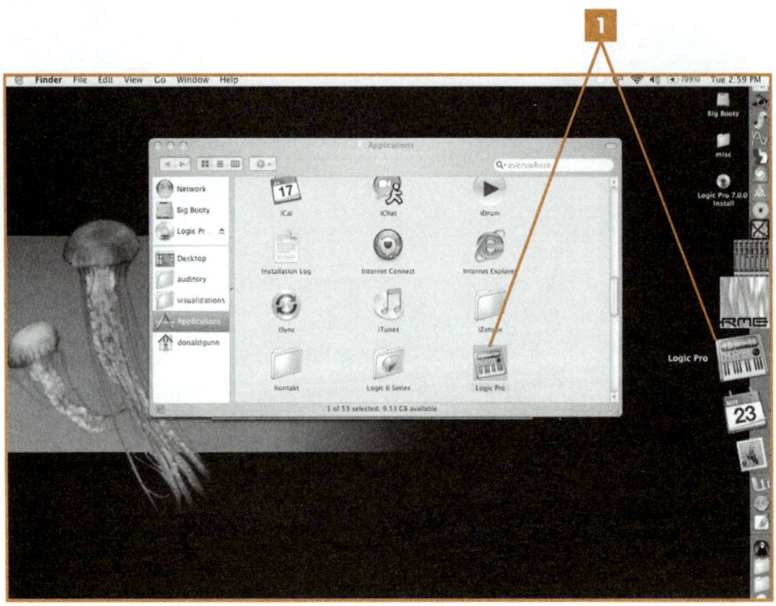

1 Drag the Logic Pro or Logic Express application icon to the Dock.

Does the Alias Have to Be in the Dock?

We have put an alias for Logic in the Dock, because that's how we like to work. However, if you prefer to double-click aliases on your desktop, you can do that easily enough as well. Simply select Logic and choose the menu command File > Make Alias (or press COMMAND + L, or use the context menu). This will give you an alias file, which you can drag to your desktop.

Running the Logic Setup Assistant

You have Logic installed, your XSkey is inserted into an empty USB port on your Macintosh (or a connected USB hub), and you've followed the instructions that came with your audio and MIDI hardware to install its drivers properly. Now you're ready to tell Logic about your hardware and what kind of mixing environment you will need. Logic includes an easy-to-use setup wizard, called the Logic Setup Assistant (LSA), to walk you through this process. The LSA will automatically ask to be run the first time you launch Logic.

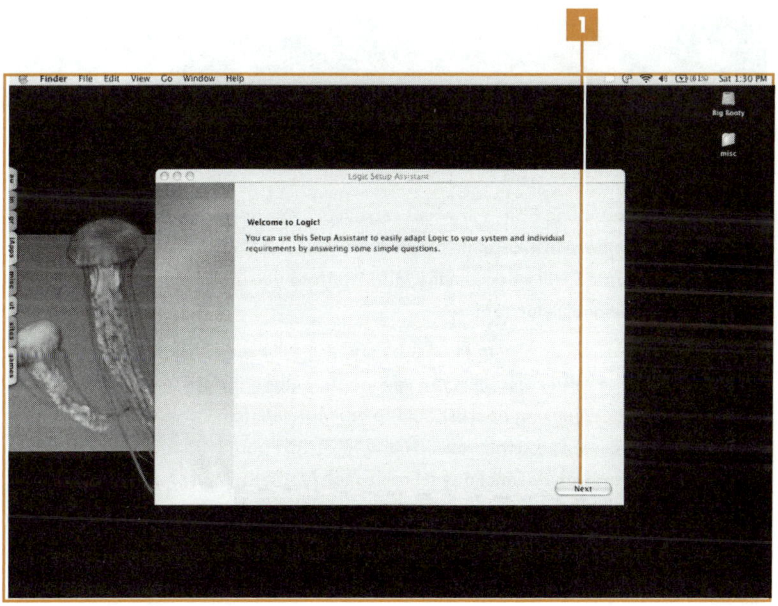

1 Read the overview on the first screen of the LSA and click Next.

2. If you have already installed your audio and MIDI hardware, choose the first option. If you want to install it after setting up Logic, choose the second. It is recommended that you install your hardware options first.
3. Click Next.

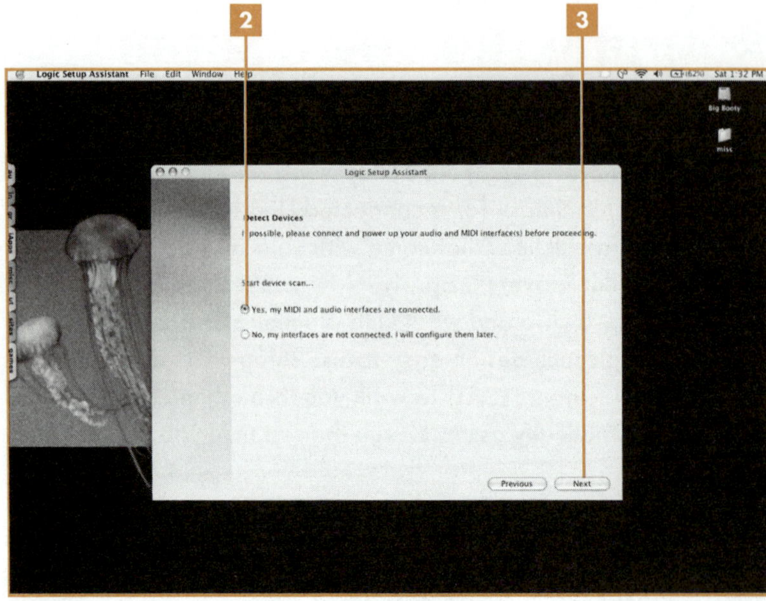

What MIDI Hardware Do I Need?

If you are upgrading from a previous version of Logic or GarageBand, or are coming from another MIDI-capable application, you most likely already have a MIDI interface. Logic 7 will work with the MIDI interface you have been using previously, with no additional setup required.

If you are completely new to MIDI software, you will need to buy a MIDI Interface in order to use MIDI controllers like keyboards, outboard sound modules, software control surfaces (mixing boards), and so on. MIDI interfaces come in all sizes, from interfaces with a single MIDI IN and MIDI OUT port, to rack-mountable multi-port interfaces with advanced synchronization functions. Many MIDI controller keyboards and audio interfaces these days also include one or two MIDI IN and MIDI OUT ports as well.

Which MIDI interface you'll need depends on how much MIDI hardware you want to use with Logic 7. If you just have a single controller keyboard you want to use with Logic, the built-in MIDI interface of the controller or the built-in MIDI port(s) of your audio interface might be enough. If you have a significant number of controllers or hardware sound modules (for example, you might have a MIDI synthesizer, a rack-mounted sound module or two, a MIDI drum controller, and a software mixer), you'll definitely want to get one of the multi-port controllers.

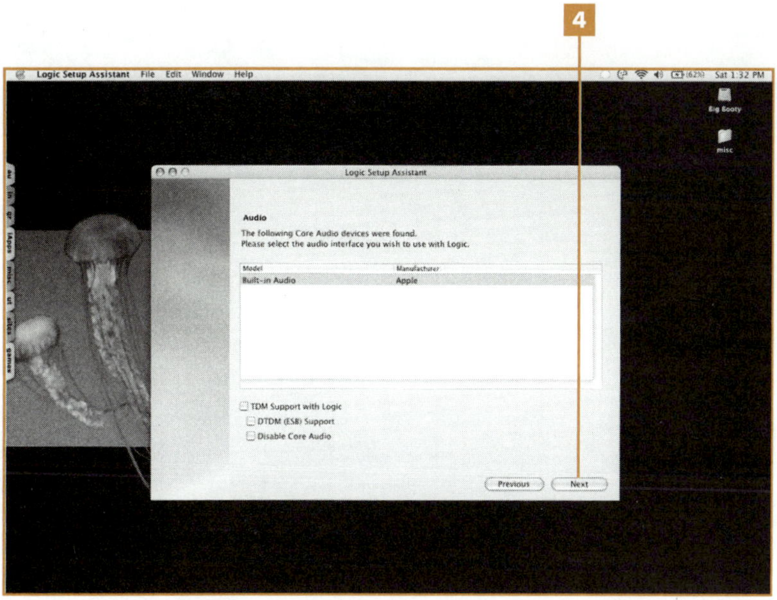

4 Your installed audio devices should appear here. If you don't have any external interfaces, Logic will default to your computer's built-in audio. Select your device and click Next.

What Type of Audio Interface Do I Need?

If you already have an audio interface that works with OS X, it will work with Logic 7. If you intend to buy one for the first time, there are many options these days for audio interfaces—so many, in fact, that the choice may seem overwhelming. It is beyond the scope of this book to offer you a hardware buying guide, but here is some advice to consider.

First, you need to determine how much recording you plan to do. Do you see yourself just recording your own performances? An interface with a single stereo input would be fine. Will you be recording entire rock bands? In this case, you'll need at least 8 inputs and, depending how many microphones you like to have on drums, maybe more like 16-24 inputs.

Nobody wants to buy an interface with poor quality, of course, but these days, even inexpensive interfaces offer 16-bit CD-quality sound. You may want a 24-bit interface with built-in microphone preamps, higher sample rate capability, and so on, but there's no need to buy more interface than you need, and there are multiple options at every price point.

Audio interfaces connect to your Macintosh in different ways. Do you want a plug-and-play USB or FireWire interface, or a PCI card that you need to install into a desktop machine? Keep in mind that laptops and iMacs don't have PCI slots, so your only options are USB and FireWire.

Finally, you'll need to take your budget into account. You can buy audio interfaces for under $100 or over $5000! You want to buy the best quality you can, but you also don't need to pay for 8 channels of mic preamps and 192kHz sample rate capability if you'll never use it! Remember that you can always upgrade your audio interface later as your needs and budget increase—you're not locked into whichever interface you choose now.

5 Here you will configure Logic's Audio Mixer. You can choose some preset configurations of channel strips from the drop-down menu, or create a Custom setup.

6 When you're done, click Next.

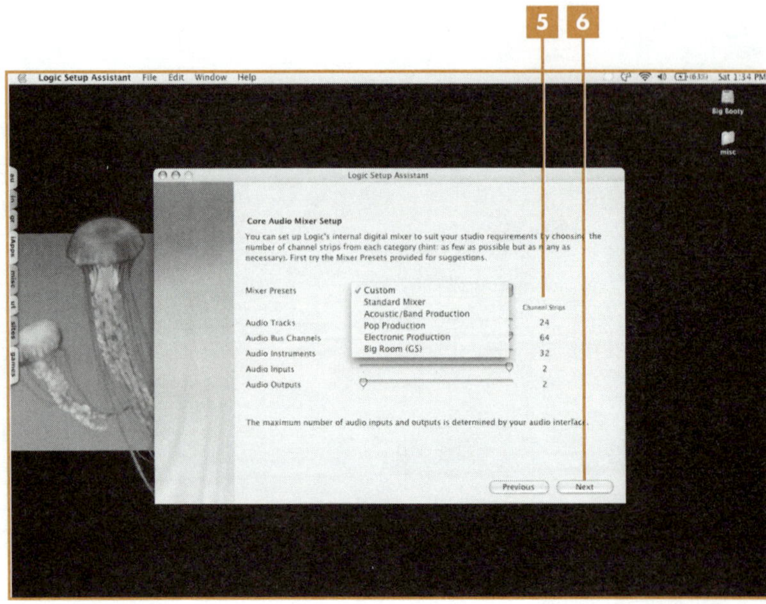

What Are These Different Channel Strip Options?

Chapter 11, "Mixing Your Project," will explore the various channel strips in detail. Here, however, is a brief description of what the various types of channel strips are.

Audio Tracks: These are the equivalent of Real Instrument tracks in GarageBand. These tracks allow you to record and play back audio data.

Audio Bus Channels: These channels accept audio signals from one channel strip, such as an Audio Track or Audio Instrument, and allow you to either process that audio or send it to another type of channel, such as an output or auxiliary channel.

Audio Instruments: These are the equivalent of Software Instrument tracks in GarageBand. These tracks allow you to use software instruments.

Audio Inputs: These channels represent how many inputs you wish to use from your audio interface's available inputs. You can never select more Audio Inputs than physically present on your interface, but you do not have to select every input.

Audio Outputs: These channels represent how many outputs you wish to use from your audio interface's available inputs. You can never select more Audio Outputs than are physically present on your interface, but you do not have to select every input.

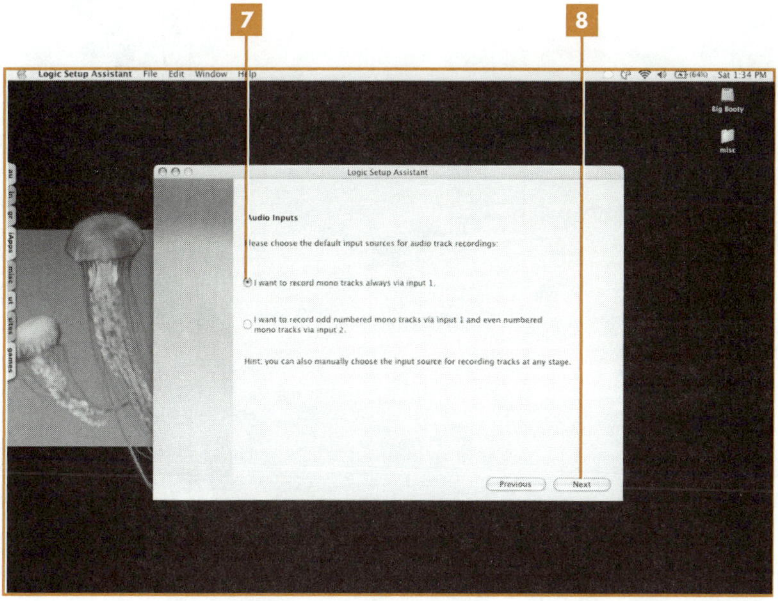

7 Set up your interface's default inputs.

8 Click Next.

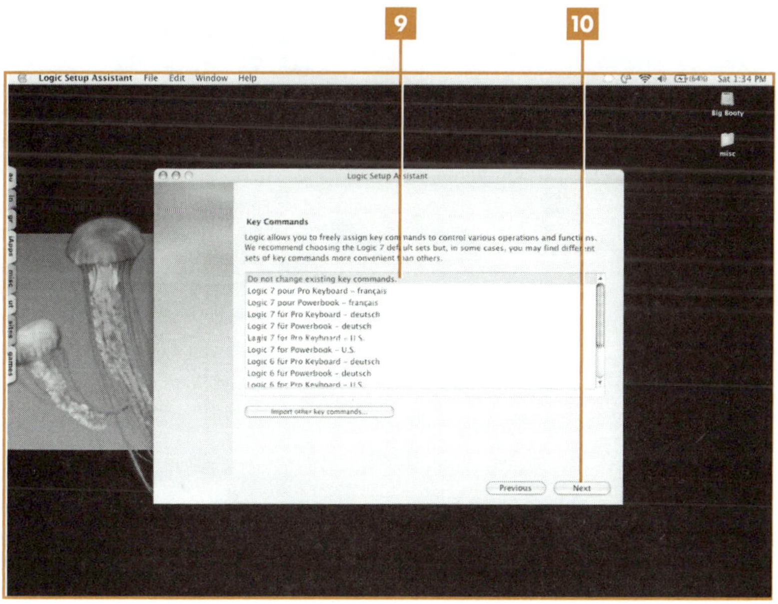

9 Choose a set of Key Commands for Logic to use as a default. If you haven't created your own customized key command set in a previous version of Logic, choosing the default Logic 7 key commands is a great starting set.

10 Click Next.

11 If you have multiple displays hooked up to your computer, you can choose which ones are used for Logic's Screensets.

12 Click Next.

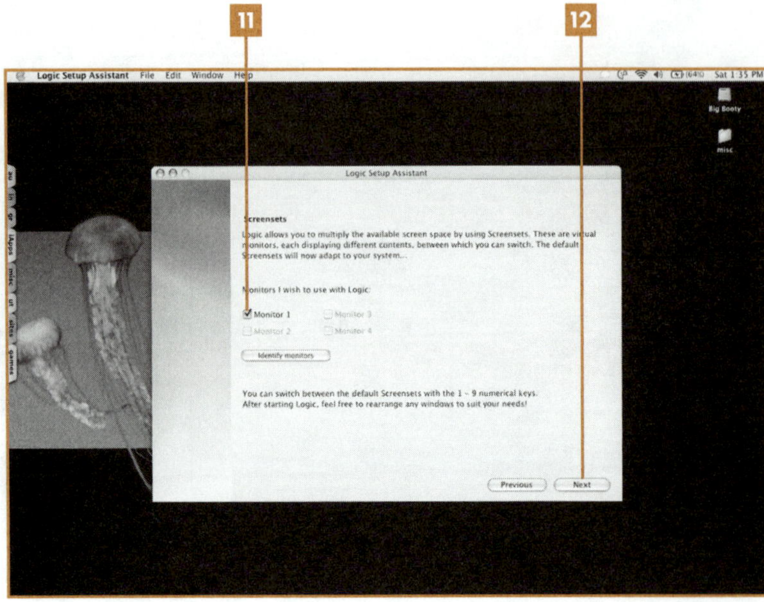

13 If you have a MIDI interface hooked up to your computer, click Add.

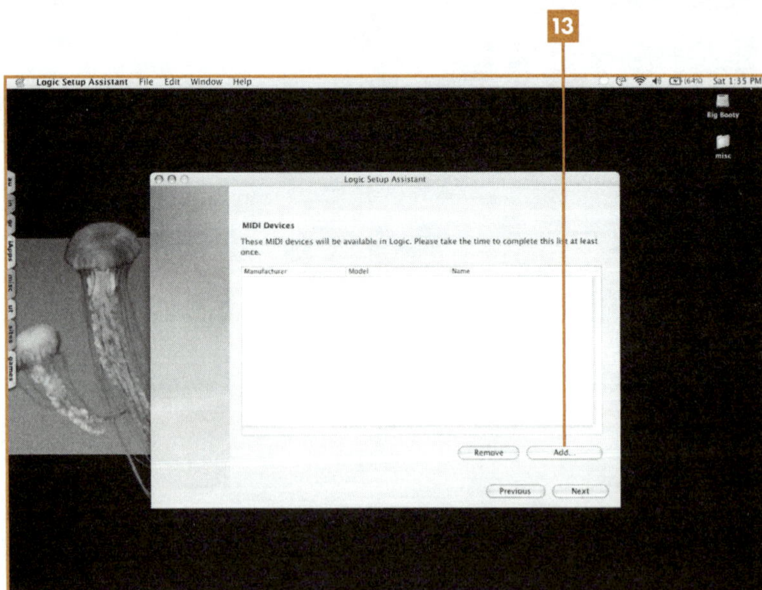

MIDI Devices and the Audio MIDI Setup Utility

If you have already used the Audio MIDI Setup utility included with Mac OS X to configure your MIDI setup, all that information will automatically be entered here. Just click Next to continue.

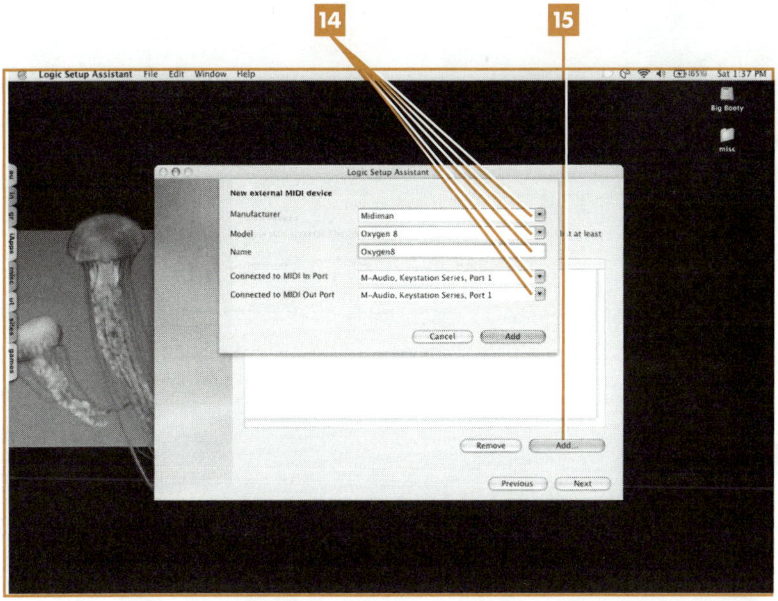

14 Enter the information for your MIDI interface.

15 Click Add.

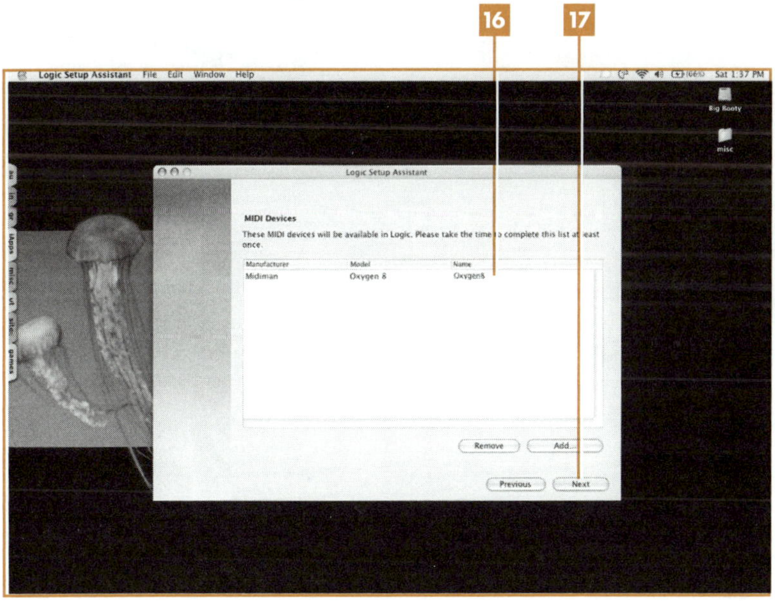

16 Your interface should now appear in the MIDI Devices window.

17 Click Next.

18 Congratulations! You can now click Finish to complete the Logic Setup Assistant and start Logic.

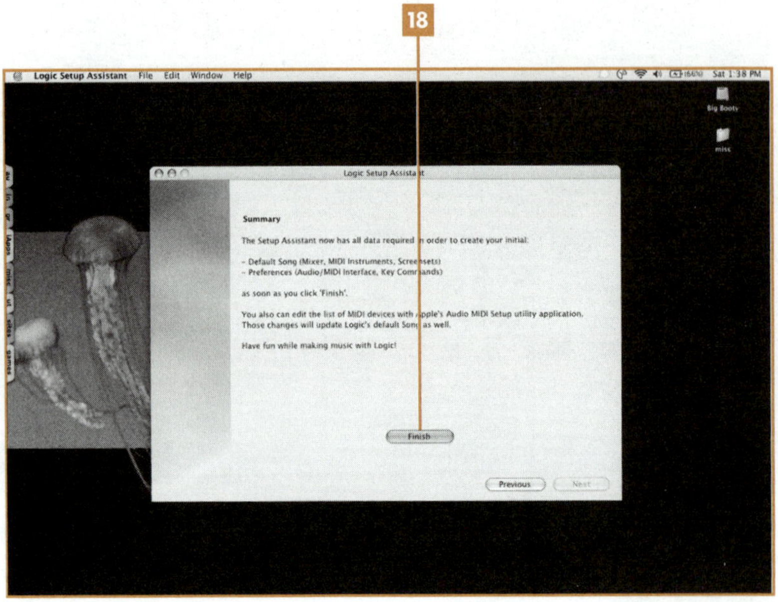

2 Basic File Management

Now that Logic 7 is installed, you're probably eager to check it out! Whether that means exploring one of the excellent demo songs included with Logic, opening one of your own GarageBand or Logic songs, or starting a new project from a song template, one of the first things you'll need is a few pointers on the fundamentals of file management and the Default Song in Logic 7. Logic includes some amazingly powerful file and media management features in the Project Manager, which we'll touch on in Chapter 13, "Advanced Topics in Logic 7," but for now, we'll stick to the basics. In this chapter, you will learn to:

- Open a Logic 7 demo song
- Open a song previously created in GarageBand or Logic
- Create a new Project in Logic
- Save your Logic Project
- Open and save song templates
- Configure Logic to open the most recent Logic song automatically

The Default Song

When you first launch Logic 7, it will automatically open a blank song called the Default Song. This is a basic Logic song template that Logic generates based on how you configured Logic in the Logic Setup Assistant, which we covered in Chapter 1. This song is designed to be a very basic starting point; nonetheless, since it's the first view of Logic you'll see, a brief overview follows.

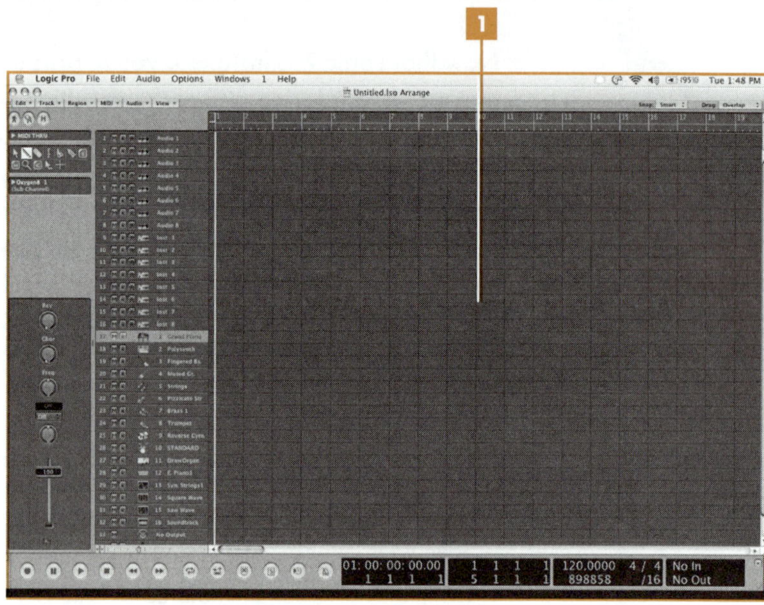

1 The Default Song

Why Is It Called Untitled.lso?

You'll note that the Default Song is called "Untitled.lso" on its title bar. It is named "Untitled" because you have not yet saved it with a title, and the extension ".lso" stands for Logic SOng.

Logic 7 Global Menus

Logic offers a number of Global menus. These menus are broadly grouped into categories based on the functions contained within each menu. Keep in mind that Logic Express 7 does not have all the menu options that Logic Pro 7 does.

1 **Logic Pro (or Express) Menu**: This menu contains options for hiding and unhiding Logic, as well as Logic's preferences, key commands, and control surface handling.

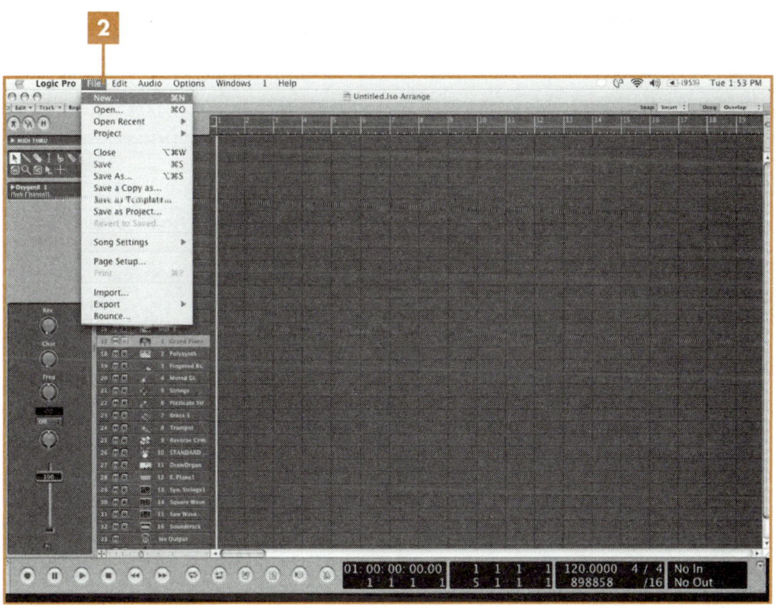

2 **File Menu**: This menu contains options to create new songs and projects, open existing ones, and save copies of songs, as well as bouncing and exporting tracks, regions, songs, and MIDI data.

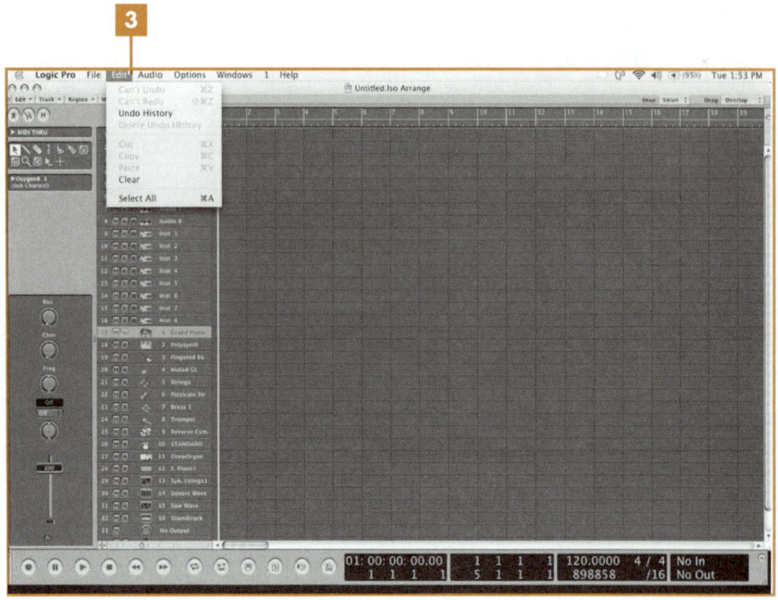

3 Edit Menu: This menu is similar to most Macintosh Edit menus with the standard Cut, Copy, and Paste commands, but also included are the abilities to Undo, Redo, and view an Undo History.

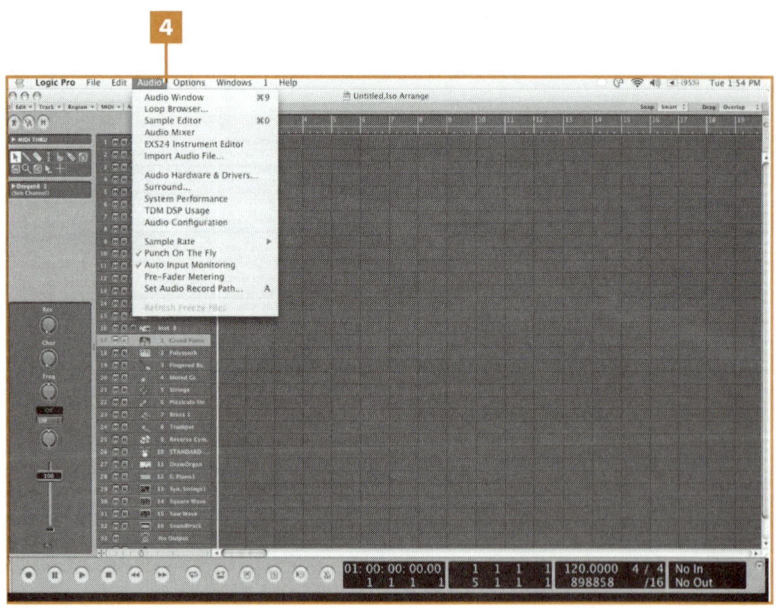

4 Audio Menu: This menu is where you set a project's Sample Rate, access the settings for your audio hardware, set a path for audio files, and handle general audio preferences.

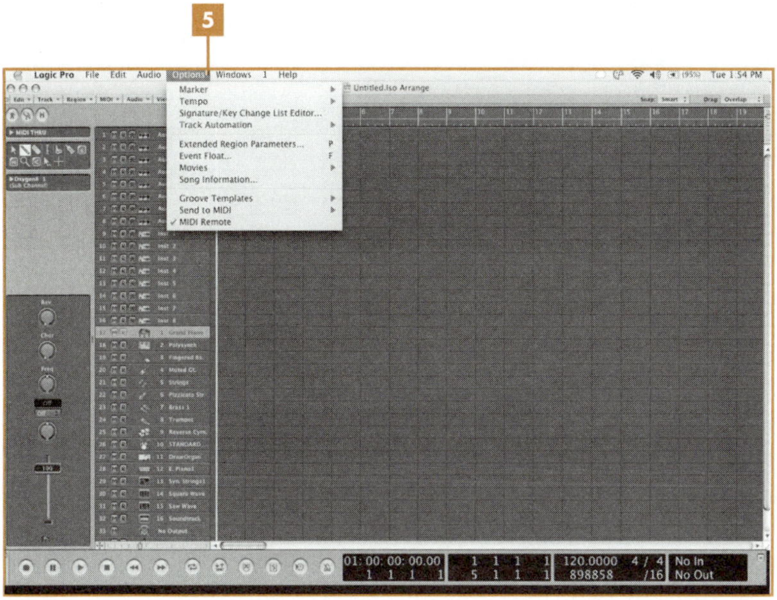

5 Options Menu: This menu provides access to Marker, Tempo, and Automation functions, as well as Groove Templates and Movie options.

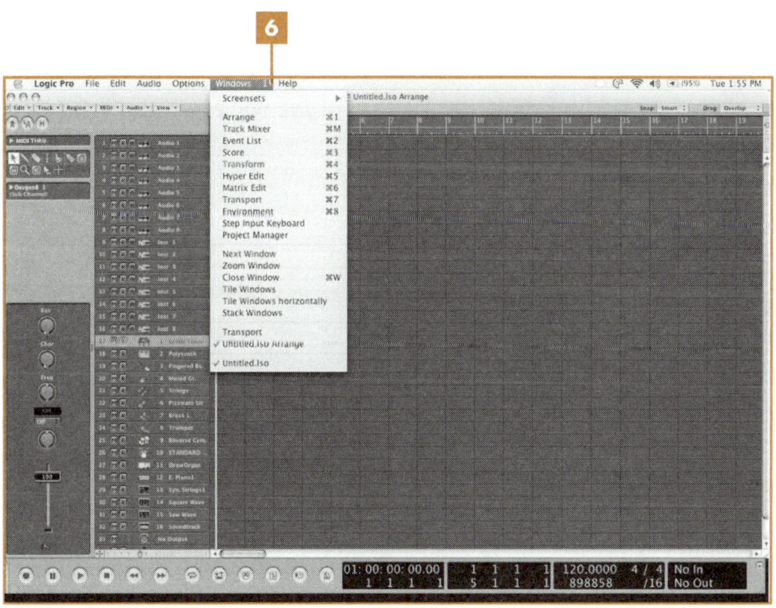

6 Windows Menu: This menu shows all open windows in the currently open file(s), allows for Screenset management, and has some shortcuts to commonly used windows such as the Track Mixer, Event List, and Matrix Editor.

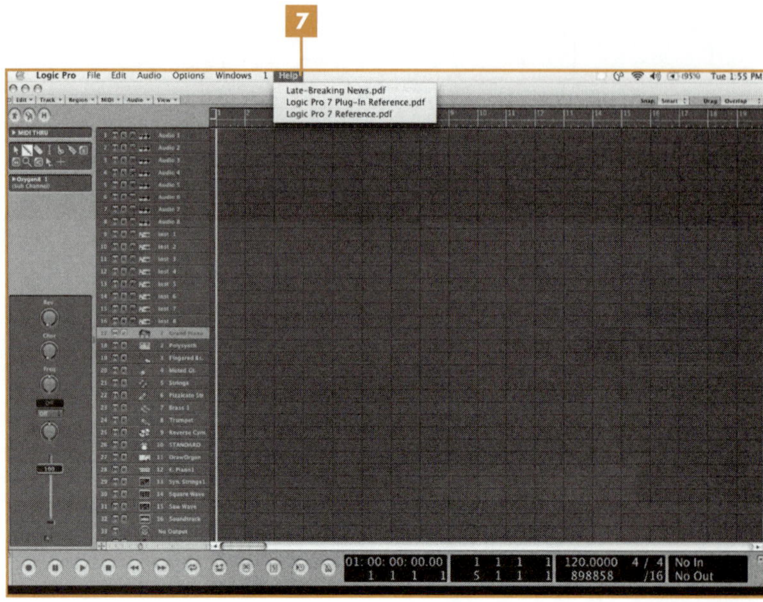

7 Help Menu: This menu will open Logic reference documents.

Default Song Elements

We will go into each of the windows in Logic in detail later in the book, but here is a simple description of the windows you'll see in the Default Song.

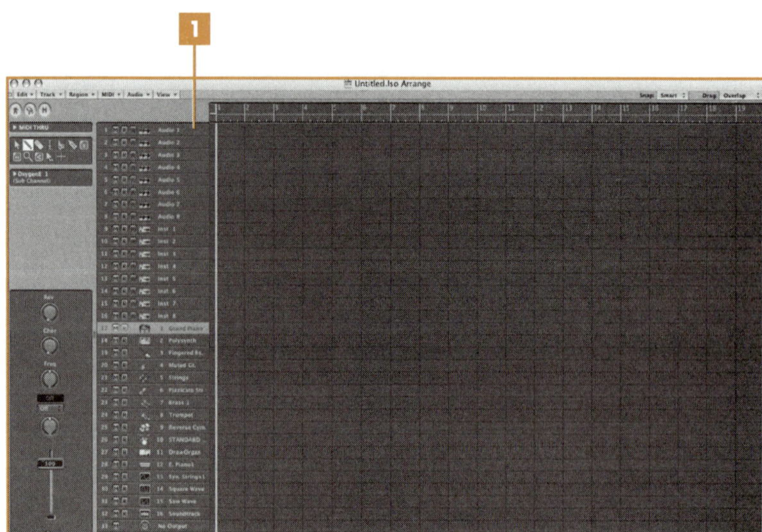

Arrange Window: This is the main compositional overview window in Logic. You can move and rearrange audio and MIDI regions, see a linear timeline of your song, and add or remove tracks and instruments.

1 Track List: These are the currently active tracks in your Logic song. You can add or remove tracks; create and edit automation; arm tracks for recording; and Freeze, Hide, and Mute tracks.

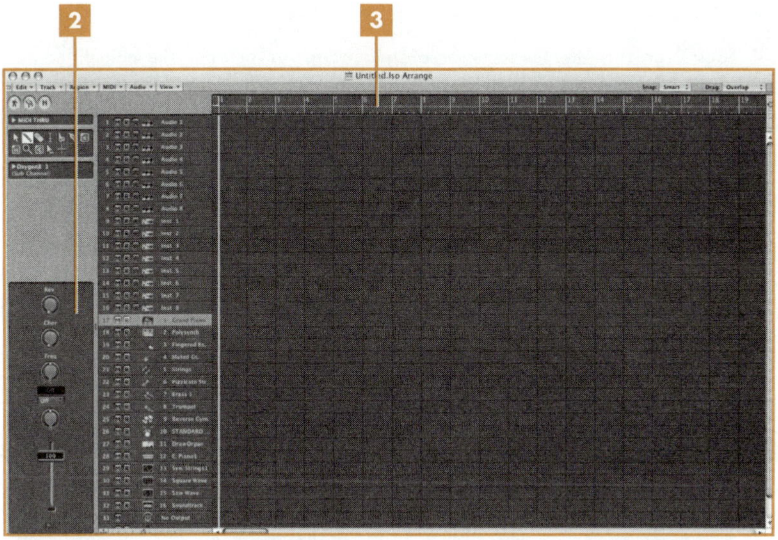

2 Channel Strip: This displays a single Channel Strip for the currently selected Arrange track. You can directly control Volume, Pan, Automation Modes, and Groups, as well as ChannelEQ, Inserts, and Sends.

3 Timeline: The Timeline is a linear representation of your song in Measures and Beats.

Transport Window: In addition to readouts for Tempo and Time Signature, the Transport window contains information on song position, Cycle locators, and MIDI monitoring.

1 Transport Buttons: Record, Pause, Play, Stop, Rewind, and Fast Forward, just like a tape recorder. There are also specialized Mode buttons like AutoDrop, Cycle, and Replace.

2 Song Position: The position in the song of the Song Position Line, displayed in SMPTE time as well as Bar, Beat, Division, and Tick.

3 Cycle Locator: The left and right position on the Timeline of a repeated section when the Cycle button is pressed.

4 Tempo, Free Memory, Time Signature, and Beat Division

5 MIDI Monitor: This displays Note In and Note Out from a connected MIDI keyboard controller or other MIDI input source.

The Logic Express Default Song

Logic Express creates the same sort of Default Song as Logic Pro. The main difference is that Logic Express has a simpler Transport window, as shown below.

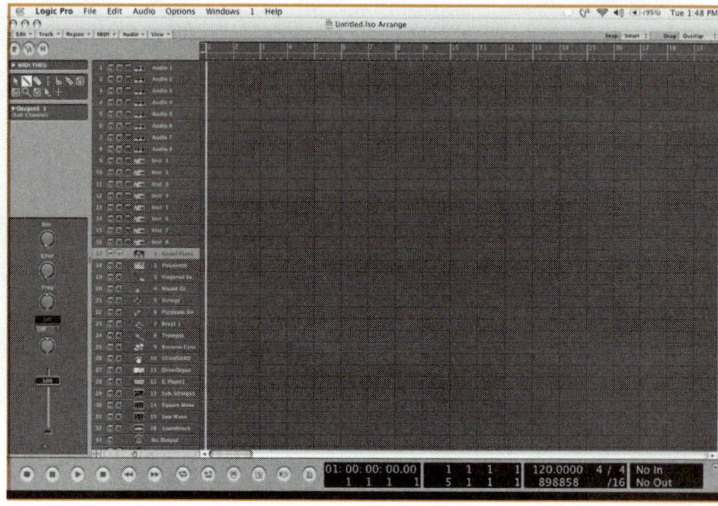

All the buttons and displays on the transport have the same function as in Logic Pro, so just ignore those items you don't have.

Can I Customize the Default Song?

The answer is yes and no.

The only way to customize the automatically generated Default Song is to enter different information into the Logic Setup Assistant. Even so, it will set up a different mixer for you, but the Default Song will still be mostly the same. The Default Song itself is not really meant to be customized extensively.

However, if you ever visit a professional studio running Logic, or even the project studio of an experienced Logic user, notice that their version of Logic opens to a custom song. This custom song is called an "Autoload" song, and Logic will automatically open this song instead of the Default Song. The Autoload song will be briefly discussed later in this chapter.

Opening a Logic 7 Demo Song

If you're unfamiliar with Logic, just staring at an empty Default Song can be fairly intimidating. An even better way to introduce yourself to Logic 7 is to open one of the Demo Songs, take a look at how a Logic song looks when it's fully loaded with audio and MIDI data, play the song, and so on. This section walks you through the process of opening and playing one of the included Logic 7 demo songs, as well as switching Screensets.

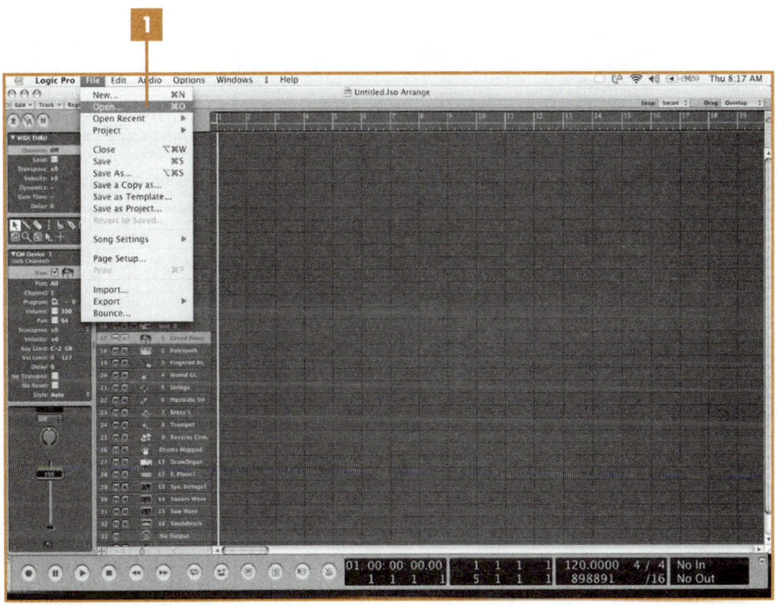

1 Click on the File menu and select Open.

2 If you still have the Default Song open, Logic will ask if you want to close the current song before opening the new one. Click Close.

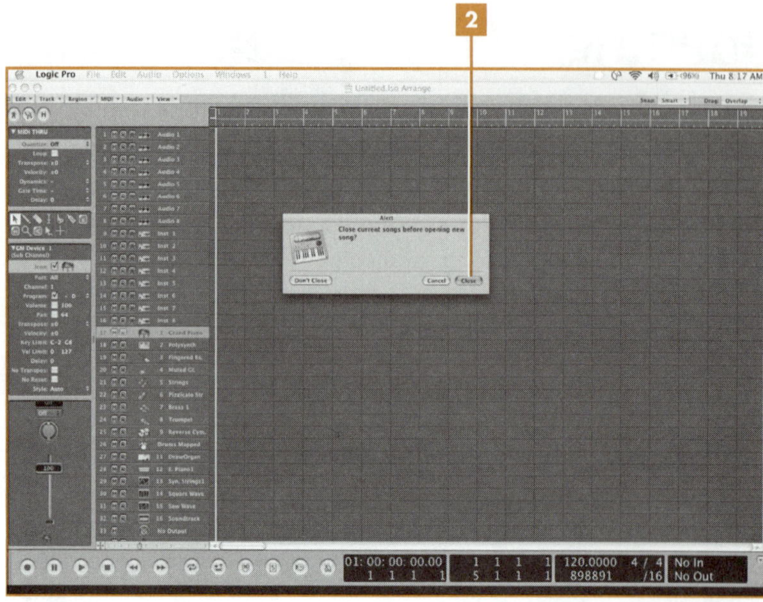

3 Navigate to the directory where you copied the Logic Demo Songs, and select a demo song to open.

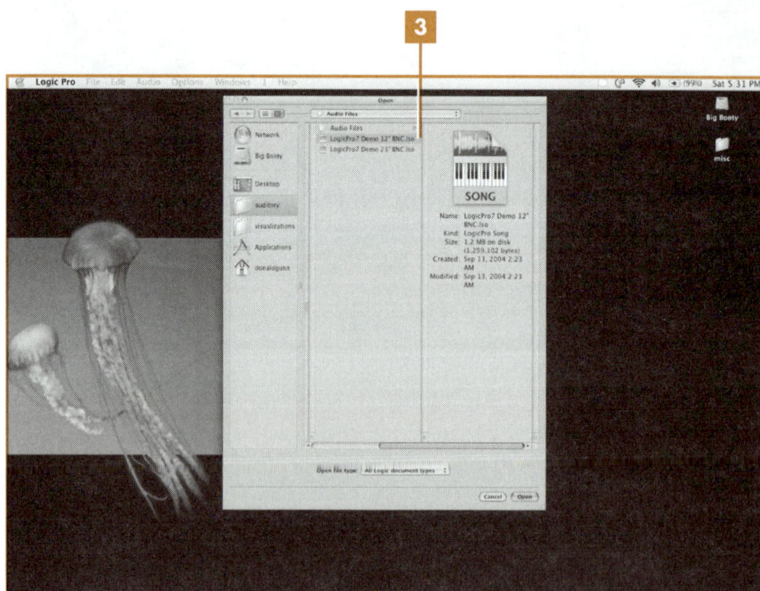

4 Logic will open the Demo Song. It may take a few moments as waveform overviews are calculated. Be patient. Once it has finished loading, press Play on the Transport.

5 Press the 2 key on the keyboard of your Macintosh. You will now see one of the most powerful features of Logic, the Screenset, in action. Pressing the numbers on your keyboard will call up different Screensets and allow you to completely change the way Logic appears for quick and easy access to any editing window.

Demo Songs, "Screensets," and Monitor Sizes

One of the most important concepts in Logic is that of Screensets. Basically, this means that when you save a Logic song, it will automatically remember where you placed its windows on the screen. As you'll learn further on, Logic's Screenset handling is best-in-class, and it's an extremely powerful tool—you can assign different window formations to different Screenset numbers, and they will automatically be saved with your song for instant recall of any window layout!

This does mean, however, that you need to be careful about where you position your windows in your Screensets if you plan on transferring your Logic song between Macs with different monitor setups. For example, I use two monitors; if I am not careful, my Logic song will look very chaotic on a single monitor system! If you have a Powerbook with a screen resolution of 1280x1024 pixels, and you then open that song on an iBook with a screen resolution of 1024x768 pixels, if you're not careful your song may look completely different than you intended.

Knowing this, Apple saved each Demo Song twice: once for a 15" Powerbook screen, and once for a 20" monitor. The 15" Demo Songs will look good on any monitor with a resolution of 1024x768 or 1280x1024. The 20" Demo Songs will look good on larger screens with higher resolutions. This way, all users can see the Logic Demo Song the way Apple meant for it to be seen.

Opening a GarageBand or Logic Song

If you have created songs in GarageBand previously, or if you are upgrading from a previous version of Logic, the best way to explore Logic 7 might be to open one of your old songs and see the differences. The process of opening and playing the song is basically the same as above.

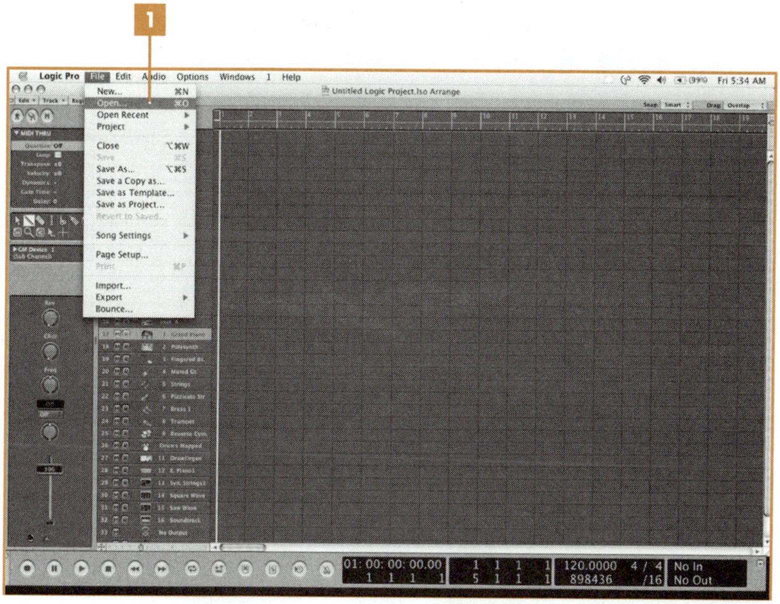

1 Click on the File menu and then click the Open option. Alternatively, use the key command COMMAND+O.

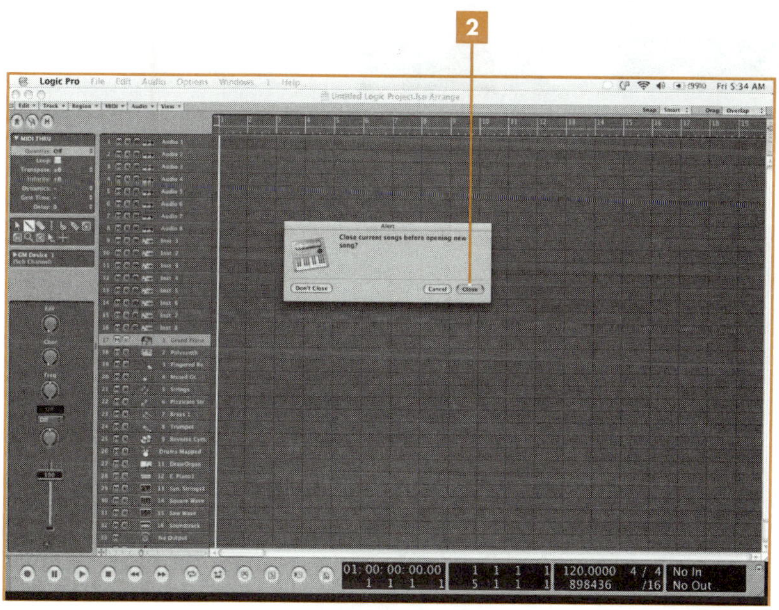

2 If you already have a song open, Logic will ask if you want to leave the current song open. Click Close.

3 When the Open dialog box appears, look at the bottom of the box for a drop-down menu for Open file type. You can select any of the various types of files Logic can open or leave it set to All Logic document types.

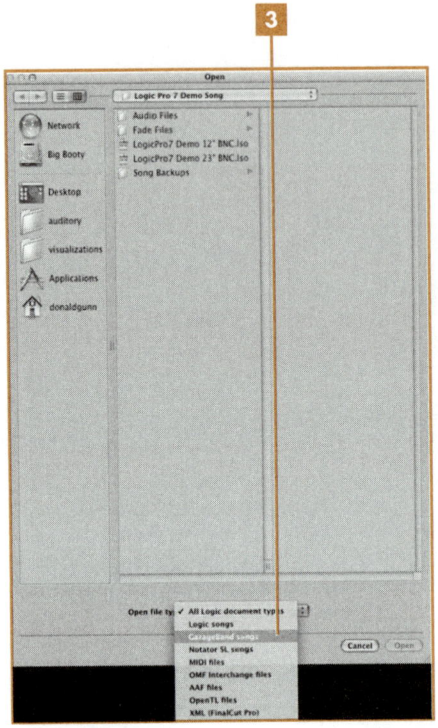

4 Navigate to your GarageBand or older Logic songs.

5 Select one and either click Open, or double-click the name of the file to open it.

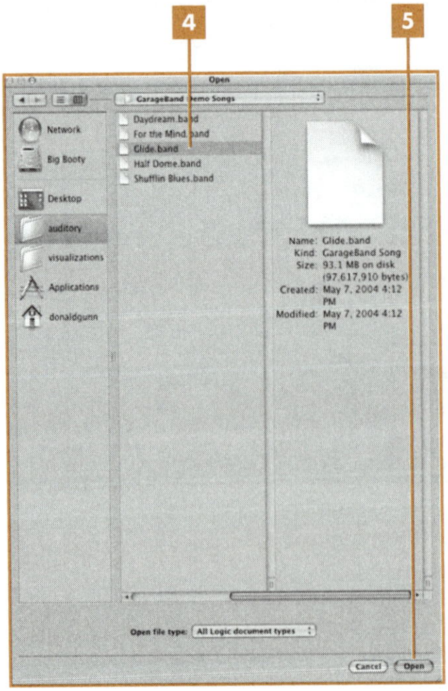

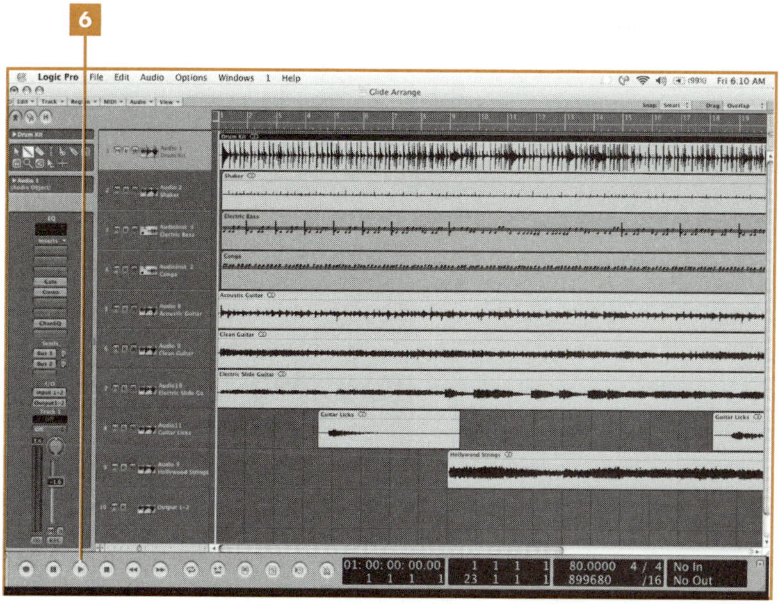

6 When your song opens, hit Play and check out the tune in Logic!

Creating a New Project

Now that you've looked around Logic 7 a bit, you'll want to start a new song. Rather than simply using the Default Song, I recommend that you begin by starting a new Project. When you begin a song as a Project, Logic automatically creates a Project folder for your Logic song, as well as a hierarchy of subfolders for each of the related files (audio files, sampler instruments, and so on) that will be associated with your song. In fact, starting your songs as Projects has even more advantages than just folder organization. Project folders also have some special abilities, such as automatically converting any audio file you import into your Logic song to the correct sample rate, and other niceties. You can also use *song templates*, or Logic songs already pre-created and optimized for particular workflows, as the basis for beginning your new Logic Project.

The first step, of course, is to select the option to create a new document as you would in any other application.

1 **Click** on the **File** menu and then **click** the **New** option. Alternatively, use the key command COMMAND+N. You will then see the **New** dialog box.

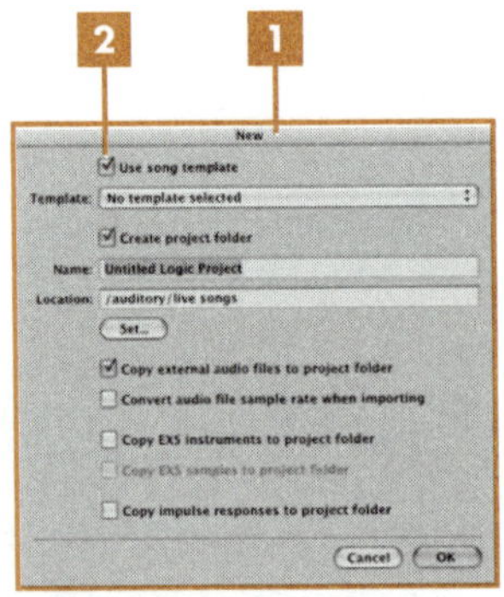

Return to the Default Song

If you want to bring up a new Default Song, click the New button with the OPTION key held down.

2 Make sure to **check** the **Create project folder** option.

Opening a Song Template

You may not want to use the Default Song as the basis for your new Project. Logic comes with a number of pre-configured song templates for you to choose from. This subsection will explain how to open a song template from the New Project dialog.

1 Make sure you have **Use song template** checked.

2 Use the **Template** drop-down menu to navigate through the song templates and **choose a template** to open.

Where Are Song Templates on My Hard Drive?

Logic 7 stores song templates in very specific locations. This way, Logic always knows where to find them, and it never needs to prompt you to guide it to them. If you're curious as to where they are, Logic 7 stores the factory compliment of song templates in the folder at the following directory path: /Library/Application Support/Logic/Song Templates. Song templates that you create yourself (as described later in the chapter) are stored at: ~/Library/Application Support/Logic/Song Templates. Don't worry if the above paths seem confusing; as I said, Logic knows where to look automatically.

Project Settings

You have a number of Project Settings options that you can use to govern the behavior of your Logic Project. Here are the options in the lower half of the New dialog.

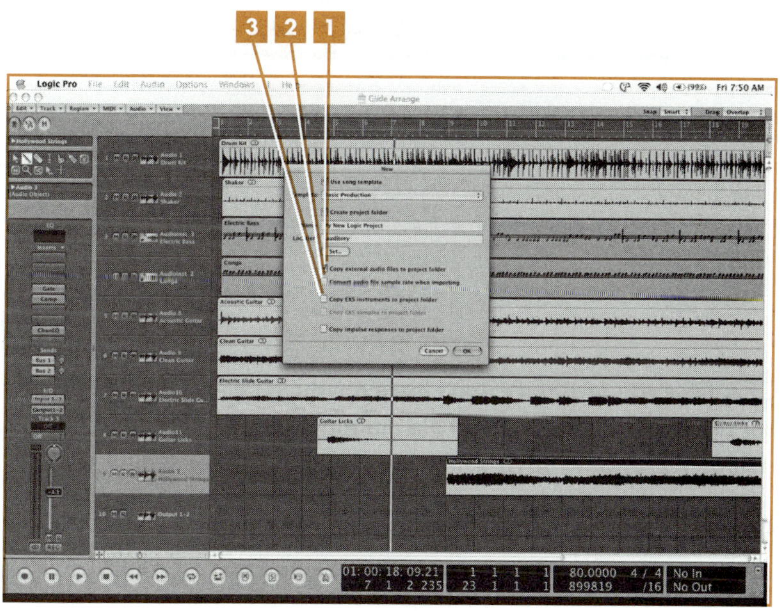

1 Copy external audio files to project folder: If you use any audio files outside the Project folder, this option will automatically copy them to the Project's audio files folder.

2 Convert audio file sample rate when importing: If you import an audio file at a different sample rate than the Project's rate, Logic will convert it to the proper rate.

3 Copy EXS instruments to project folder: If you use the EXS24 sampler in a project, Logic will copy the sample instruments to the Project.

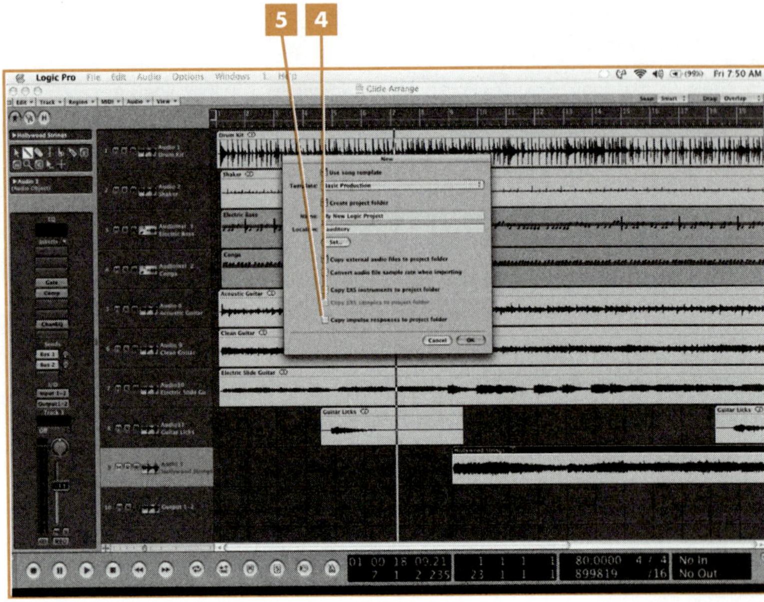

4. **Copy EXS samples to project folder**: This option becomes active if the Copy EXS instruments option above is checked. This can be handy if you have to move your Project to another user's computer and you use custom samples. Keep in mind that this doubles the required hard drive space for your EXS samples for this song.
5. **Copy impulse responses to Project folder**: This will copy impulse responses used in Logic's Space Designer reverb plug-in. Keep in mind that this will double the required hard drive space for your impulse responses for this song.

Saving Your Logic Project

Of course you probably don't have anything to save just yet, but since we're talking about file management, it makes sense to include the steps to save your project in this chapter.

Saving a Logic Song That's Already Part of a Project

If your song started as a Project, saving the Project couldn't be simpler.

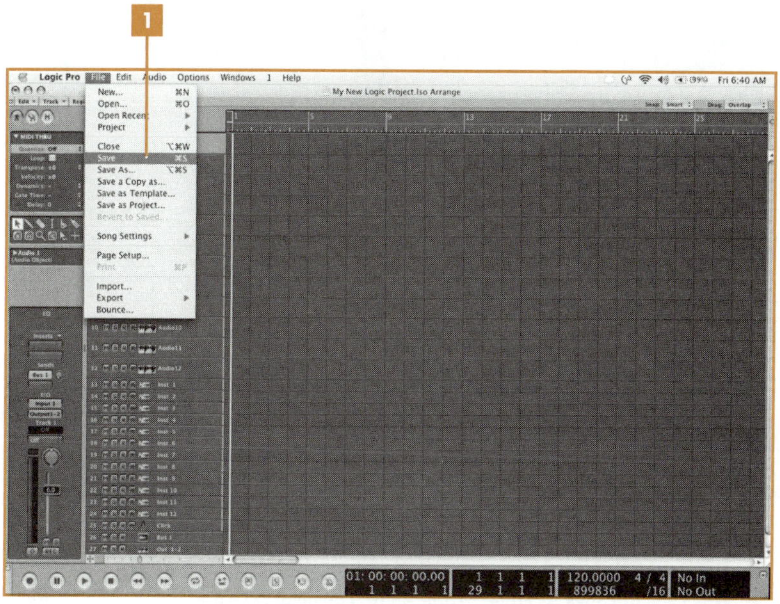

1 **Click** on the **File** menu and then **click** the **Save** option. Alternatively, use the key command COMMAND+S.

Saving a Logic Song as a Project

If you just started working on the Default Song without saving it as a Project first, don't worry—you can still save it as a Project now.

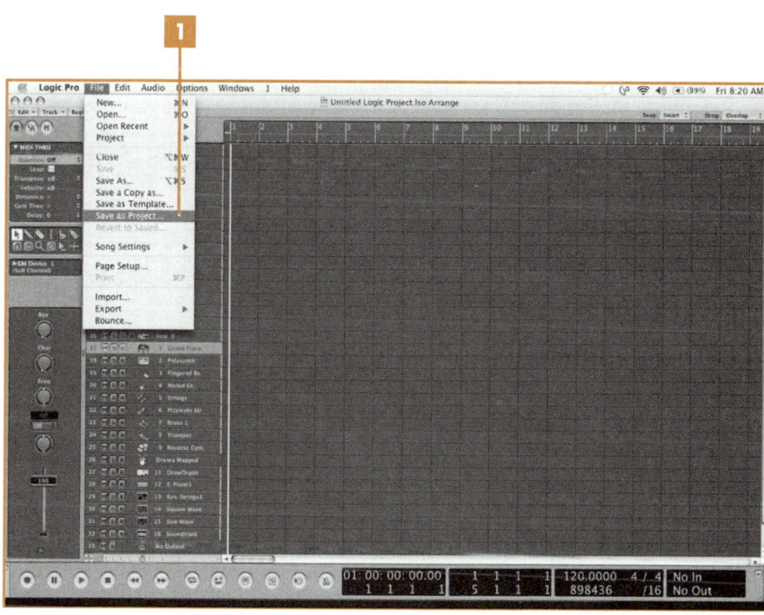

1 **Click** on the **File** menu and then **click** the **Save as Project** option.

2 Here you have the same options as when creating a new Project, but you are also given the opportunity to Move files in addition to Copy. Be careful using the Move option as this can cause problems with other Song or Project files that may share the same files.

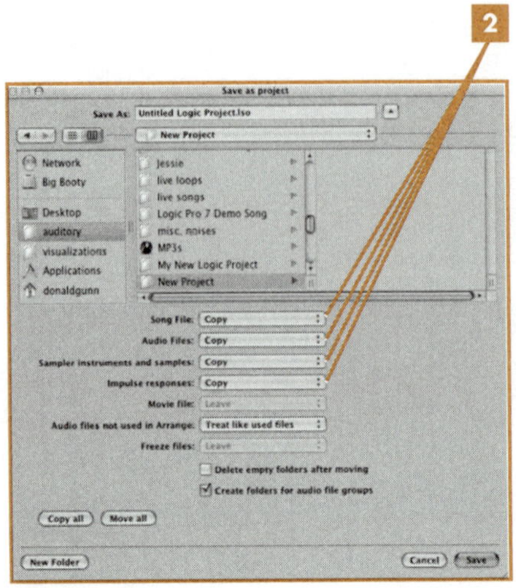

Don't Forget Your Project Settings!

When you use Save As Project, Logic doesn't automatically present you with all the Project Settings options. You can still set them by selecting File > Project > Settings. This will launch the Project Settings dialog, which contains the same five preferences discussed above in the Project Settings subsection.

Adding an Additional Logic Song File to an Existing Logic Project

If you already have done a Save As Project to save a song as a Project, and then you want to save an alternate version of that song or save an additional song to an already created Logic Project, use the Save As command. This will allow you to rename your Logic song file and save it in the existing project folder.

Saving a Logic Song as a Template

Perhaps you have reorganized one of the factory song templates the way you like it, and you want to save it as a new song template. Or maybe you've created an entirely new song and like the way you set it up so much that you want it available as a song template. Either way, Logic lets you save your song as a song template very easily. Once you do this, your song will be available in the New dialog in the list of song templates.

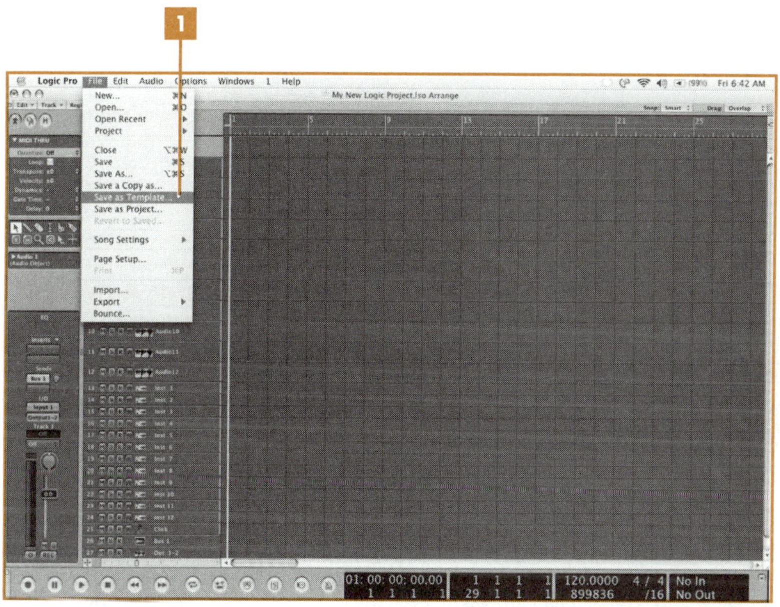

1 Click on the File menu and then click the Save as Template option.

2 Name your new template.

3 Click Save.

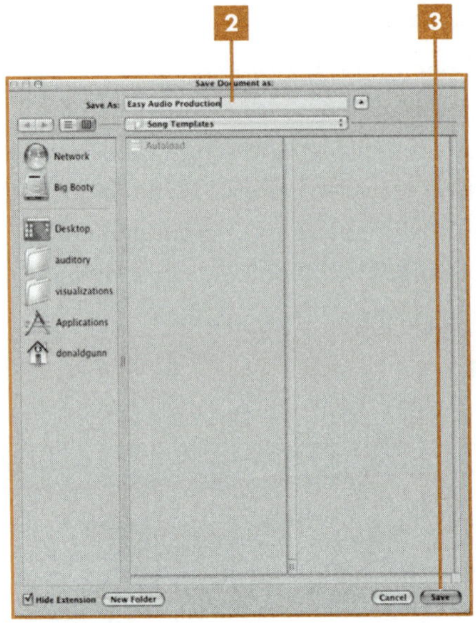

The Automatically Loading Song Template: Autoload

There is one special song template that not only is available in the song template list, but also replaces the Default Song as the song that opens every time you launch Logic. This automatically loading song template is named—appropriately enough—Autoload. If you create a song that you like so much that you want it to be the song that opens automatically every time you launch Logic, simply choose File > Save As Template and name it "Autoload" (without the quotes, of course!). From then on, your Autoload will replace the Default Song.

Having only read through Chapter 2, don't feel you need to create your Autoload now. This is an ongoing process that you will continually revisit as you learn more about Logic and develop your working methods. It is beyond the scope of this book to go into too much detail on tips for creating your own Autoload, but if you want more information, please check out *Logic Pro 7 Power!* (Muska & Lipman, 2004), which has an entire chapter on creating your Autoload song.

Configuring Logic to Open with Your Most Recent Song

Finally, you may not want Logic to open the Default Song (or an Autoload) when you launch the application. You may want Logic to automatically launch the song you were working on previously, just like GarageBand does. This is also easy to configure.

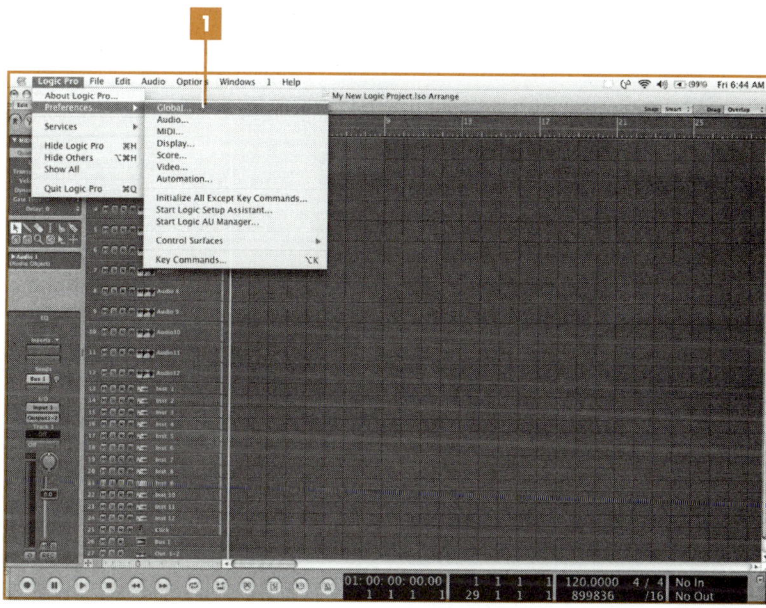

1 Click the Logic Pro menu and go to Preferences > Global.

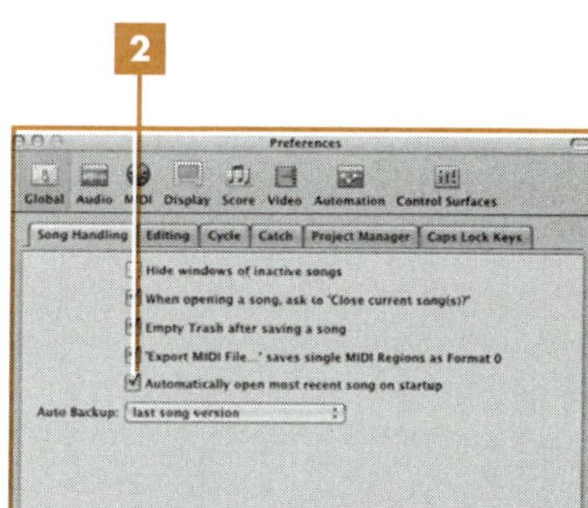

2 In the Song Handling dialog box, check the Automatically open most recent song on startup option.

3 Recording Audio and MIDI

Checking out Logic 7's menus and Demo Songs is a great way to get acquainted with Logic, but pretty soon you'll want to jump right in and start recording new tracks. Considering how architecturally deep Logic is, you'll find that basic recording of audio and MIDI is quite simple! There's a bit more setup involved than in GarageBand, of course, but nothing that you won't be able to master quickly. In this chapter, you will learn how to:

- Configure your audio driver in Logic
- Set up an Audio Track for recording
- Record an Audio Track
- Record multiple Audio Tracks simultaneously
- Record a MIDI or Audio Instrument Track
- Record multiple Audio Instrument Tracks simultaneously
- Record multiple MIDI Tracks simultaneously
- Use Cycle recording and Autodrop recording

The Audio Driver Preferences Window

Before you start recording, you'll want to take a look at the Audio Driver Preferences. Logic will already be set up to use the audio interface you selected in the Logic Setup Assistant, but it may not be configured to give you the best performance. This section will walk you through the Audio Driver Preferences tab to help you optimize your audio performance in Logic.

Opening the Audio Driver Preferences Window

The Audio Driver Preferences window is accessible through the Preferences menu in the Logic Pro menu.

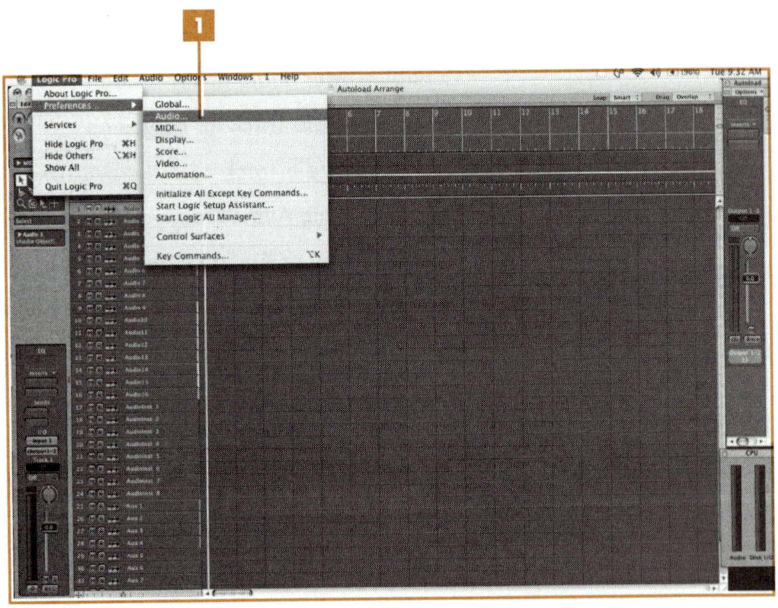

1 Accessing Audio Driver Preferences.

The Audio Hardware and Drivers Menu

You can also access the Audio Driver Preferences window directly by selecting Audio > Audio Hardware & Drivers.

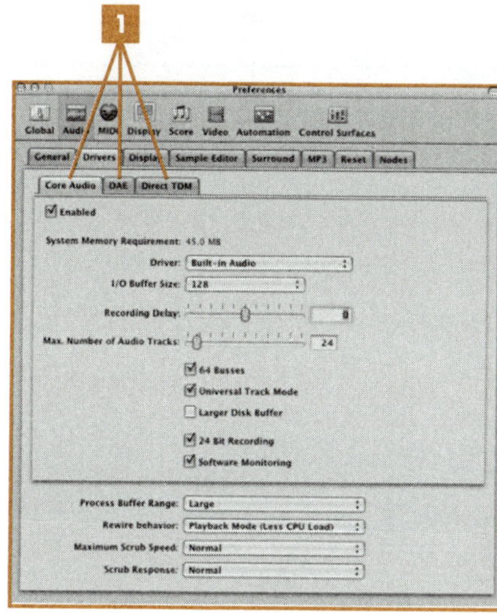

The Audio Driver Preferences

1 The three driver tabs.

Three Driver Tabs in the Logic Pro 7 Audio Driver Preferences Window?

If you're a Logic Pro 7 user, you've probably noticed that there are actually three different tabs for drivers on the Audio Driver Preferences window: Core Audio, DAE, and Direct TDM. You only need to concern yourself with the Core Audio tab, since Core Audio is the way that your Mac interfaces with all audio hardware except Digidesign Pro Tools TDM hardware, such as a full Pro Tools HD or Pro Tools HD|Accel system. If you do have a Pro Tools TDM system, you'll need to consult the Logic Pro 7 TDM Guide for specific information on using DAE and TDM with Logic Pro.

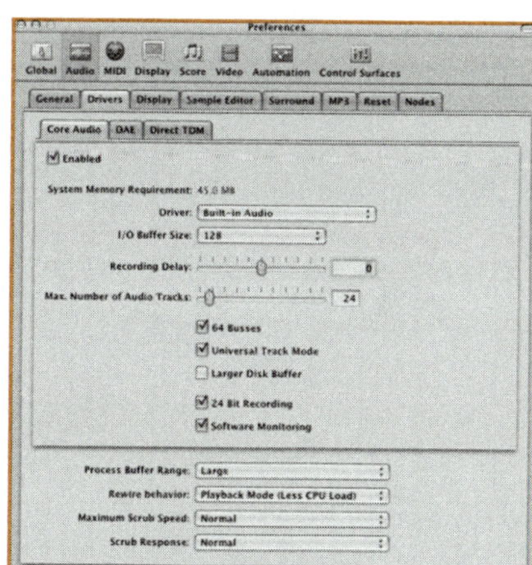

Each of the preferences available in the Audio Driver Preferences window affects a different aspect of Logic 7's audio performance. Don't feel that you need to adjust every preference just because it's included here—the defaults are usually good enough. If you find yourself pushing your Macintosh or audio interface to its limits, here are the various options that can make a significant difference in performance.

1 **Driver**: This option allows you to choose between the Macintosh's Built-In Audio and the driver(s) for any third-party audio hardware you have installed. If you have another device installed with it's own drivers, be sure to select it here.

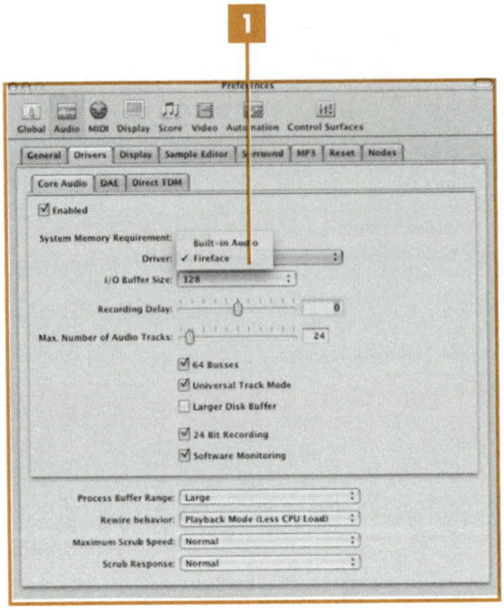

2 **I/O Buffer Size**: The lower the buffer, the more work the computer has to do to process audio in real time; larger sizes are better for mixing, but smaller sizes, like 64 and 128, may be necessary when recording to compensate for latency (see the **I/O Buffer Size and Latency** sidebar later in this section).

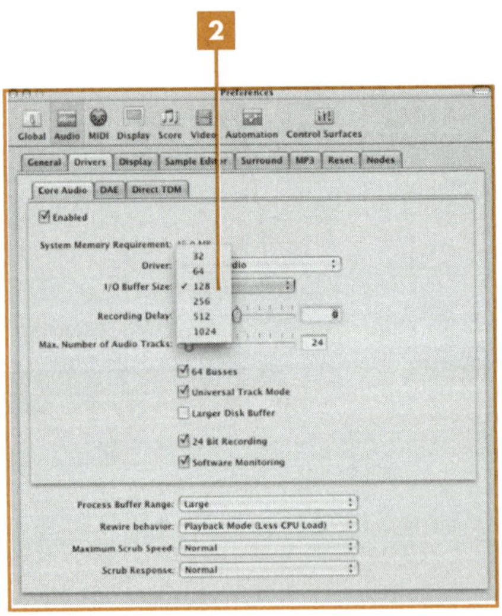

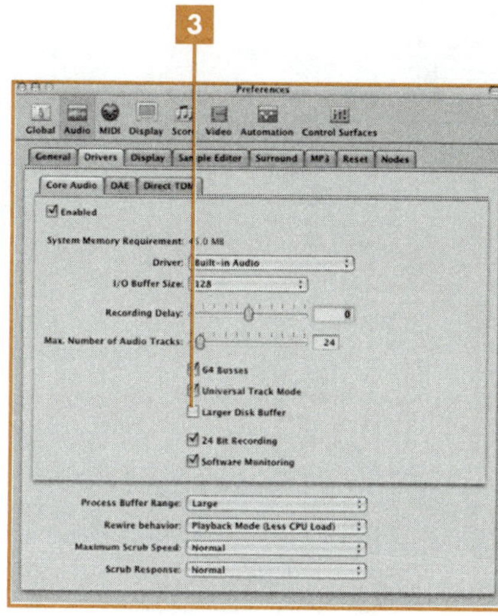

3 Larger Disk Buffer: Checking this option makes Logic read more data from the hard drive before playing; this requires more RAM but can improve performance with higher track counts.

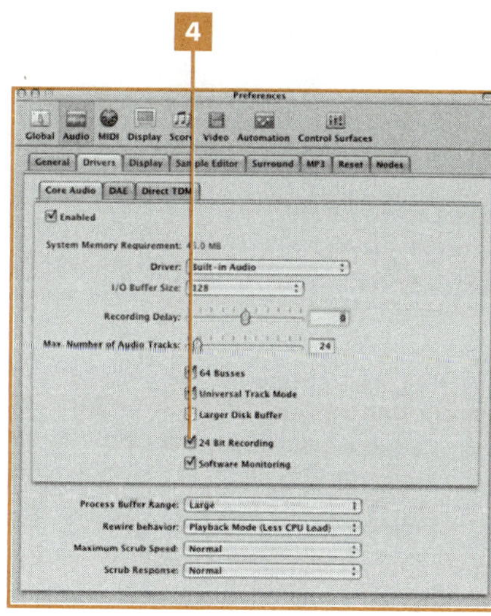

4 24-Bit Recording: Click this button to record 24-bit audio instead of 16-bit audio. 24-bit audio has 256 times the resolution of 16-bit audio, but it takes up more hard-drive space, and 24-bit files also require more processor power when running effects.

5 **Process Buffer Range**: This sets the size of Logic's internal buffer for audio processing. Your choices are Small, Medium, and Large. Larger sizes can increase the latency, but the smaller the size, the more the CPU has to work. Medium is usually a safe default.

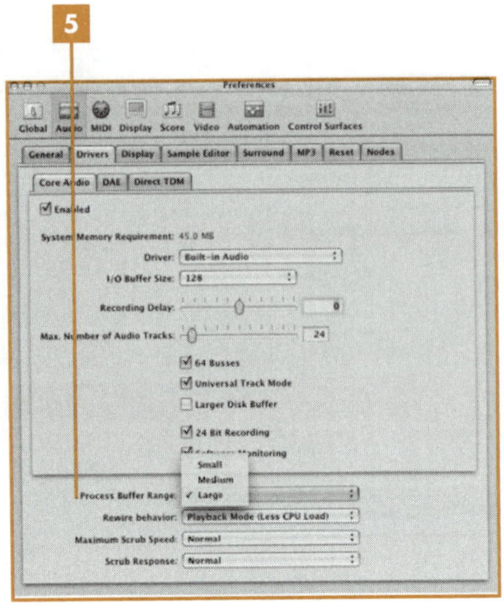

6 **ReWire Behavior**: You can set the ReWire behavior to either Live Mode or Playback Mode. Live Mode is only necessary if you need to use your MIDI controller to play your ReWire application in real-time from within Logic (see the sidebar **What Is ReWire?** for more details). Unlike many options in the Audio Drivers tab, you can change this one without relaunching the audio engine.

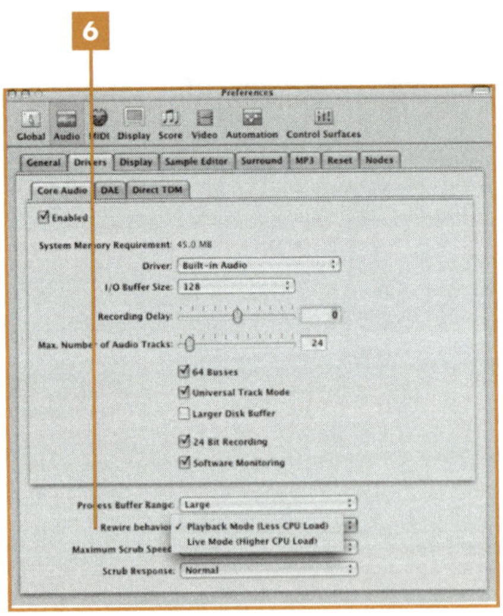

What Is ReWire?

ReWire is an inter-application communication protocol, developed by Propellerheads Software, that allows one computer application to send and receive MIDI and audio data to another application. Logic can be configured to be a ReWire "master," meaning it can receive audio and MIDI data from a ReWire "slave" application. Many audio applications—such as Propellerheads' own Reason, Ableton Live, Arturia's Storm, and so on—can be slaved to Logic this way.

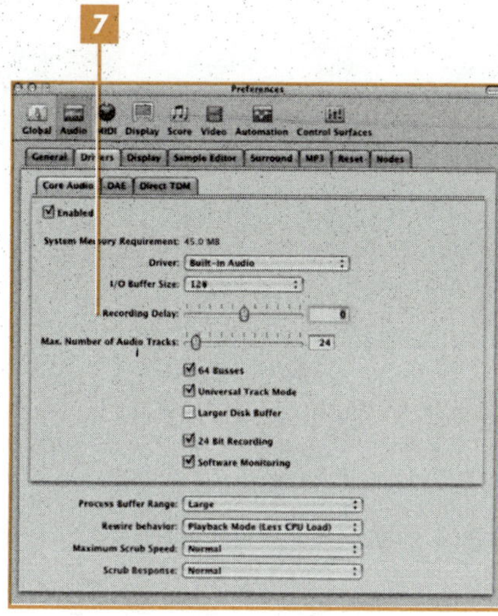

7 **Recording Delay slider: This slider allows you to adjust for record offset (see the sidebar Audio Buffers and Record Offset for details).**

Audio Buffers and Record Offset

The way computers are able to process streaming audio data is by grabbing some samples of audio, performing a process (recording it to disk, for example), then grabbing more samples of audio to process. Since the computer has to wait for one group of samples to be processed before the next group can be processed, this will result in a delay between what you perform live and when Logic can process your audio.

Luckily, Logic is very good at automatically compensating for that delay—assuming your audio interface properly communicates how many samples it will delay the audio it streams into Logic. If your audio interface doesn't properly report its delay, the difference between when you perform something and the position at which it appears on the timeline in Logic's Arrange window is called the record offset. Normally, this number is so small you don't need to worry about it. If you want to correct it, however, you can use the Recording Delay parameter.

8 Software Monitoring: This button allows you to listen to (monitor) your audio signal after it goes through Logic's audio engine. This button, along with the I/O Buffer Size menu, determines if you will experience monitoring latency (see the sidebar Latency and I/O Buffer Sizes for details).

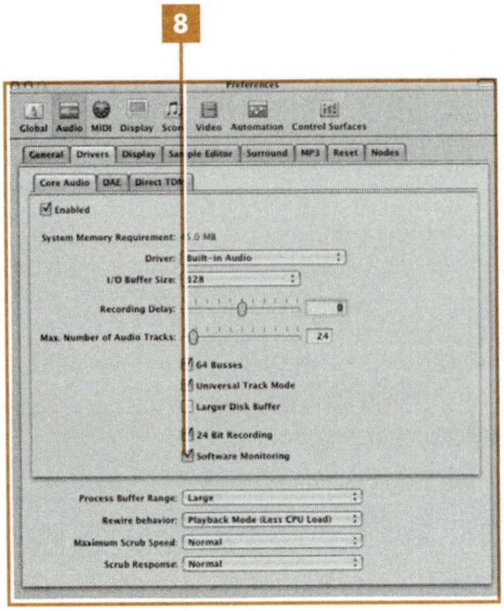

Latency and I/O Buffer Sizes

If you listen back through Logic with Software Monitoring turned on, your audio will be grabbed in samples to be processed on the way in, as described in the Audio Buffers and Record Offset sidebar, and will be returned to your audio interface in groups of samples as well. This round-trip delay is called monitoring latency.

Your I/O Buffer Size determines the number of samples of audio Logic will grab at once. If you set your audio buffer to a very low number, such as 32 or 64 samples, Logic will grab audio data very quickly from your audio interface, resulting in a monitoring latency so small you won't be able to hear it. Unfortunately, buffers this small make your computer work extremely hard and are too much for all but the fastest computers.

Setting your audio buffer to a very high value, such as 1024 or 2048 samples, is very gentle on your CPU, so you'll have the maximum amount of processing power left over for high track counts, audio processing, and so on. But it will result in very long monitoring delays—so long that it will be virtually impossible to perform.

In other words, if you are monitoring through your hardware, not Logic, you should set your I/O Buffer Size high—to 1024 samples, for example—to maximize how much CPU power is available for processing. If you are using Software Monitoring, you should set your I/O Buffer Size low to minimize the delay, but be aware that if it is too low you will overload your computer.

Recording Audio

With your audio interface configured, and your instruments and microphones properly hooked up, you're ready to begin recording! It may seem like there are a large number of steps involved, but you'll find that in practice they take no time at all.

Selecting and Preparing One or More Audio Tracks for Recording

The first thing you'll want to do is to select the Audio Track onto which you will record your performance and prepare it for recording.

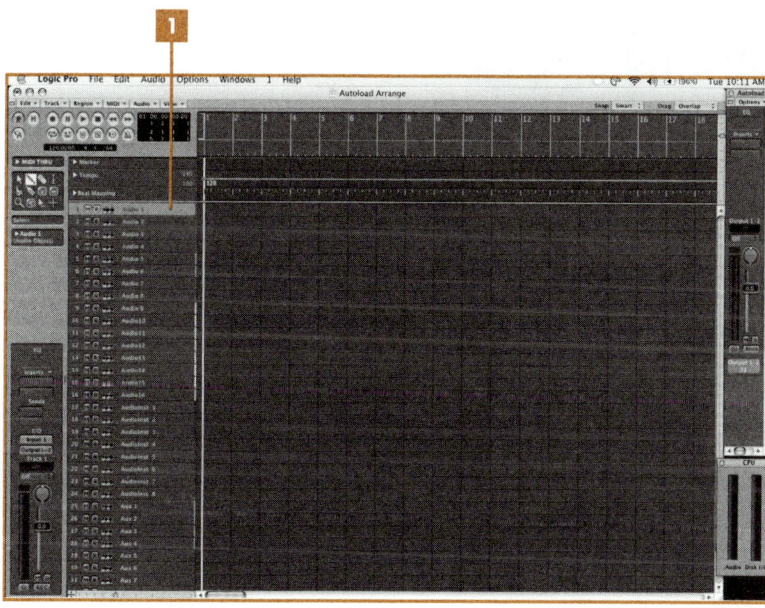

1 Select the track you want to record to in the Track Column of the Arrange window.

Naming the Audio Channel

While this step isn't strictly necessary, we cannot stress how important it is to properly label and identify each audio channel that you have assigned to a track.

2 The first method you can use to name your track is to hold the OPTION key and double-click on the track name in the Tracks column.

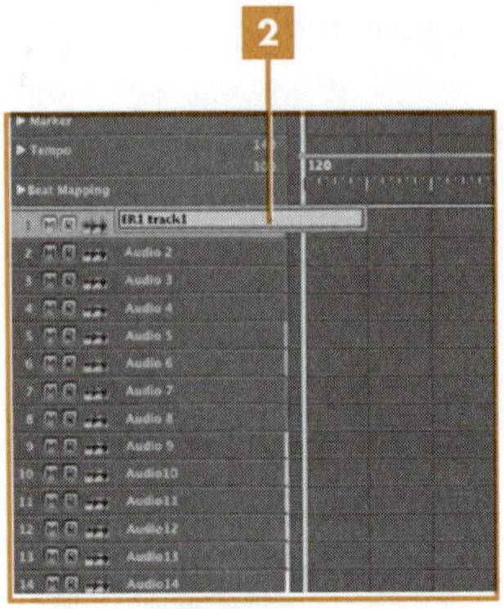

3 Alternatively, you can click on the track name in the Parameter pane to the left of the Tracks column.

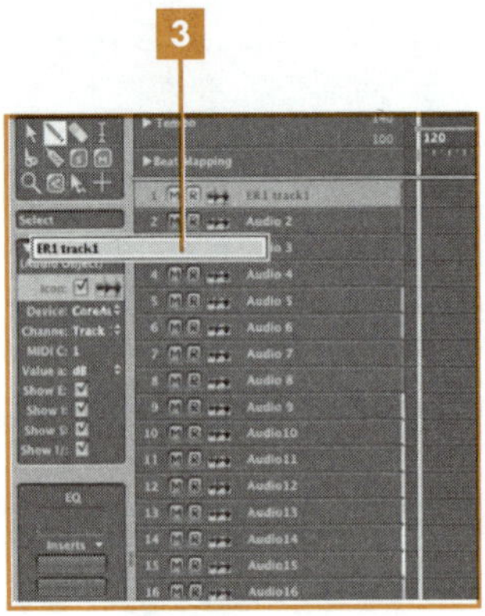

Setting the Input

You won't be able to record on your track unless you've selected an audio input from which it will receive audio data.

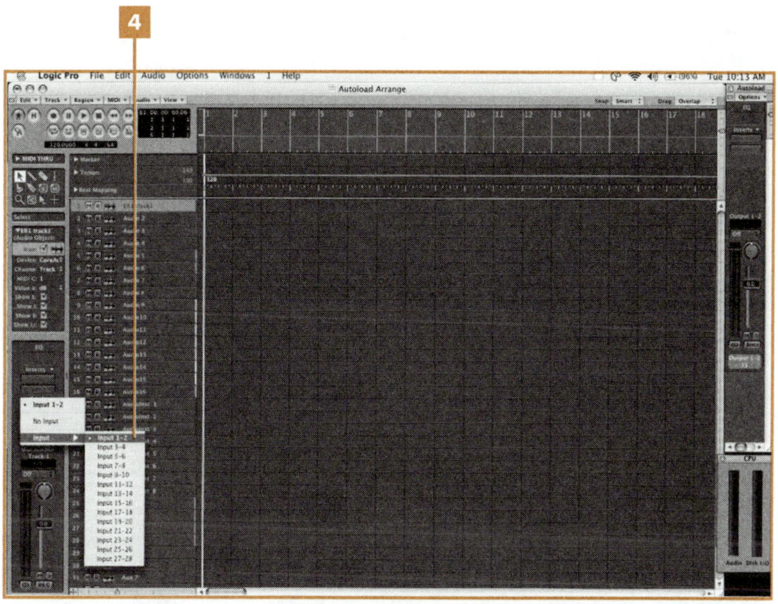

4 Click and hold on the Input tab in the Channel Strip for your selected track. This will pop open the list of available inputs based on your selected driver. Choose the input to which you have connected your source.

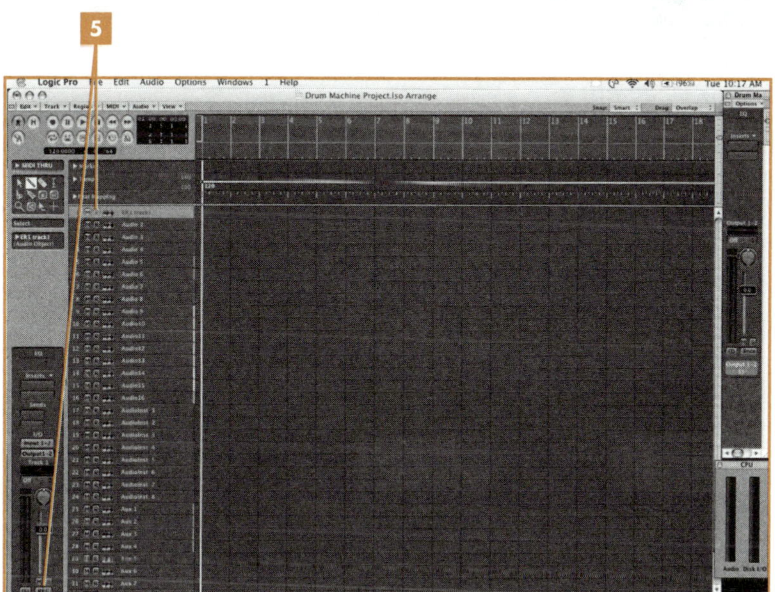

Record-Enabling the Audio Track

Once your track has an audio input assigned, you can record-enable the track.

5 Click the R button (R for "Record") in the Track column or the REC button at the bottom of the Channel Strip to record-enable the track.

Record-Enabling Multiple Audio Tracks

Unlike GarageBand, you are not limited in regards to how many tracks at a time you can record in Logic. You can simultaneously record on as many tracks as you have audio inputs on your audio interface.

6 After naming each track and setting the respective input on each one, click Record on all the tracks you want to record.

6

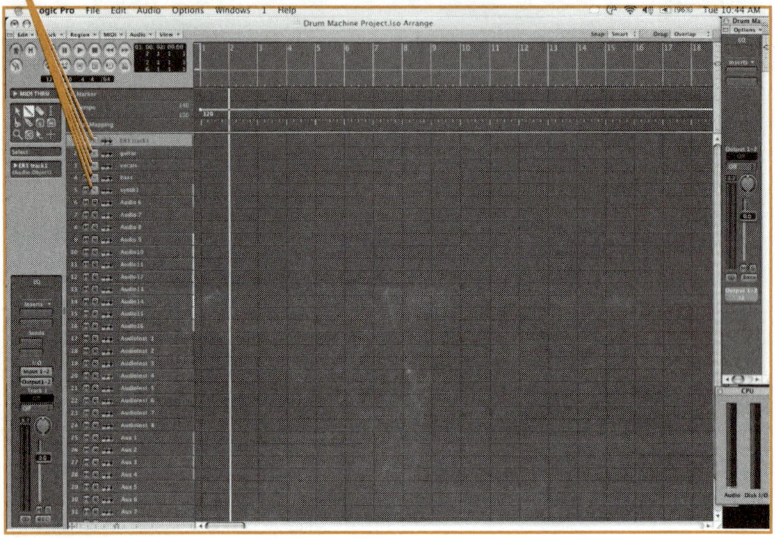

Where Did My Inputs Go?

If your audio interface has more audio inputs than are available in the Input menu in Logic, the chances are good that you didn't enable all of them in the Logic Setup Assistant. You can always re-run the LSA by selecting it from Logic Pro > Preferences > Start Logic Setup Assistant and, in the Audio Mixer window, enabling all your audio inputs.

Entering Record and Recording Audio

Now that you've named tracks, set inputs, and record-enabled your Audio Track(s), you're ready to start recording!

1

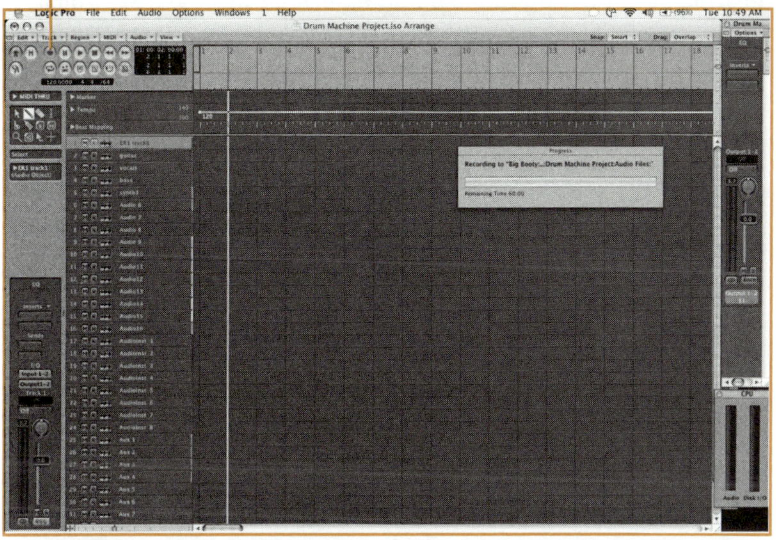

1 Click Record in the Transport to start recording.

Key Command Alert: Record

You can also begin recording by pressing * on your QWERTY keyboard or numeric keypad.

2

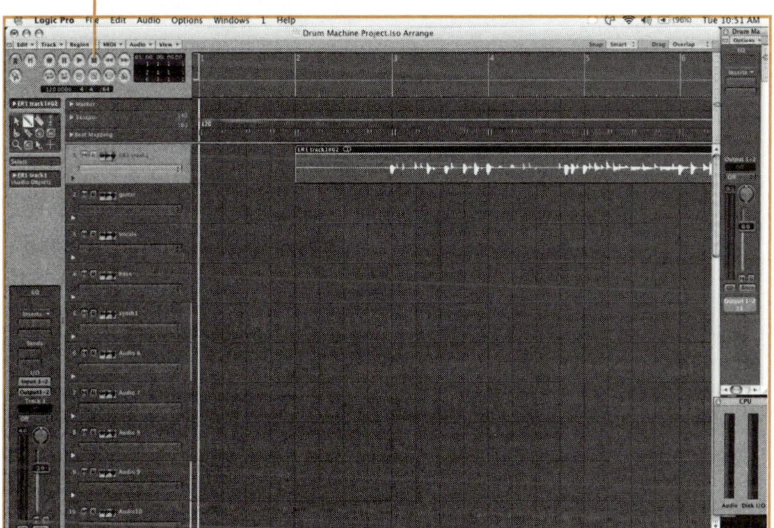

2 When you are finished recording, click the Stop button in the Transport, or press the Space Bar.

Key Command Alert: Play/Stop

You can start and stop the Transport, for both recording and playback, by pressing the Space Bar.

Recording MIDI

Logic makes recording MIDI as intuitive as recording audio! There are two kinds of instruments that rely on MIDI data—Audio Instruments, which are software synthesizers (called Software Instruments in GarageBand), and external MIDI devices, which are hardware synthesizers. Once again, recording MIDI data, like recording audio data, requires a little setup first.

Selecting and Preparing One or More Audio Instrument Tracks for Recording

The process for selecting and preparing Audio Instrument Tracks for recording is very similar to that of Audio Tracks.

Naming Your Audio Instrument

While this step isn't strictly necessary, we cannot stress how important it is to properly label and identify each Audio Instrument channel.

1 Just as you did with your Audio Track, either OPTION+ double-click on the track name, or click on the name in the Parameter pane.

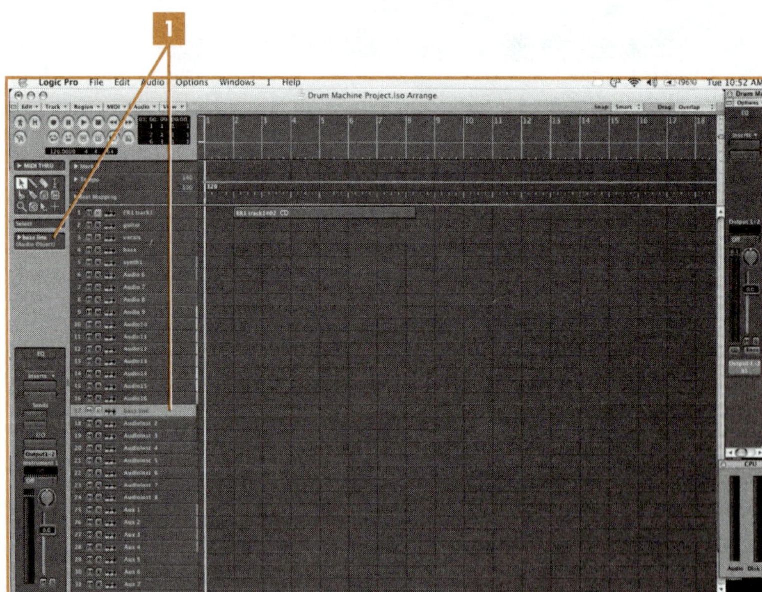

Selecting Your Audio Instrument

Logic 7 comes with a huge selection of professional quality Audio Instruments, as well as all the Software Instruments from GarageBand. Exactly which instruments come with your version of Logic will depend on whether you are using Logic Express or Logic Pro. You can also use any virtual instruments compatible with the Audio Units format inside Logic 7. Whether using a built-in Logic Audio Instrument or an Audio Unit plug-in, the process for selection is the same.

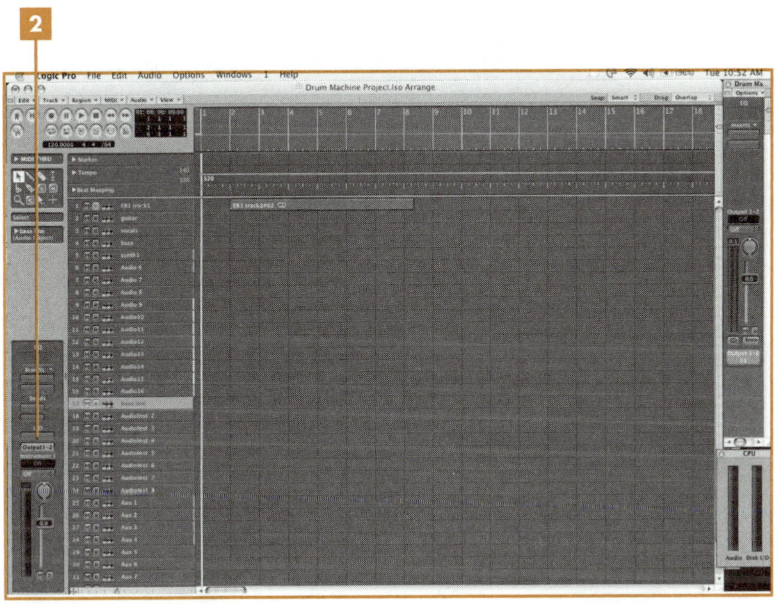

2 Click and hold on the blank Audio Instrument slot above the Output setting in the Channel Strip.

3 From the list that pops up, **choose** the **Audio Instrument** you want to insert in the track.

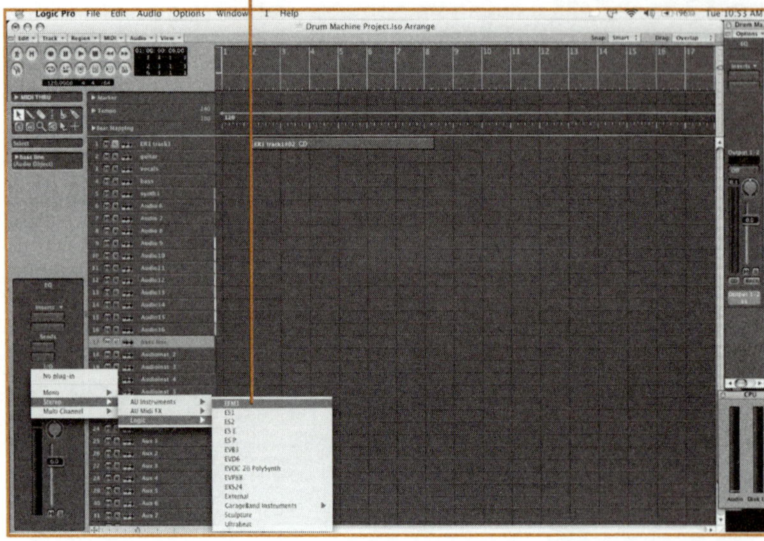

4 The Instrument you select will open, allowing you to change its parameter or open presets if necessary. We will discuss the particulars of Audio Instruments in Chapter 8, "Working with Audio Instruments."

Record-Enabling Multiple Audio Instrument Tracks

Unlike GarageBand, you are not limited to recording a single track at a time in Logic. As you probably already noticed, as soon as you selected your Audio Instrument Track, it automatically became record-enabled. However, if you want to record multiple Audio Instrument Tracks simultaneously, you'll need to manually record-enable them.

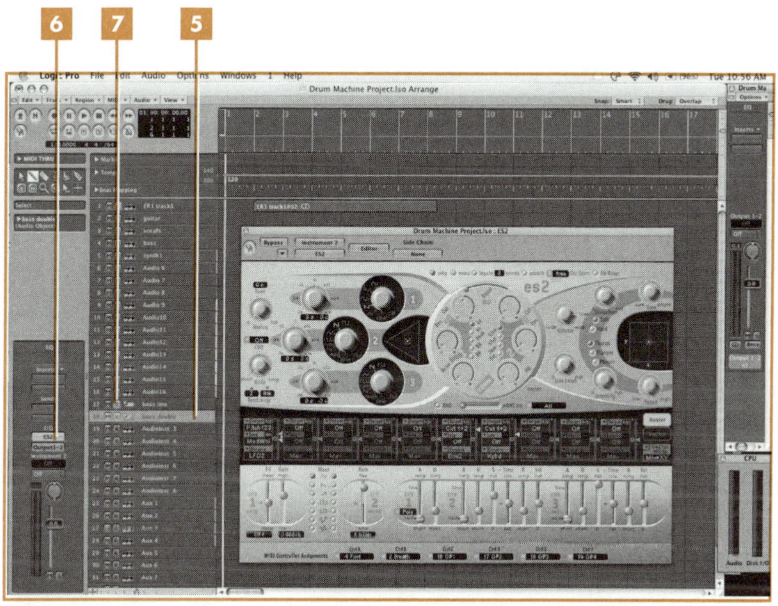

5. Choose a second Audio Instrument. Name the new instrument by OPTION+double-clicking, or by using the Parameter pane.
6. Insert another Audio Instrument. It will be automatically record-enabled.
7. Record-enable the first instrument again.

Selecting and Preparing a MIDI Track to Record

Recording onto a MIDI track is one of the simplest things to do in Logic.

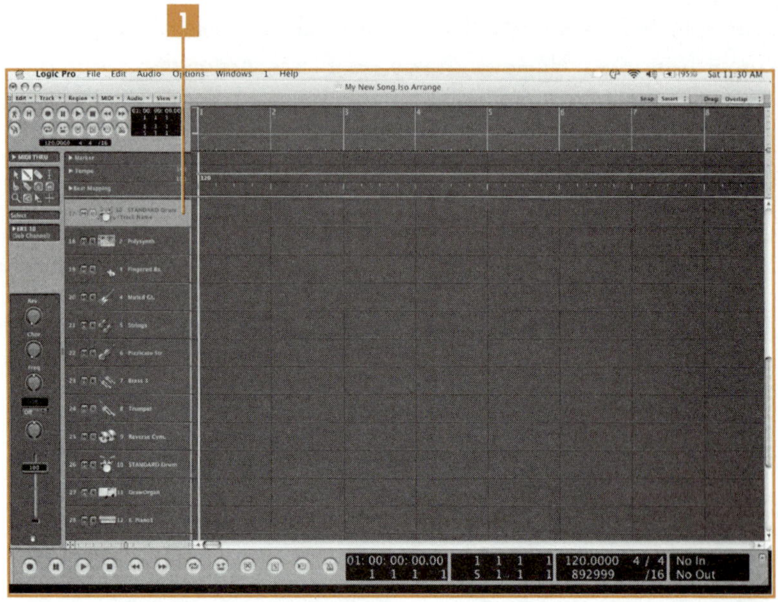

1 Select a MIDI Track in the Arrange window.

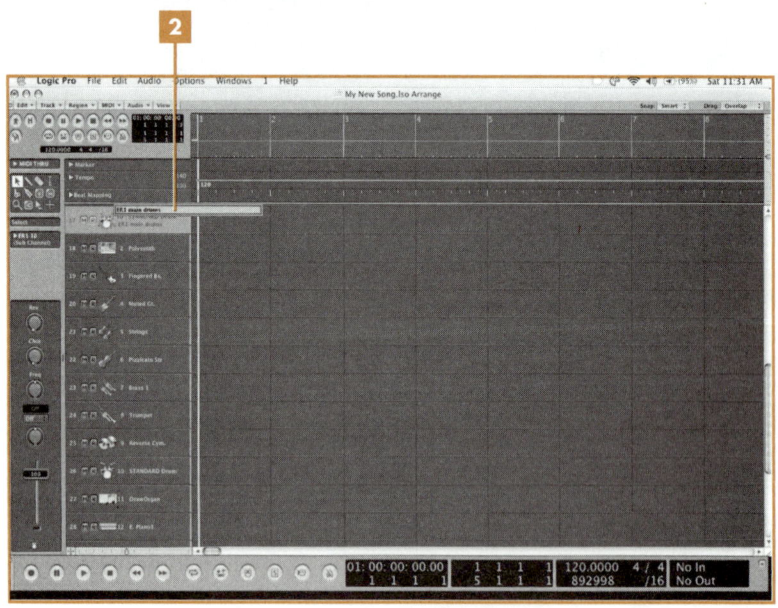

Naming Your MIDI Track

While this step isn't strictly necessary, we cannot stress how important it is to properly label and identify each track.

2 SHIFT+double-click on the track to rename it.

Selecting Your MIDI Instrument

All the MIDI synthesizers and sound modules you own should be readily available to you after you set them up in the Logic Setup Assistant. If they are not, you can always re-run the LSA by selecting it from Logic Pro > Preferences > Start Logic Setup Assistant and, in the MIDI window, enabling MIDI instruments.

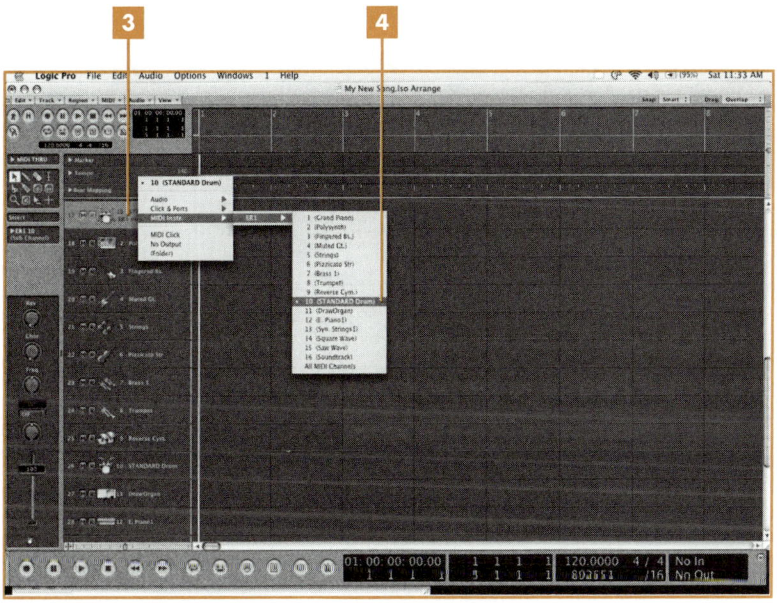

3. Click on the track name and hold the mouse button for a couple of seconds to open the list of MIDI Instruments.
4. Select the Instrument you want to use from the list.

Setting up Logic for Recording Multiple MIDI Tracks

In fact, Logic only records onto a single MIDI track at a time, even when you are recording multiple MIDI channels at once. So what Logic will do when you are recording multiple channels is automatically split out the MIDI channels to their own track after they are recorded, based on the tracks you have record-enabled.

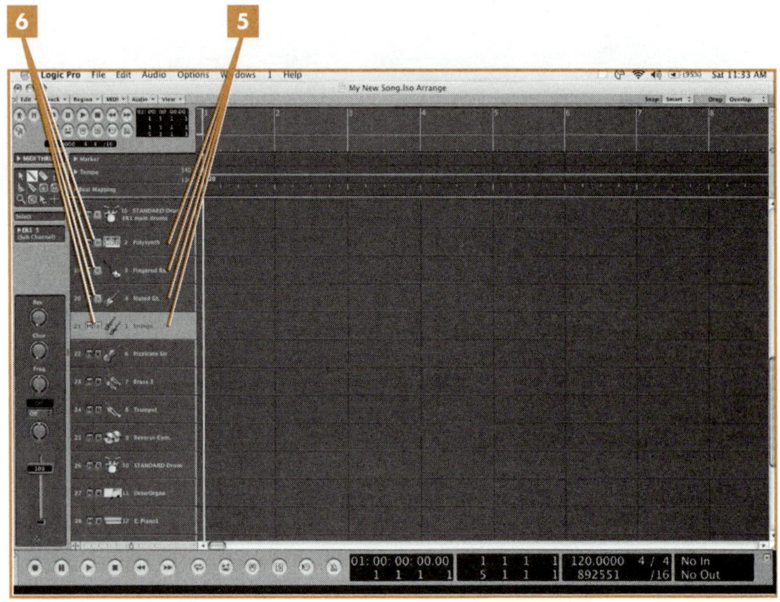

5. As you did previously, name the MIDI Tracks and select instruments for each track that you want to record.
6. Record-enable each track.

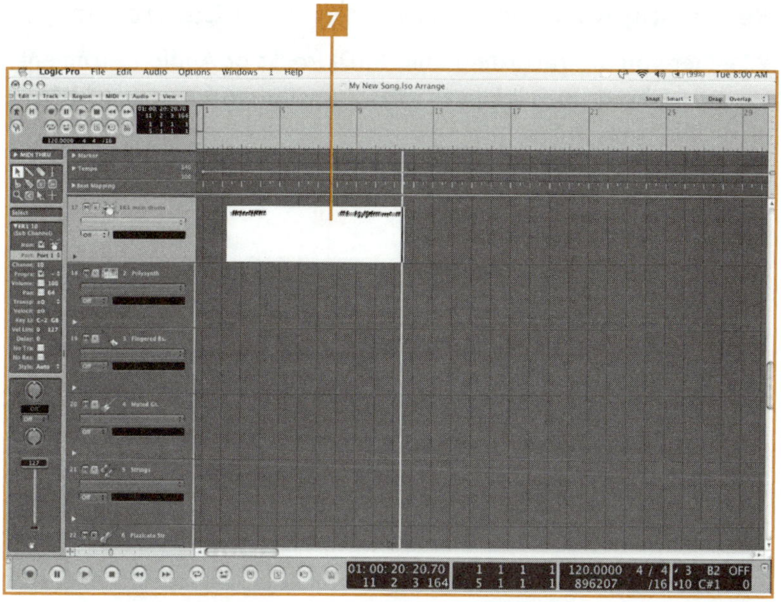

7 When you press the Record button and play your parts into Logic, the multiple MIDI channels will appear on one track while recording.

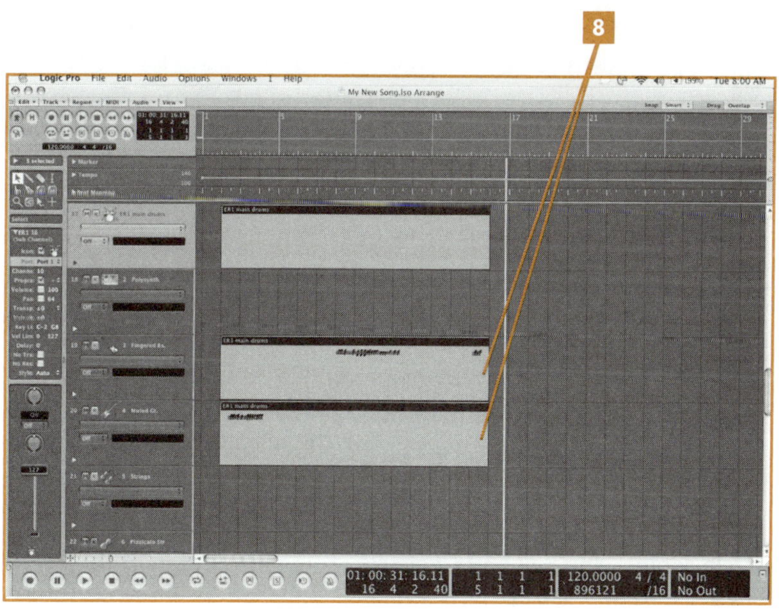

8 After you press Stop in the Transport, the individual MIDI tracks will be placed on the tracks that correspond to their respective channels.

Note

You will need to enable "Auto demix by channel if multitrack recording" in File > Song Settings > Recording to tell Logic to split your multichannel MIDI tracks to their individual channels.

Recording MIDI Data with Your MIDI Controller

Whether you are recording onto MIDI tracks or Audio Instrument tracks, the basic procedure to record MIDI data from your MIDI controller is the same.

1 **Press** the **Record** button in the Transport.

2 As Logic plays in Record mode, you'll see the notes appear as you play them on your controller.

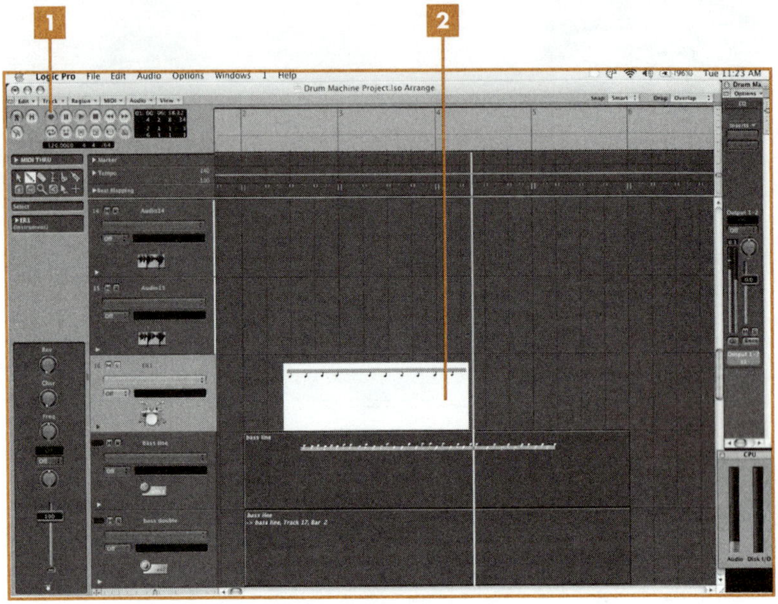

Cycle Recording

Whether recording audio or MIDI, a single track or multiple tracks, you may want to limit your recording to a specific amount of time or number of bars in your song. Or perhaps you want to automatically record multiple passes and not have to worry about constantly setting up new tracks. Cycle Recording is the answer! Cycle Mode allows you to constrain Logic to a certain length of measures in the timeline, and then continually repeat within that Cycle region. You will find Cycle recording invaluable for building MIDI drum parts, layering synths, recording multiple takes of audio, and so on.

Setting the Cycle Region

Logic makes setting the Cycle region as easy as dragging the mouse!

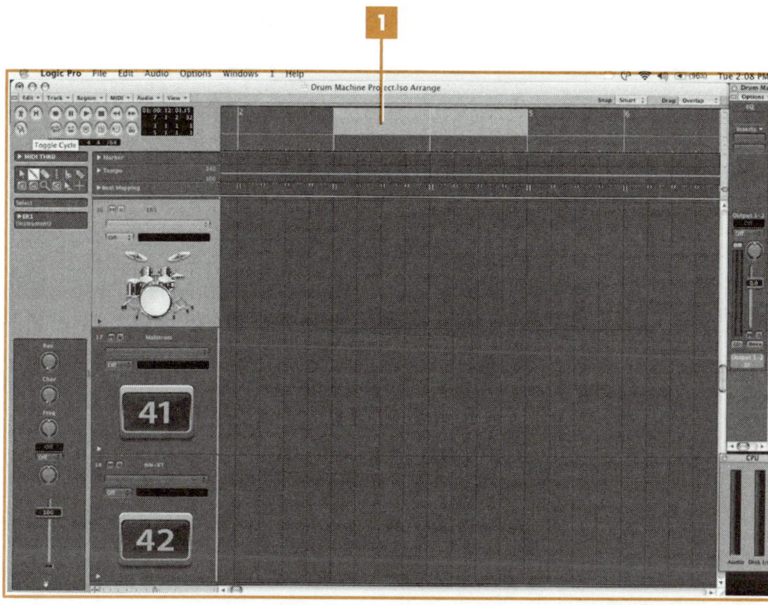

1 Click in the upper-half of the Timeline and drag it to set your Cycle region.

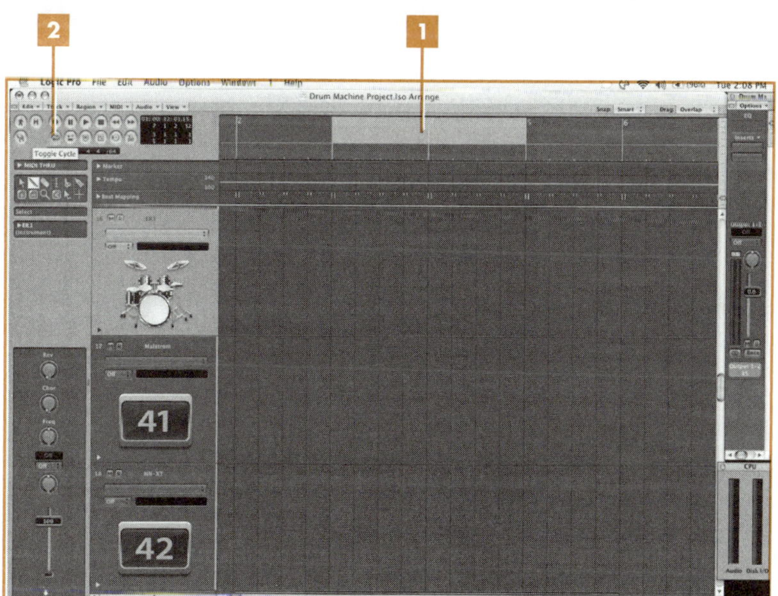

Turning on Cycle Mode

You can turn on Cycle Mode a number of ways in Logic:

1 Once your Cycle is set, you can turn it on and off by clicking within the Timeline.

2 You can also click the Toggle Cycle button in the Transport.

Creating a New Track for Each Cycle Pass

When you record audio, Logic can automatically create a new track each time you record one entire cycle. To enable this feature, there are a couple of Record settings that need to be confirmed first.

1 You get to the Record settings by clicking File > Song Settings > Recording.

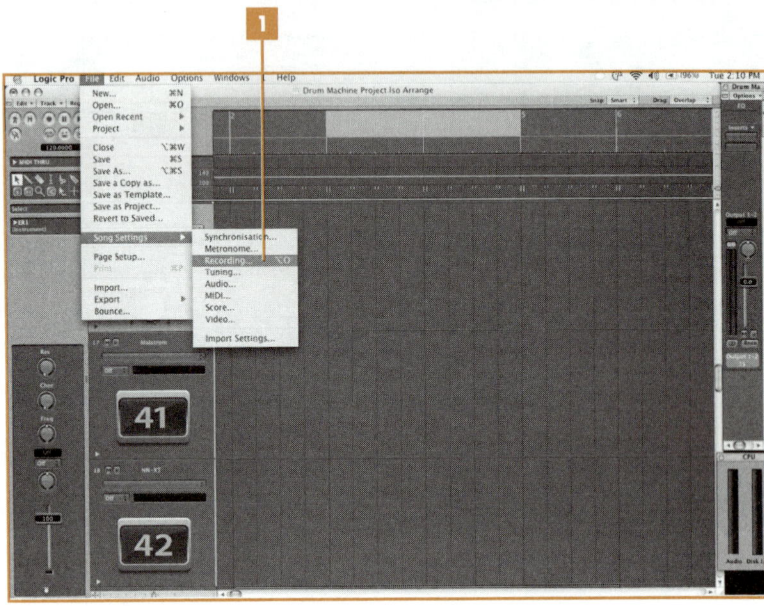

2 You can also click and hold the mouse button on the Record button in the Transport to pop open a small menu of recording options. Select Recording to go to the settings.

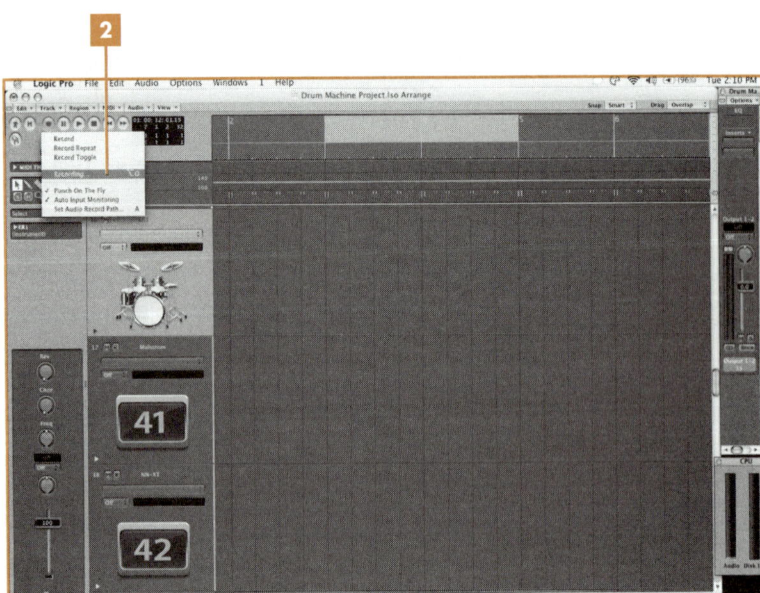

Key Command Alert: Record Settings

You can also access the Record settings by holding the OPTION key and pressing the letter O.

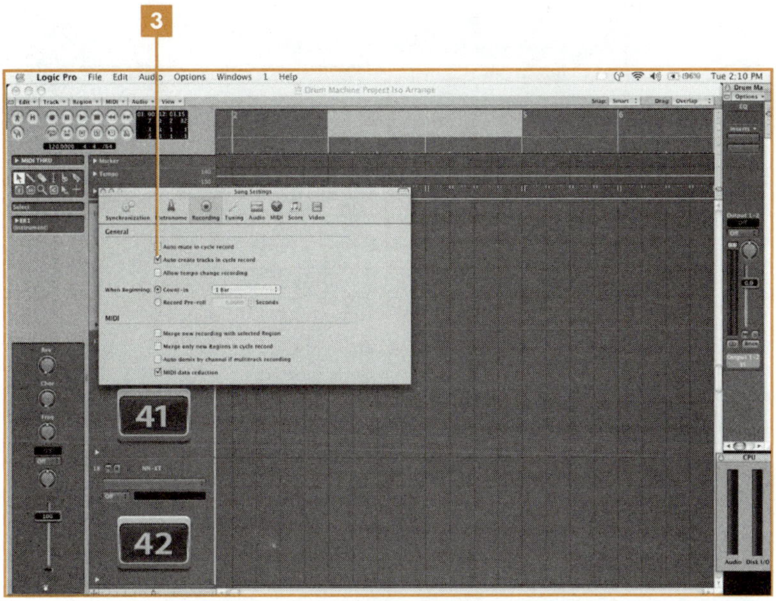

3 Make sure Auto create tracks in cycle record is checked.

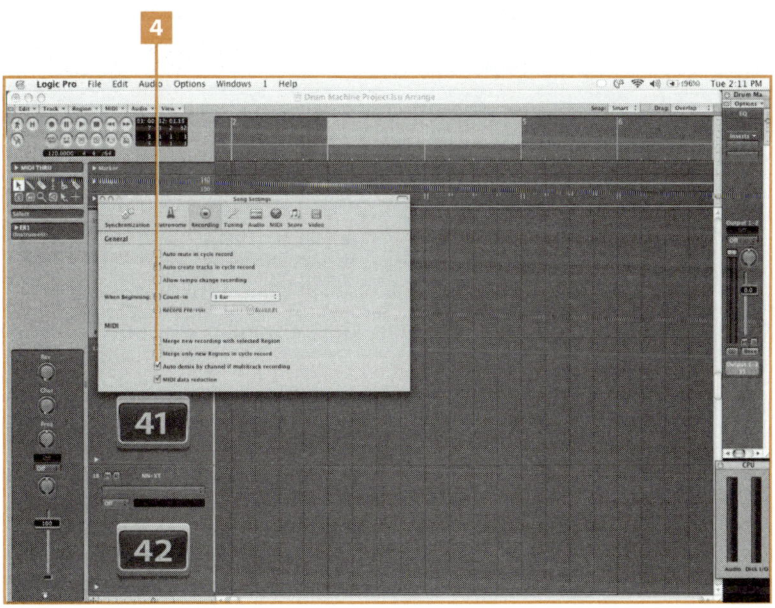

4 If you are recording multiple MIDI tracks simultaneously, you should also check the Auto demix by channel if multitrack recording option.

5 Checking Auto mute in cycle record will prevent Logic from playing back earlier recorded takes.

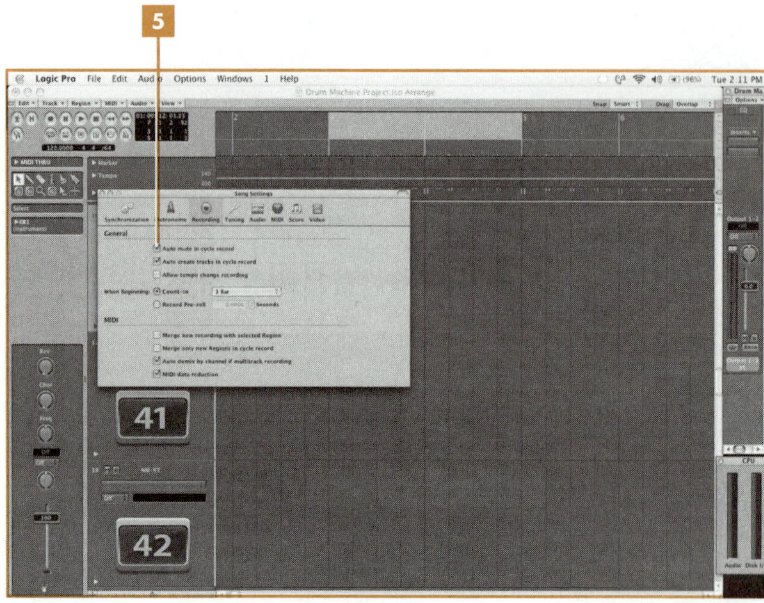

6 Press Record in the Transport, and Logic will play through your Cycle, recording your Audio or MIDI and creating a new track with each pass of the Cycle.

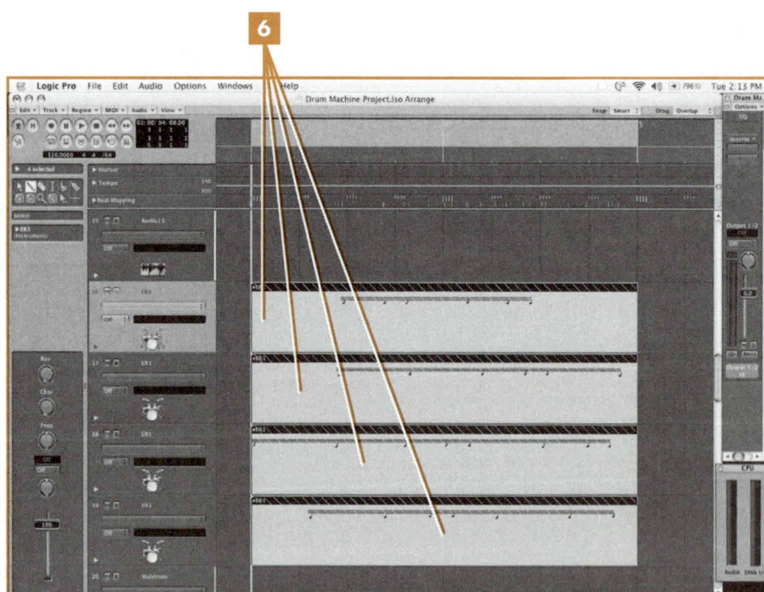

Replacing an Existing Recording with Each Cycle Pass

You can also configure Logic to automatically erase whatever you have just recorded with each new Cycle pass.

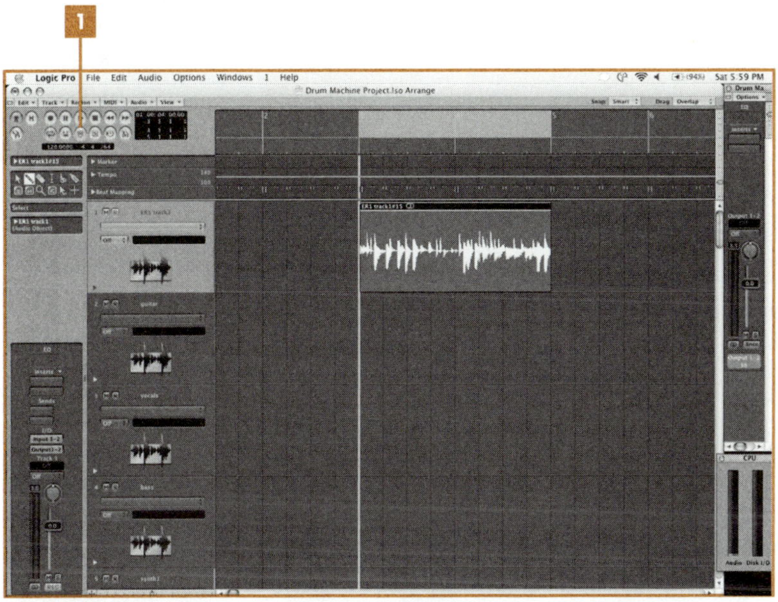

1. With a track recorded, click the Erase mode button in the Transport.

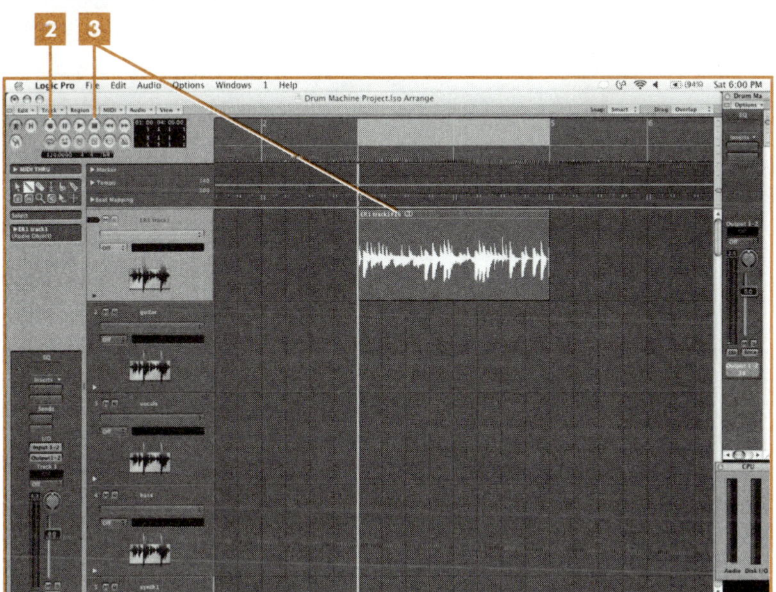

2. Click Record and record your new part.
3. Click Stop after the Cycle begins to repeat. You will see that the original part has been replaced by the new recording. This only works for one pass, and is best combined with Autodrop recording, explained below.

Autodrop Recording

If you want "hands-free" recording, Logic allows you to define a point in time at which Logic will automatically enter and then exit record mode. This is called "Autodrop" recording.

1. Click the Autodrop button in the Transport.
2. You will see a green line appear in the Timeline, just as in Cycle Mode, but it will only occupy the bottom half of the Cycle area.

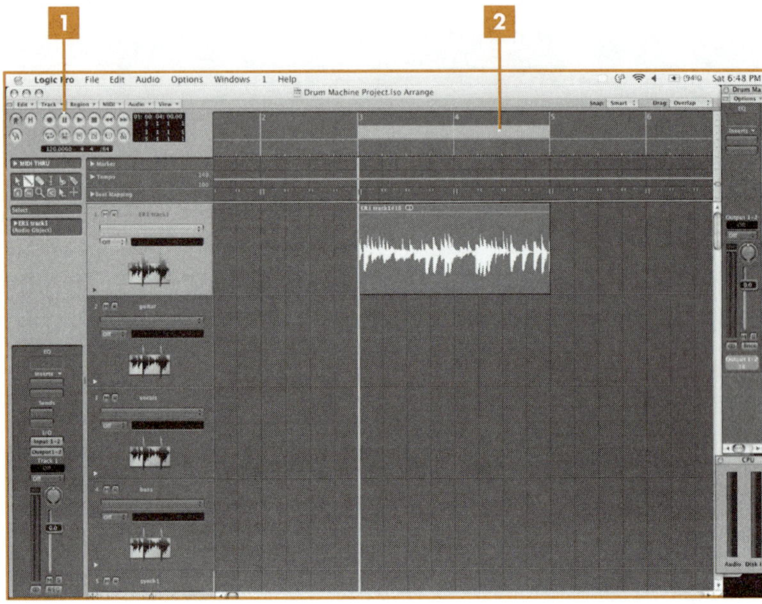

3. To change the length of the Autodrop region, double-click the locator values in the Transport, or Shift+click and drag to the left or right of the Autodrop region in the Timeline.

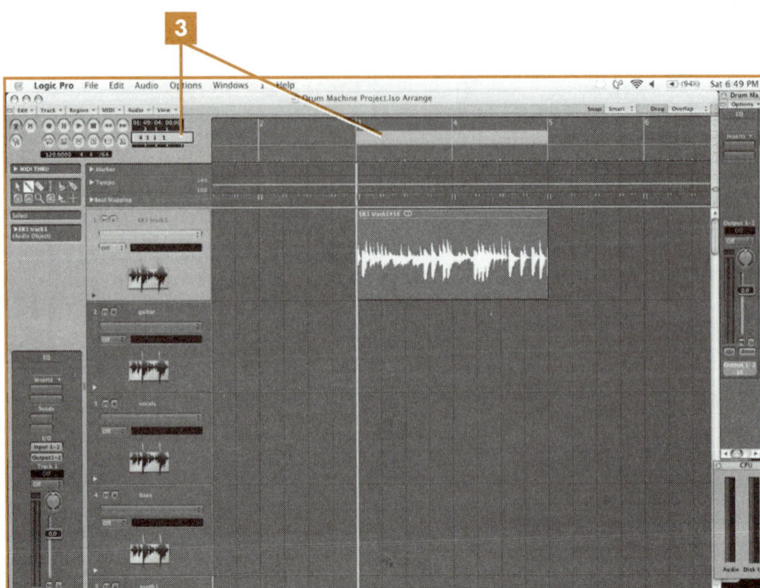

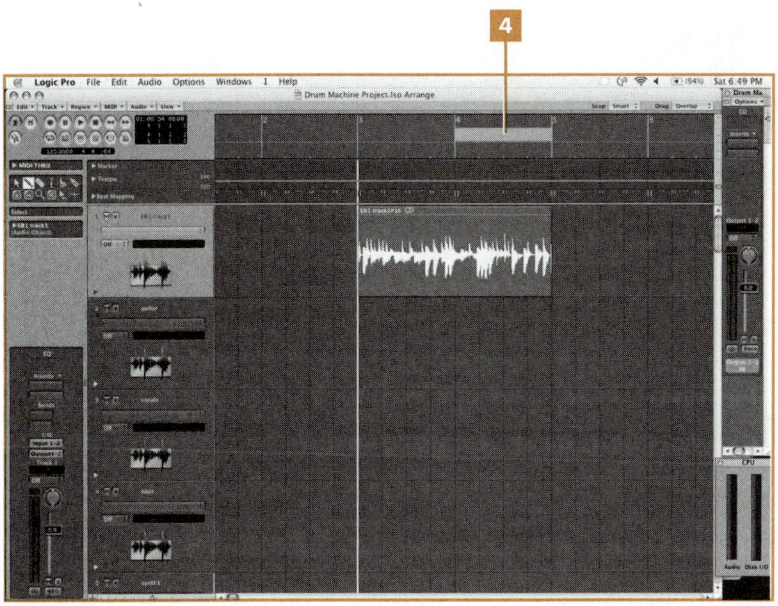

4 You can see that the Autodrop region now starts at measure 4 and ends at measure 5.

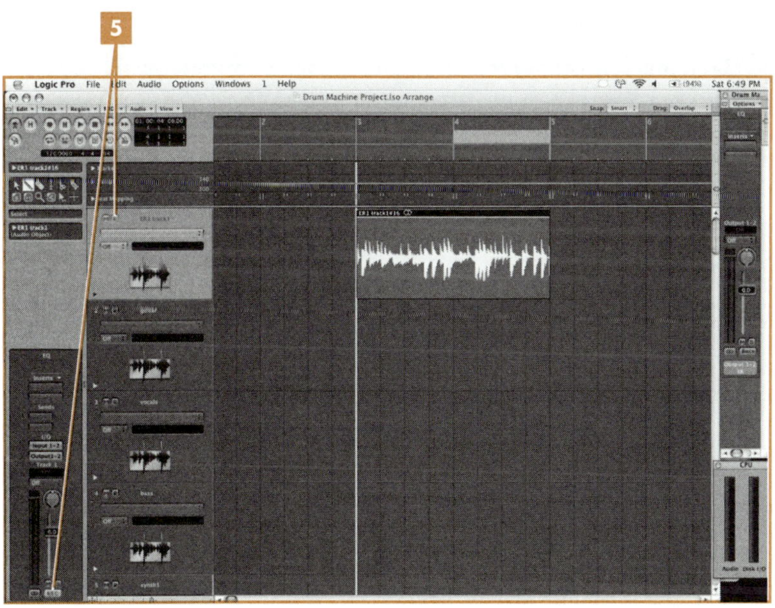

5 Record-enable the track.

6. **Press Record** in the Transport.
7. When the Song Position Line reaches the Autodrop start at measure 4, recording will start and then stop automatically at measure 5.
8. **Press Stop** in the Transport or press the Space Bar and you will see the newly recorded region.

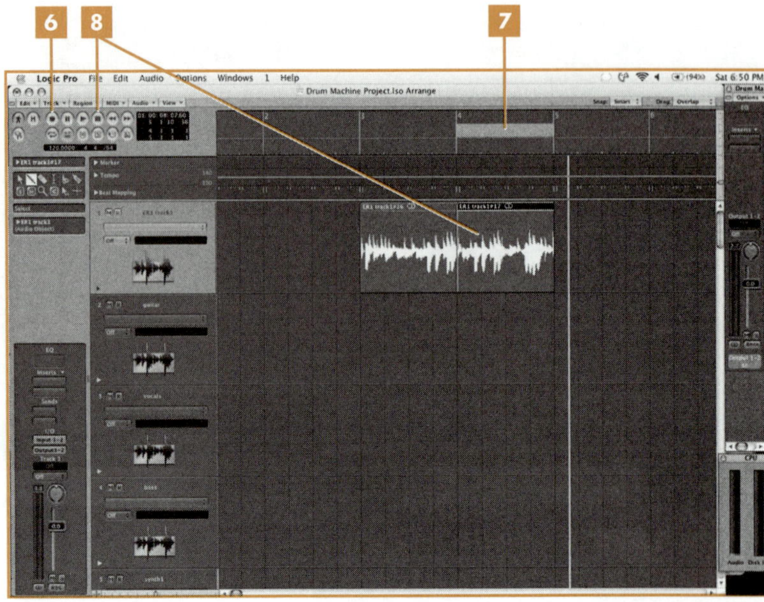

Why Is It Called Auto*drop* Mode?

The term goes back to the days of using reel-to-reel tape machines for recording. Back then, when an engineer defined a point at which the machine would automatically enter record mode, the machine would physically "drop" its record head onto the tape. Even now, in the digital age, the term has stuck.

4 Apple Loops and the Loop Browser

New with Logic 7, both Logic Pro and Logic Express now support Apple Loops. First introduced in Apple Computer's Soundtrack application, Apple Loops really took off after their inclusion in GarageBand. Basically, an Apple Loop is a sound file that, in addition to standard audio or MIDI information, contains additional information (called metadata) regarding its tempo, pitch, channel strip, and Audio Instrument information! This means that Apple Loops will automatically play back in the proper key and tempo of your song, and even bring up the proper Audio Instruments and effects, so you don't need to do any of it manually! In some cases, an Apple Loop includes both MIDI (for an Audio Instrument track) and audio (for an Audio Track). Trust us, you will love Apple Loops as much as I do! In this chapter, you will learn how to:

- Browse through your Apple Loops
- Add new Apple Loops to your Loop Browser
- Add an Apple Loop to your song
- Open the Apple Loops Utility to create your own Apple Loops

Browsing Apple Loops

Logic 7 ships with gigabytes' worth of high-quality, free Apple Loops for you to explore. Logic makes it very easy to locate and audition (preview) Apple Loops, so you can choose the right Apple Loop. There are a number of different ways to browse your Loop library, depending on your personal preferences.

Opening the Loop Browser

Before you can browse and audition your Apple Loops, you'll need to open the Loop Browser.

1 Click on the Audio menu and go to Loop Browser.

1

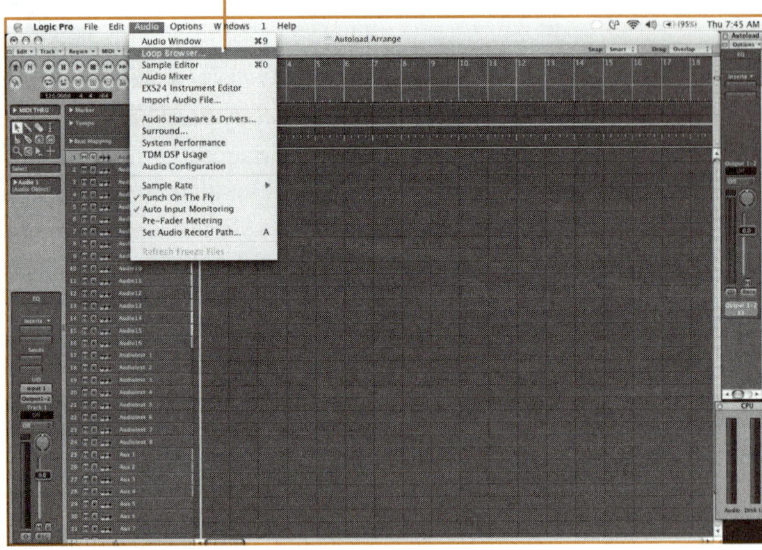

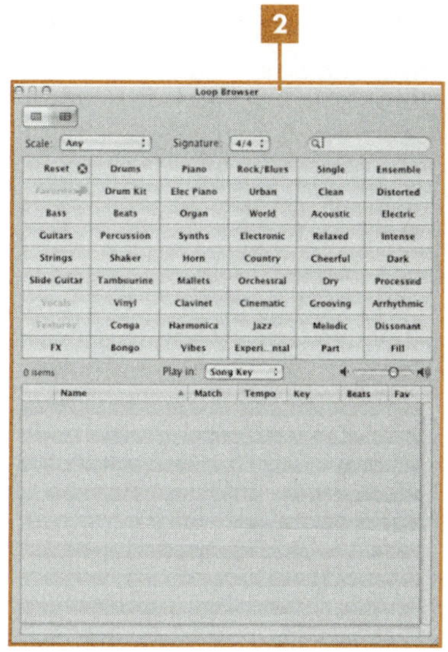

2 The Loop Browser will appear.

Exploring the Loop Browser

If you are familiar with GarageBand, it won't take long to get comfortable with Logic's Loop Browser. The Loop Browser has two modes: button view and column view. How to browse your loops in each mode is explained in the subsections below. However, there are common elements in the Loop Browser with which you should be familiar.

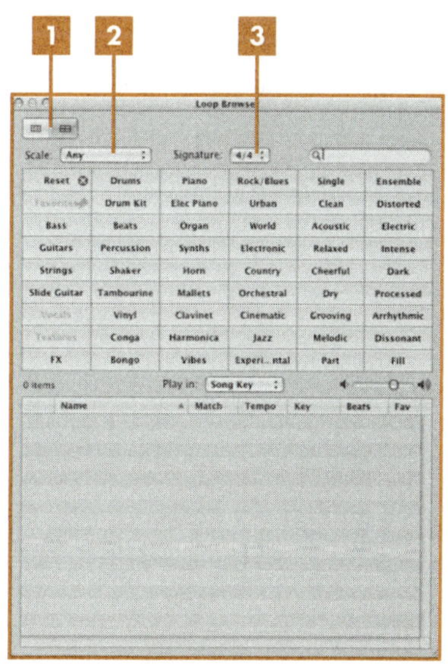

Button View

1 Browser Mode: Choose between button view and column view.

2 Scale: A method for limiting the scales of loops browsed or searched. Any, Major, Minor, Neither, and Good for Both are the options available.

3 Signature: Choose from some common time signatures when searching or browsing.

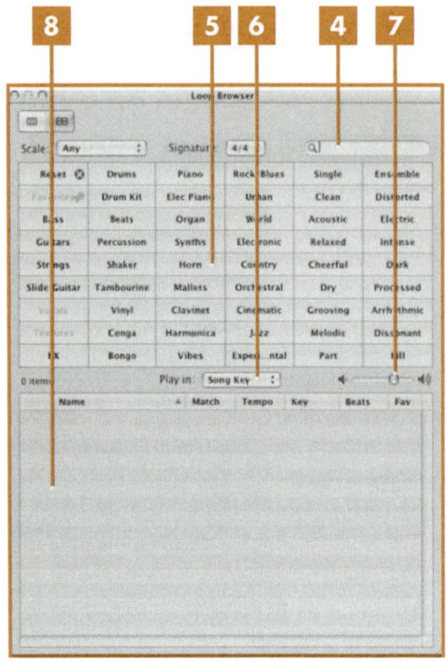

4 **Search**: Type in the name of a loop, a style, or an instrument to find all relative loops.

5 **Loop Categories**: Use the categories to find and refine your search for a type of loop. The more options chosen, the narrower the search.

6 **Play in (Key)**: Depending on the selection, the loop will audition in its original key, the Global key of the song, or the selected key from the menu.

7 **Volume slider**: Adjust the playback volume of the loops as you audition them.

8 **Results list**: As you browse and make selections, the results will display here. You can click on any loop to audition it. Click again to stop it.

Column View

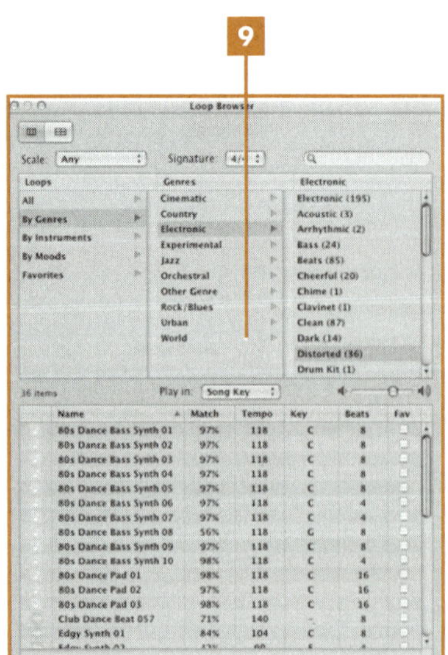

9 Column view provides the same options as button view, but the buttons are replaced by a standard Mac OS X column display. Instead of buttons for each choice of Genre, Instrument, or Mood, these are represented by categories. Selecting a category populates the column to the right with the available categories and/or keywords.

You should also be familiar with what information is presented in the results list for each loop.

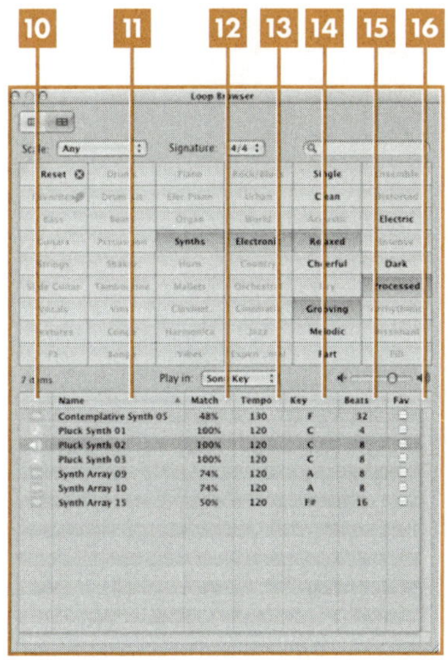

10 Type. This column will display a musical note if the loop is a Software Instrument (audio and MIDI data), Apple Loop, or an audio waveform graphic if the loop is a Real Instrument (audio) loop.

11 Name. The name of the loop.

12 Match. The accuracy percentage of the found loops based on the search criteria.

13 Tempo. The original tempo of the loop.

14 Key. The key at which the loop was originally performed.

15 Beats. This column lets you know how many beats long the loop is.

16 Favorites. A check in this box will select a loop for inclusion in your list of Apple Loop favorites.

The Loop Browser Isn't Just for Apple Loops

You may have noticed that other than for Software Instrument Apple Loops, all references in this section are made to the more generic term "loops." This is because Logic 7 and its Loop Browser actually support more varieties of audio loops than just Apple Loops. For example, you can also use ACID Loops from Sony Digital Media with Logic 7 and with the Loop Browser. Since Logic 7 and its Loop Browser are optimized for Apple Loops, you may find that some ACID Loops do not work as smoothly with Logic 7 as your Apple Loops. Nonetheless, if you do have some CDs of Sony Digital Media ACID Loops, you should be able to use them as you would Apple Loops.

Browsing Loops in Button View

The first browsing view we'll explain is button view.

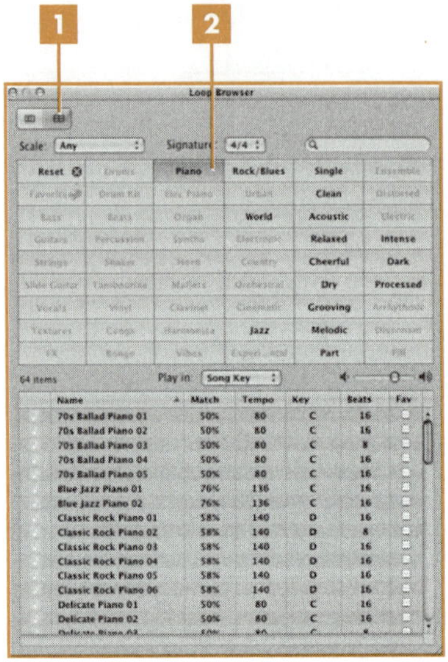

1 Click on the button view button. If the Loop Browser is not already in button view, it will switch to button view.

2 Click on the button of the musical instrument for which you are searching. Loops will appear in the results list. Only those buttons relevant to your selection will remain available.

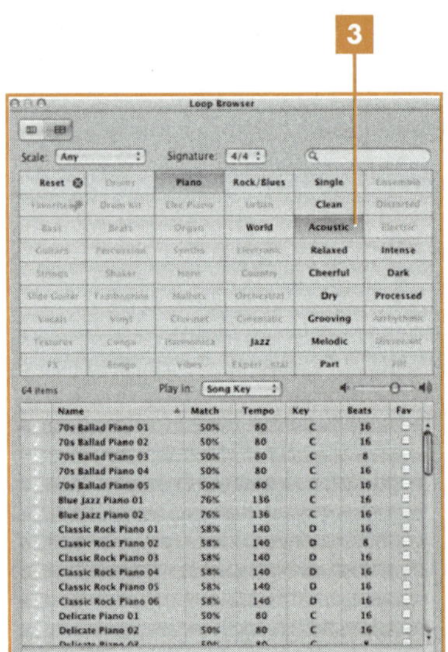

3 Click on the button of the musical style that you want for your instrument. The loops in the results list will conform to your selection. Only those buttons relevant to your selection will remain available.

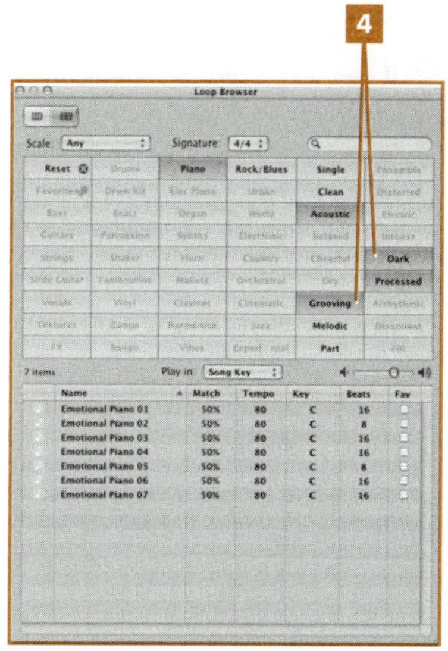

4 Click on any remaining buttons that are available to further narrow your selection.

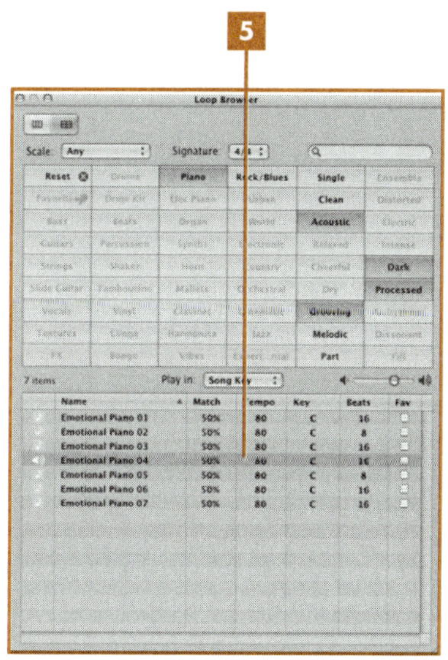

5 Click on a loop in the results list. The loop will play repeatedly at the current song tempo and key. This is called "auditioning" a loop. Loops will always audition out of Outputs 1-2 in Logic.

Stopping Loop Auditioning

If you want to stop playback of the selected loop, just click on the loop again.

Adjusting Tempo and Key When Auditioning

If the loop you audition has a different tempo and/or key in its Tempo and Key column than the tempo and key of your song, the loop may not sound the way it was intended to sound. This is neither good nor bad—you may prefer the way the loop sounds at the tempo of your song, as opposed to the original tempo, for example. But be aware that if you want to audition an loop as it was originally meant to be used, you'll need to match the tempo of your song to the tempo and key of the loop. You can match the key by selecting Original Key from the Play In pull-down menu.

Playing Your Song and Loops Together

If your song is currently playing when you click on a loop to audition, both the song and the loop will play. If you want to audition your loop in the context of the song, this is a great way to hear both together. However, this might end up sounding pretty jumbled if you're auditioning a number of loops one after the other, so, depending on your material, you might want to make sure the song itself isn't playing.

6 Click in the Favorites checkbox if you want to save this loop among your Favorites. You can then recall these loops from the Favorites button.

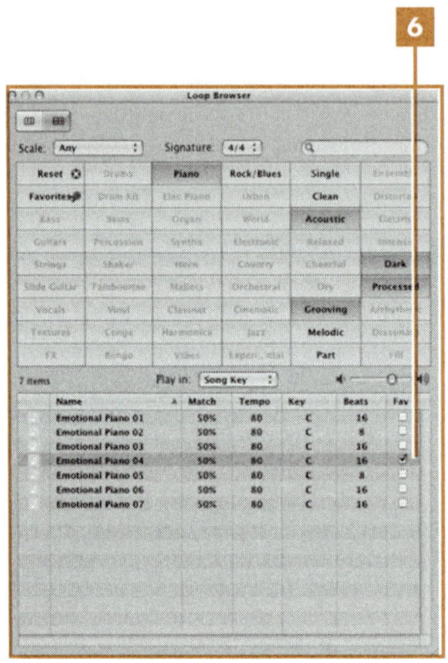

7 Repeat steps 5 and 6 for as many loops as you want to audition.

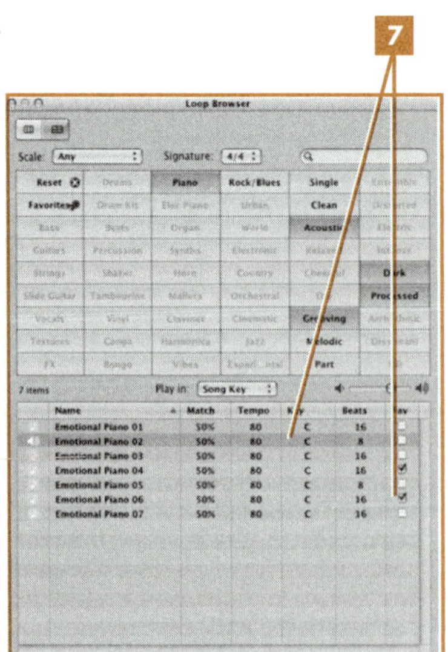

Browsing Loops in Column View

If you prefer to browse your loop collection in a more "explorer" or list-view style of interface, you can choose column view.

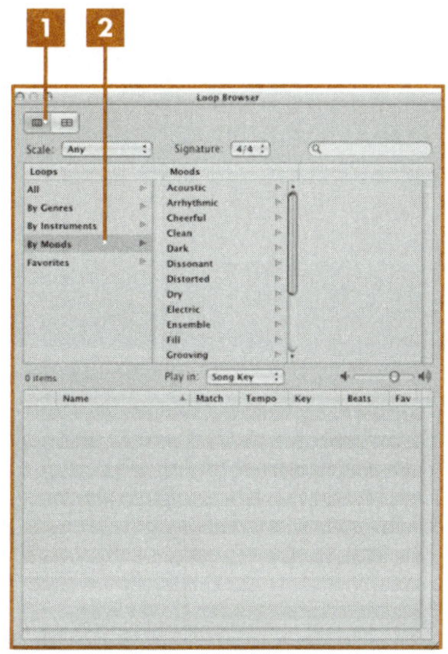

1 **Click** on the **column view** button. If the Loop Browser is not already in column view, it will switch to column view.

2 **Click** on the **entry in the Loops column** for the type of loop you would like to find. The category column will fill with the loop categories that match your selection (instrument categories if you chose By Instrument, genre categories if you chose By Genres, and so on).

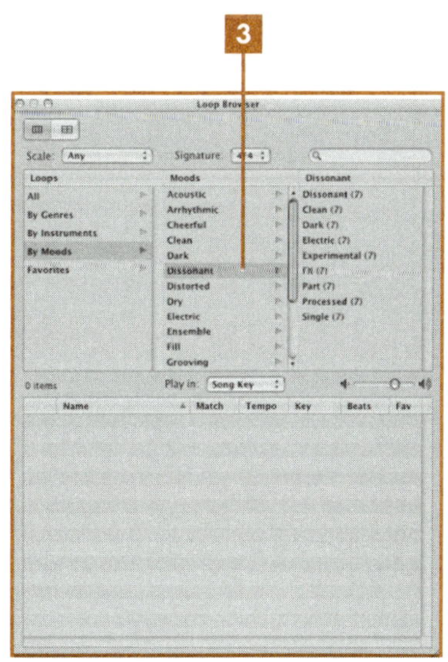

3 **Click** on the **entry in the category column** that you want for your loop. The keyword column will fill with loop libraries that conform to your selection.

4. **Click** on the **entry in the instrument column** to select those instruments. The selected instruments will appear in the results list.

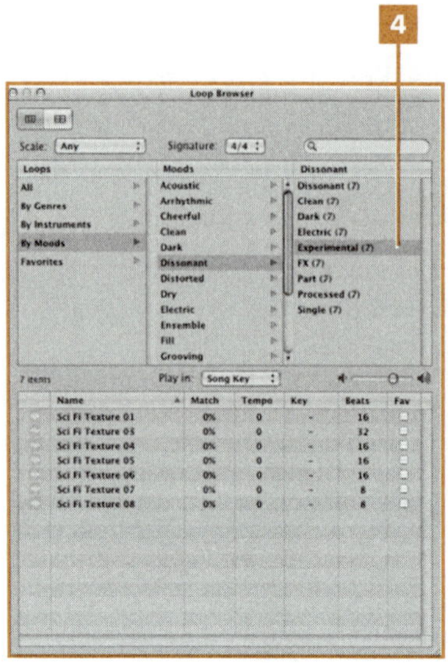

5. **Click** on a **loop** in the results list. The loop will play repeatedly at the current song tempo and key. This is called "auditioning" an Apple Loop.
6. **Click** in the **Favorites** checkbox if you want to save this loop among your Favorites. You can then recall these Apple Loops from the Favorites button.

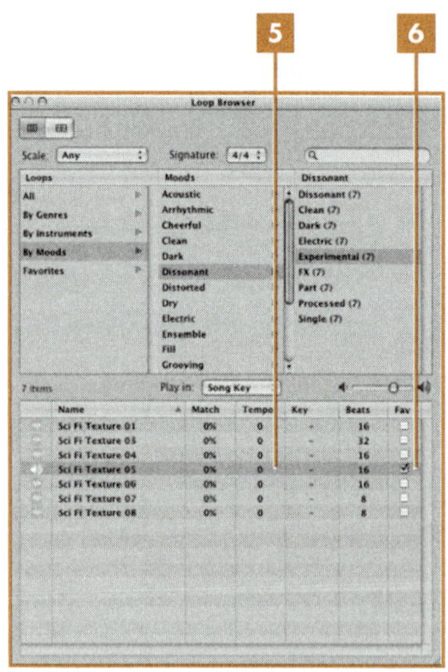

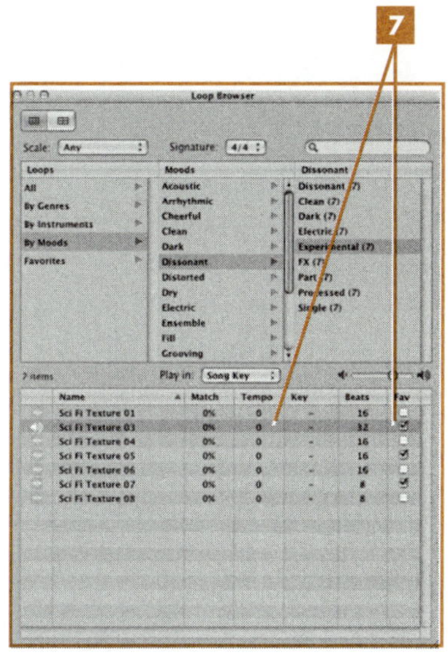

7 Repeat steps 5 and 6 for as many loops as you want to audition.

Refining Results by Keyword

In either button view or column view, you can type in a keyword to further refine your results.

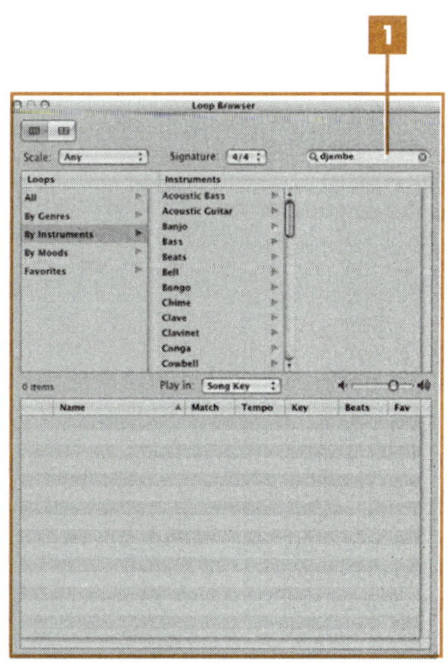

1 Type a keyword for your loop search.

2 **Press** the **Return key**. The remaining loops in the results list will all have the keyword you typed in their description.

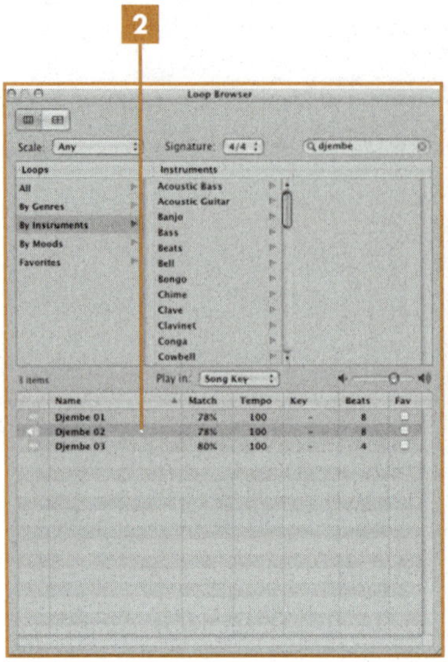

3 **Click** on a **loop** in the results list. The loop will play repeatedly at the current song tempo and key.

4 **Click** in the **Favorites checkbox** if you want to save this loop among your Favorites. You can then recall these loops from the Favorites button.

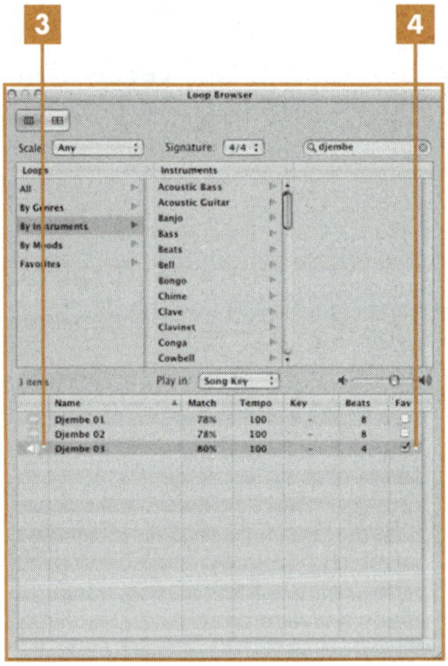

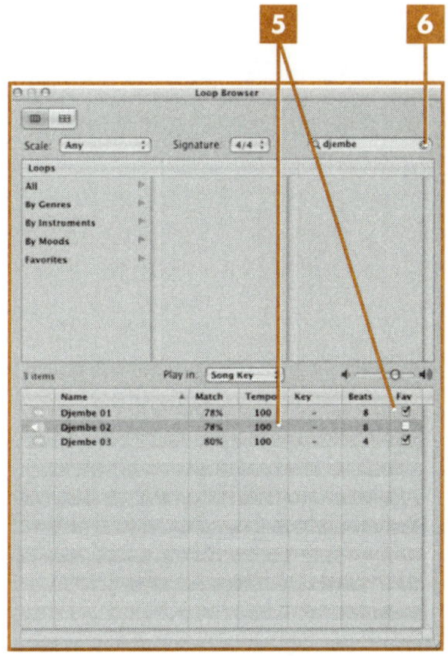

5 **Repeat steps 3 and 4** for as many loops as you want to audition.

OPTIONAL

6 **Click** on the **Cancel** button in the text box if you wish to return to the complete results list.

Refining Results by Scale

Apple Loops will automatically conform to the key of your song. However, if the Apple Loop has to change its key to fit your song, it may sound and feel different than it did in its original key. One way to reduce this effect is to stick to Apple Loops that have the same scale type (major, minor, and so on) as your song.

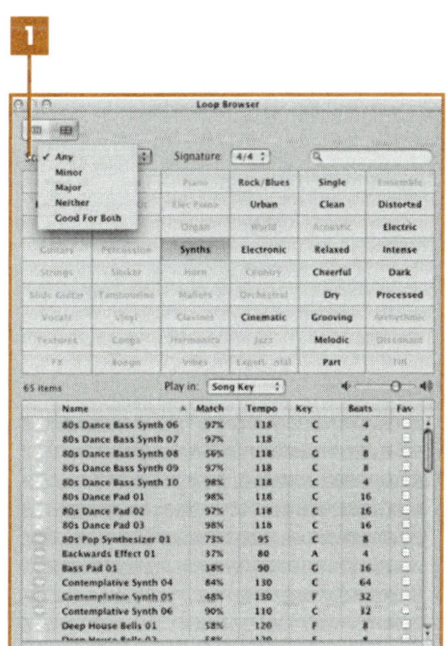

1 **Click** on the **Scale** drop-down menu. A menu will appear.

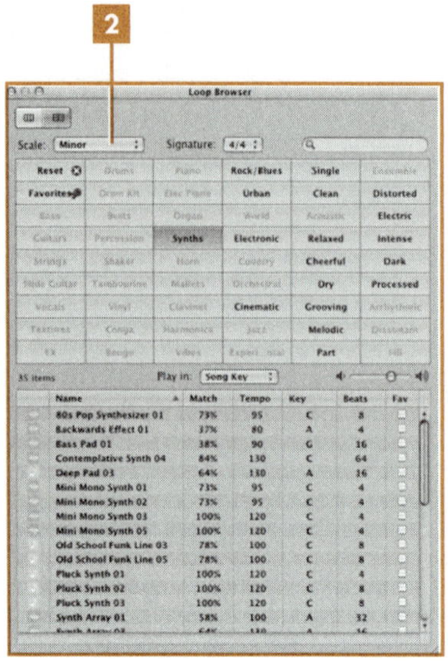

2 Click on the scale type of your song. The results list will now contain only Apple Loops matching the scale type you selected.

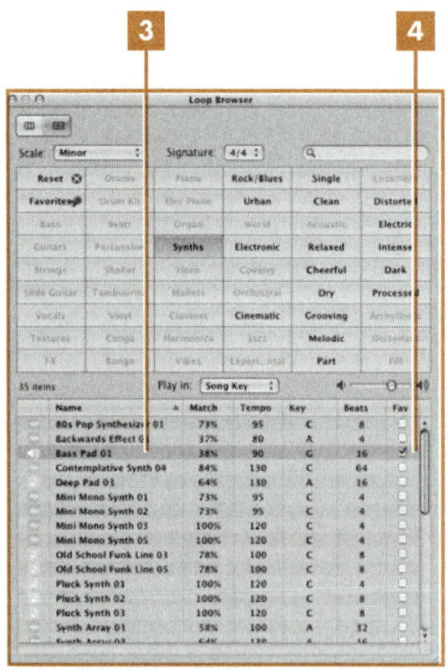

3 Click on an Apple Loop in the results list. The loop will play repeatedly at the current song tempo and key.

4 Click in the Favorites checkbox if you want to save this loop among your Favorites. You can then recall these Apple Loops from the Favorites button.

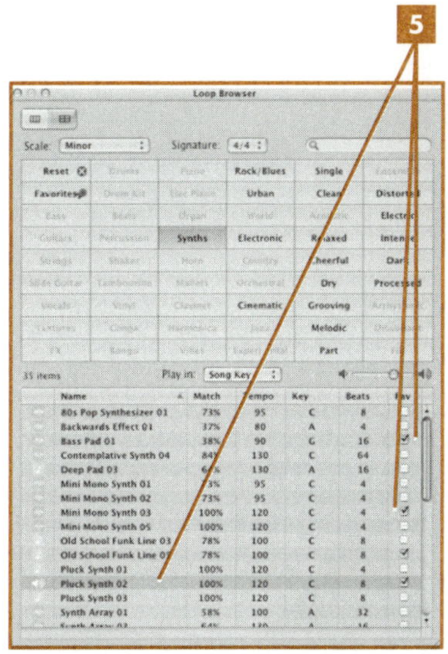

5 **Repeat steps 3 and 4** for as many Apple Loops as you want to audition.

Adding Loops to the Loop Browser

Of course, you are not limited to only the Apple Loops that were included with Logic 7! There are many companies selling CDs of Apple Loops, and you can find free Apple Loops on the Internet as well. The easiest way to access these loops from within Logic is to first add them to the Loop Browser. Adding new loops to Logic's Loop Browser is as easy as adding songs to iTunes!

1 **Open** the **Loop Browser**.

2 **Switch** to the **Finder**.

3 Click on the Apple Loops folder in the Finder or on your desktop (or on the disk that is mounted on the desktop).

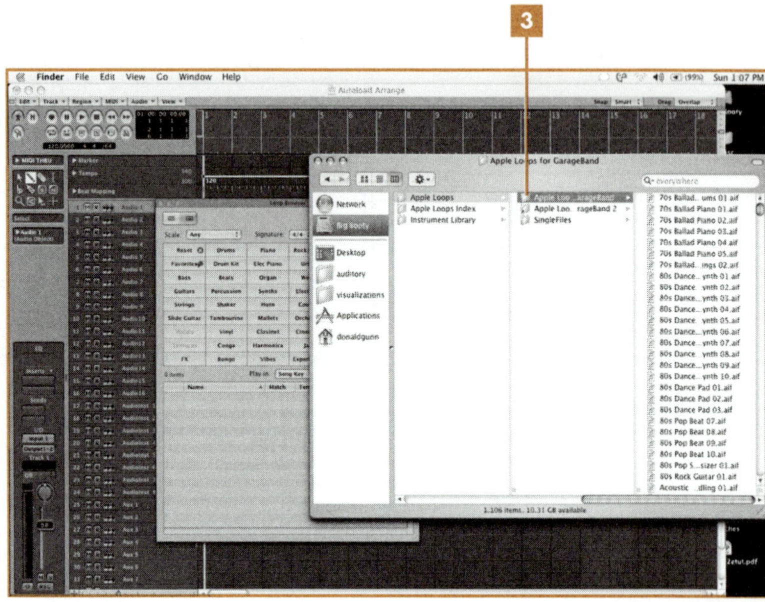

4 Drag the Apple Loops folder onto the results window of the Loop Browser.

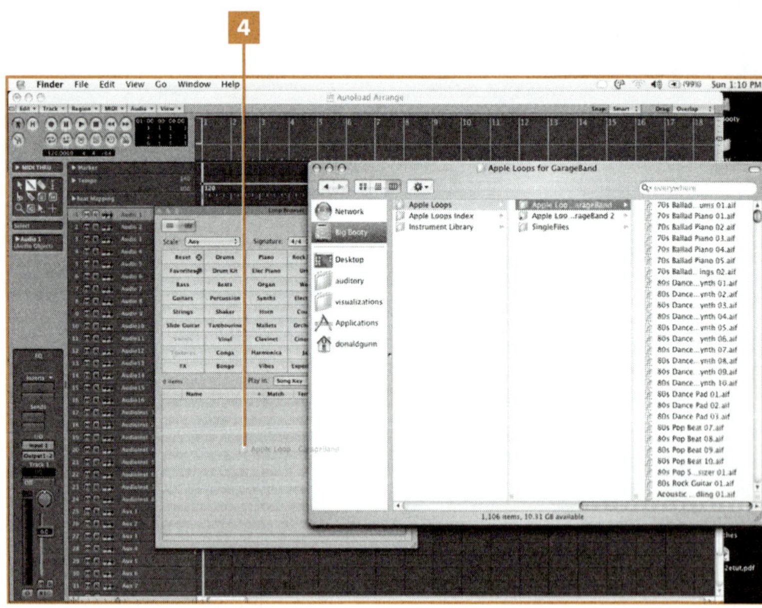

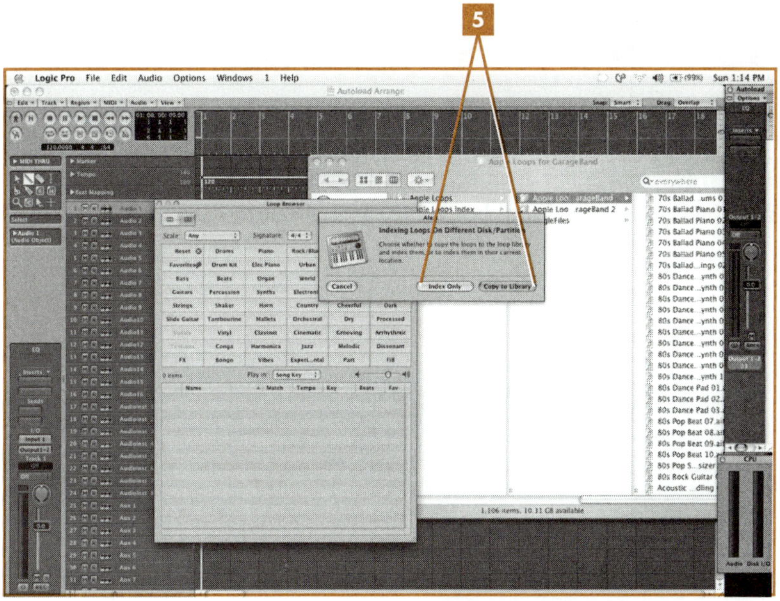

5 You will be asked if you want to copy the loops to the loop library and index them or index them in their current location. Select the option you prefer, and then confirm that your loops are now searchable in the Loop Browser.

To Copy, or Not to Copy—That Is the Question

Should you have Logic add your loops to its private Apple Loops folder, or simply index the loops in their current location? If your loops are currently located on a removable storage media such as CD-ROM, Logic should absolutely copy them. But if they are already on your hard drive, you may just want to index your loops and not make a separate copy of them just for Logic. Finally, if you're running out of space on your system hard drive, you'll want to index your Apple Loops instead of copying them.

Adding ACID Loops to the Loop Browser

ACID Loops do not contain the categorization data that Apple Loops do. Instead, the categories for ACID Loops are generated by their folder structure. This means that when you add ACID Loops to the Loop Browser, in order for them to be properly categorized, you will need to drag in their entire folder hierarchy from their original CD-ROM or folder structure.

Adding an Apple Loop to Your Song

After auditioning the Apple Loops you want in your song, you'll no doubt want to add them. Logic makes this very easy.

1 Click and hold on the loop you wish to add to your song.

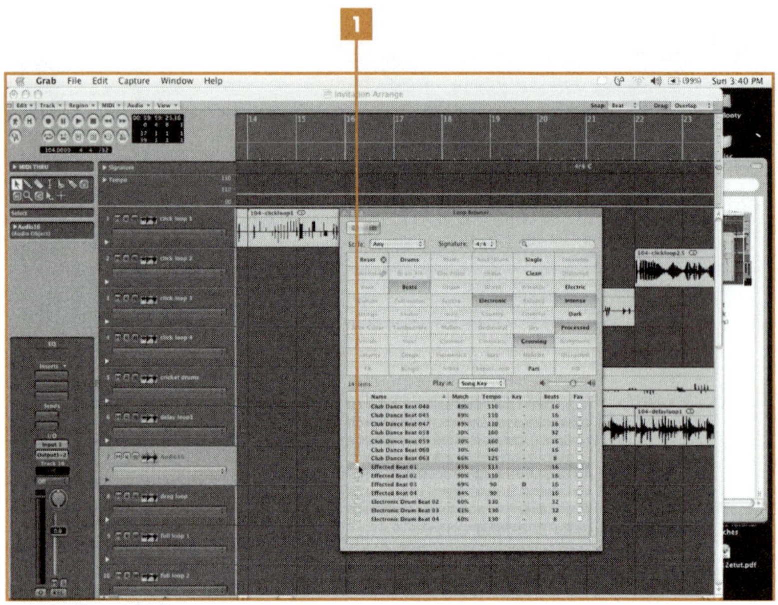

Software Instrument and Real Instrument Apple Loops

As mentioned in the introduction of this chapter, there are two kinds of Apple Loops in GarageBand, named after their respective track types: Real Instrument Apple Loops, which consist only of audio files and related metadata, and Software Instrument Apple Loops, which consist of both MIDI and audio data, as well as metadata relating to both (tempo and pitch of the audio performance, and channel strip and audio instrument of the MIDI performance).

This means that if you drag a Software Instrument Apple Loop onto an Audio Track, the Apple Loop will turn into an audio waveform just like a Real Instrument Apple Loop. This means that you will lose a Software Instrument's features, such as MIDI editing its notes and automatically loading its audio instrument and effects with the loop. The Apple Loop will, however, still play at the proper tempo and transpose to the proper key of your song.

Real Instrument Apple Loops cannot be dragged onto Audio Instrument Tracks, as they contain no MIDI data.

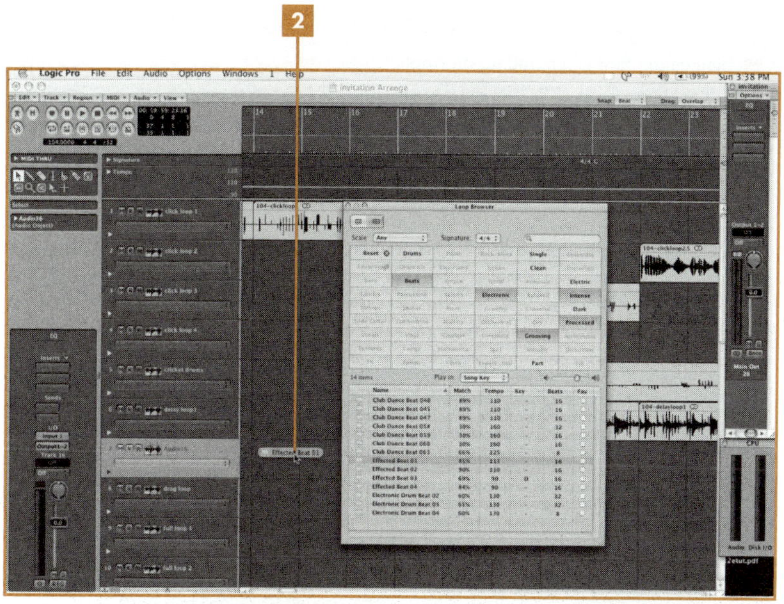

2 **Drag** the **loop** to an area inside the track lane of the empty track.

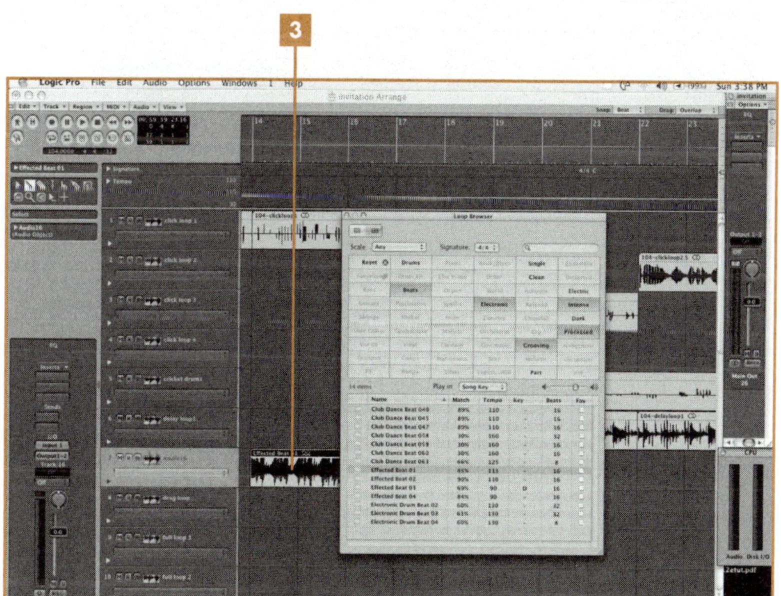

3 **Release** the **mouse** button. Logic will place your loop on the track. You will see its audio region in the track lane for that track.

Real and Software Instrument Apple Loops Redux

Remember that when adding an Apple Loop to an Audio Track, you can add either a Real Instrument or Software Instrument Apple Loop. Either loop contains audio data. When adding an Apple Loop to an Audio Instrument track, you can only add a Software Instrument Apple Loop. Real Instrument loops do not contain MIDI data.

Adding an Apple Loop to an Existing Track with Material Already Present

You may want to add an Apple Loop to a track that already has material on it. You can add an Apple Loop to a track with other Apple Loops, Software Instrument performances, or Real Instrument performances.

1 Click and hold on the loop you wish to add to your song.

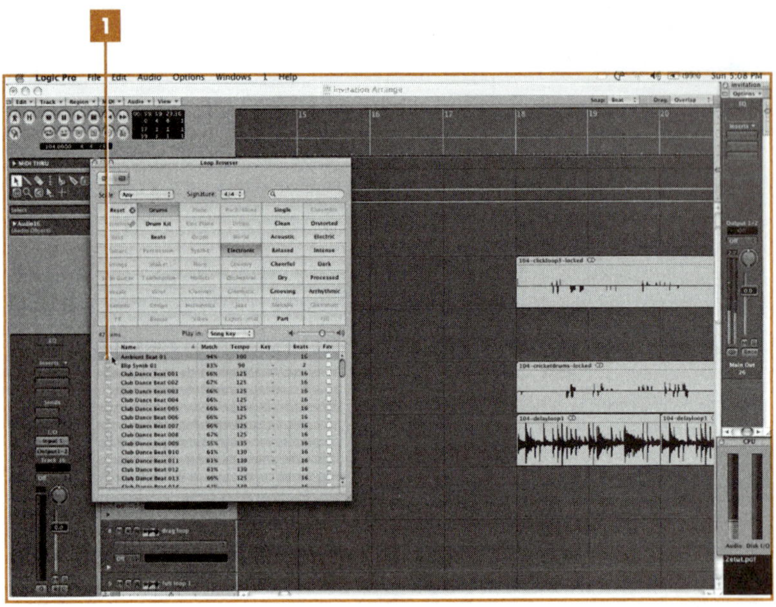

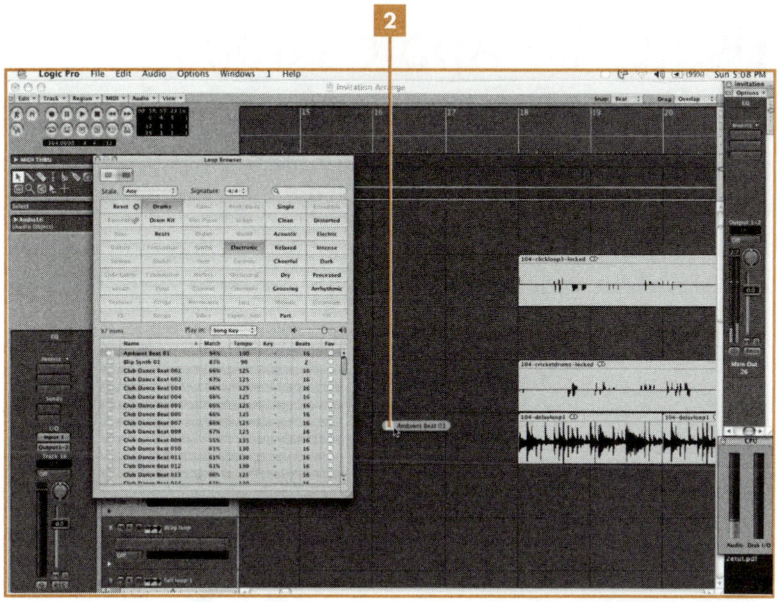

2 Drag the loop to an area of the track lane before or after the existing regions on that track.

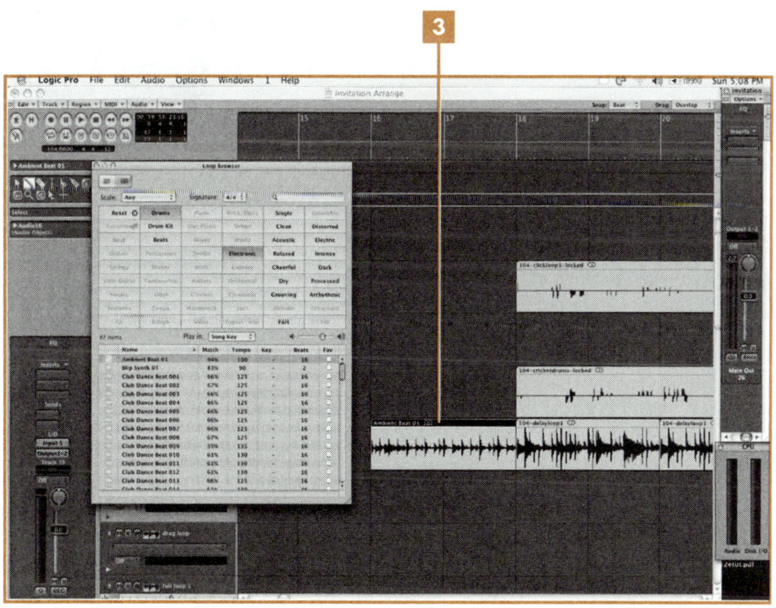

3 Release the mouse button. Logic will place your loop on the track at the location you have specified. The loop's region will display either its audio waveform or MIDI notes, depending on whether it was added to an Audio or Audio Instrument Track.

Using the Apple Loops Utility to Create Apple Loops

Unlike GarageBand, Logic 7 ships with a helper application that allows you to turn your own audio files into Real Instrument Apple Loops. While it is beyond the scope of this book to go into the art of designing and editing loops, we at least want to familiarize you with the basic steps involved in using the Apple Loops Utility.

1 In the Finder, navigate to the Soundtrack Loop Utility in your Applications folder. Double-click to launch the program.

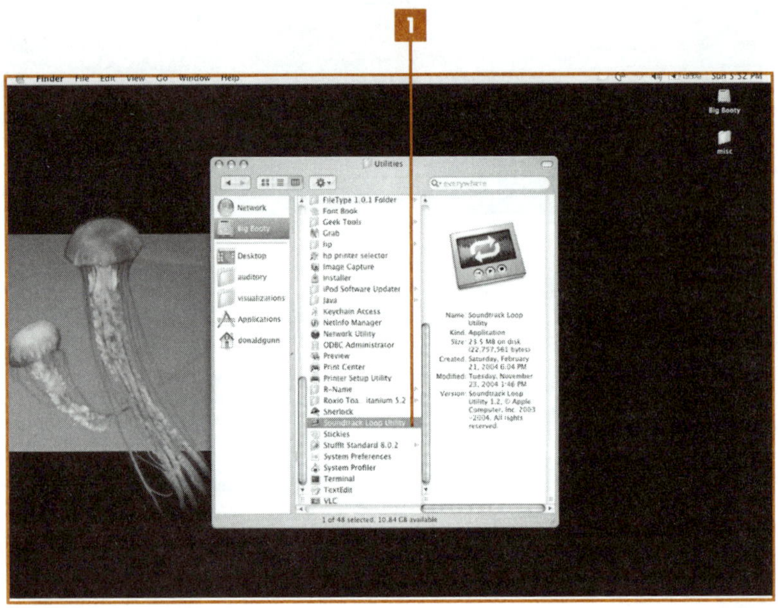

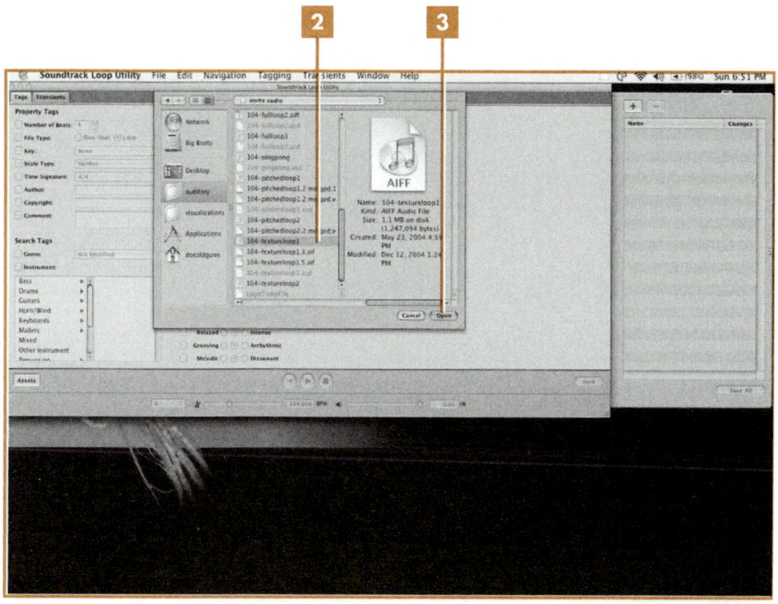

2 When the Soundtrack Loop Utility opens, you will be prompted with a dialog box to select a file to open. Click the file you want to open in the utility.

3 Press Open to open the file, or double-click the name to open it.

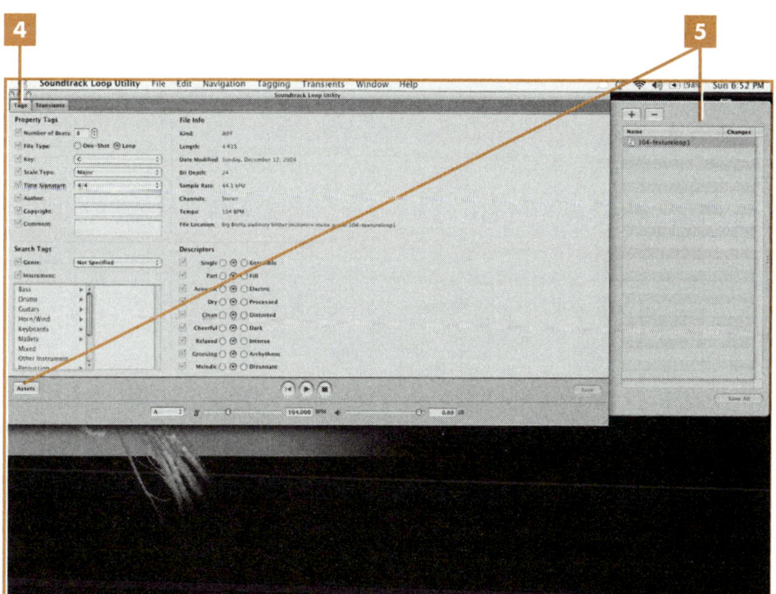

4 Your loop will open with the Tags page visible. If you see a waveform display, press the Tags tab in the upper left of the window. This page displays the metadata associated with the loop and can be modified and saved with the Apple Loop. This will be discussed further a little later.

5 The Assets button will open and close the drawer to the right that displays a list of open files.

6 Click the Transients tab to switch to the waveform display. In this window, the transients of a loop are detected and best guessed at in their rhythmic location by the Utility.

7 The Sensitivity slider adjusts how finely the transients are detected.

8 At the leftmost position, transients will be placed based on the setting in the Transient Division menu. Moving the slider to the right will result in more transients being detected.

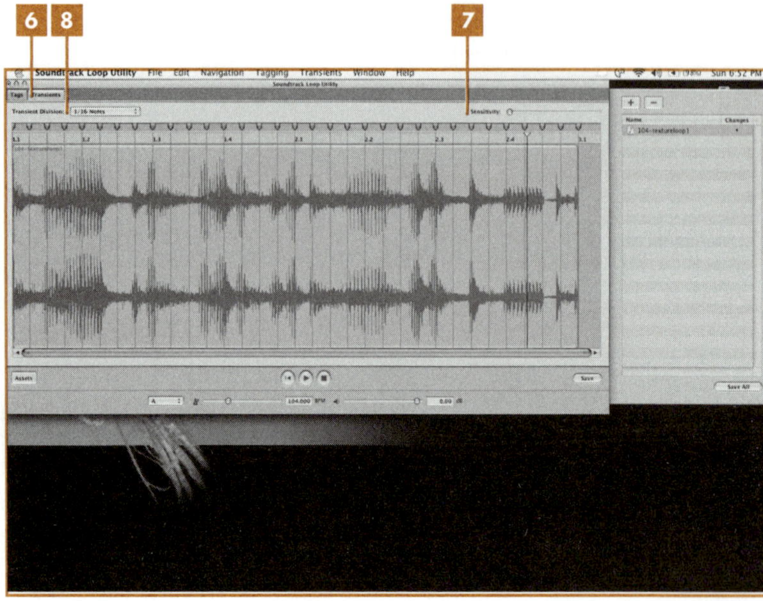

9 Click and drag left or right on the handles on either end of the scroll bar to zoom in on the transients.

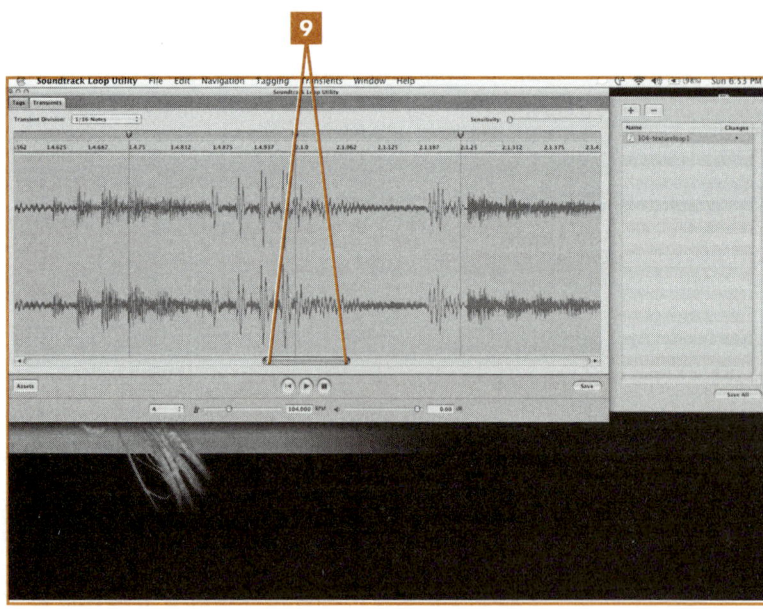

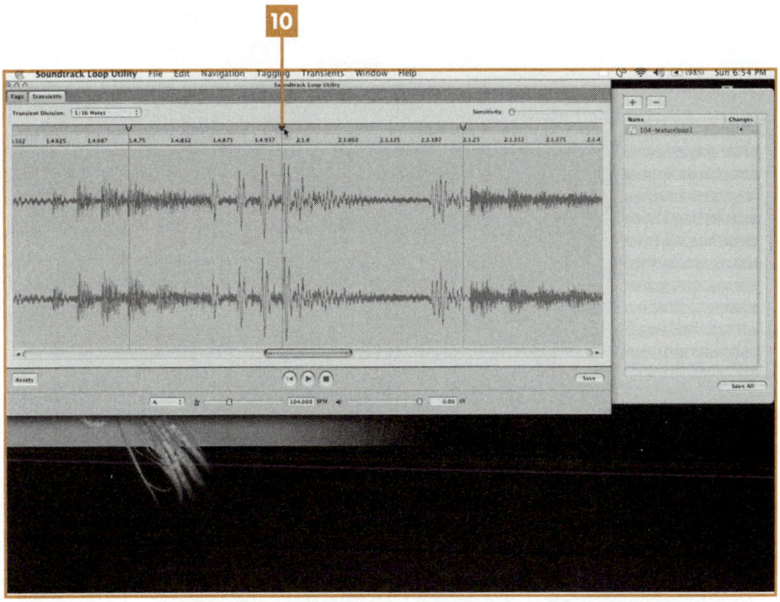

10 Click and drag the Transient markers if you want to move where a beat is falling.

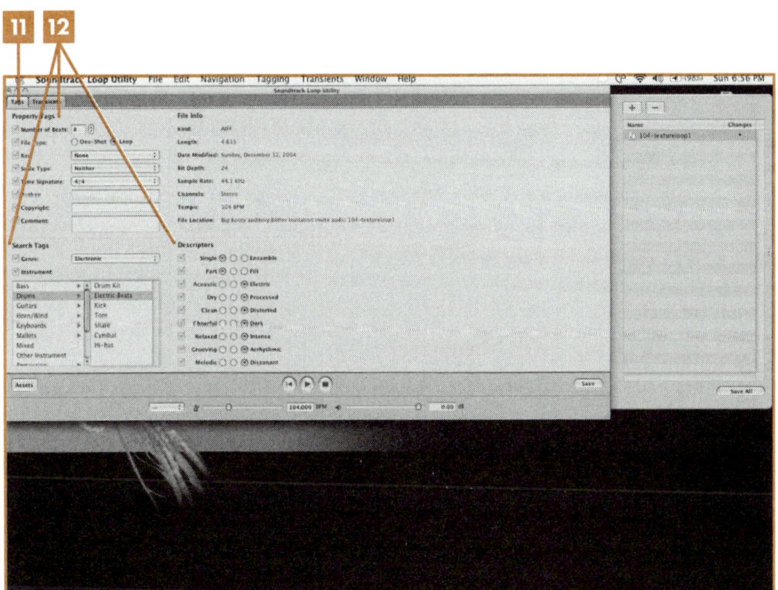

11 Click the Tags tab to return to the Tags page.

12 Enter your information for the Property Tags, Search Tags, and Descriptors.

13 Click the **Save** button to save a new copy of your file as an Apple Loop.

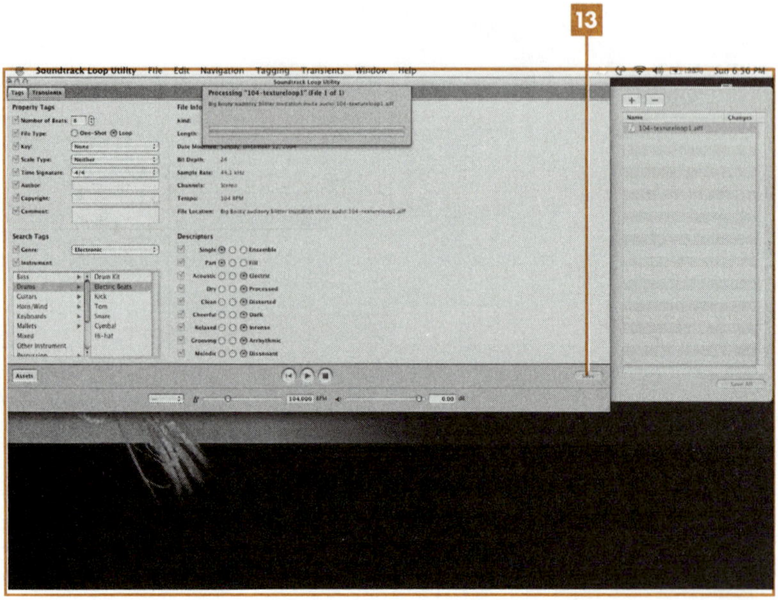

Is It the Apple Loops Utility or the Soundtrack Loops Utility?

The utility to make your own audio files into Apple Loops originally shipped with Apple Computer's Soundtrack application, and it was named the Soundtrack Loop Utility. When Apple Computer's other audio applications gained Apple Loops support, this name made less sense. While the Apple Loops Utility currently shipping with Logic is named Soundtrack Loops Utility, Apple Computer intends to change the utility's name to the more inclusive Apple Loops Utility.

Converting ACID Loops

If you find that Logic is having trouble using your ACID Loops, the easiest solution is to simply drag them to the Apple Loops Utility and resave the ACID Loops as Apple Loops. Since the Apple Loop Utility can recognize the ACID transients, there is very little for you to do except select Save All!

5 The Arrange Window

You've set up your audio and MIDI equipment. You've configured Logic's mixer, and you have recorded some audio and MIDI. You've even got some Apple Loops in your song. Now it's time to start arranging! In Logic, this will be done in the Arrange window.

In all likelihood, the Arrange window is where you will spend most of your time when using Logic. You already know this is where your tracks live, and you have recorded audio in the Arrange window. You will also use the Arrange window to get a global overview of your song, to edit your audio and MIDI regions, to move around your audio and MIDI regions, and to loop regions. With its exhaustive number of commands in its local menus and its extensive Toolbox of cursor tools, it can seem quite complicated. But in fact, there is an elegance and—dare we say—logic, to all of it. Trust us—you'll find yourself getting comfortable with the Arrange window in no time!

In this chapter, you will learn how to:

- Navigate the Arrange window
- Use the Track buttons
- Adjust the zoom
- Freeze tracks
- Use Logic Nodes (Logic Pro only)
- Create and use Markers on the Marker Track (Logic Pro only)
- Add files to the Arrange window

A Look Around the Arrange Window

You already should be somewhat familiar with the Arrange window elements from the previous chapters. But let's take a more detailed look at the Arrange window.

Arrange Window Buttons

The Arrange window includes a few buttons that control how the Arrange window interoperates with other windows. Here are Logic's Arrange buttons:

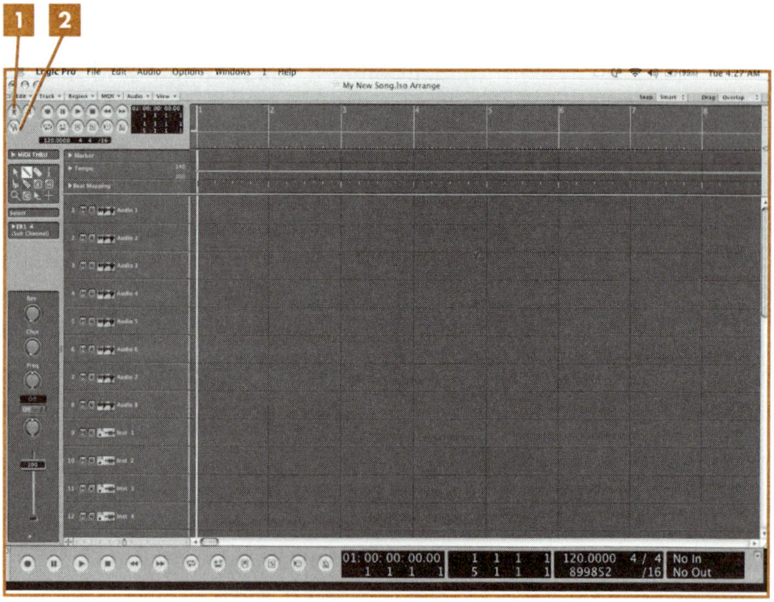

1 Catch Button: Clicking this button will ensure that the visible section of the Arrange window will display the current song position. This is especially important when in playback or record mode. If you move the visible section of the Arrange yourself, the Catch button is automatically disengaged so that you don't lose the section you're working on.

2 Link Button: Clicking the Link button will ensure that the contents of the Arrange window will always be linked to any window that is "topped," or in front of all other windows. You can double-click this button to engage Contents Link mode, in which the Arrange window will always show whatever region is selected in the linked editor.

Using the Catch and Link Buttons Together: Contents Catch

If you have both the Catch and Link buttons enabled , Logic will be in Contents Catch mode. This acts like Contents Link mode until you start playback. When Logic is playing and the Arrange is in Contents Catch mode, the selected region will change in a linked editor as the song position line moves along the song.

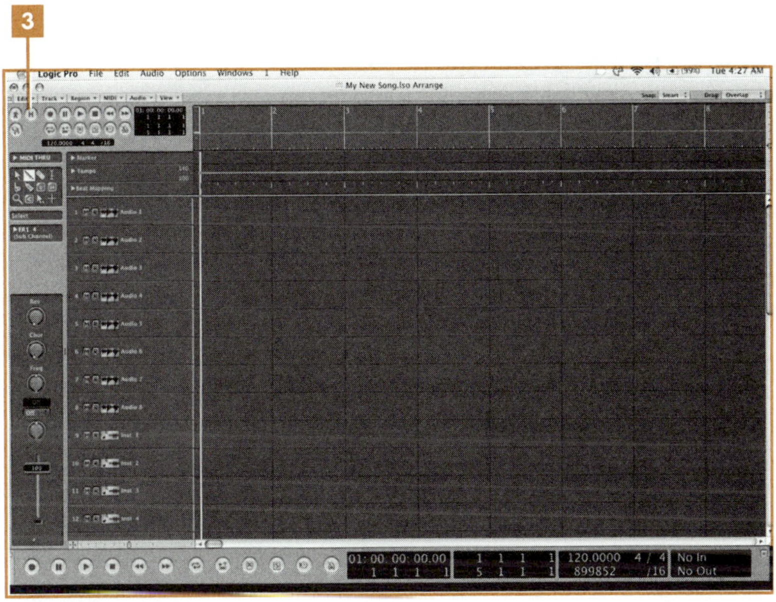

3 Hide Button (Logic Pro only): Toggle this button to hide some of the tracks on your Arrange window, or to choose which tracks to hide.

Global Tracks

One of Logic 7's new features is Global Tracks. Global Tracks contain Global Events—data that affects or organizes your Logic song as a whole. Logic Pro offers seven Global Tracks; Logic Express offers four. These tracks can be displayed in most MIDI editors and in the Arrange window. A brief introduction of each Global Track follows.

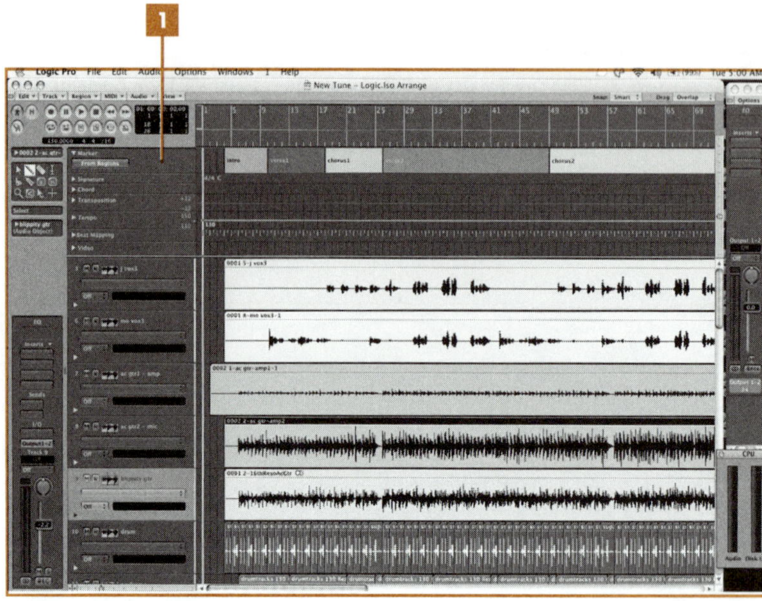

1 Marker Track (Logic Pro only): The Marker Track contains song markers that can help you organize and navigate your song.

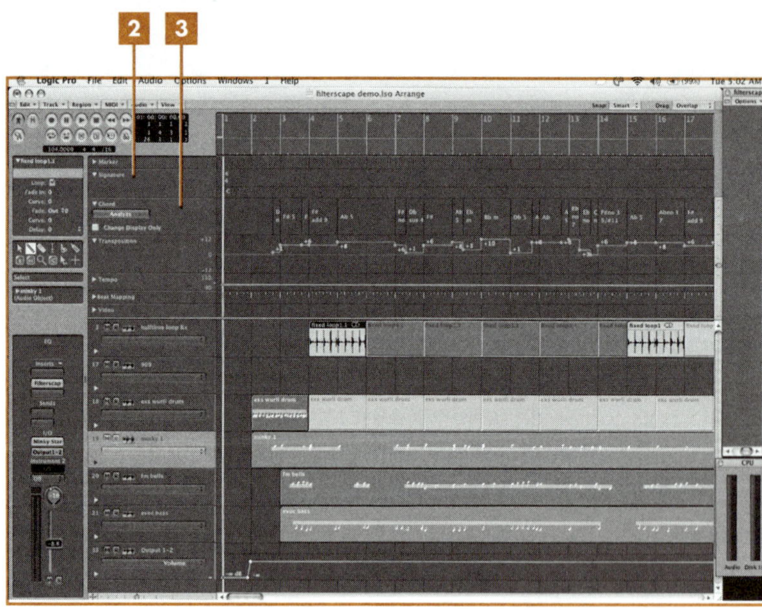

2 Signature Track: This track contains key signature and time signature events for your song. You can use this information along with the Chord Track and Transpose Track to automatically transpose MIDI data and Apple Loops as your song plays.

3 Chord Track (Logic Pro only): This track contains Chord events that display your song's chord changes. This information can be used along with the key signature and Transpose Track to automatically transpose MIDI data and Apple Loops as your song plays.

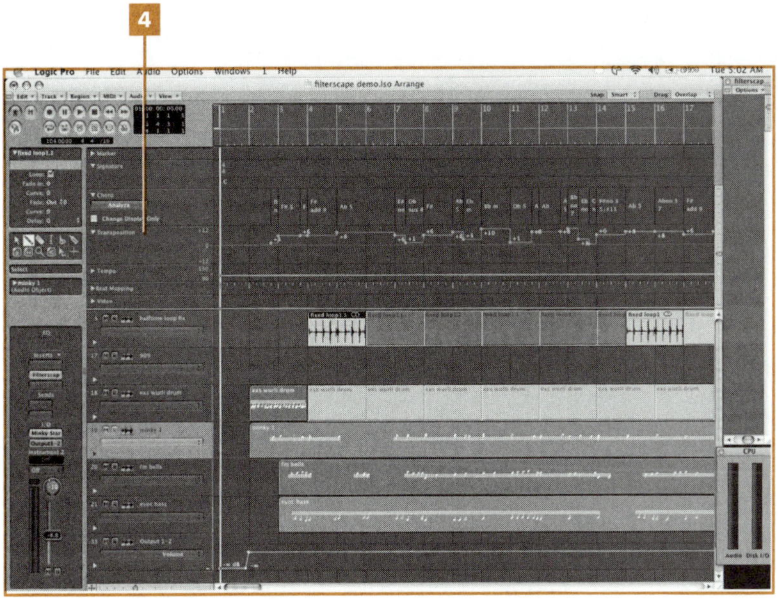

4 Transposition Track: This track contains Transpose events that you can use to automatically transpose MIDI data and Apple Loops. The Transpose Track has a range of +/- 12 semi-tones (one octave) as your song plays.

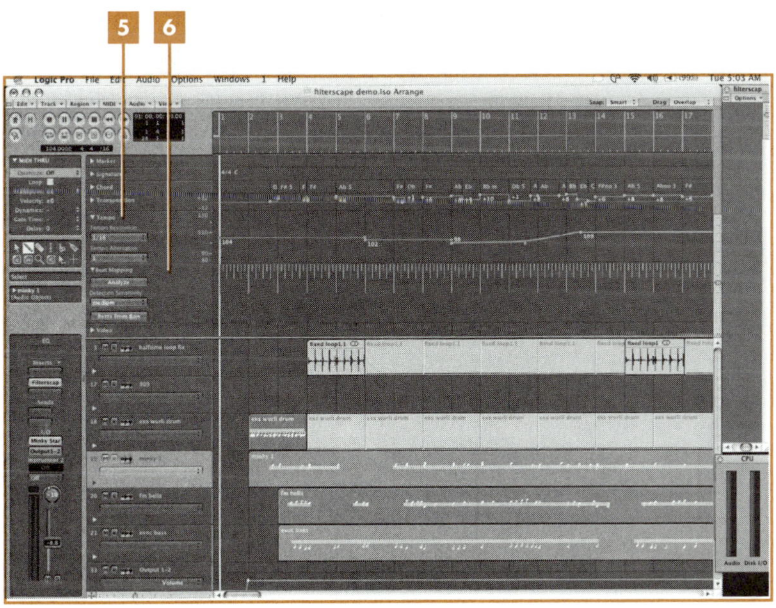

5 Tempo Track: This track contains the tempo map of your Logic song. You can create tempo events to automatically change Logic's tempo as your song plays.

6 Beat Mapping Track (Logic Pro only): This track can be used to automatically beat map (create a tempo map) for your song based on musical information from the regions in your Logic song.

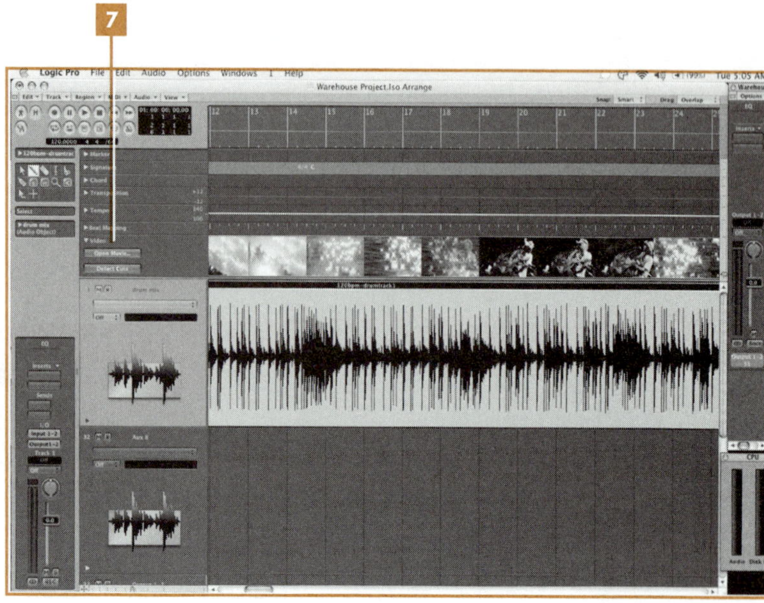

7 Video Track: You can use this track to display video thumbnails of a QuickTime video you open with your Logic song.

Arrange Window Local Menus

Most commands that relate to the Arrange window can be found in these local menus. While going into each command is beyond the scope of this book, we do want to familiarize you with the contents and organization of the local menus to help you in your own exploration.

1 Edit Menu: This menu contains commands relating to the selection and editing of regions in the Arrange window.

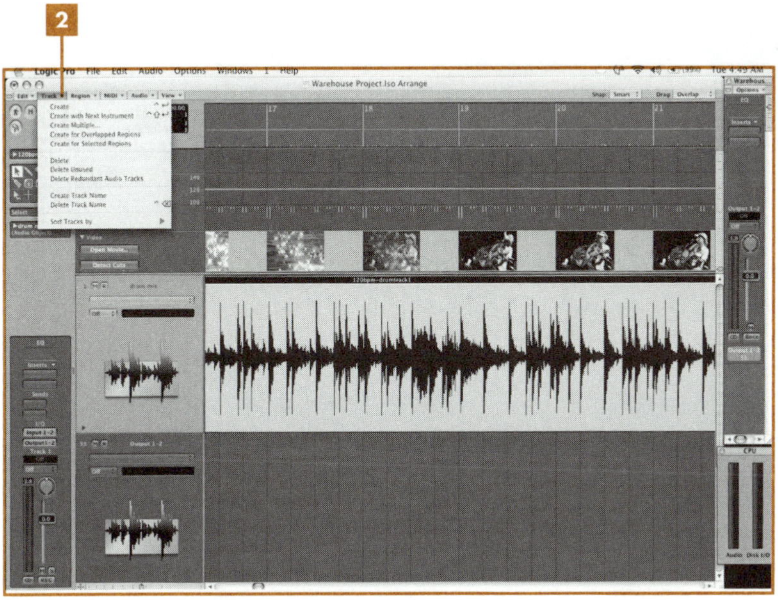

2 **Track Menu**: This menu contains operations that function on tracks in the Arrange window.

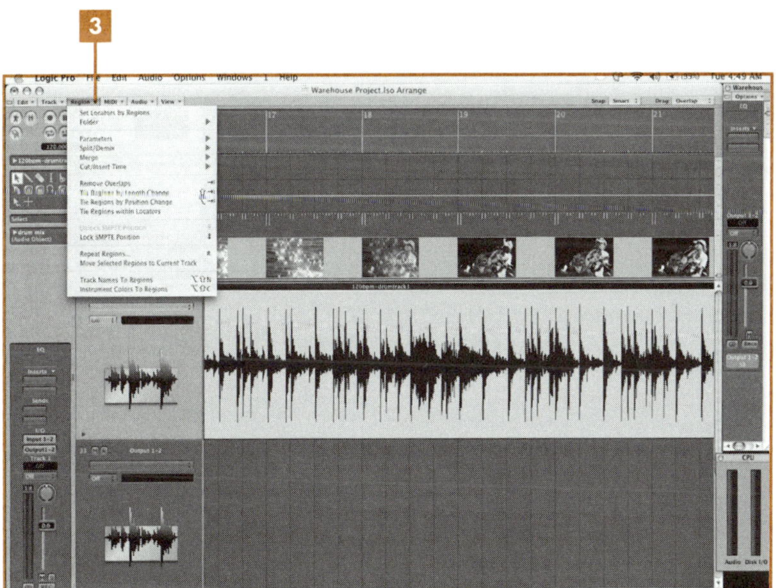

3 **Region Menu**: This menu contains operations that function on regions in the Arrange window.

4 **MIDI Menu**: This menu contains operations that function on MIDI regions in the Arrange window.

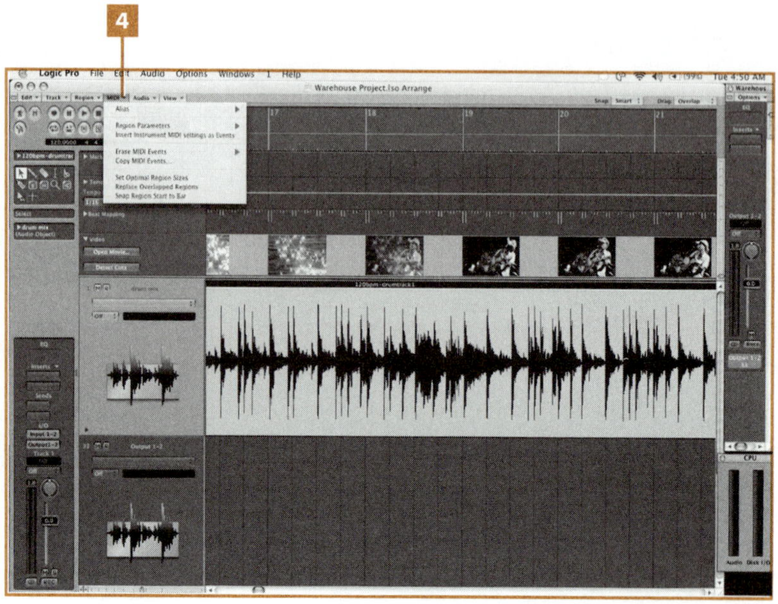

5 **Audio Menu**: This menu contains operations that function on Audio regions in the Arrange window.

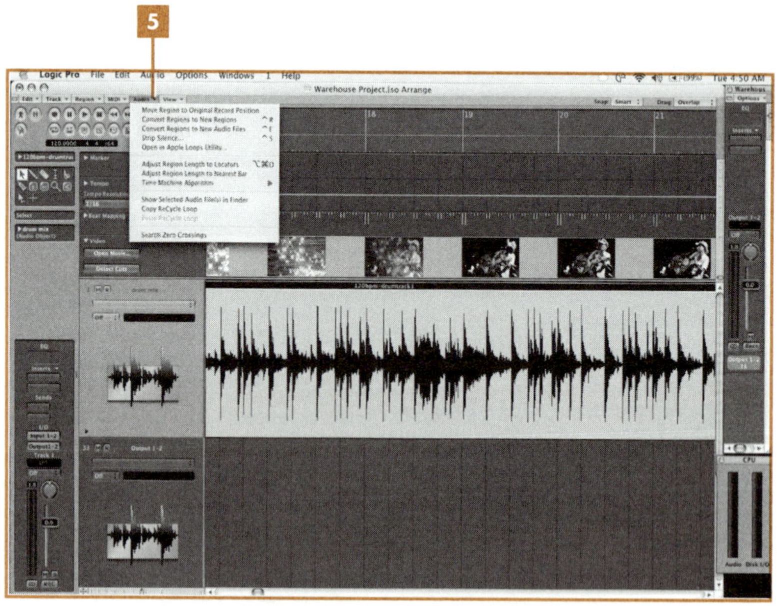

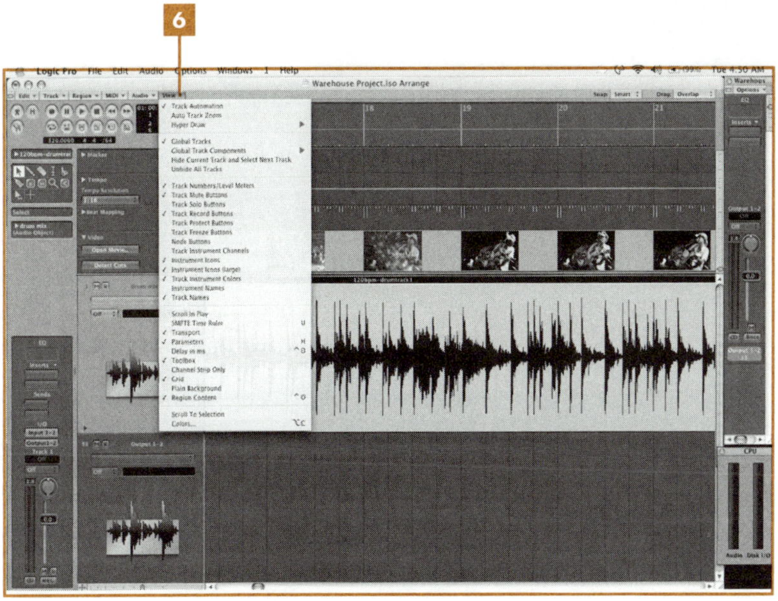

6 **View Menu**: This menu allows you to select elements to be displayed in the Arrange window.

Arrange Window Parameter Area

The leftmost column of your Arrange window is called the parameter area. This is where you will find the Arrange Channel Strip that you saw in Chapter 2, the parameter boxes for the track, regions, and the Toolbox. In the View menu of the Arrange window, you can configure exactly which of these items, if any, you want displayed. Below is a brief exploration of each window that you can choose to view in the parameter area of the Arrange window.

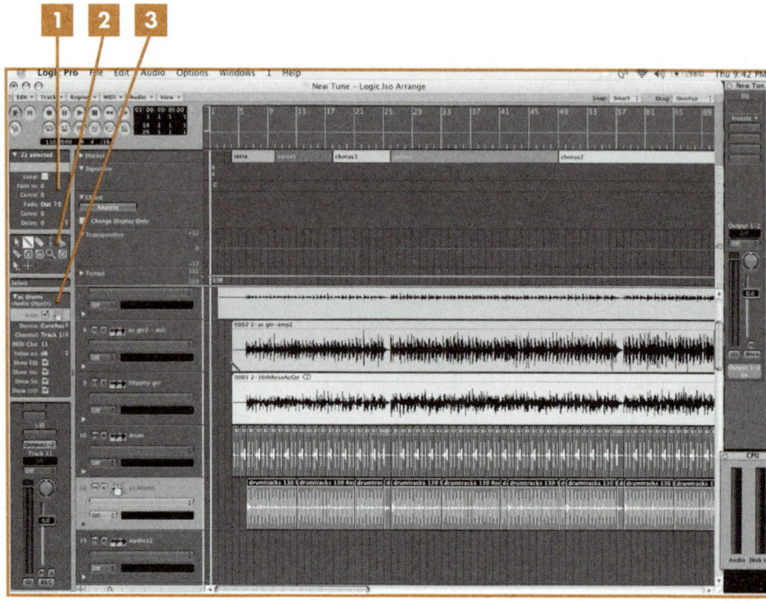

1 **Region Parameter Box**: Here you can adjust parameters that control the selected region(s) in the Arrange area. The specific parameters available in this window will change depending on whether your selection consists of audio, MIDI, or Apple Loop regions.

2 **Arrange Toolbox**: These are all the different tools you can use in the Arrange window. This is explored in more detail in the next section.

3 **Object Parameter Box**: This box offers the parameters that adjust the properties of the MIDI device, Audio Instrument, or Audio Channel that is playing back the regions on that track.

4 **Arrange Channel Strip**: You can also elect to view the Channel Strip for the selected track in the parameter area of the Arrange window. This is explored in more detail in the next section.

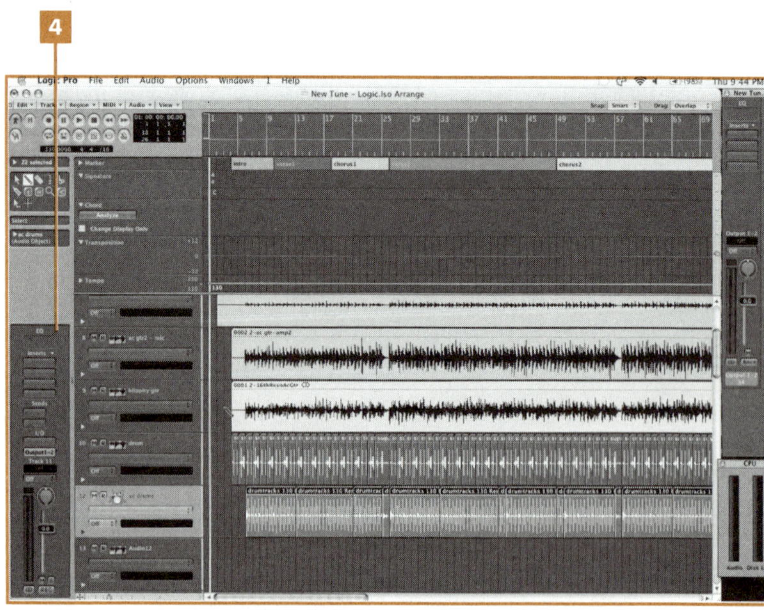

My Parameter Area Doesn't Have All This!

If you don't see an item in your Parameter area that you see here, make sure there is a checkmark next to the item in the Arrange > View local menu.

A Closer Look: The Arrange Window Toolbox

The Toolbox contains tools for nearly every basic editing function. Most operate by clicking on one or more regions, or by dragging over a section of the Arrange area. Most tools will be described in detail later, but here is a brief look at them.

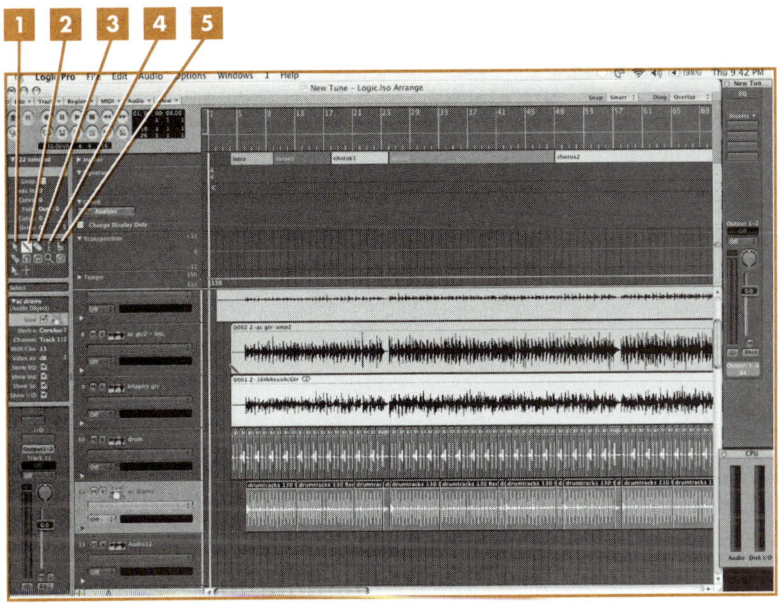

1. Pointer: The Pointer tool is your basic selection tool. It is also a "smart" tool, meaning if moved to specific "hot spots" in a region, it can change into the Resize, Move, or Loop tool, as we'll discuss later in the chapter.
2. Pencil: You can use the Pencil tool to create new regions or add audio files to the Arrange window.
3. Eraser: The Eraser tool deletes regions from the Arrange window.
4. Text Tool: If you click a region with the Text tool, you can type in a new name for that region.
5. Scissors: You can use the Scissors tool to split regions, as we'll discuss later in the chapter.

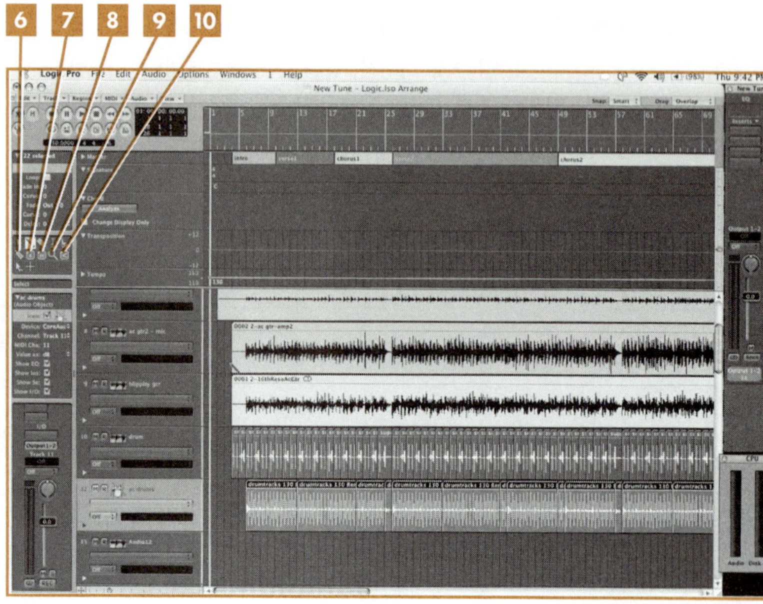

6 **Glue**: You can use the Glue tool to merge one or more regions into a single region.

7 **Solo Tool**: You can use the Solo tool to solo regions, as we'll discuss later in the chapter.

8 **Mute Tool**: You can use the Mute tool to mute regions, as we'll discuss later in the chapter.

9 **Magnifying Glass**: You can use the Magnifying Glass tool to zoom in to a specific area of the Arrange window.

10 **Fade Tool**: You can use the Fade tool on audio regions to create fade outs, fade ins, and crossfades. This is discussed further in Chapter 7, "The Audio Window and Sample Editor."

11 **Automation Tool (Logic Pro only)**: The Automation tool allows you to make smooth automation curves, and offers some special automation features. This tool is explained in more detail in Chapter 13, "Advanced Topics in Logic."

12 **Marquee Tool (Logic Pro only)**: Whereas the Pointer tool can only select entire regions, the Marquee tool allows you to select portions of regions, as we'll discuss later in the chapter.

The Floating Toolbox

Unlike the Parameter boxes or Channel Strip, you can actually call up the Toolbox anywhere your mouse is by using the ESC key, or by right-clicking with a two- (or more) button mouse.

The Track List

To the right of the Parameter area of the Arrange window, but to the left of the Arrange area, is the Track List. This list contains all the tracks in the Arrange window, and shows you all of your tracks that aren't hidden (Hide Tracks is a Logic Pro feature only). Each row in the Track List contains all the control buttons for that specific track. Some buttons are specific to certain types of tracks. Below we'll explore the Track List and the various buttons you will find on a track.

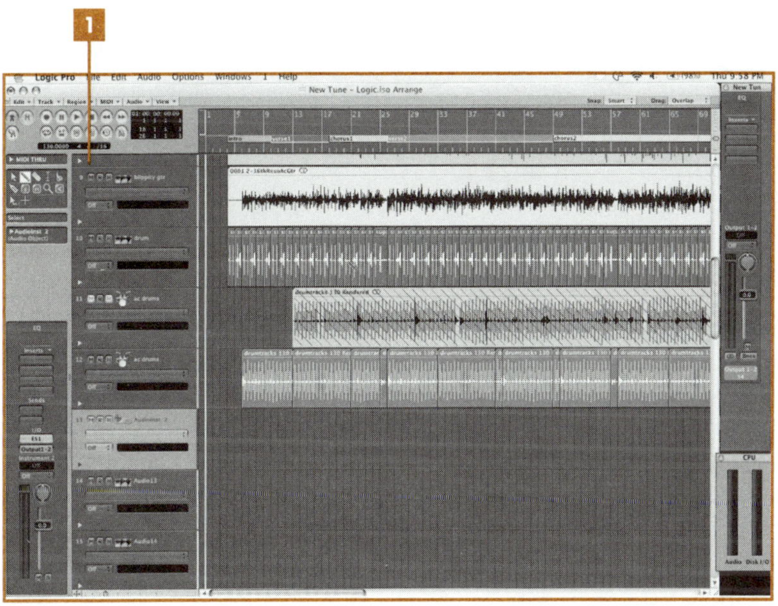

1 **Track List**: This is the list of all the tracks in your Arrange window.

2 **Track Number**: The number of the specific track.

3 **Mute Button**: The Mute button will mute all the regions on this track.

4 **Solo Button**: The Solo button will solo all the regions on this track.

5 **Record-Enable Button**: As described in Chapter 3, use this button to enable recording on an Audio or Audio Instrument Track.

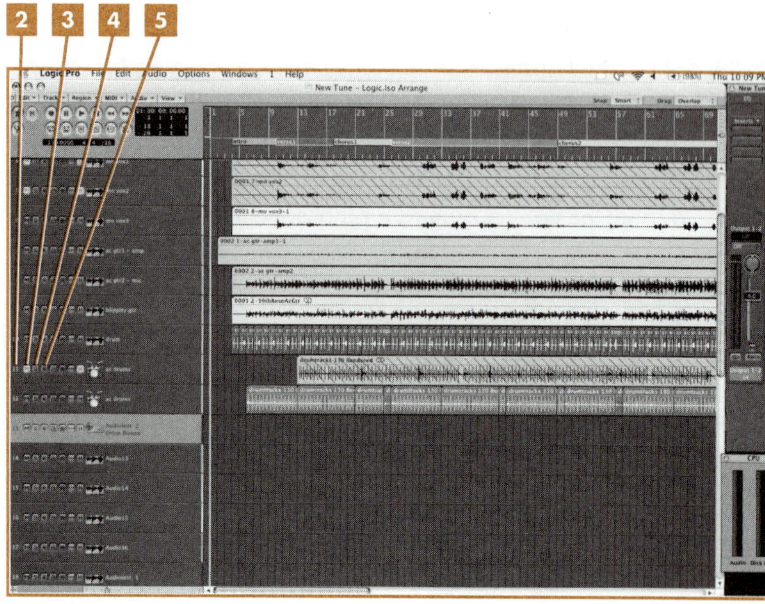

6 **Track Protect Button**: The Track Protect button keeps the regions on the track from moving as you arrange the song.

7 **Track Freeze Button**: The Track Freeze button allows you to "freeze" Audio and Audio Instrument Tracks to conserve CPU resources, as will be explained later in this chapter.

8 **Nodes Button (Logic Pro only)**: If you have Nodes activated, you can press this button to send the Logic built-in effects (and instrument, if any) to be processed on the Node computer. This is briefly explored later in this chapter.

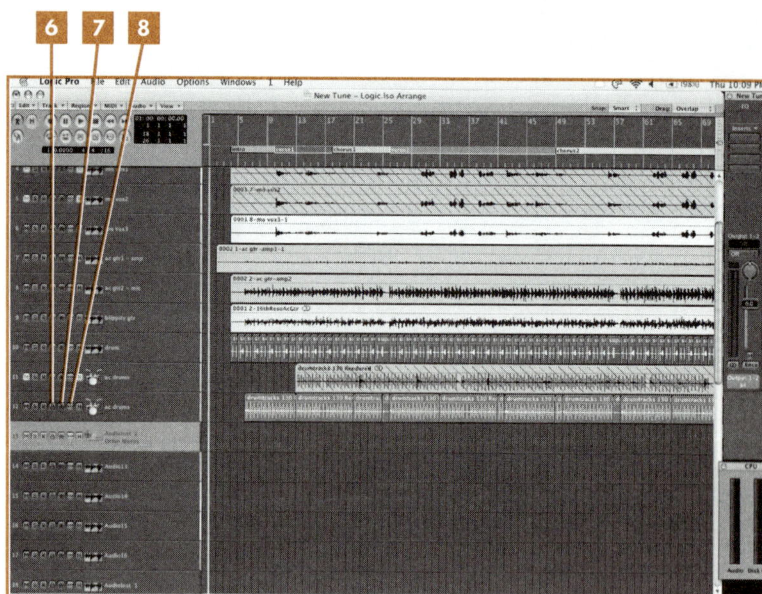

9 **Hide Track Button (Logic Pro only)**: Pressing this button and then selecting the main Hide button at the top of the Arrange window will hide the selected tracks to help clean up your Arrange window.

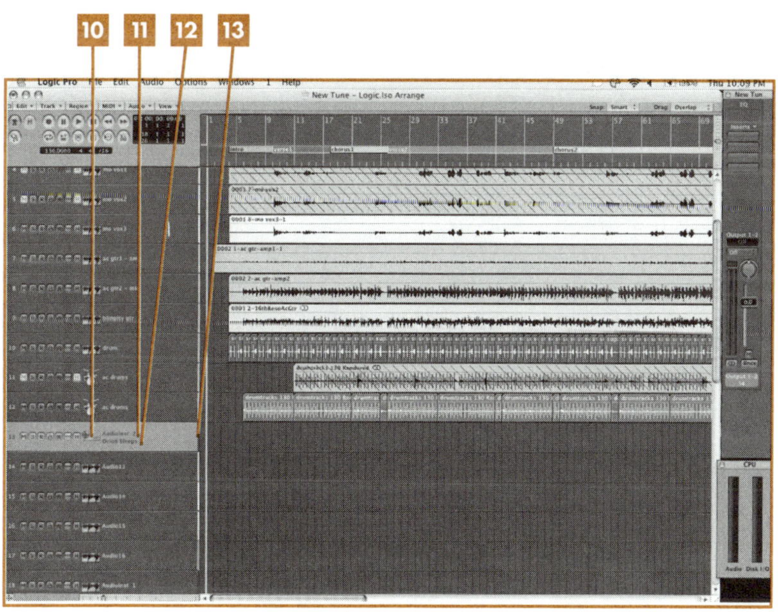

10 **Instrument Icon**: The icon that you select for each track in the Object Parameter Box is displayed here.

11 **Track Name**: The name of your track.

12 **Instrument Name**: If you are using a patch from a Logic Audio Instrument, the patch name will be displayed here.

13 **Track Color**: If you have Track Colors turned on, the color of your track will be displayed here.

My Track Row Doesn't Have All This!

If you don't see a button or other item in the Track row that you see here, make sure there is a checkmark next to the item in the Arrange > View local menu.

The Arrange Area

By far the most spacious portion of the Arrange window is the Arrange area, which includes the scroll bars, zoom sliders, Arrange Area, and Bar Ruler.

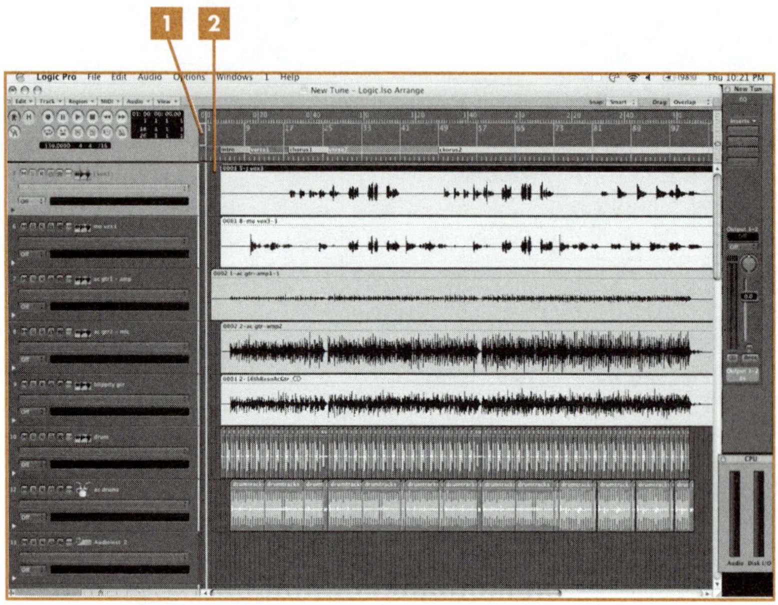

1 Bar Ruler: This ruler displays where you are in your song in measures (bar, beat) and, if you turn it on in the View menu, SMPTE Frames (minutes, seconds).

2 Arrange Area: This is where all the regions that fill your tracks and comprise your song are located. This is the actual workspace in which you "arrange" your song.

3 Zoom Sliders: These sliders adjust both vertically and horizontally to focus the Arrange window zoom from the macroscopic (an entire song) to the microscopic (sample-level viewing of a waveform) and everything in between.

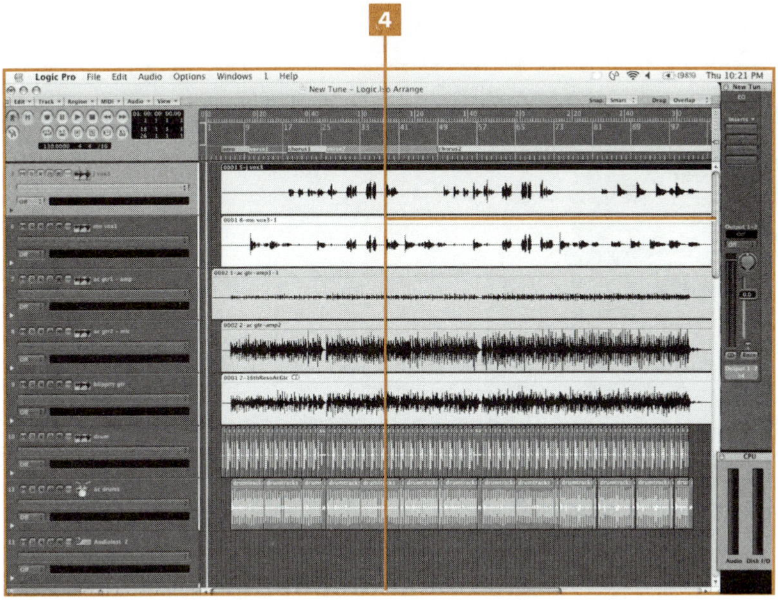

4 **Scroll Bars**: These are standard Macintosh scroll bars that allow you to scroll the Arrange window.

Zooming in the Arrange Window

As you start to look at the regions in your song and think about editing, you'll likely want to focus on specific parts of your song or get a look at the entire song at a glance for perspective. This is called zooming, and Logic lets you adjust the zoom level in the Arrange window a number of ways.

Adjusting the Zoom Level Using the Zoom Sliders

The most straightforward way to adjust the zoom level for the entire Arrange Area is to use the Zoom sliders.

1 Click and hold the mouse on either the horizontal or vertical Zoom slider.

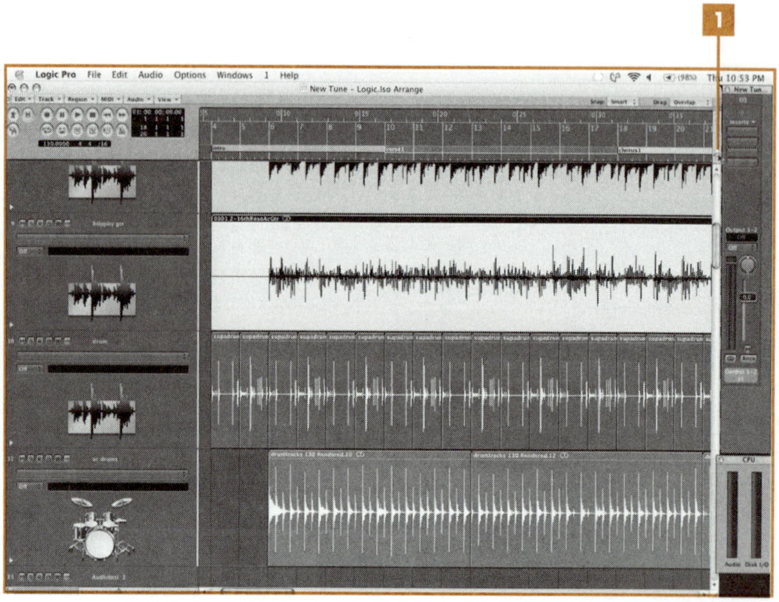

2 Drag the slider with the mouse to zoom in or out.

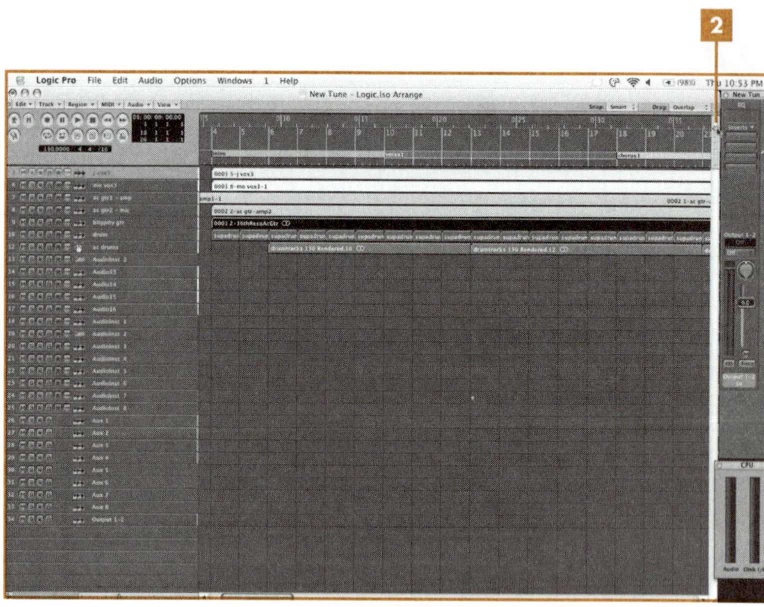

Adjusting Horizontal and Vertical Zoom from a Single Zoom Slider

If you hold down the OPTION key while moving the horizontal Zoom slider, it will adjust the vertical zoom. If you hold down the OPTION key while moving the vertical Zoom slider, it will adjust the horizontal zoom. This way, you can adjust both horizontal and vertical zoom using only a single slider!

Adjusting the Zoom Level Using the Magnifying Glass

If you want to zoom in close to a section of the currently displayed Arrange Area, you can use the Magnifying Glass tool.

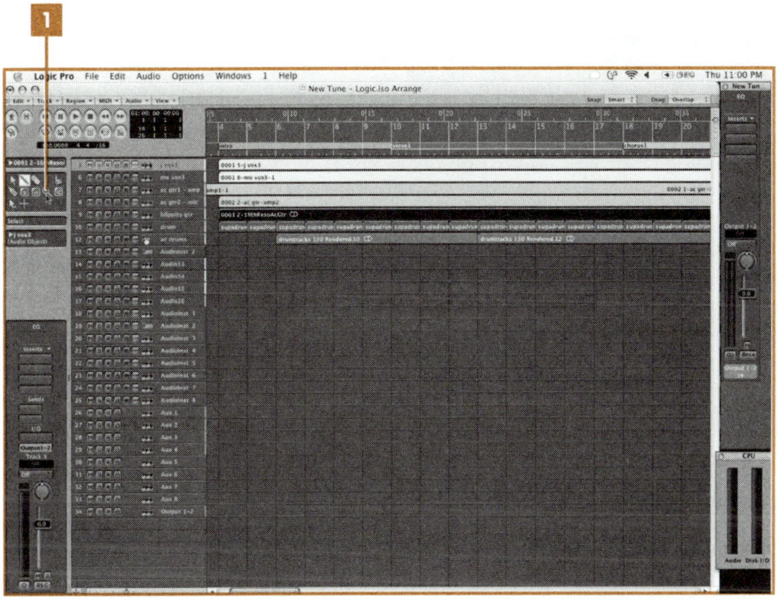

1 Select the Magnifying Glass from the Tool Palette (or press Esc with the mouse over the Arrange Area).

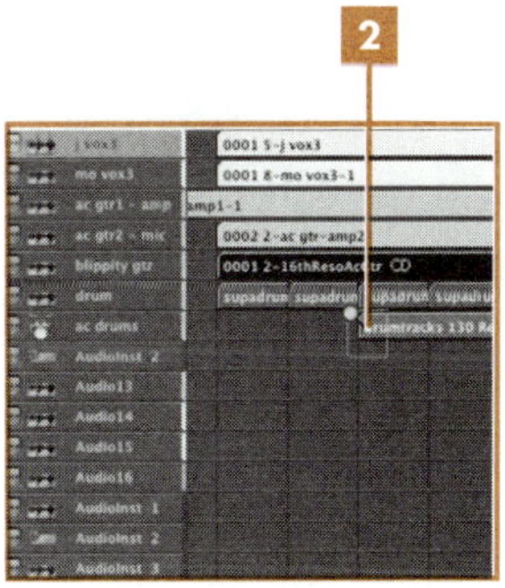

2 Click and drag over a region of the Arrange window to which you want to zoom more closely.

3 **Confirm** your **region** now fills the Arrange Area. Once you have zoomed in to the level you want, returning to the previous zoom level is as easy as clicking the Magnifying Glass in an empty portion of the Arrange Area without dragging.

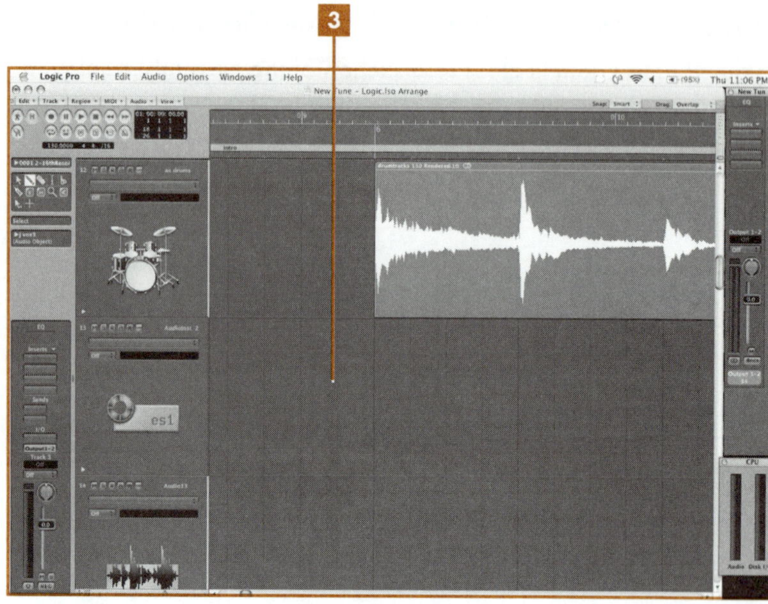

Key Command Alert: Magnifying Glass

You can temporarily change the current tool to the Magnifying Glass by holding down the **CONTROL** key.

Adjusting the Zoom Level for a Single Track

You can use the pointer to make individual tracks larger or smaller.

1 Position the mouse over the lower-left corner of a track in the Track List until the cursor changes to a single pointing finger.

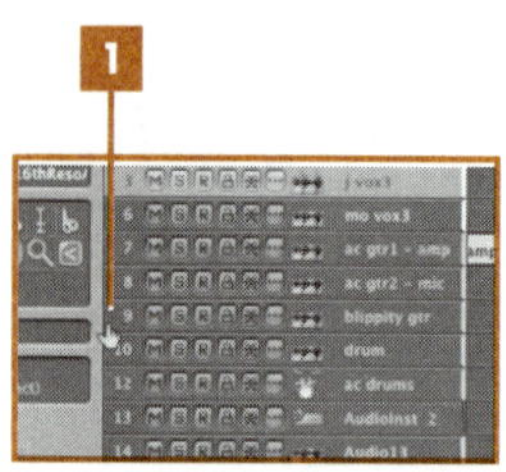

2 **Click** and **drag** up or down to change the size of the track.

Using Auto Track Zoom

One of Logic's unique and clever features is a View mode that automatically increases the horizontal zoom level of the selected track while leaving the general zoom level unchanged.

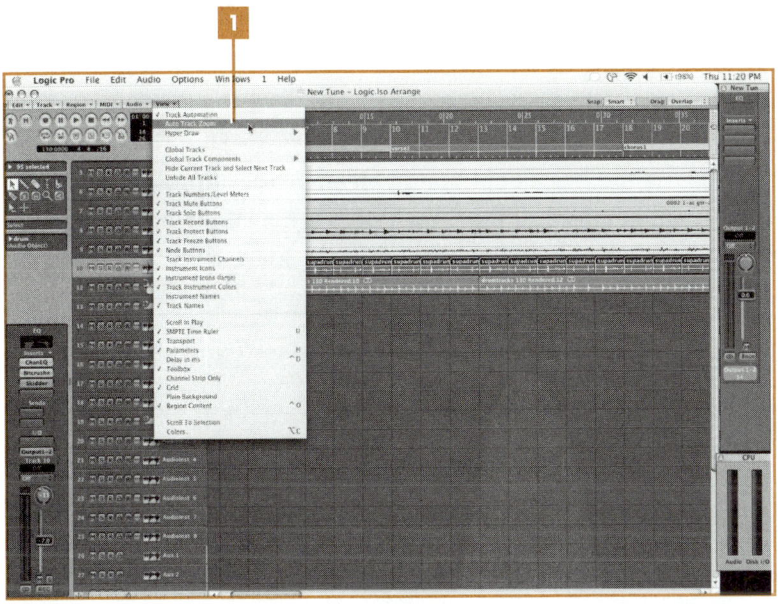

1 Click on the View menu and select Auto Track Zoom.

2 Any track that you select in the Arrange window will now automatically zoom in vertically.

Soloing

One of the first things you'll want to do once you've recorded more than one region is to listen to a single region without everything else playing. Isolating one or more regions for playback is known as **soloing**. Logic actually offers three kinds of soloing—Track Solo, Region Solo, and Channel Solo.

Soloing Tracks in the Arrange Window

You can use the Track Solo button on each track to solo all the regions on that track. If the Solo button is not visible on the Tracks, check the **Track Solo Buttons** option in the View menu.

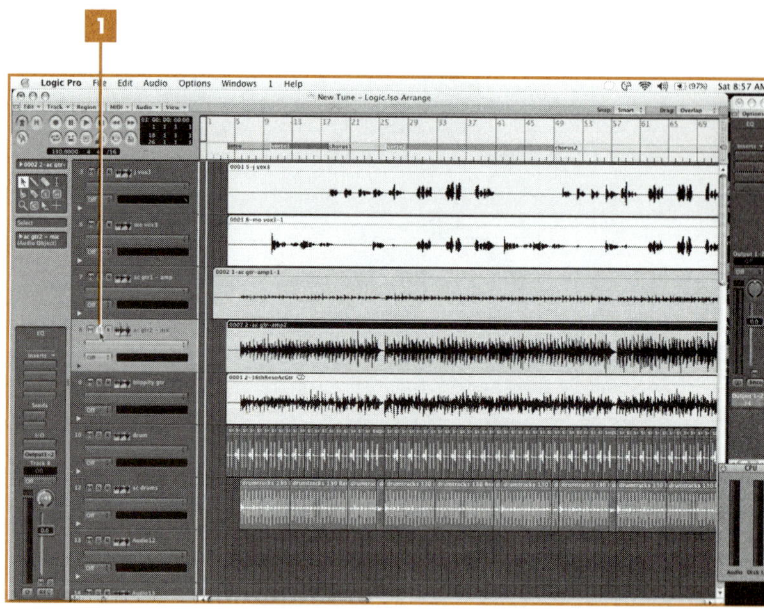

1 Press the Track Solo button on the track you want to solo. You will notice the Time Ruler changes to yellow and the regions on the selected track will have a light yellow outline to them.

Do the Solo Drag!

Click and hold the mouse over a Track Solo button. While continuing to hold the button, drag up or down over additional Arrange tracks to solo them all with one effort.

Soloing Regions in the Arrange Window

You can use the Solo Tool in the Toolbar to solo individual regions in the Arrange window.

1

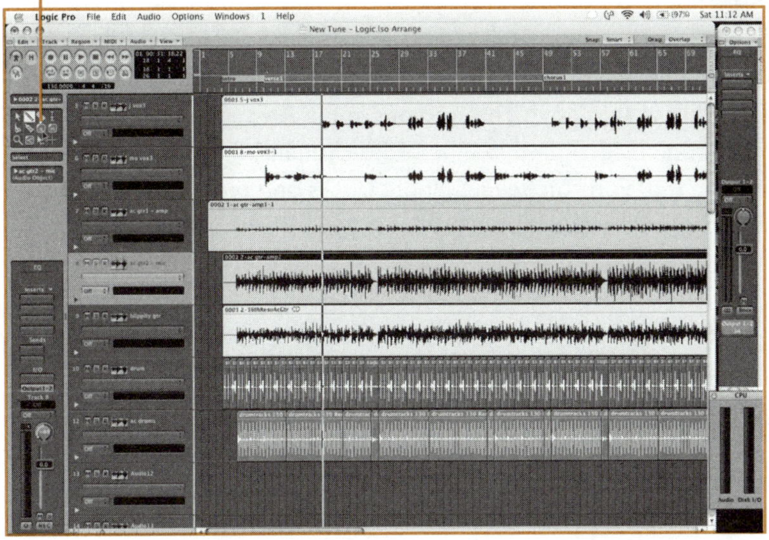

1 **Select** the **Solo Tool** in the Toolbar.

2

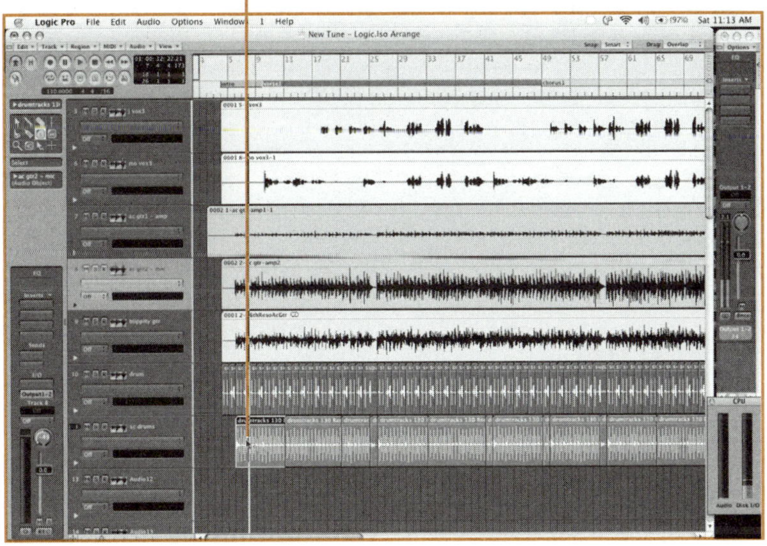

2 **Click** and **hold** on a **region** in the Arrange window with the Solo Tool. Playback will start from the position of the cursor.

Key Command Alert: Solo

You can also solo the selected region(s) by pressing the S key on your computer keyboard.

Selecting Non-Soloed Regions: Solo Lock

If you want to change selected regions without changing the solo status of those or other regions, you can double-click the Solo button on the Transport to engage Solo Lock mode. You will see a padlock in the lower-left corner of the Transport's Solo button to indicate that you are in Solo Lock mode and that you are free to select and edit any regions in the Arrange window without affecting their solo status.

Soloing Audio Channels Using the Arrange Channel Strip

Sometimes you may want only a single audio channel to play. You can do this by using the Solo button on the track's Channel Strip. This will not solo any of the regions in the Arrange window—only those regions assigned to that audio channel will be heard. Keep in mind that you can have multiple tracks and regions assigned to the same audio channel.

1 Press the Solo Button in the Channel Strip of the track you want to solo.

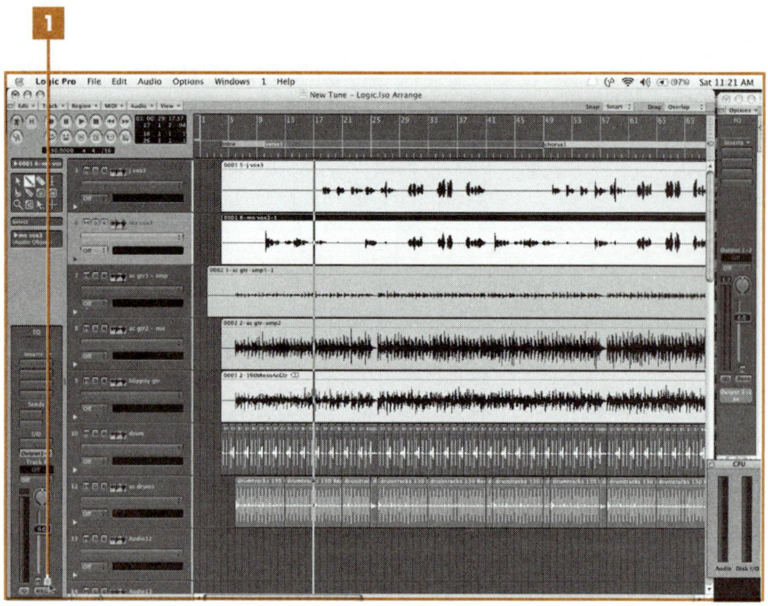

Solo Safe Mode

You may wish to ensure that some audio channels always play, even when other channels are soloed. You can do this by CONTROL-clicking on the audio channel's Solo button. You will see a red '/' over the Solo button of the channel strip, indicating that the channel is in Solo Safe mode. In Solo Safe mode, the channel will always play, regardless of what other channels are soloed.

Muting

Sometimes, rather than only hearing a specific element of your song, you may wish to silence a particular element of your song. This is called muting. Just like soloing, Logic offers three kinds of muting—Track Mute, Region Mute, and Channel Mute.

Muting Tracks in the Arrange Window

You can use the Track Mute button on each track to mute all the regions on that track.

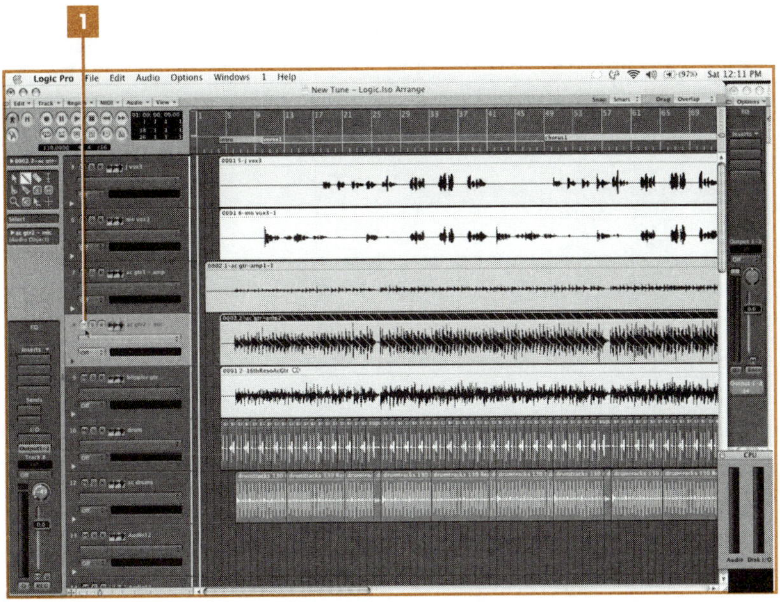

1 **Press** the **Mute** button on the Arrange track you wish to mute.

Do the Mute Drag!

Click and hold the mouse over a Track Mute button. While continuing to hold the button, drag up or down over additional Arrange tracks to mute them all with one effort.

Muted Regions Are Textured

There is a setting in Preferences > Display > Arrange to select whether muted regions have a visual texture to them. This can make for easier viewing of muted regions.

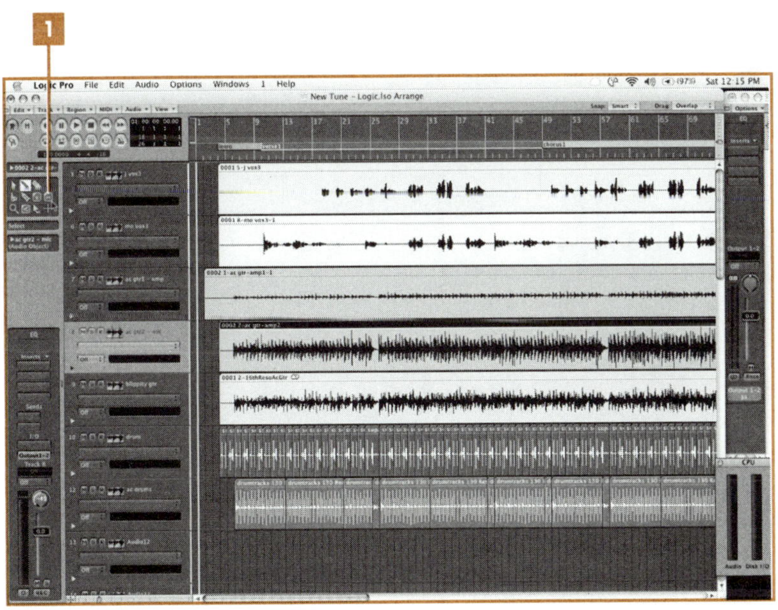

Muting Regions in the Arrange Window

You can use the Mute tool in the Toolbar to solo individual regions in the Arrange window.

1 **Select** the **Mute** tool in the Toolbar.

2 **Click** on a **region** in the Arrange window and it will become muted. There will be a bullet point in front of the name of the region. You can click multiple regions if you need to mute more than one.

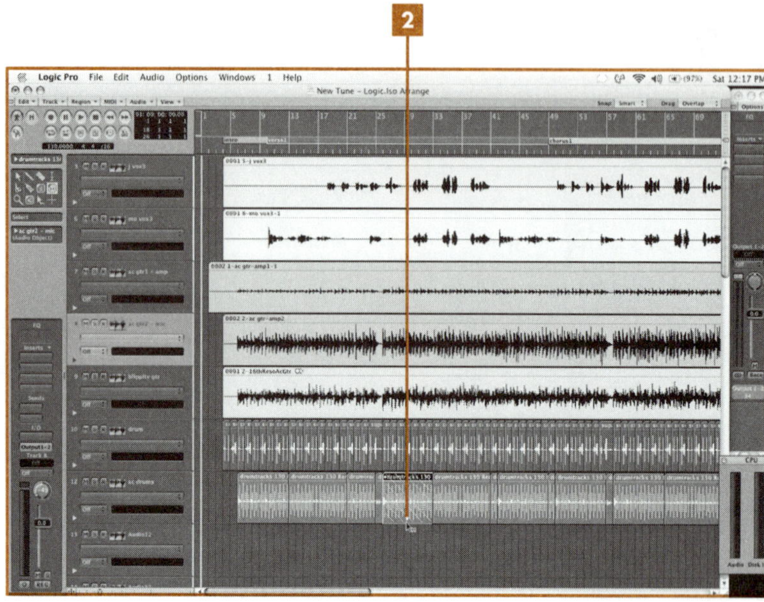

Unmuting a Region

Clicking a muted region with the Mute tool will unmute it and return it to normal status.

Key Command Alert: Mute

You can also mute the selected region(s) by pressing the **M** key on your computer keyboard.

Muting Audio Channels Using the Arrange Channel Strip

Sometimes you may want to silence an entire audio channel. You can do this by using the Mute button on the track's Channel Strip. This will not mute any of the regions in the Arrange window, but any regions assigned to that audio channel will not be heard.

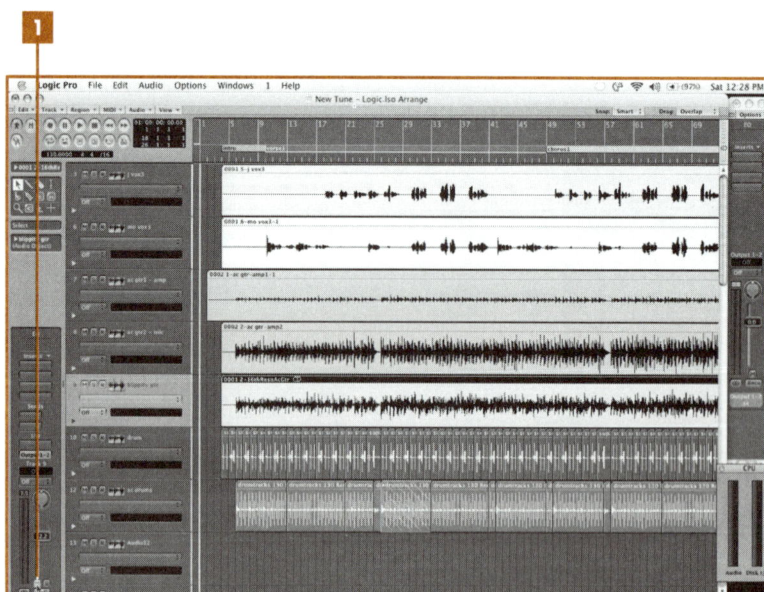

1 **Press** the **Mute** button in the Channel Strip of the track you want to mute.

Freezing Audio and Audio Instrument Tracks

You've already learned how to select Audio Instruments in Chapter 3, "Recording Audio and MIDI." Those Audio Instruments take a fair amount of your Macintosh's processing power to generate sound in real time. When we get into mixing your song and adding effects in Chapter 11, "Mixing Your Project," you'll find that those effects also take your Macintosh's processing power to affect your audio in real-time. If you try to ask your Macintosh to do more real-time processing than it can handle, it will start throwing out overload errors, and it will refuse to play.

Thankfully, Logic offers the Freeze function for when your real-time processing is too much for your Mac. What the Freeze function does is print an audio file that includes the regions, automation, and all the real-time processing of your track—in effect, "freezing in place" all the processing. This way, instead of needing to process the track in real time, Logic needs only to reference the printed track. When you start to overload your computer, the Freeze function is a lifesaver!

While Freeze is a complicated function to explain, using it is as easy as pushing a button!

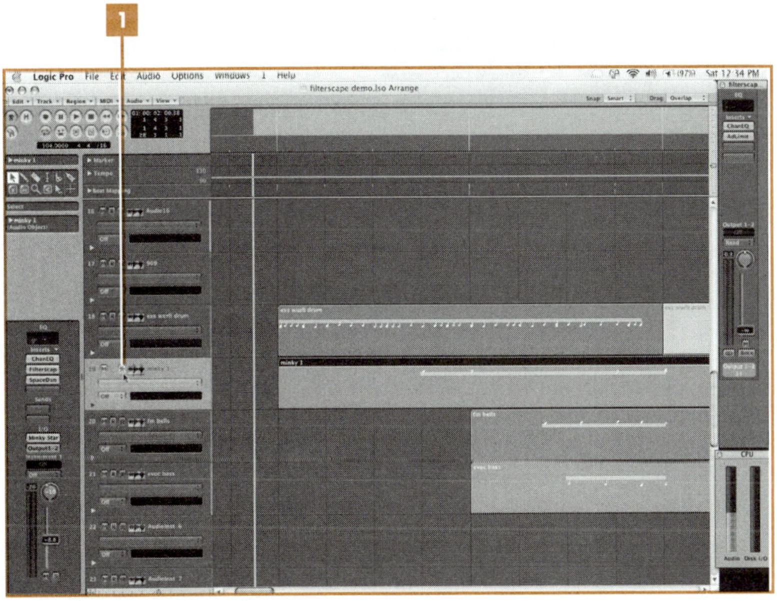

1 Select the Freeze button on the Arrange track you want to Freeze. If the Freeze button is not visible on the Tracks, check the Track Freeze Buttons option in the View menu.

2 Press Play in the Transport to begin the Freeze process. Logic will freeze the track until the Song End marker unless you cancel the action.

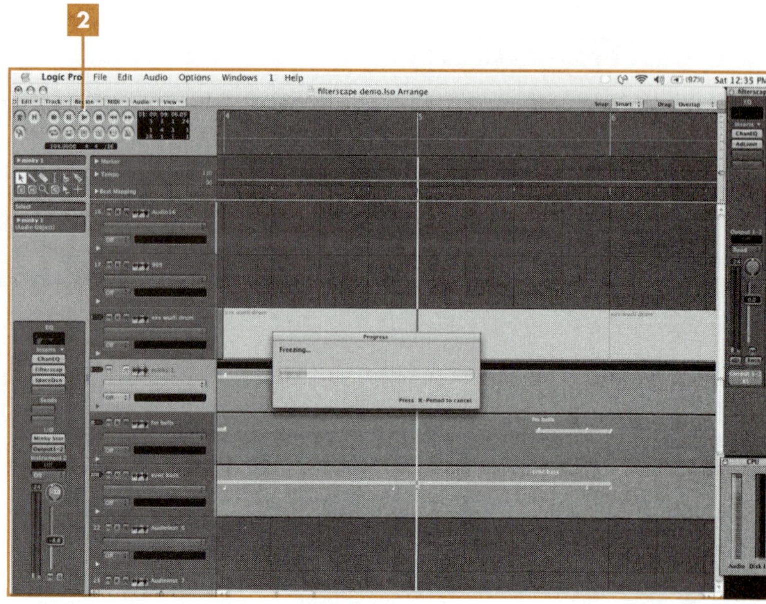

3 Logic will now play your frozen track.

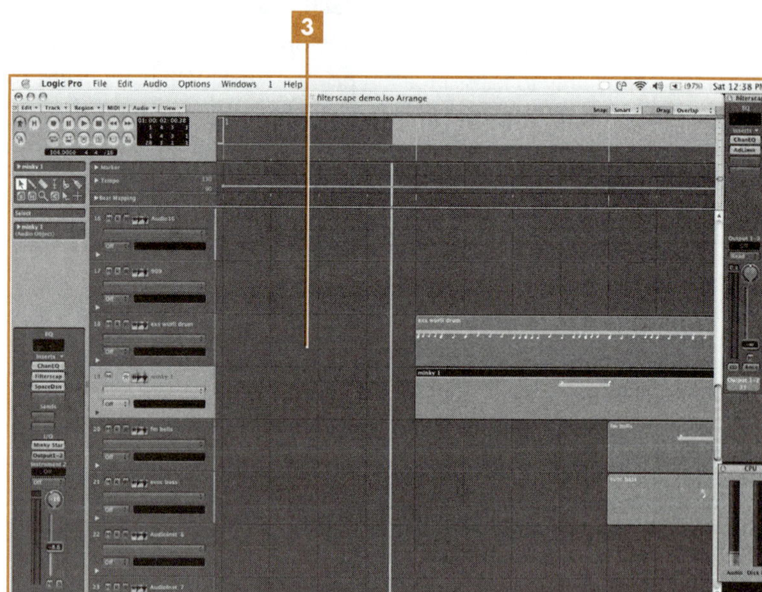

Editing Frozen Tracks

Remember that when a track is Frozen, Logic isn't actually playing the Arrange track at all, but rather the Freeze file. Since what you hear and what's on the Arrange track are "disconnected" during Freeze, Logic won't let you edit a Frozen track. This ensures that you won't be confused by not hearing a change on a region in a Frozen track.

If you do want to edit a Frozen track, just unfreeze the track, then re-freeze it when you are done.

Logic Nodes (Logic Pro Only)

If you're using Logic Pro 7 and you start running out of processor power, you have an amazingly innovative and powerful way to add nearly infinite amounts of processing power by adding Logic Nodes. A Logic Node is another Macintosh computer connected to your main Logic Pro computer by a Gigabit Ethernet cable. You simply install the Logic Node application that came on your Logic Pro Install DVD onto your Logic Node computer, and you can now use the Logic Node computer to distribute the audio processing load of your Logic song!

Can I Use My Old Mac as a Logic Node?

Technically, Logic Pro only recommends that G5 computers with Gigabit Ethernet be used as Logic Nodes. The reason for this is that the transfer of the audio data takes a lot of bandwidth, and the Logic Node application and audio processing take a lot of processor power. So a G5-based Macintosh and Gigabit Ethernet offer the most available processing power. But there's no *technical* reason your older Macintosh with a slower processor or without Gigabit Ethernet will not work as a Logic Node. Just be aware that it will not give you nearly the audio processing benefit of a faster Macintosh with Gigabit Ethernet.

1

1 Once your two computers are connected with a Gigabit Ethernet cable, launch the Logic Node application on the computer that will act as the Node.

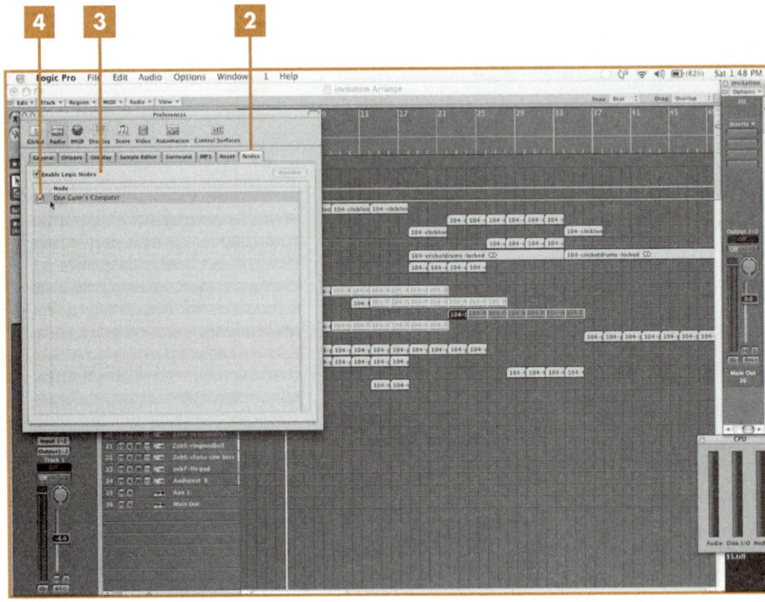

2 Launch Logic Pro 7 on your other computer. Make sure you have enabled Logic Nodes by going to the Nodes tab in Preferences > Audio.

3 Check the Enable Logic Nodes box.

4 Select the name of the computer that will be used as the Node.

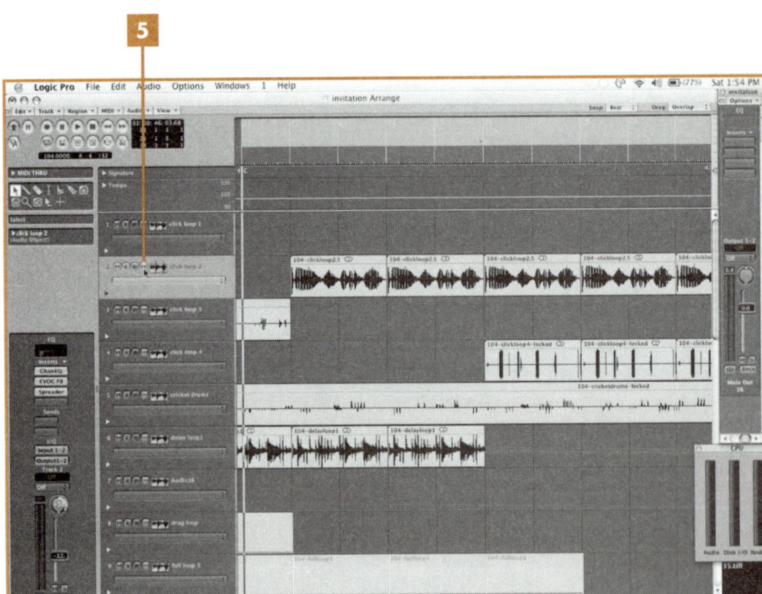

5 Press the Node button on the Arrange Track on which you want to distribute the processing.

Current Limitations of Logic Nodes

Since Logic Pro 7.0 was the first version of Logic to include distributed audio processing, naturally there are some limitations to it. First, Logic Nodes-distributed audio processing is only available for Audio and Audio Instrument tracks. More important, you can only process Logic's own effects and synthesizers on Logic Nodes, not Sampler Instruments or any third-party Audio Unit plug-ins. These limitations may very well change with future updates to Logic Pro 7, so check out Apple's Web site for the latest information.

Using Markers (Logic Pro Only)

One of the best ways to organize your song into sections is by creating Markers—graphic indicators that separate song sections—in the Marker Track of your song.

Marker Track versus Bar Ruler Markers

If you are upgrading from an older version of Logic, you may be used to seeing Markers on the Bar Ruler. In fact, Logic will still display your Markers in the Bar Ruler if you do not have the Marker Track displayed in the Arrange window. But since it is far simpler to create Markers using the Marker Track, which was specifically designed for this purpose, that is what we are focusing on in this book.

For a more detailed exploration of Markers, please check out *Logic Pro 7 Power!* by Orren Merton, also published by Course Technology.

Creating Markers on the Marker Track

Creating Markers on the Marker Track couldn't be easier!

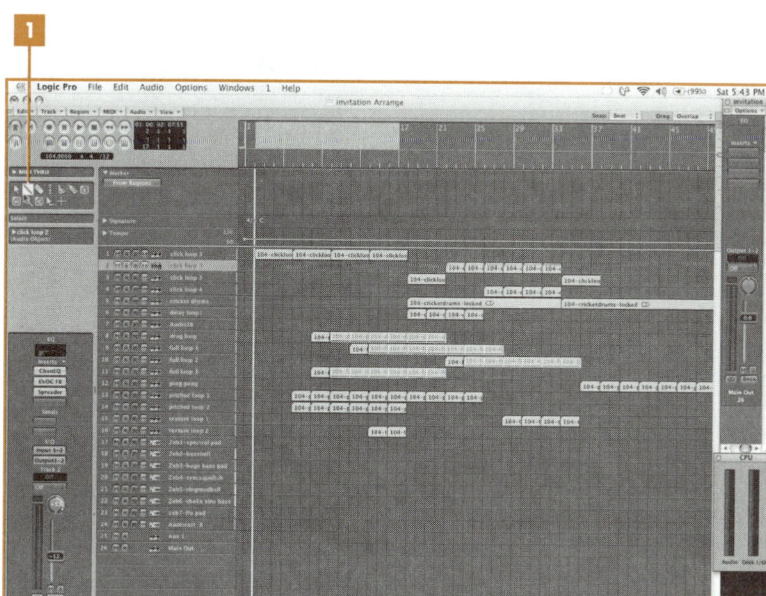

1 Select the Pencil tool from the Tool Palette.

2 Click on the Marker Track with the Pencil tool to create a Marker.

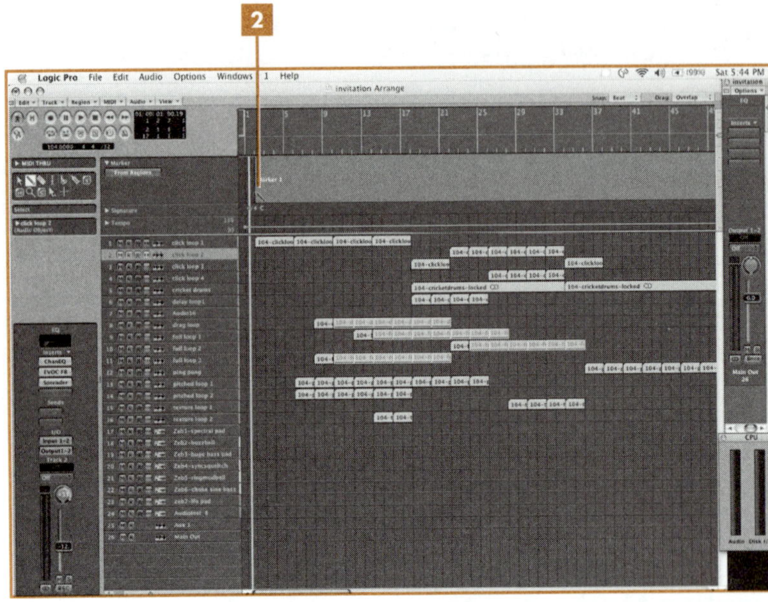

3 To name your Marker, select the Pointer tool in the Tool Palette.

4 Double-click on the Marker to open the Marker window.

5 Rename the Marker to your liking.

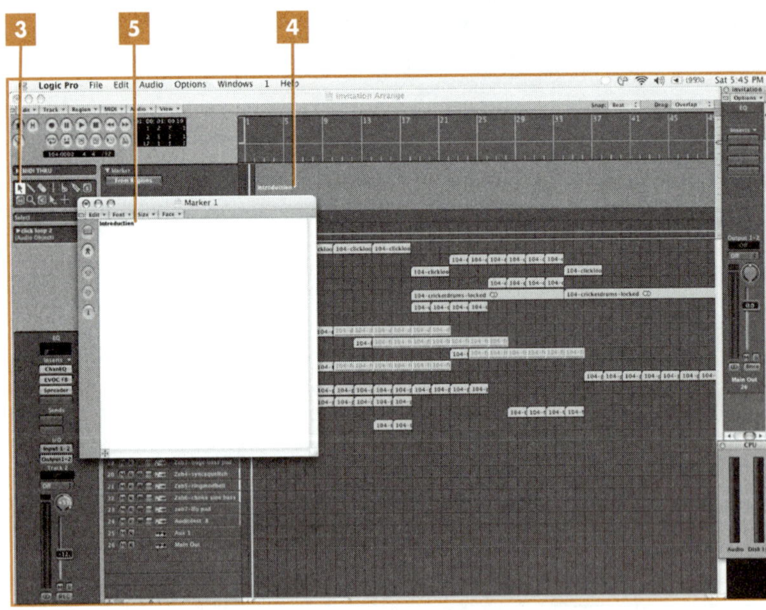

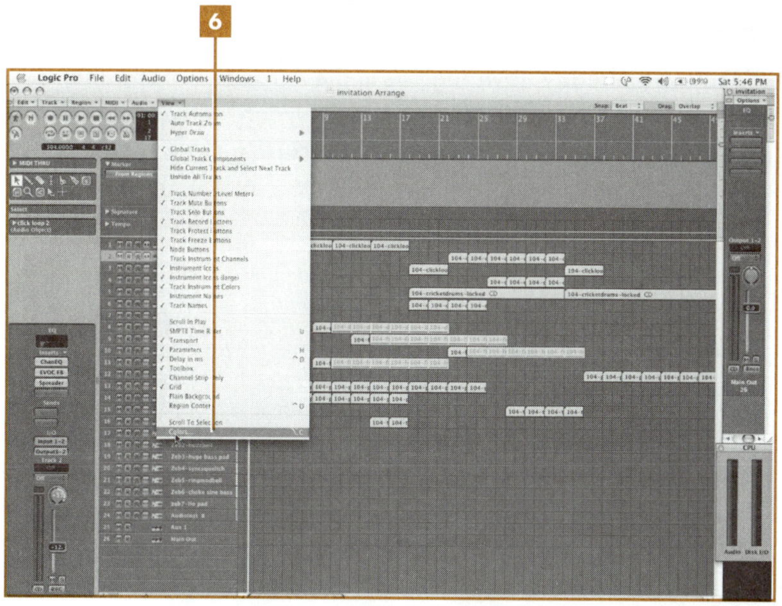

6 To apply a color to your Marker, open the Color Palette from the View menu.

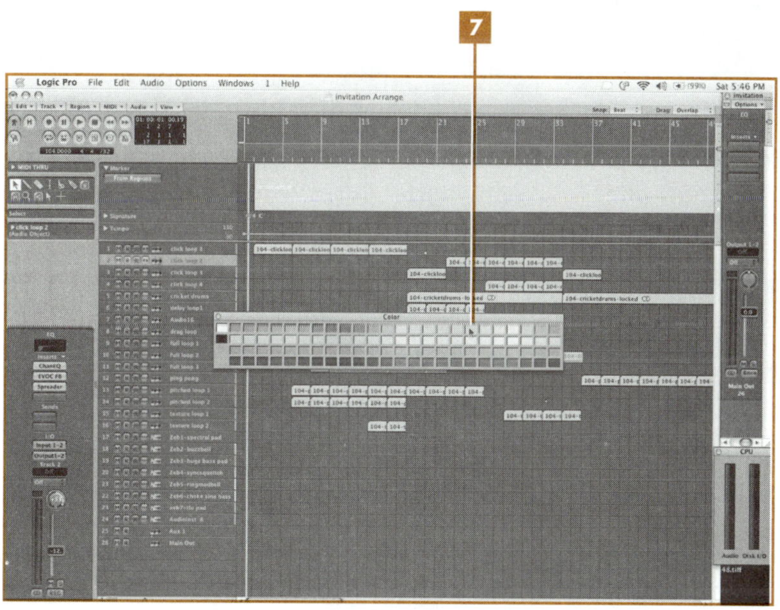

7 Click on a color in the Color Palette to change the Marker color.

Key Command Alert: Color Palette

You can also use the key command of OPTION+C to open the Color Palette.

Creating Markers from Existing Regions

Let's say you already have regions in the Arrange window that have the exact boundaries you would like your Markers to have. Logic makes it very easy to create Markers from those regions.

1 **Select** one or more **regions** in the Arrange window.

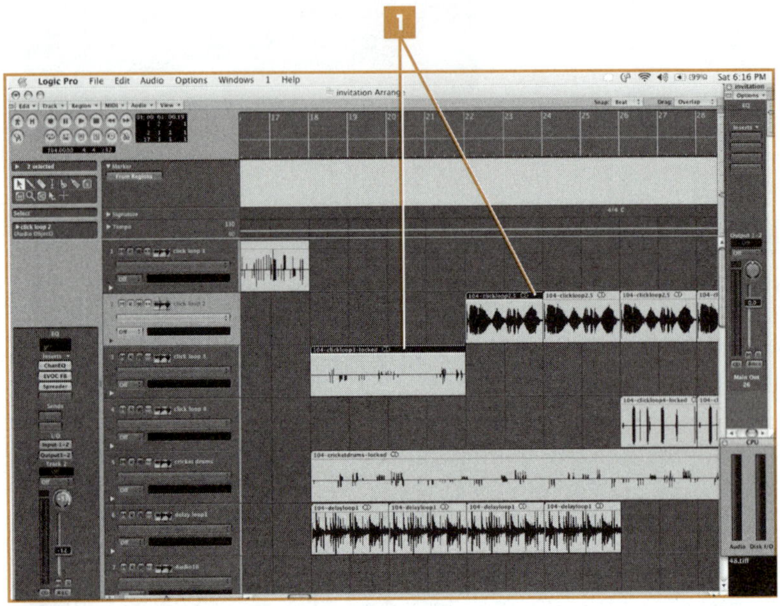

2 **Click** the **From Regions** button in the Marker Track. Your new Markers will be created in the Marker lane.

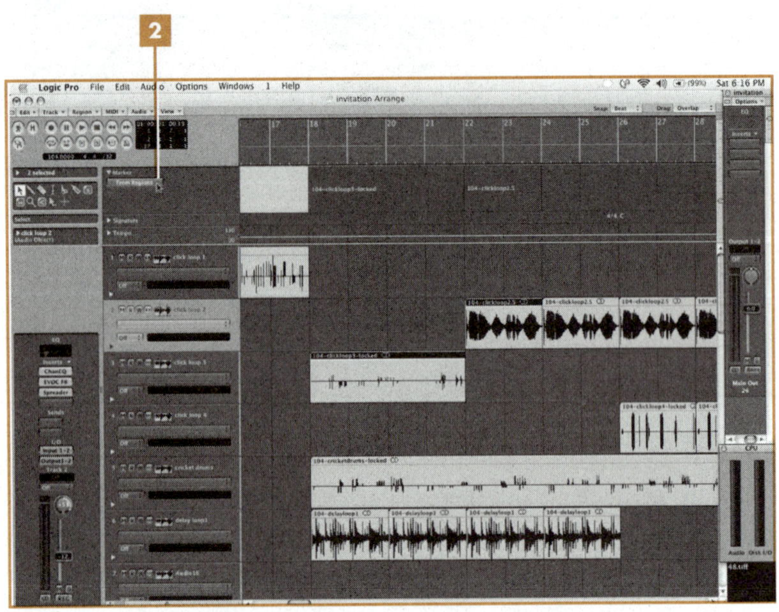

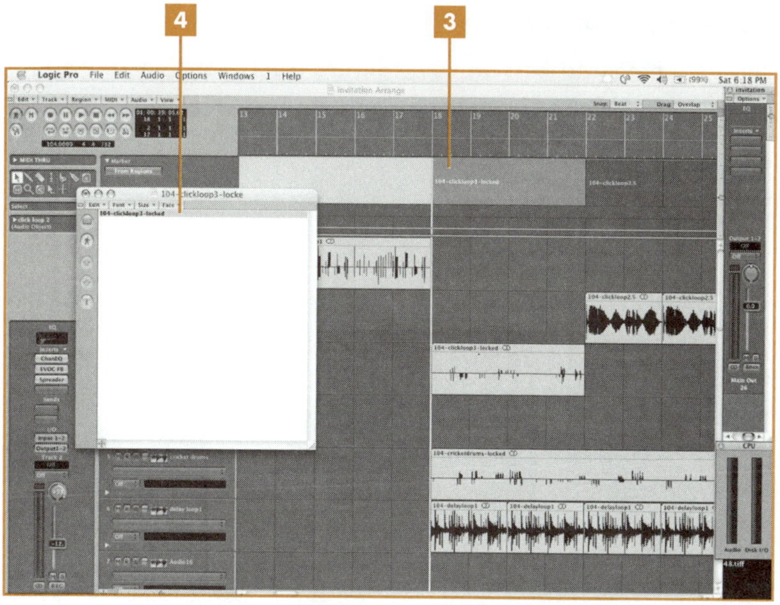

3 Double-click one of the new Markers to open the Marker window.

4 Rename the Marker in the Marker window.

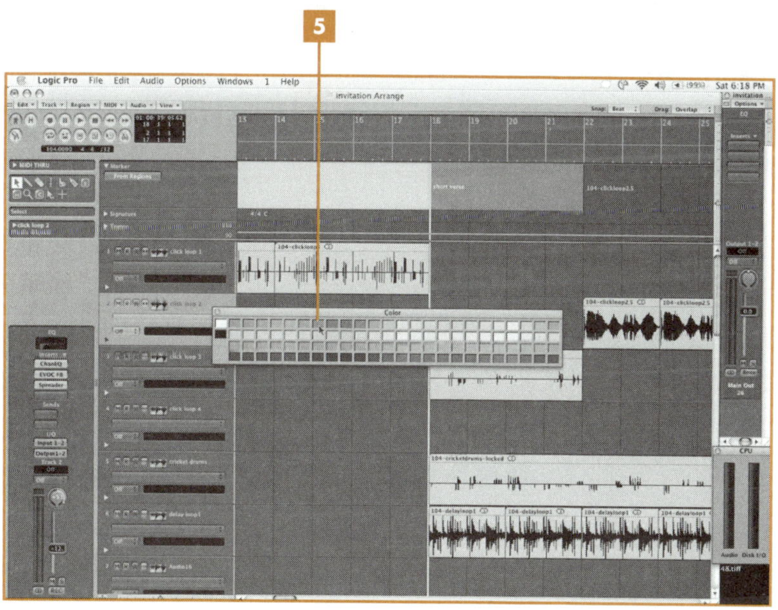

5 Open the Color Palette, either from the View menu or using the key command, and select a color for your new Marker.

Adjusting Markers on the Marker Track

Once you have Markers on your Marker Track, you can very easily move them around and resize them.

To move your Markers around:

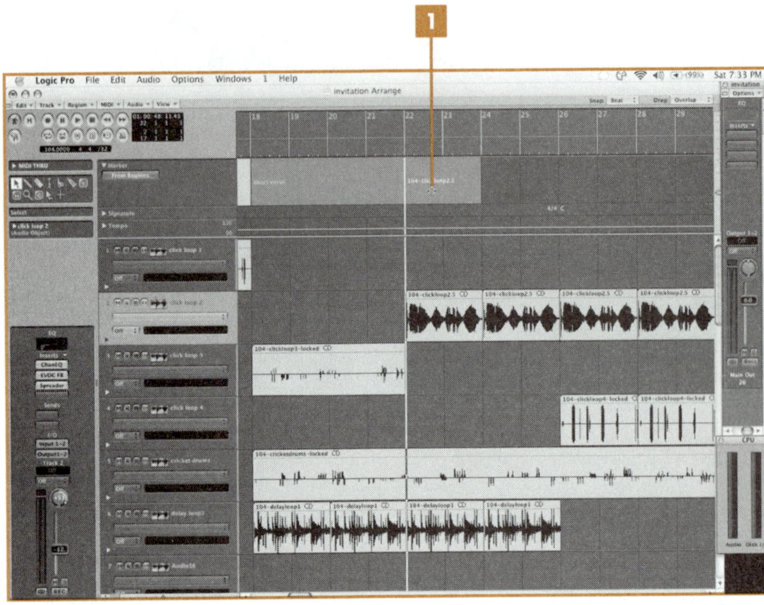

1. **Hover** the mouse pointer over a **Marker**; you will see the pointer change to a left and right arrow.

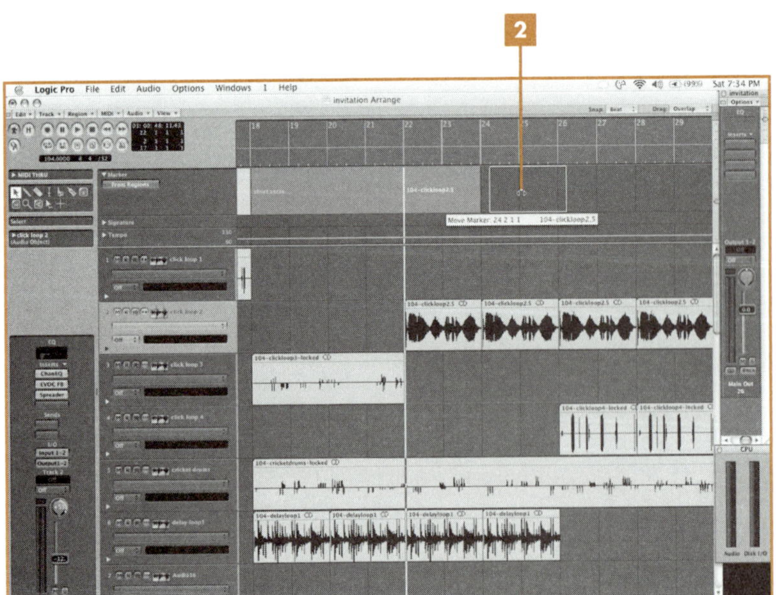

2. **Click** and **drag** the **Marker** either left or right; you will see an outline of the Marker as you drag.

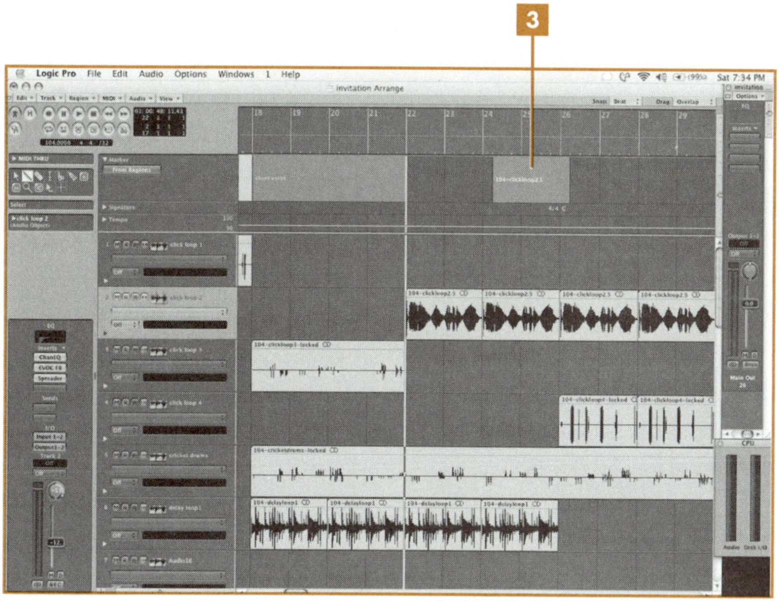

3 Release the mouse when the Marker is where you want it to be.

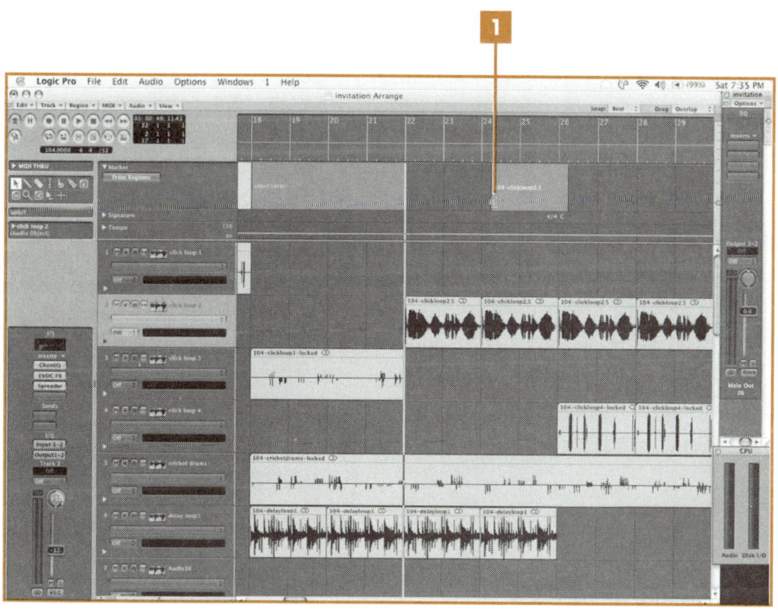

To resize your Markers:

1 Hover the mouse pointer over the left or right edge of a Marker. The pointer will change to a bracket surrounded by arrows.

2 Click and drag left or right to move the border of the Marker; let go of the mouse button when the border is where you want it to be.

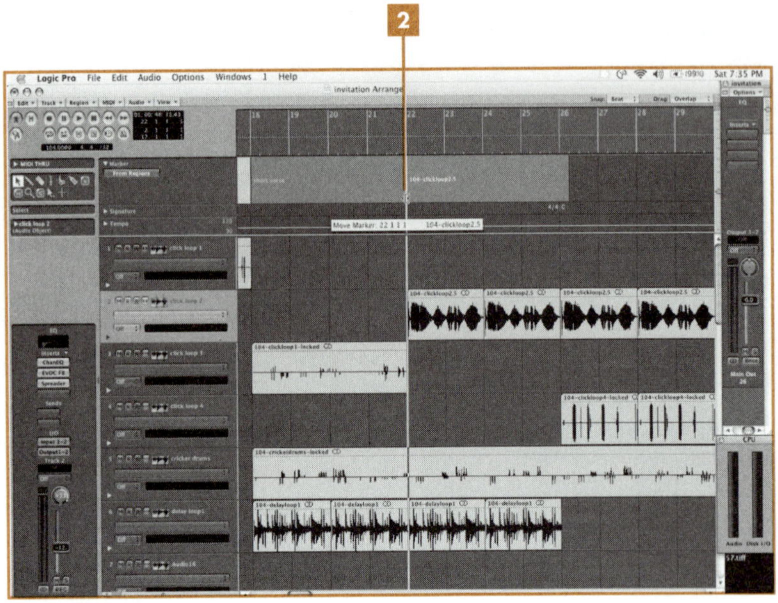

Navigating the Arrange Window Using Markers

Markers function as more than simply visual cues. You can also use them to navigate around the Arrange window.

1 Click on Options > Marker and you'll see the Goto Next and Goto Previous commands (as well as their associated key commands). These commands let you jump quickly from Marker to Marker within the Arrange window.

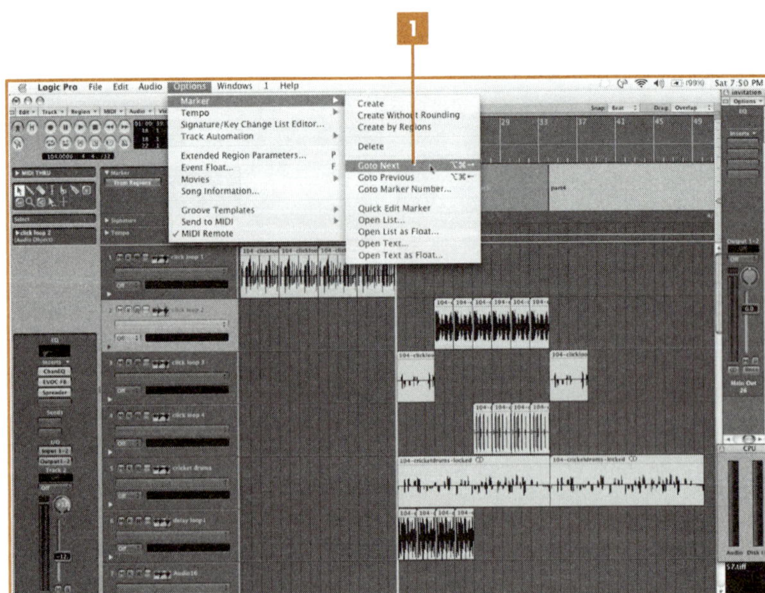

Quick Marker Navigation

If you hold the OPTION key and click on a Marker in the Marker Track, the Song Position Line will jump to the beginning of that Marker.

Setting the Cycle Area Using Markers

Finally, you can set the Cycle Area using Markers as well.

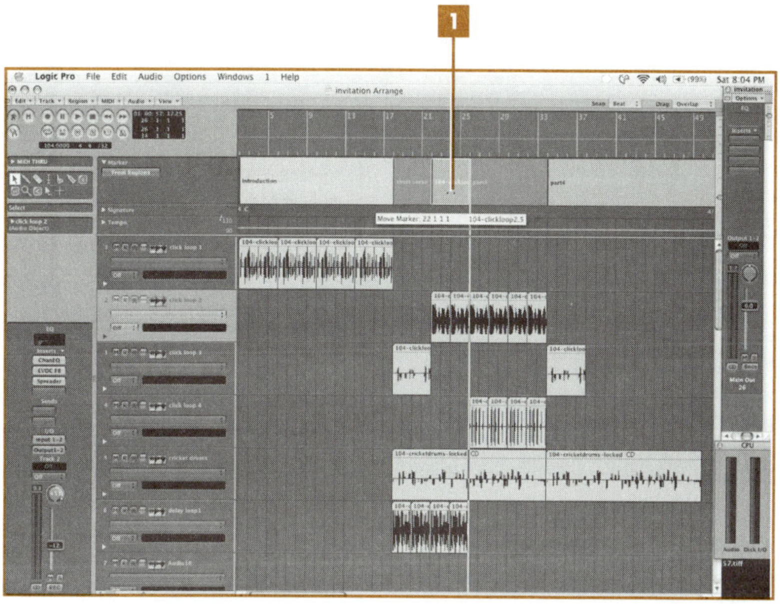

1 Click on a Marker with the mouse.

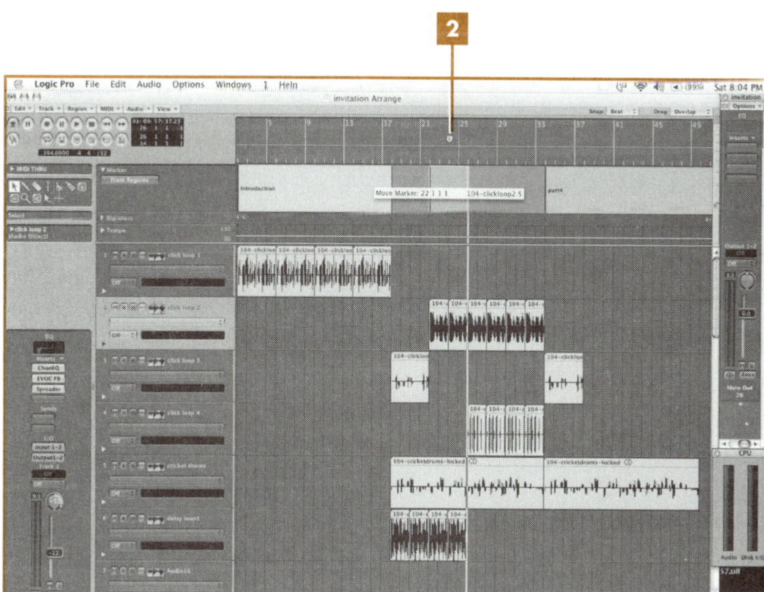

2 Drag the Marker up into the Time Ruler; you will see the cursor change to a closed hand.

3 Let go of the mouse, and you will see the Cycle Area expand to match the length of the Marker.

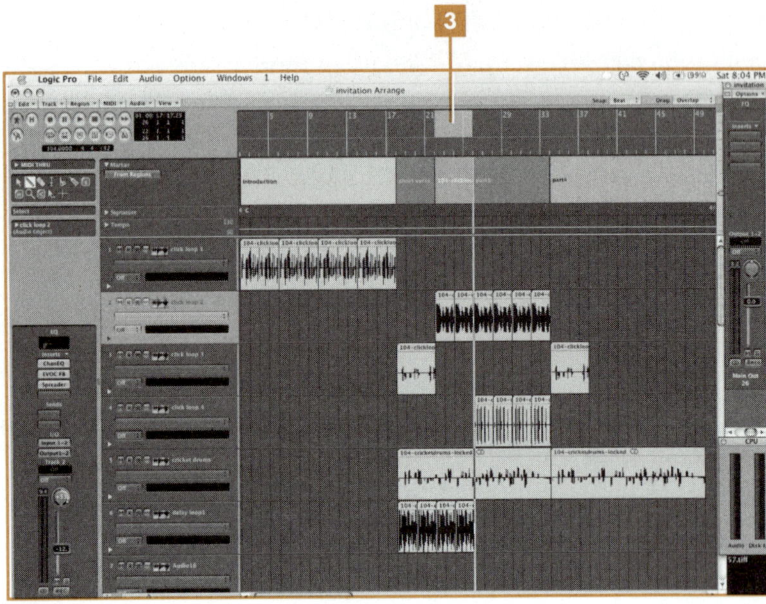

Adding Files to the Arrange Window

You may find that you want to add either Audio or MIDI files to a song that comes from a collaborator or additional source. These files may have been generated in a different application, imported from a CD, etc. Logic makes it incredibly easy to add these files to your project! You can simply drag files from the Finder or use the Import command.

Adding Audio Files to the Arrange Window

Dragging files from the Finder:

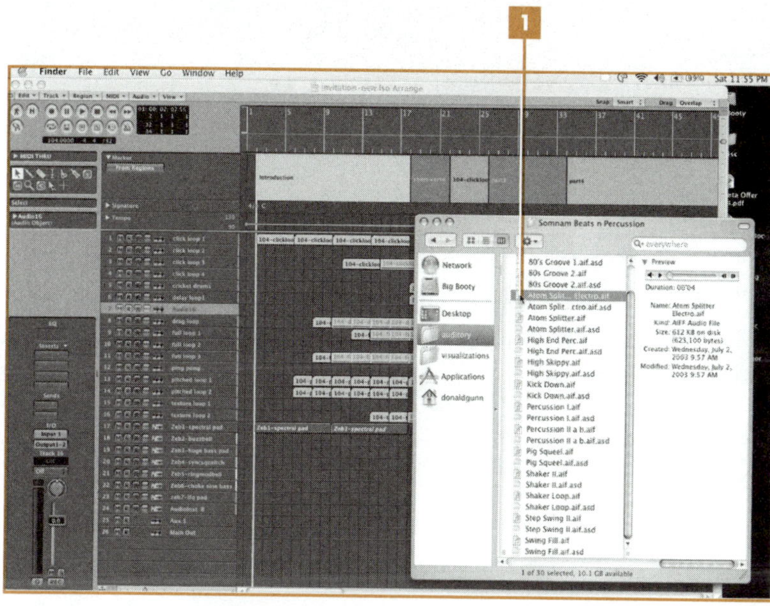

1 From the Finder, navigate to the directory that contains the file you want to add.

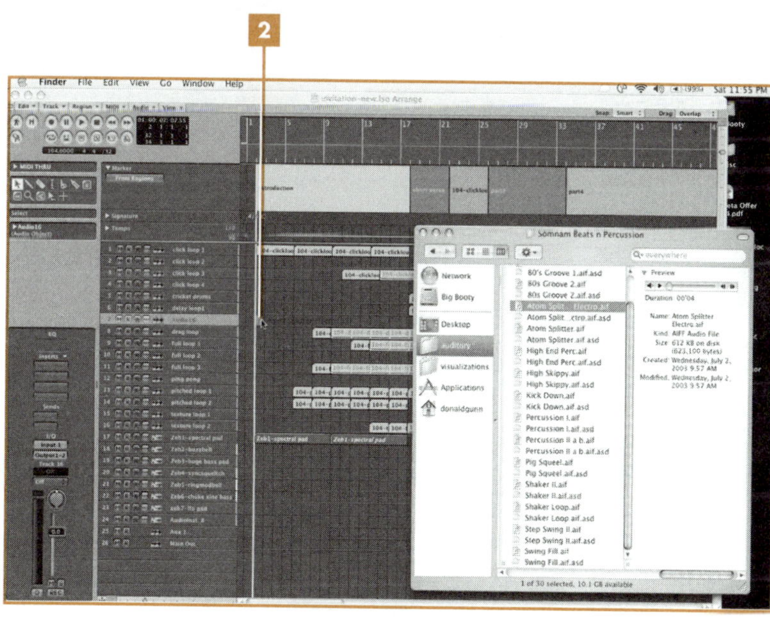

2 Drag the file to a track in the Arrange window.

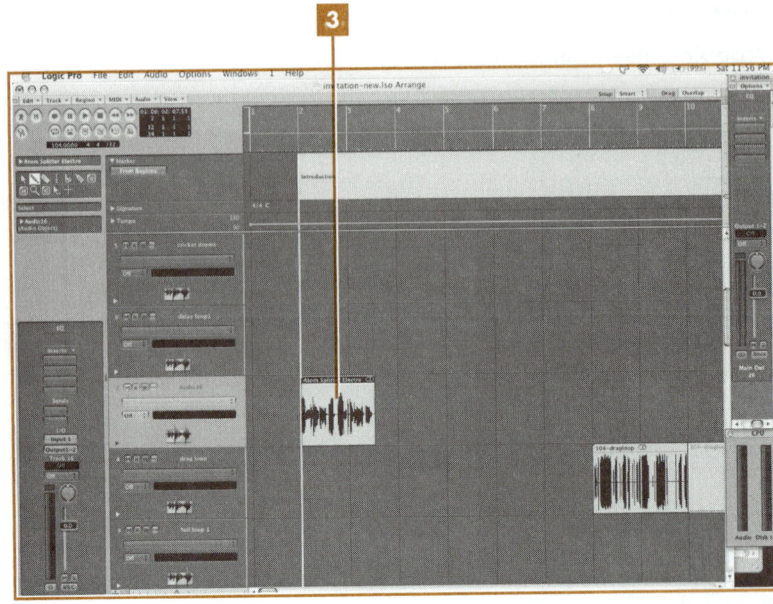

3 **Release** the **mouse** button, and the file will appear on the Arrange track.

Using the Import Audio File command:

1 **Select** the **Arrange Track** on which you want the file to be placed.

2 **Go to Audio > Import Audio File**.

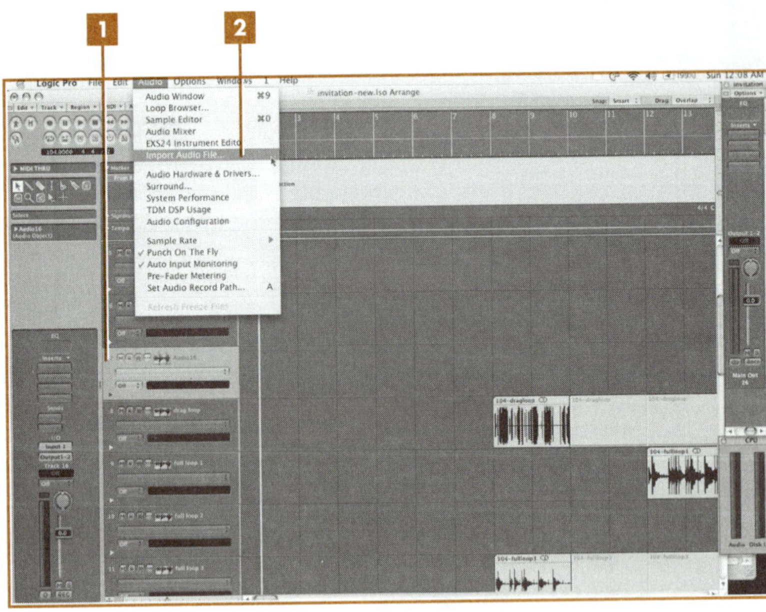

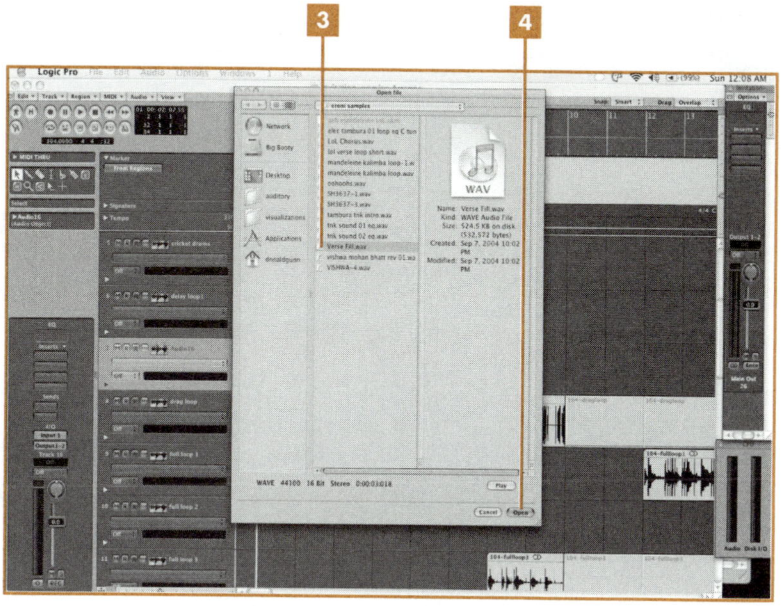

3 Select the file you want to import from the dialog box.

4 Click Open.

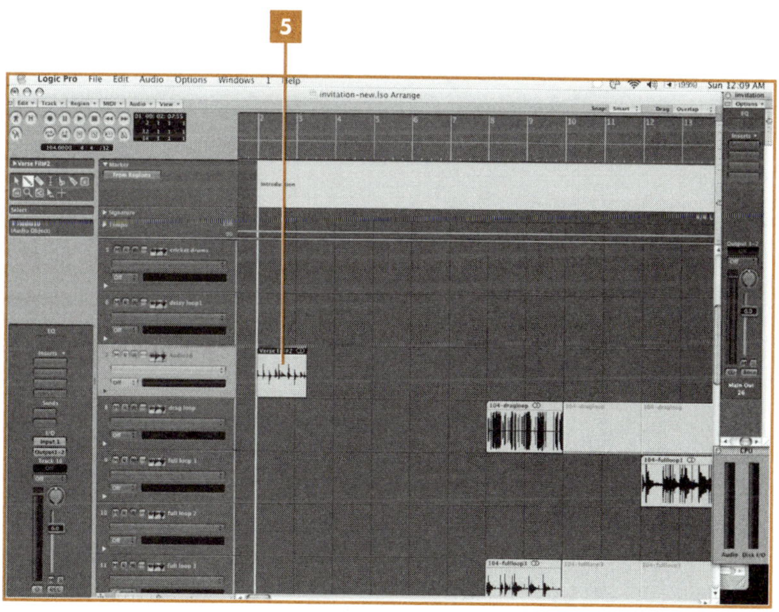

5 The file is added to the selected Arrange Track.

Adding MIDI Files to the Arrange Window

Dragging files from the Finder:

1 From the Finder, navigate to the directory that contains the file you want to add.

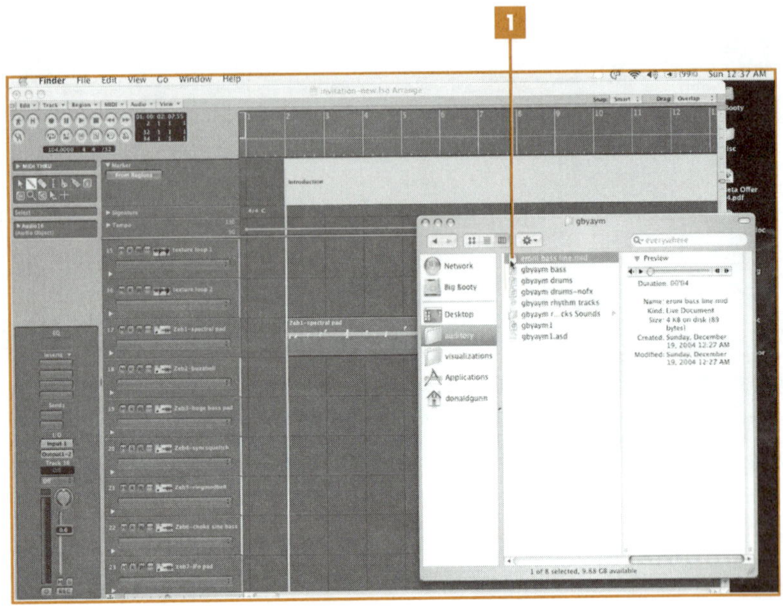

2 Drag the file to a track in the Arrange window.

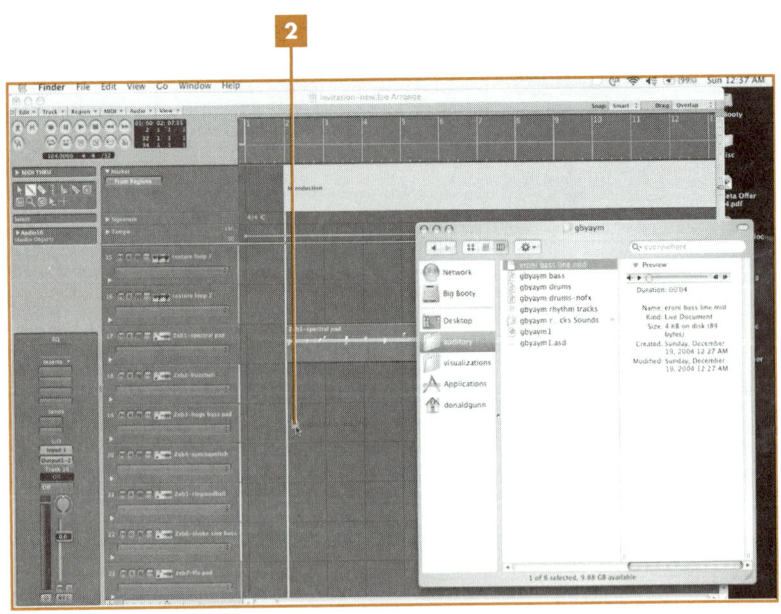

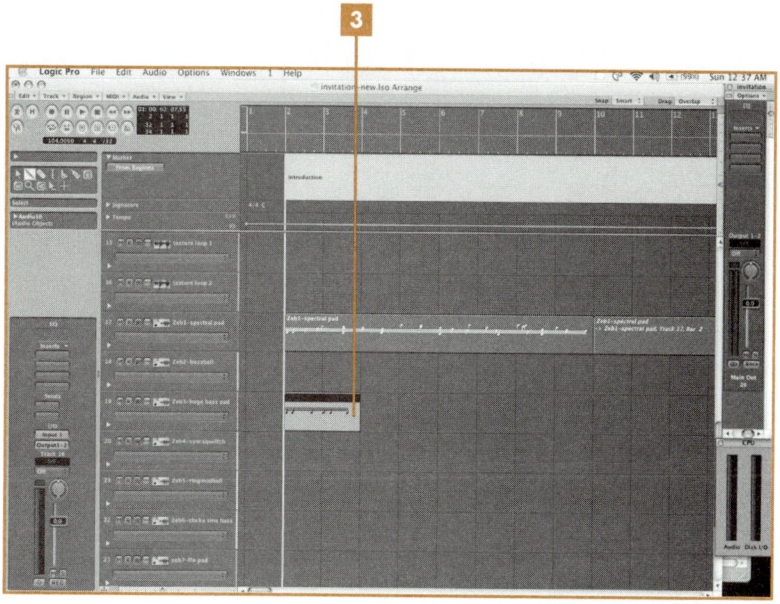

3 Release the mouse button and the file will appear on the Arrange Track.

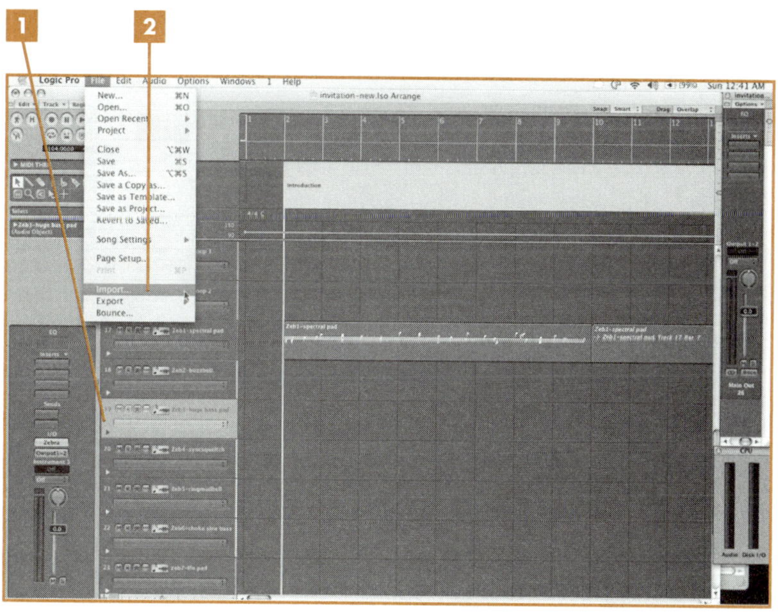

Using the Import command:

1 Select the Arrange track on which you want the file to be placed.

2 Go to File > Import.

3 Select the file you want to import from the dialog box.

4 Click Open.

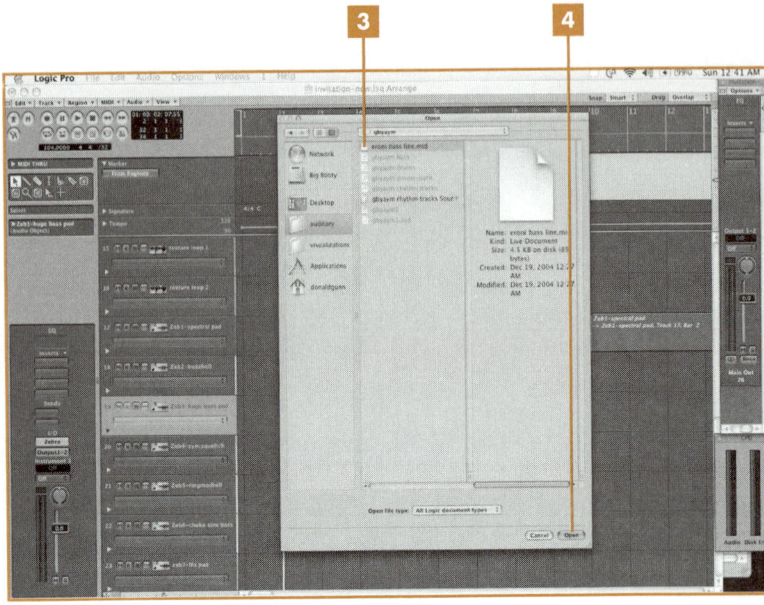

5 The file is added to the selected Arrange track.

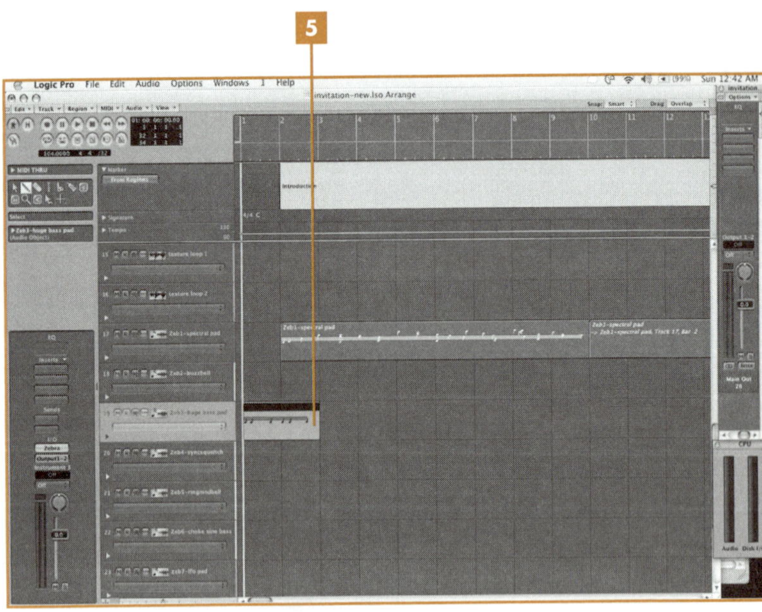

6 Arranging Your Song

Now that you know your way around the Arrange window and have explored the track functions, it's time to engage in the most fun part of using the Arrange: actually *arranging* your music! Logic's Arrange features are simply the most elegant and intuitive available, and after getting used to Logic's workflow, we're sure you'll agree! In this section you will learn how to:

- Move regions
- Loop regions
- Resize regions
- Time stretch/compress regions
- Split regions
- Copy regions

Moving Regions

One of the most basic ways you'll want to arrange your song is by moving around the regions in the Arrange Area.

1 Click on a region in the Arrange window to select it.

1

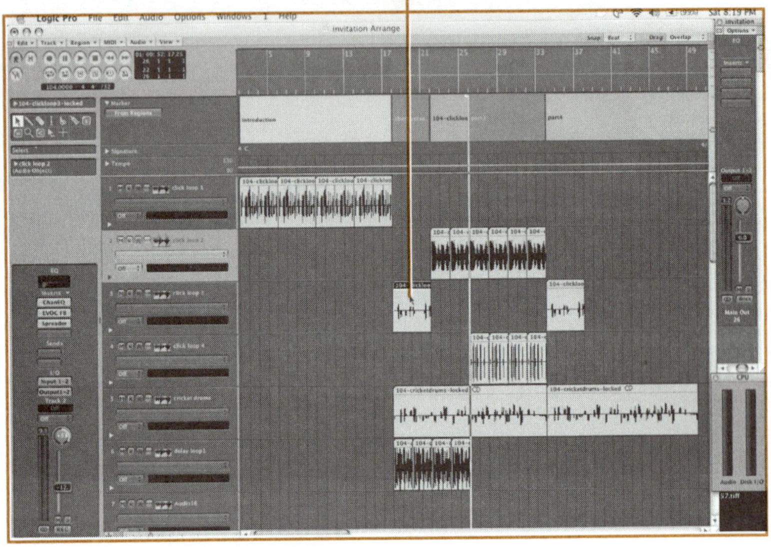

2 While holding the mouse button down, drag the region where you want it to go; you will see an outline of the region as you drag it around the window. You can move it within the track it is on or to another track.

2

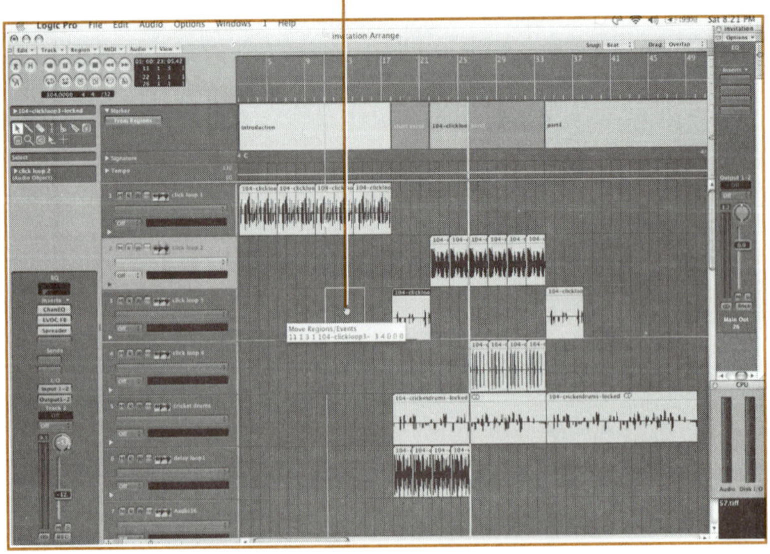

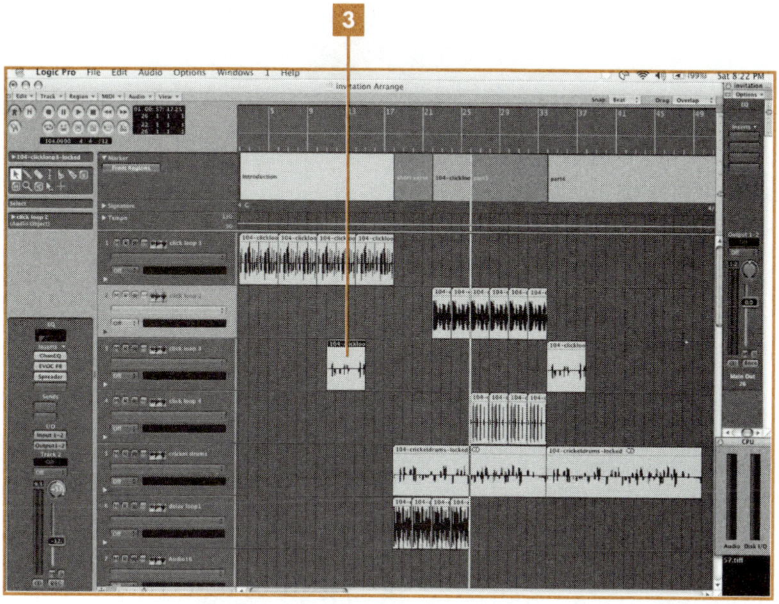

3 **Release** the **mouse** button to place the region.

Looping Regions

Popular music very often relies on repeating various musical phrases and song elements to hook the listener. When you instruct Logic to repeat a specific region or regions in your song, it is called "looping." Looping doesn't actually create any new regions; it really just creates pointers to the original region you are looping—this is why loops look like empty gray boxes originating from a region. Logic, in our opinion, offers the most intuitive and powerful looping functions and tools of any digital audio sequencer!

Looping a Region Using the Loop Cursor

New in Logic 7 is the Loop cursor, which allows you to intuitively drag loops back and forth to any position in the Arrange Area that you wish. Users of GarageBand, ACID, and other modern looping applications will find this method of looping a snap!

1. Move the mouse pointer to the top right edge of a region in the Arrange window. The cursor will change to the Loop cursor.

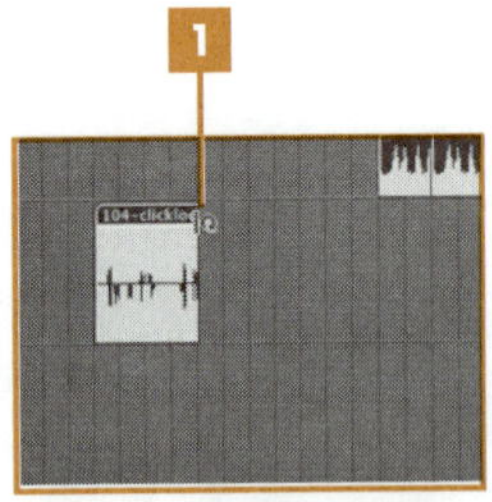

2. Click and drag the loop to the length you want the region to repeat. It doesn't have to match the exact length of the region, either!

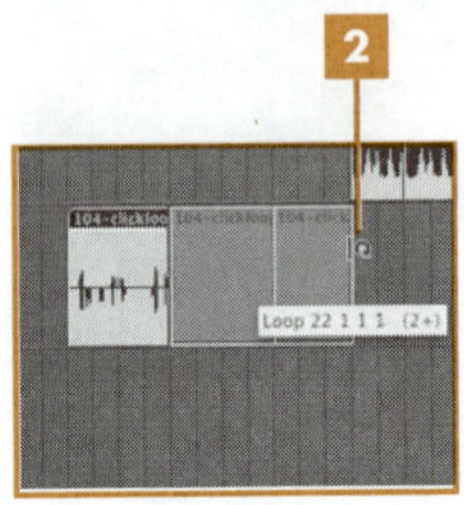

Looping a Region Using the Loop Parameter

If you want a loop to extend for the entire length of your song, you can easily do this with the Loop parameter in the Region Parameter box. Users of older versions of Logic will already be familiar with this method of looping. Logic 7, however, offers some new twists, as you'll see later.

1. Select a region in the Arrange window.
2. Click the Loop box in the Region Parameter box. Your region will loop until the end of the song.

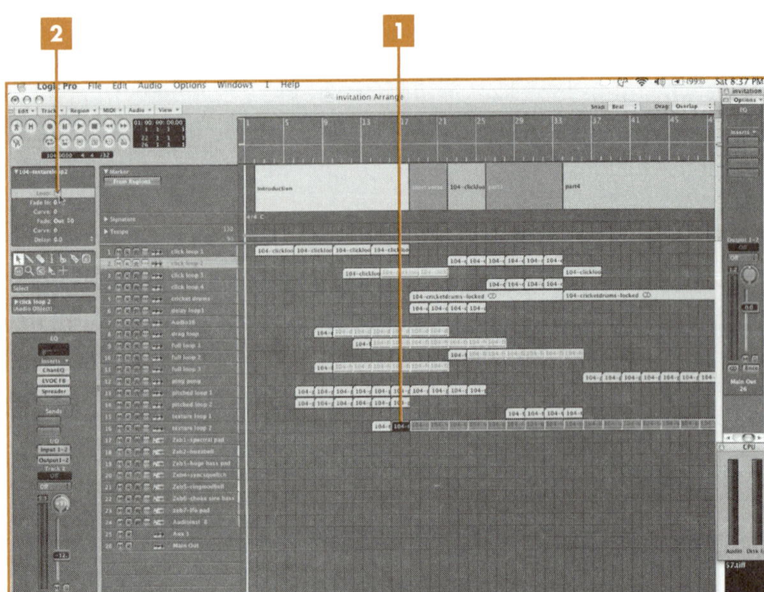

Key Command Alert: Toggle Loop

The L key will turn a loop on or off on selected regions in the Arrange window.

Cutting Loops

Whether your loop was generated using the Loop cursor or the Loop parameter, if you decide you want to shorten your loop, you can easily do so.

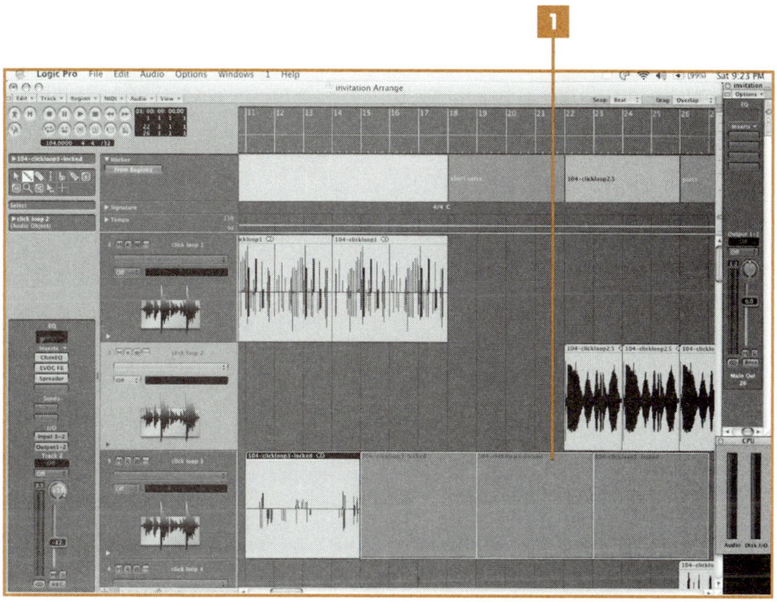

1 Select the loop whose length you want to change.

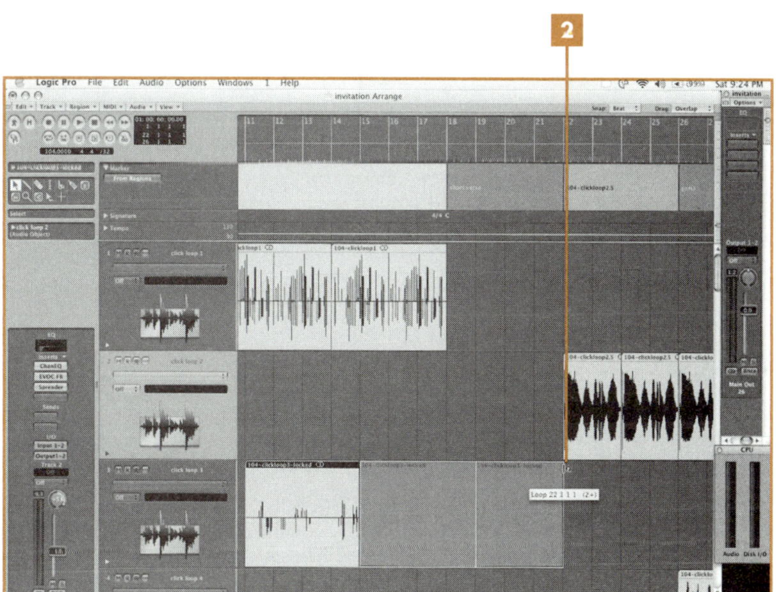

2 Click in the loop with the Loop cursor; the loop will be cut where you click.

Resizing Loops

Just as you can cut loops, you can also extend and contract them using the Loop cursor.

1 Click the mouse pointer on the right edge of a loop in the Arrange window. The cursor will change to the Loop cursor.

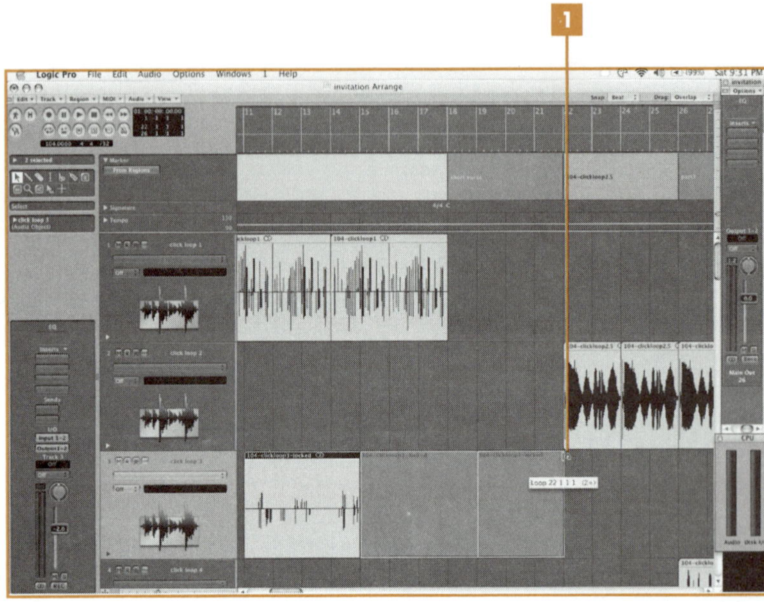

2 Click and drag the loop to the length you want the region to repeat.

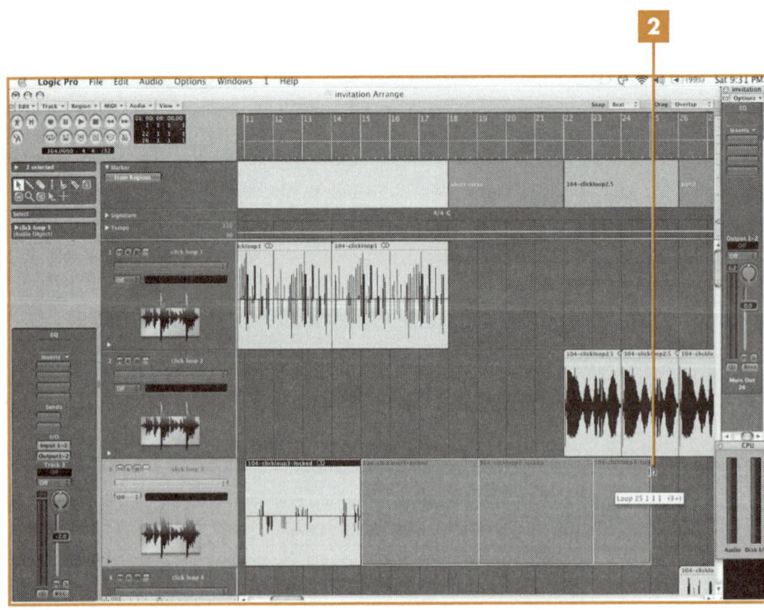

3

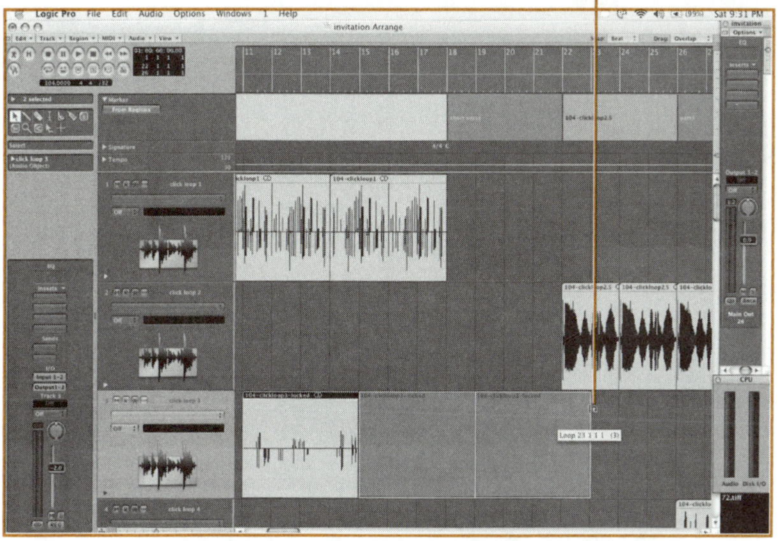

3 Drag again if you want to lengthen or shorten a loop.

Resizing Regions

There are different methods of resizing regions, depending on whether you have an audio or MIDI region. You may merely want to extend or reduce a region or simply adjust the timing of the region.

1

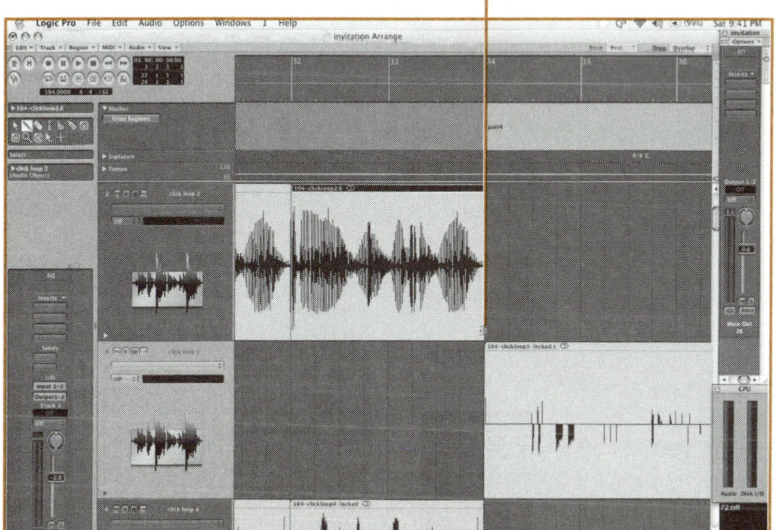

Resizing Regions Without Changing Their Timing

If you just want to expand or reduce the length of a region, this couldn't be easier, thanks to Logic's smart Resize tool!

1 Click on the lower left or right edge of a region in the Arrange window; the pointer changes to the Resize tool when you are near or over the edge.

2 Click and drag the region to change its length.

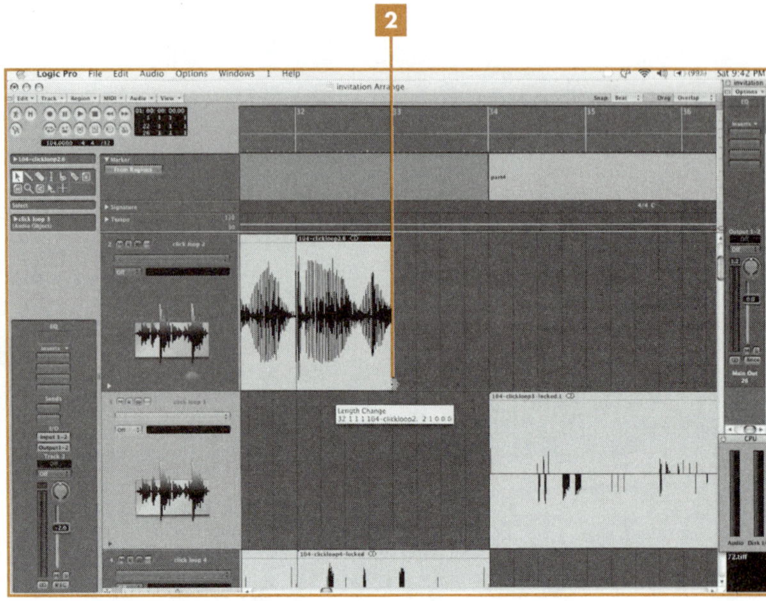

Resizing Regions and Adjusting Their Timing

You may want to not only expand or reduce the length of a region, but also have all the audio or MIDI data in the region adjust to the new region length. This process is known as time stretching. Time stretching is very easy for MIDI regions, but it takes a few extra steps for audio regions.

Time Stretching MIDI regions

Time stretching MIDI regions couldn't be simpler.

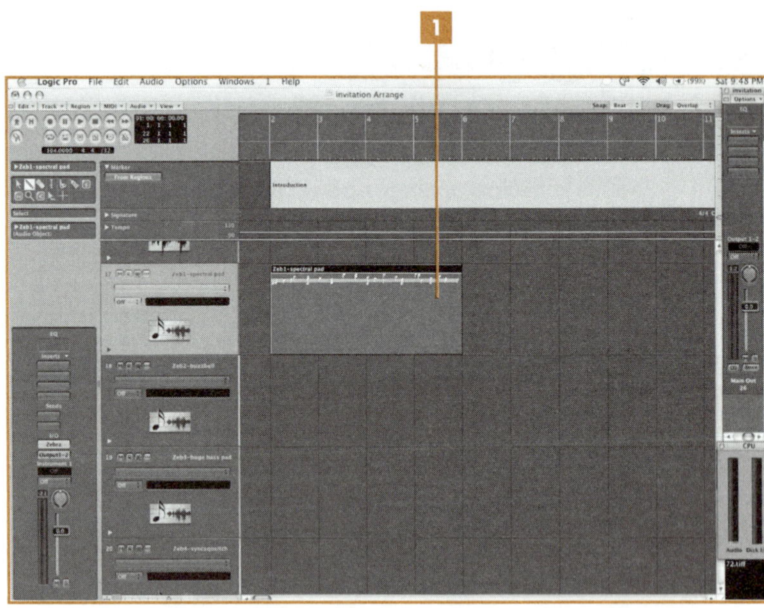

1 Select a MIDI region in the Arrange window.

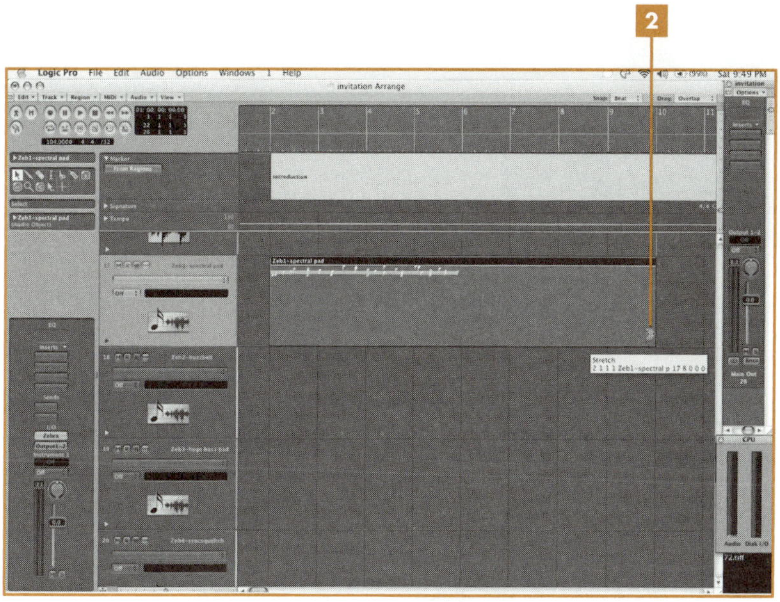

2 Hold the OPTION key and drag the edge of the region to the desired length.

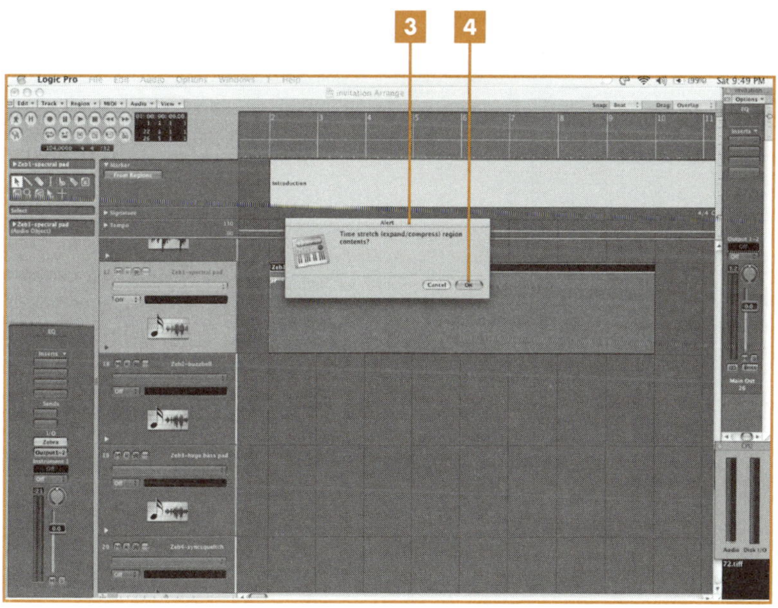

3 Release the mouse button and Logic will ask if you want to Time stretch (expand/compress) region contents.

4 Click OK.

5 You will see the original MIDI notes now stretched (or compressed) over the new length of the region.

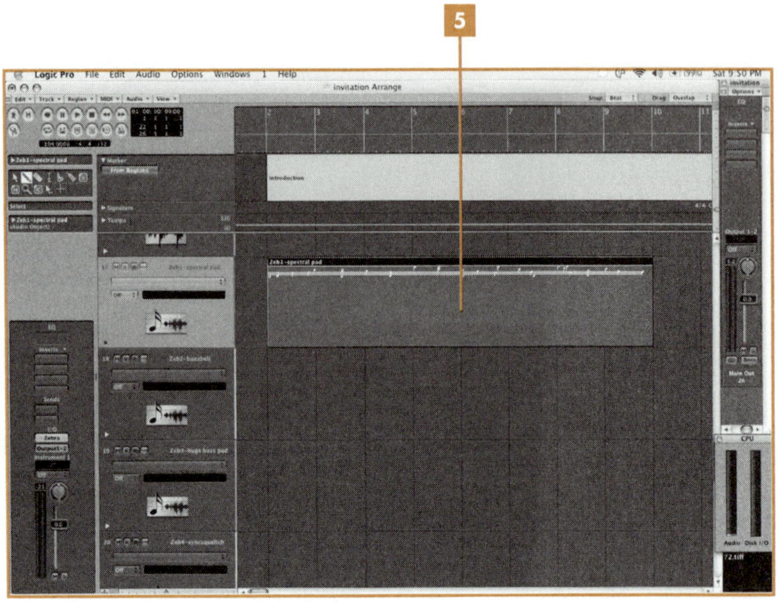

Time Stretching Audio Regions

Time stretching audio regions is conceptually the same as time stretching MIDI regions, but unlike MIDI data, time stretching audio data requires using complicated algorithms to modify the audio data on your hard drive. Because of this, it requires a few more steps.

1 Select the region you want to stretch in the Arrange window.

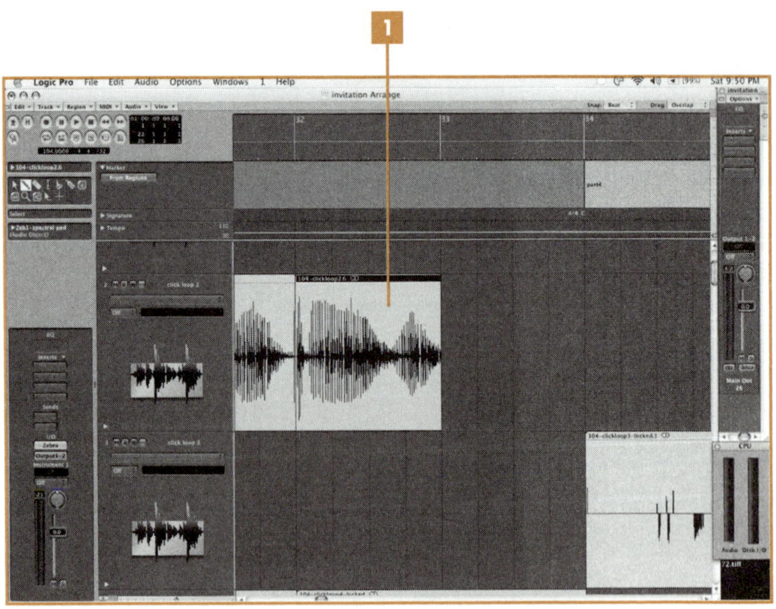

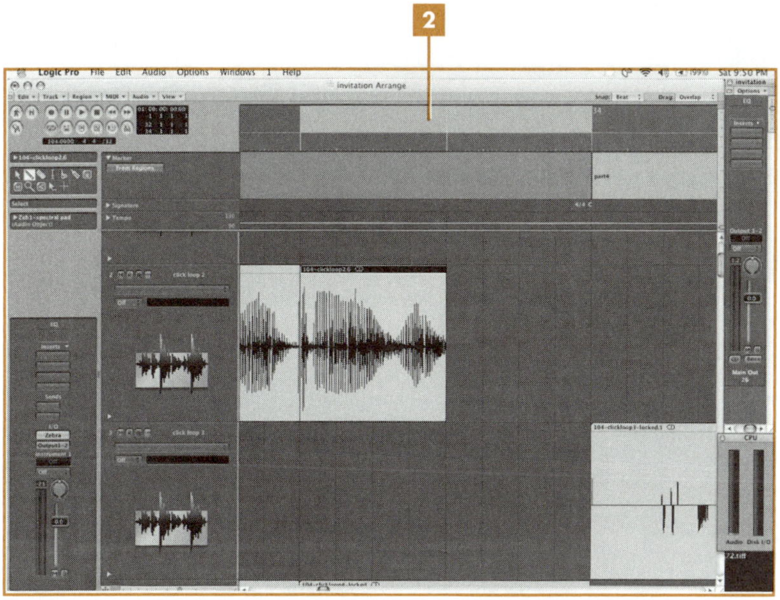

2 Create a Cycle in the Time Ruler that corresponds to the length to which you want to stretch the region.

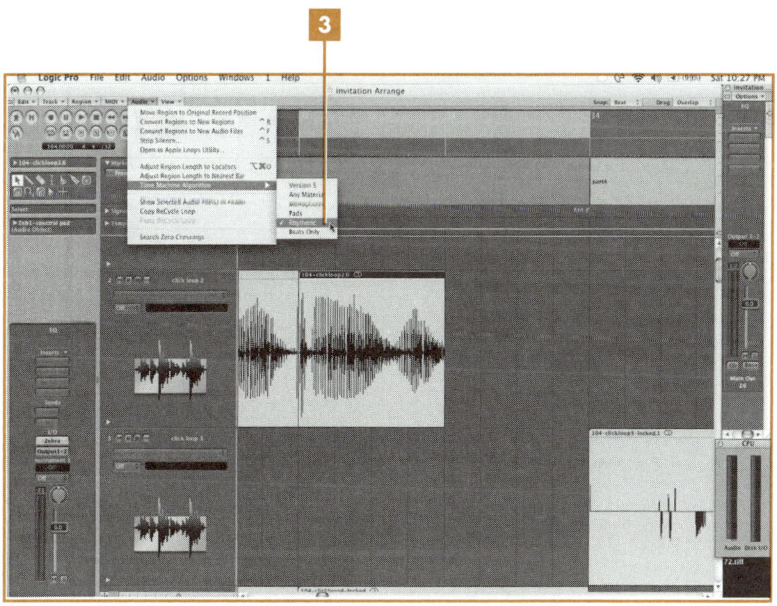

3 Go to Audio > Time Machine Algorithm, and choose the one most appropriate for the type of region you are stretching.

Time Machine Algorithm

The Time Machine is an element of the Sample Editor and will be discussed in Chapter 7, "The Audio Window and Sample Editor." The Algorithm components of the Time Machine are optimized for various types of source material and will produce better results in the stretched audio if the appropriate one is chosen before the operation is performed.

4 Go to Audio > Adjust Region Length to Locators and select the command. Logic will then perform the time stretching.

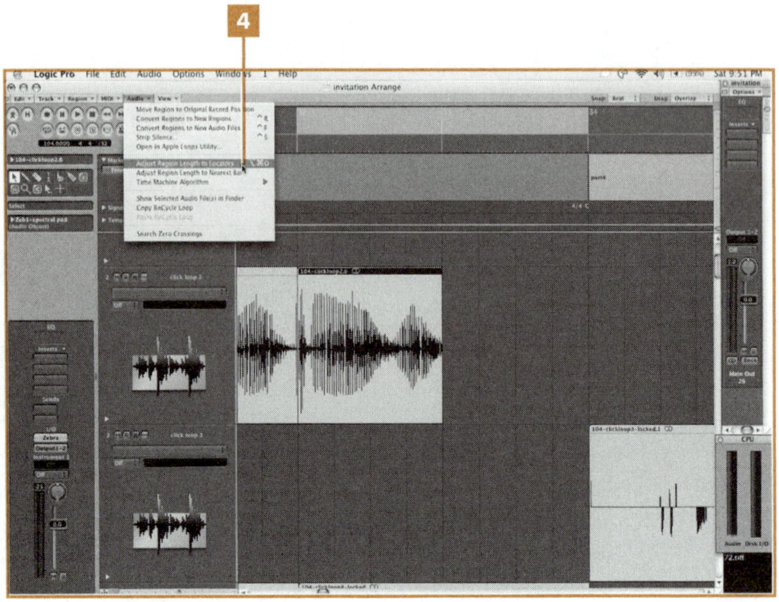

Key Command Alert: Adjust Region Length to Locators

Pressing OPTION+COMMAND+O will perform the time stretch adjustment on your region in the Arrange window.

5 Confirm that the resulting file will be stretched over the length of the locators set by the Cycle range.

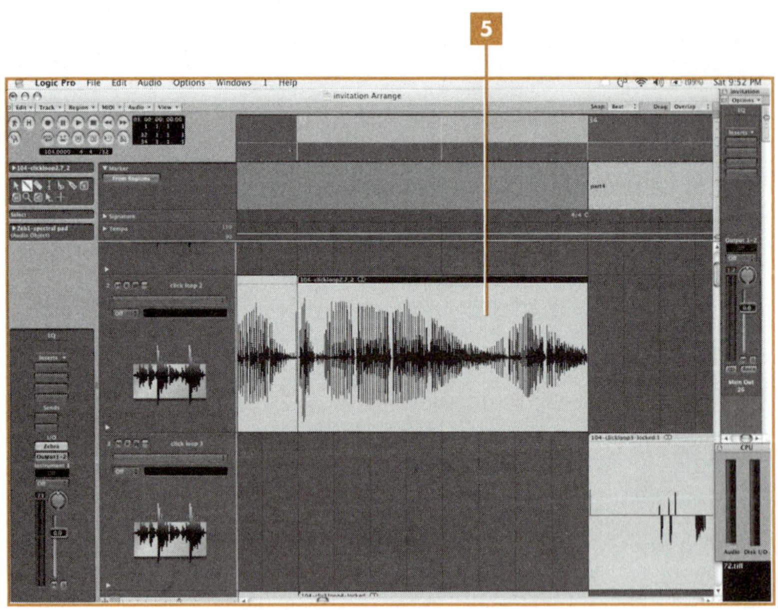

Splitting Regions

Another important arrangement function is splitting regions into two or more regions. Logic's Scissors tool and key commands make this very simple!

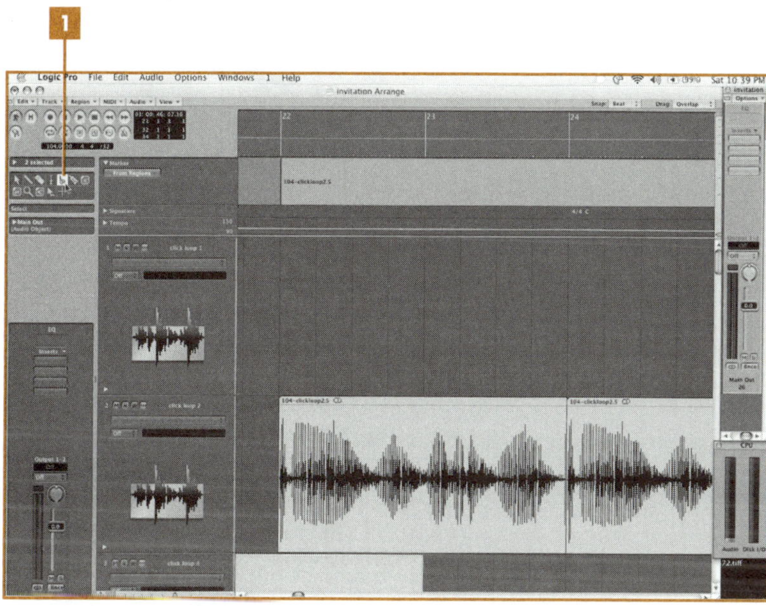

Splitting a Region

Splitting a region with the Scissors tool is a very intuitive process.

1. Select the Scissors tool from the Toolbox.

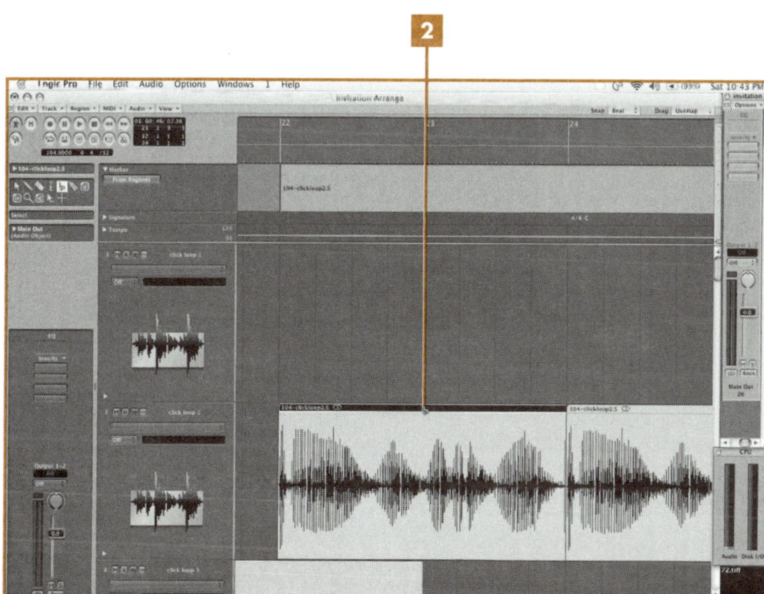

2. At the location within the region that you want the split to occur, click the Scissors tool.

3 The region will be split into two parts.

Scrubbing to Find the Right Split

If you aren't certain where you want to split a region, click and hold on it with the Scissors tool while dragging left or right to audibly scrub the audio.

Making a Split at the Song Position Line

If the Song Position Line (SPL) happens to be where you want to split your region(s), you can use the menu command Regions > Split/Demix > Split at Song Position or the key command /.

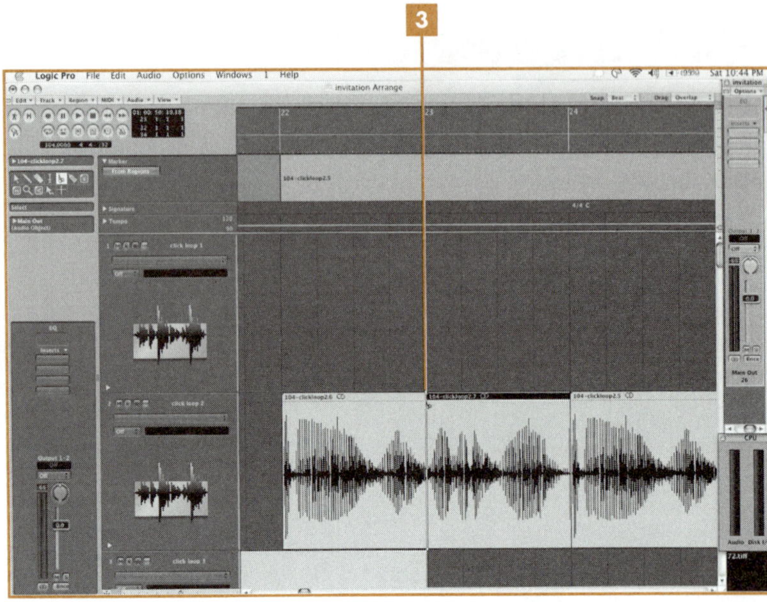

Splitting a Region into Multiple Regions

You can use key modifiers with the Scissors tool to split a region into multiple regions.

1 Move the Song Position Line within a region by the division you wish to split it. In this example, it is moved an 1/8-note from the beginning of the region.

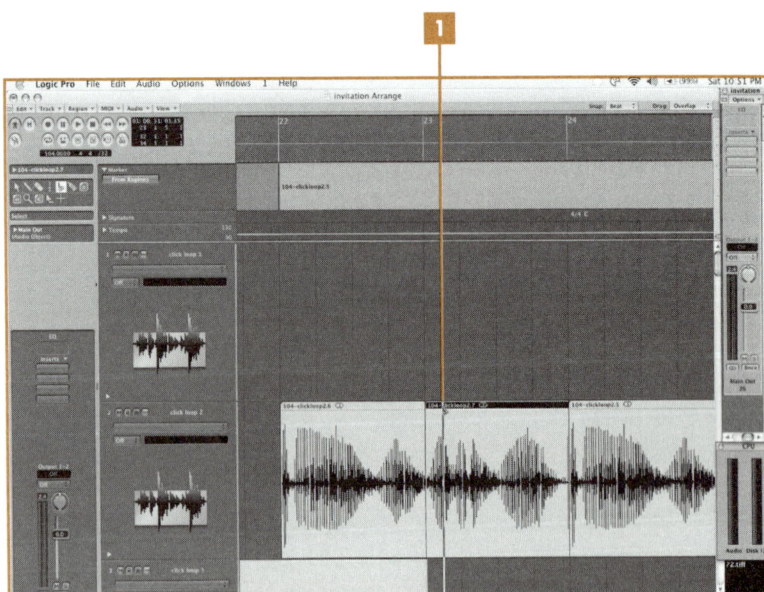

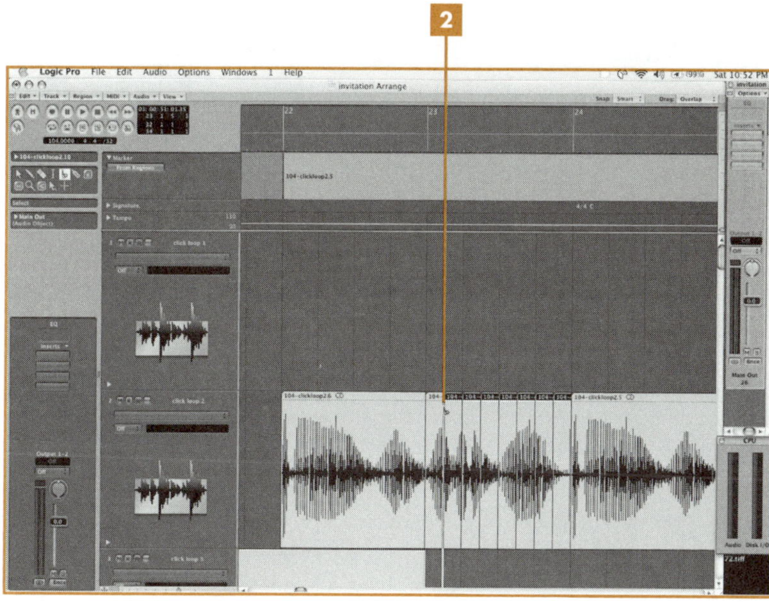

2 OPTION+click on the Song Position Line with the Scissors tool. The region will be split by 1/8-notes for its duration.

Copying Regions

Many times, you may wish to use a region more than once in your song, but you may not want to loop it. For these situations, Logic offers a number of very flexible copying functions. First of all, your copies can be either a separate duplicate of all the data from the original region, or your copies can be aliases—empty containers referencing the original region. The advantage to aliases is that any change you make in the original region will be automatically reflected in the aliased copies—however, you may not want this to happen!

Copying Regions by Moving Them

You can copy regions as easily as moving them by simply adding a key modifier.

Creating a Copy:

1 Click and drag on a region while holding the OPTION key

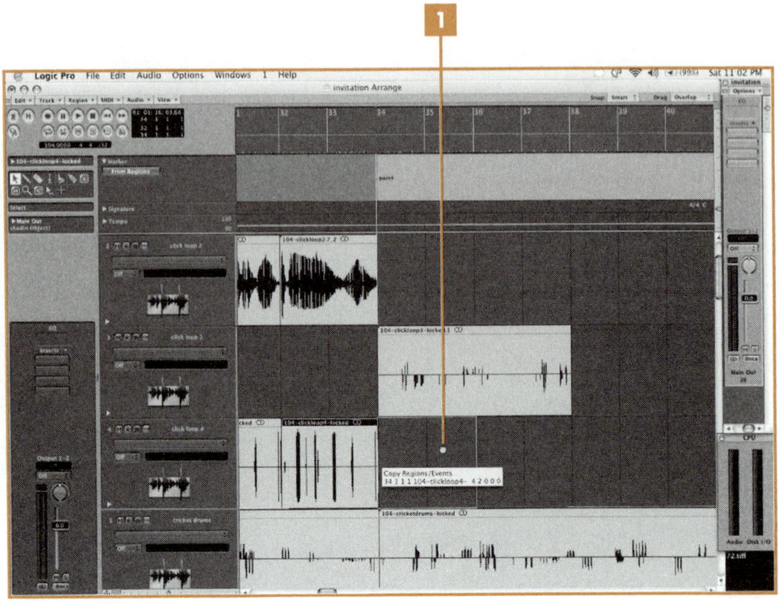

2 The result is a perfect copy of the original region.

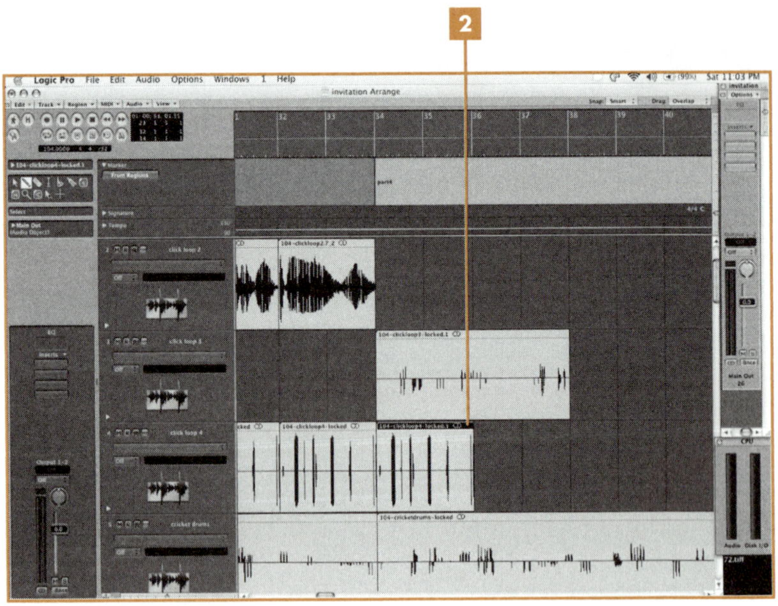

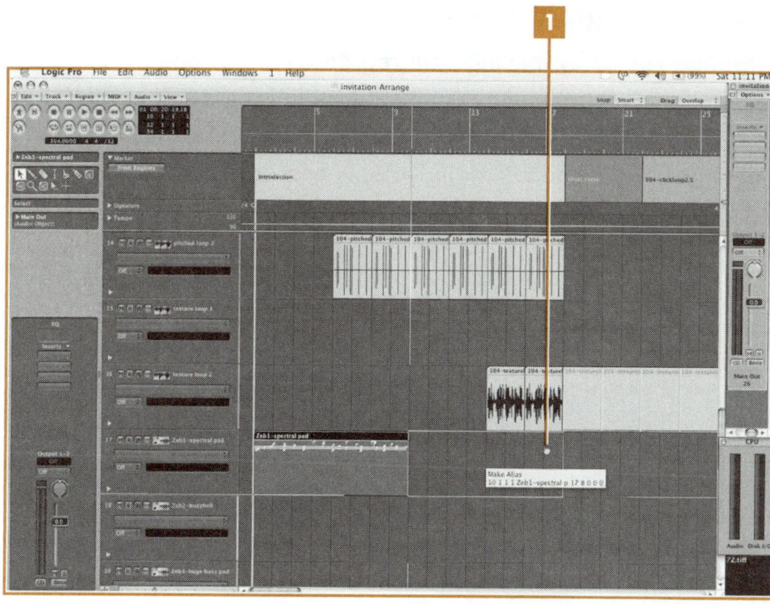

Creating an Alias:

1. Click and drag on a region while holding the OPTION+SHIFT keys.

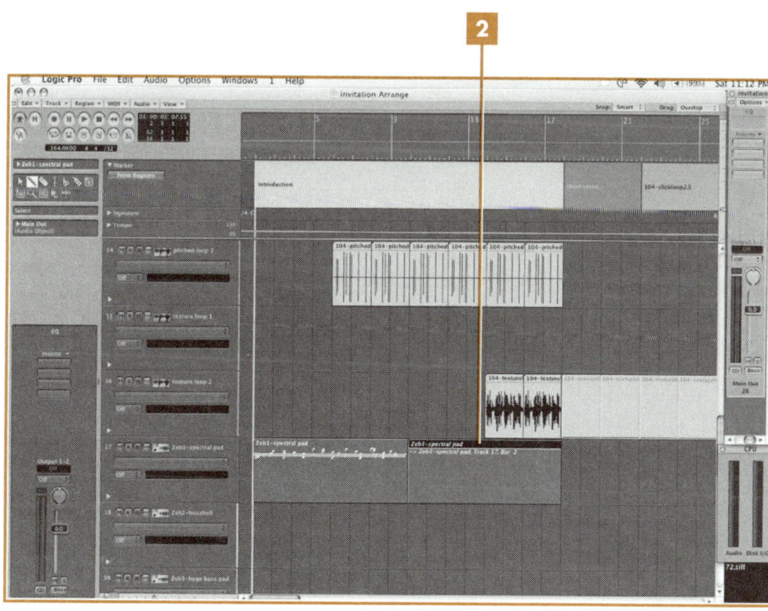

2. The resulting alias has no information in it like the original, but is merely a reference to the original.

Copying Regions Using the Repeat Command

Creating copies by moving your region works for one or two copies, but if you want to make a number of copies, it can be pretty tedious. Thankfully, you can also use the Repeat command in the Arrange local menu to create multiple copies and aliases.

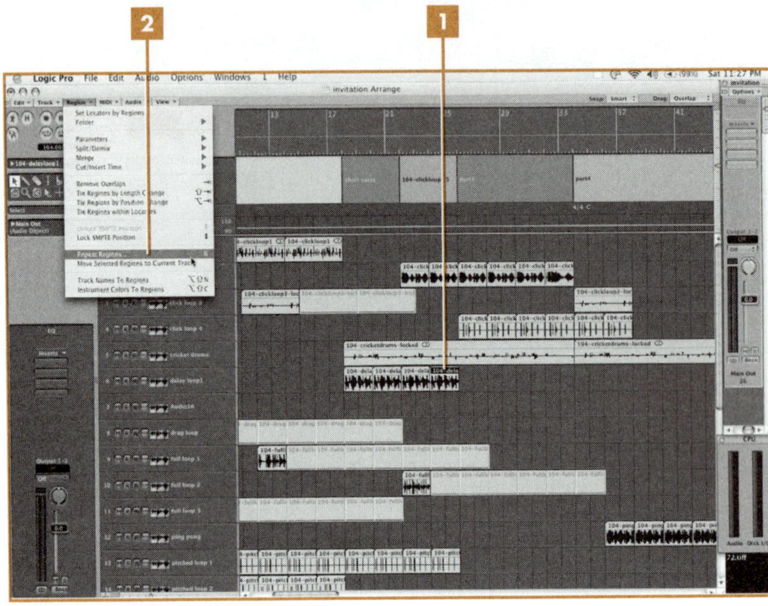

1. Select a region in the Arrange window.
2. Go to Region > Repeat Regions.

Key Command Alert: Repeat Regions

Pressing R will open the Repeat Regions/Events dialog box.

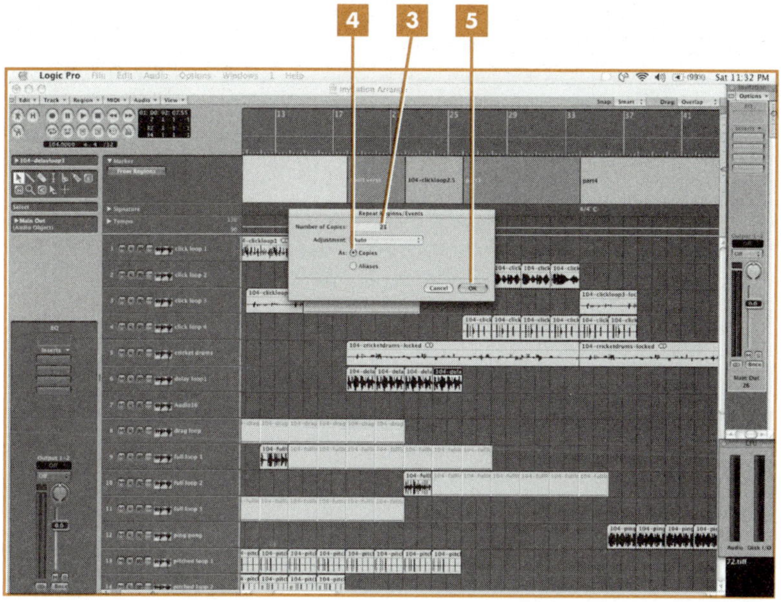

3 In the Repeat Regions/Events dialog box, enter the number of times you want the region to repeat.

4 Select whether you want the repeated regions to be Copies or Aliases.

5 Click OK.

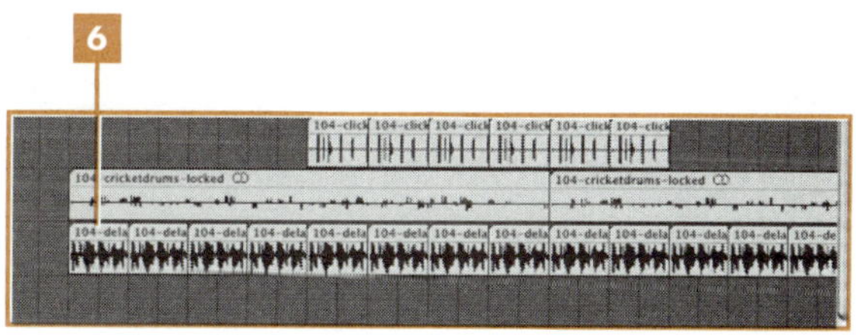

6 As simply as that, you now have a large number of copies of your original region!

7 The Audio Window and Sample Editor

Using Logic's Arrange window is almost deceptively easy; you might think that's all Logic has to offer! But from here on in the book, we'll start exploring some of the more specialized and powerful aspects of the program. First, we'll introduce you to some of the powerful ways Logic lets you work with audio files.

You've already learned how to work with audio regions in the Arrange window. In fact, in its Audio window, Logic gives you access to more audio regions and audio files than you might have in your Arrange window. Also, you may find that sometimes you want to not only edit an audio region but its actual audio data. To help you do this, Logic offers a fully-featured Sample Editor.

In this chapter, you will learn how to:

- Navigate the Audio window and Sample Editor
- Audition audio in the Audio window and Sample Editor
- Add files to the Audio window
- Delete files from the Audio window
- Sort audio regions in the Audio window
- Adjust audio region boundaries in the Audio window
- Add audio regions from the Audio window to the Arrange window
- Use the Strip Silence function
- Edit audio files in the Sample Editor
- Process audio files in the Sample Editor

A Brief Tour of the Audio Window

The Audio window has many of the elements you are already familiar with—buttons, tools, local menus, a list on the left, and a workspace on the right. The list, however, doesn't consist of tracks like the Arrange window, but rather is a list of all the audio files and audio regions that you have recorded or added to your Logic project. Logic supports all the major audio file formats: AIFF, Wave, Broadcast Wave, and Sound Designer 2 files. Many other common compressed file formats, such as MP3 and AAC, are also supported, although they are converted to AIFF files inside of Logic. Let's start by taking a look at the Audio window.

First, open the Audio window:

1 Go to Audio > Audio Window.

Key Command Alert: Open Audio Window

You can also use the key command COMMAND + 9 to open the Audio window.

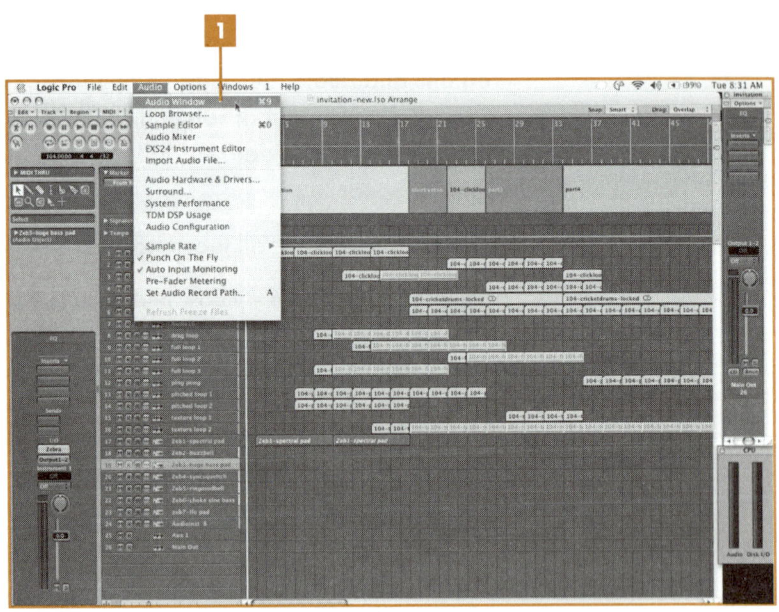

Audio Window Buttons

The Audio window contains three buttons.

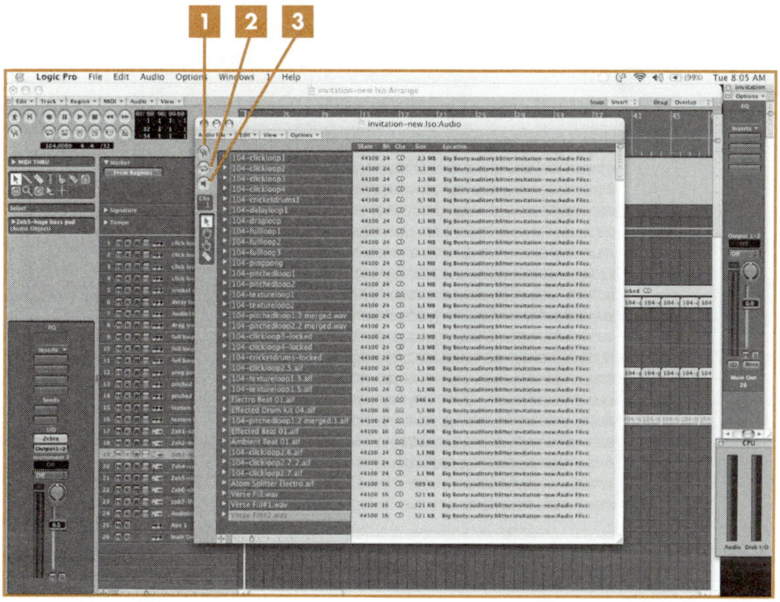

1. **Link Button**: Clicking the Link button will ensure that the contents of the Audio window will always be linked to any window that is "topped," or in front of all other windows.
2. **Region Cycle Button**: If this button is clicked, regions being monitored in the Audio window will repeat continuously. See "Auditioning Audio Regions in the Audio Window" later in this chapter for more details.
3. **Monitor Button**: Click this button to monitor regions in the Audio window. See "Auditioning Audio Regions in the Audio Window" later in this chapter for more details.

Audio Window Local Menus

Most of the commands that relate to the Audio window can be found in these local menus. While going into each command is beyond the scope of this book, we do want to familiarize you with the contents and organization of the local menus to help you in your own exploration.

1 Audio File Menu: Here you'll find most of the commands relating to adding, exporting, converting, or otherwise manipulating audio files.

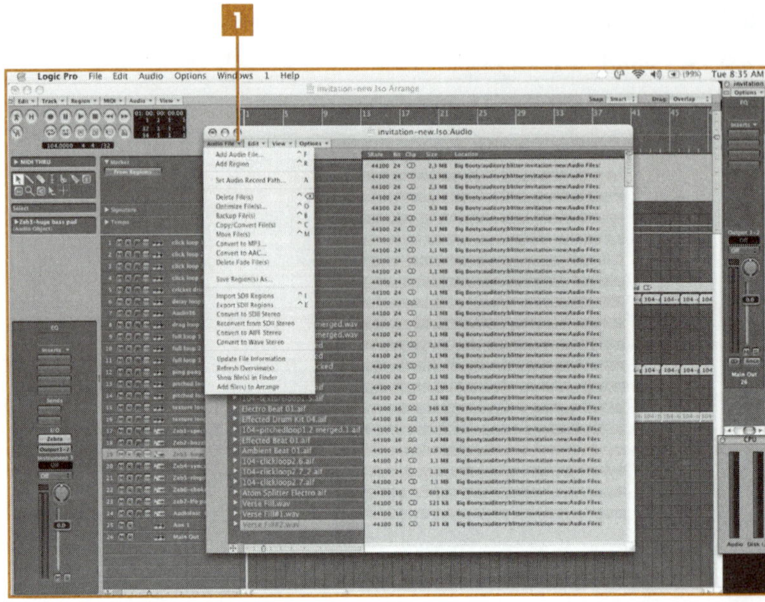

2 Edit Menu: This menu contains commands relating to the selection and editing of audio files.

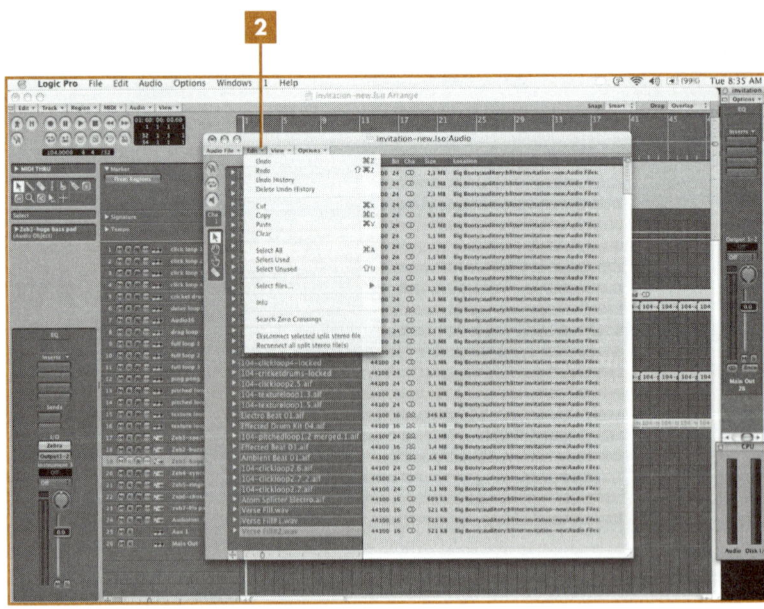

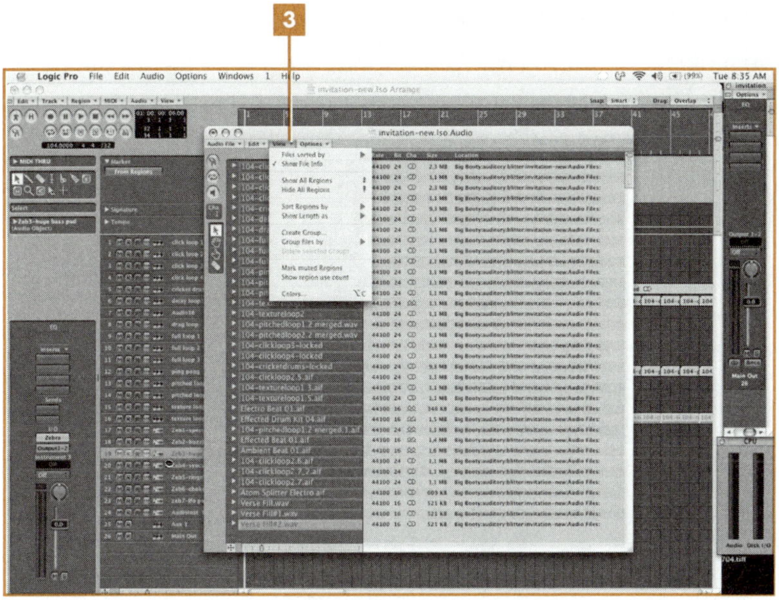

3 **View Menu**: The View menu contains options for organizing and viewing your audio files and audio regions in the Audio window.

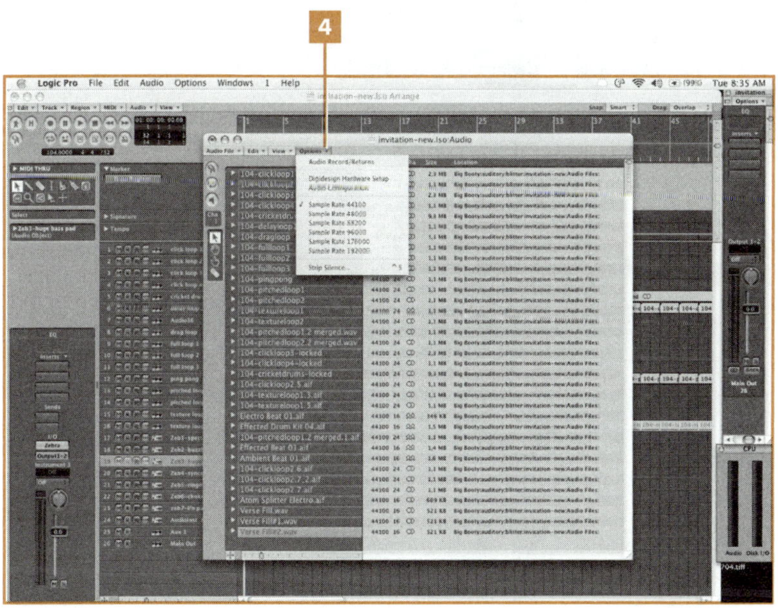

4 **Options Menu**: The Options menu is a catch-all local menu for additional commands in the Audio window.

Audio Window Main Area

The main workspace in the Audio window contains the list of audio files and their regions, and the large space for information and working with your audio regions.

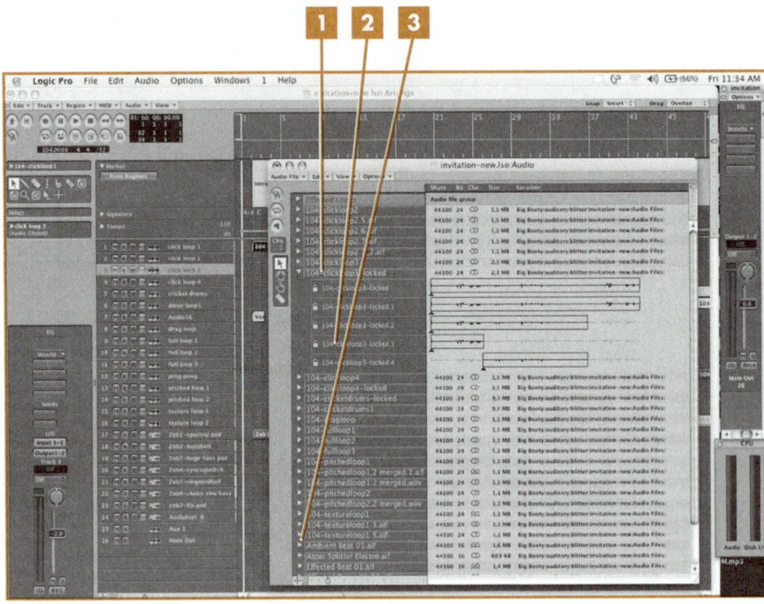

1 An audio file as it was originally recorded or imported.

2 An audio region underneath its parent audio file. The region is not a separate physical file but a set of pointers that tell Logic what portion of the file to play.

3 The region triangle will open the audio file to expose its associated audio regions.

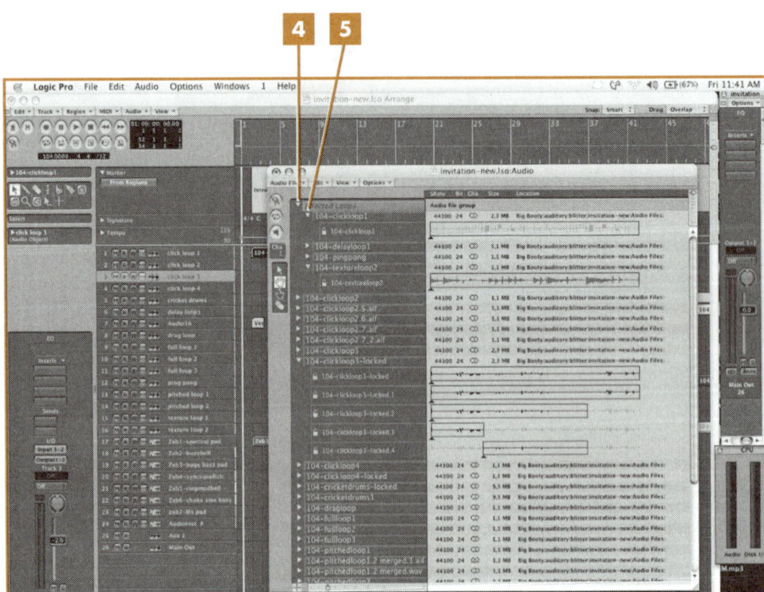

4 An audio file group.

5 Audio files within a group.

Auditioning Audio Regions in the Audio Window

The most basic operation you'll want to do in the Audio window is to listen to your various audio regions. You can choose to audition an entire region or only a specific part of a region.

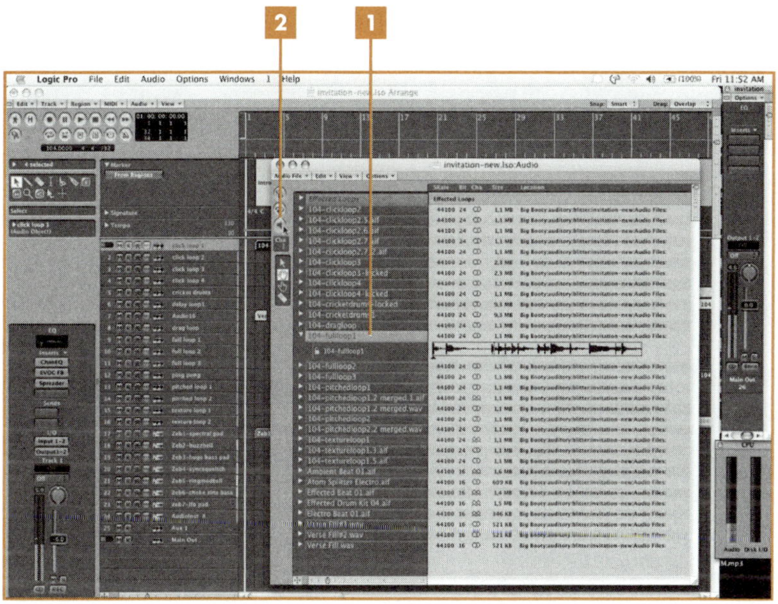

To audition an entire audio region:

1. **Select** the **audio file** or **audio region** you want to hear.
2. **Click** the **Monitor** button to hear the region play from the beginning.

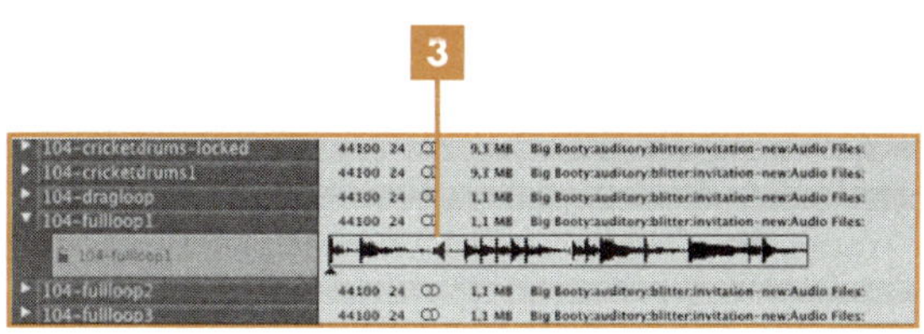

To begin auditioning from a specific point within an audio region:

3. **Hold** the pointer over an **audio region** and the cursor will change to a **speaker** icon. **Click** and **hold** the **mouse** button to play the region from the point of your click.

Adding Audio Files to the Audio Window

Whether you prefer to add audio files via dragging and dropping file icons or by using the Add Audio File menu command, adding audio files to the Audio window couldn't be easier!

Dragging Audio Files into the Audio Window

The most intuitive way to add audio files to the Audio window is to simply drag them from their current directory to the Audio window.

1 Select one or more audio files from a Finder window.

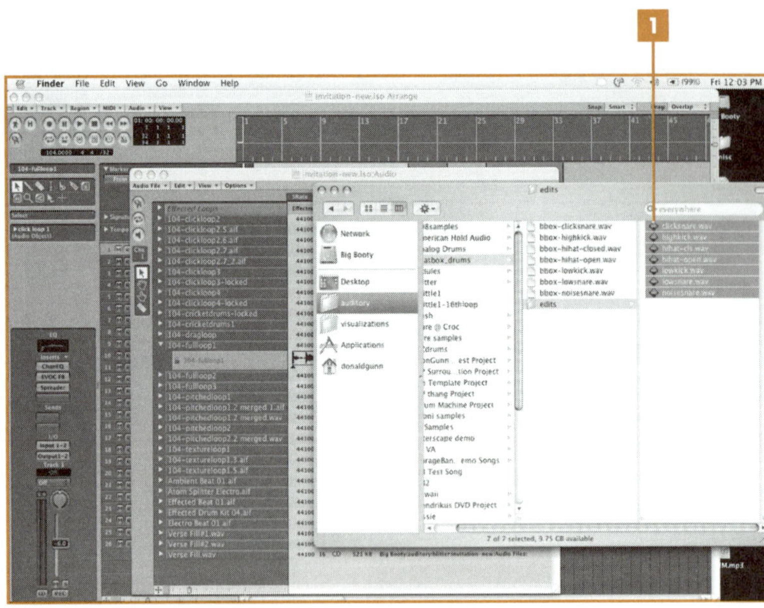

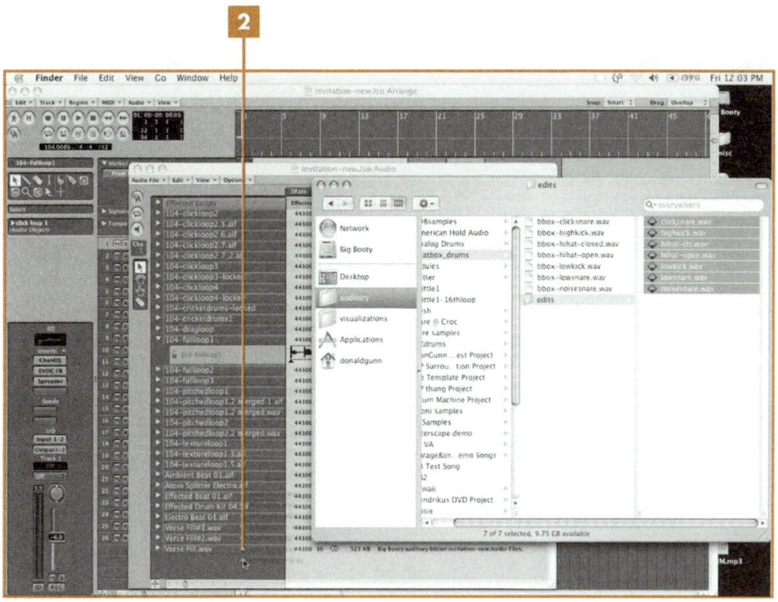

2 Drag them to the Audio window.

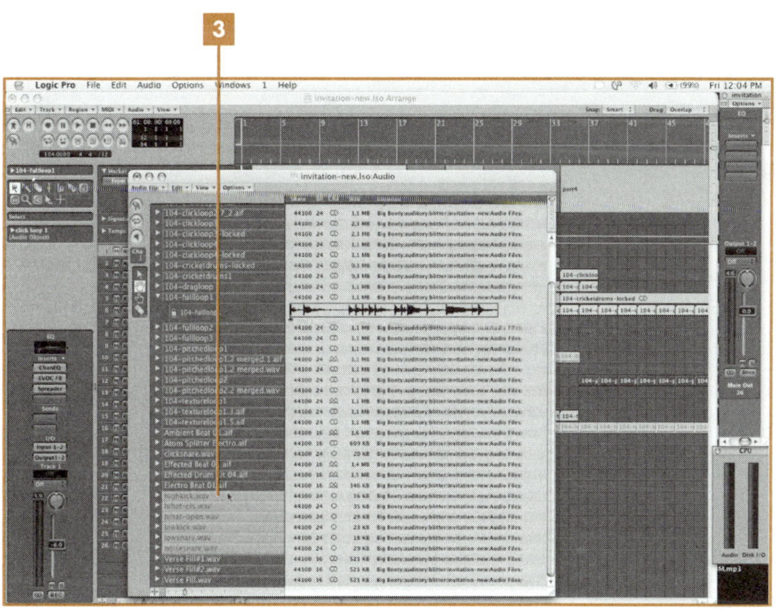

3 The files have been added to the Audio window.

Using the Audio Window's Add Audio Files Command

If you'd rather not drag files from the Finder to the Audio window, or if you want to audition your files before you add them, you can use the Add Audio Files command from the local Audio Files menu of the Audio window.

1 Select Audio File > Add Audio File.

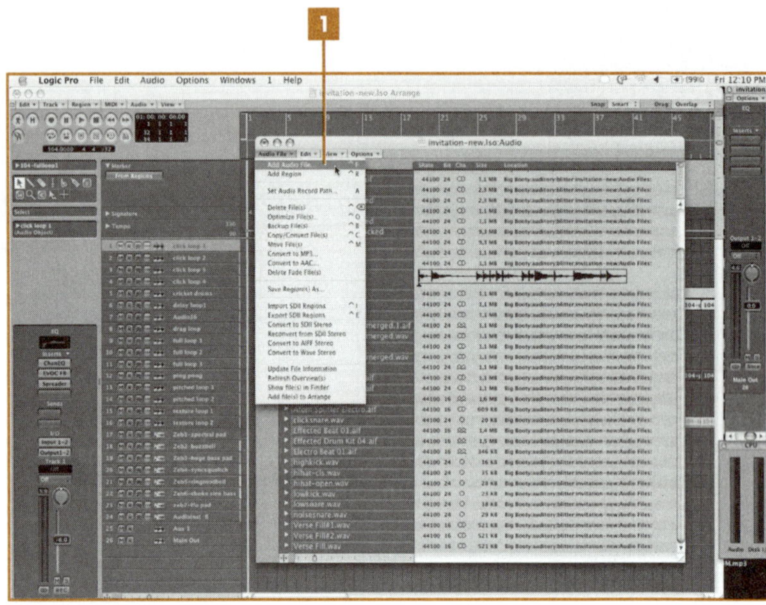

Key Command Alert: Add Audio Files

You can use the key command CONTROL + F to launch the Add Files dialog.

2 Choose a file to add.

3 If you would like to preview the file before adding it, press the Play button.

4 Click Add, or double-click the file name to add it to the list.

5 Click Done when all the files have been added.

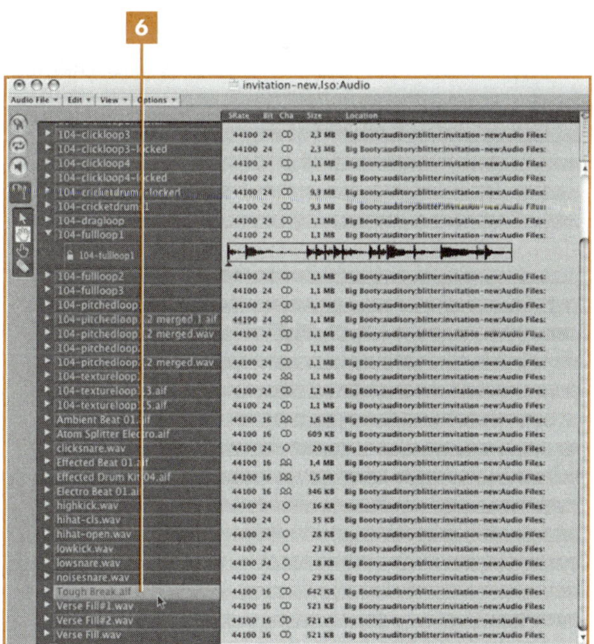

6 The files have been added to the Audio window.

Removing Audio Regions and Files from the Audio Window

You can very easily remove audio regions and audio files from your Logic project by simply selecting them in the audio list and pressing the DELETE key. This will remove the audio from your song, but it won't affect the audio files on your hard drive. If you want to, however, you can also delete the actual audio file on your hard drive from the Audio window.

Be Careful with the Delete Files Command!

Remember, when you delete a file from your hard drive, it's gone, gone, gone! The Undo command in Logic can't restore a file that you've wiped from your hard drive. Be *very* sure you want to get rid of your audio file(s) when you use this command!

1. Select the audio file you want to delete.
2. Go to Audio File > Delete File(s).

Key Command Alert: Delete Audio Files

You can use the key command CONTROL + DELETE to permanently remove audio files from the Audio window and your hard drive.

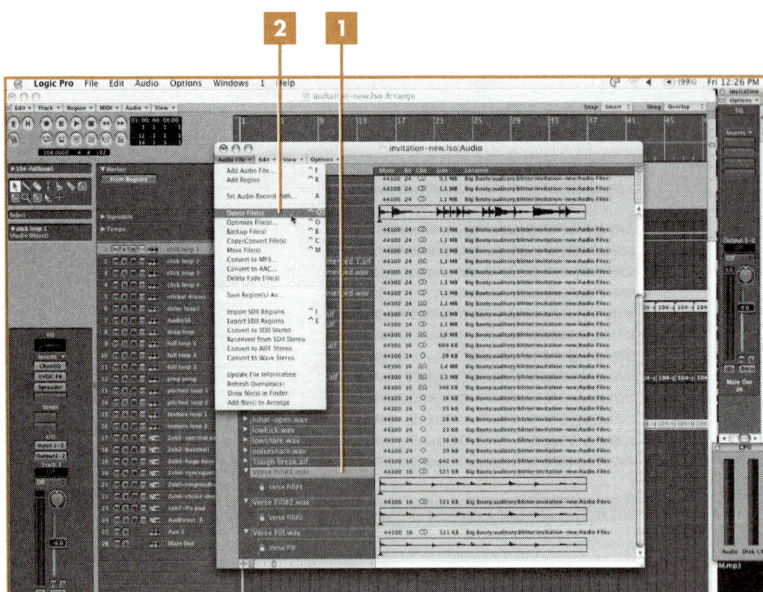

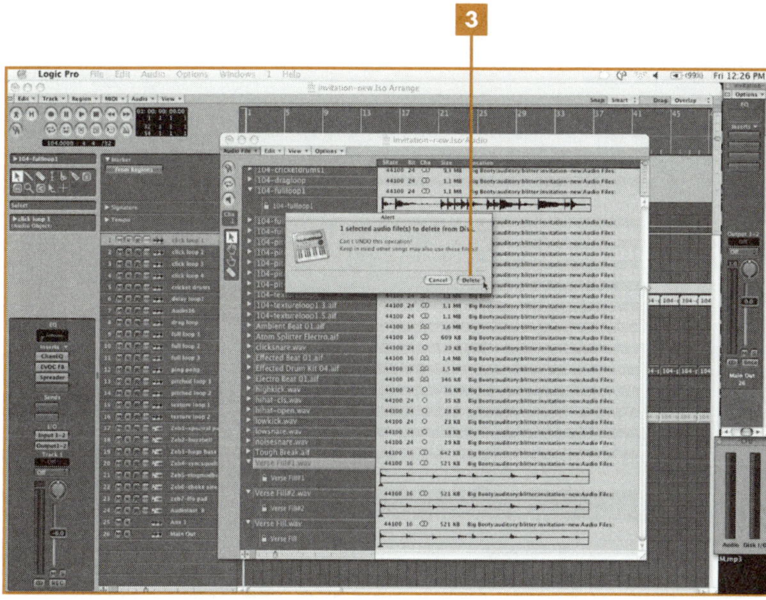

3 You will be alerted that proceeding with the operation will permanently remove the audio files from your hard drive. You have one last chance to cancel or press Delete.

Sorting Audio in the Audio Window

One of the main uses for the Audio window is as a convenient audio manager to keep all your audio regions and audio files organized. The Audio window allows you to sort audio files, audio regions, and, in Logic Pro 7, even create your own groups of files and regions.

Sorting Audio Files

Logic automatically lists your audio files in the order that they were added or recorded. However, you can choose to sort your audio files in the Audio window by Name, by Size, or by which Drive they are located on by using the Files sorted by command.

To sort your audio files by name:

1 Select View > Files sorted by > Name.

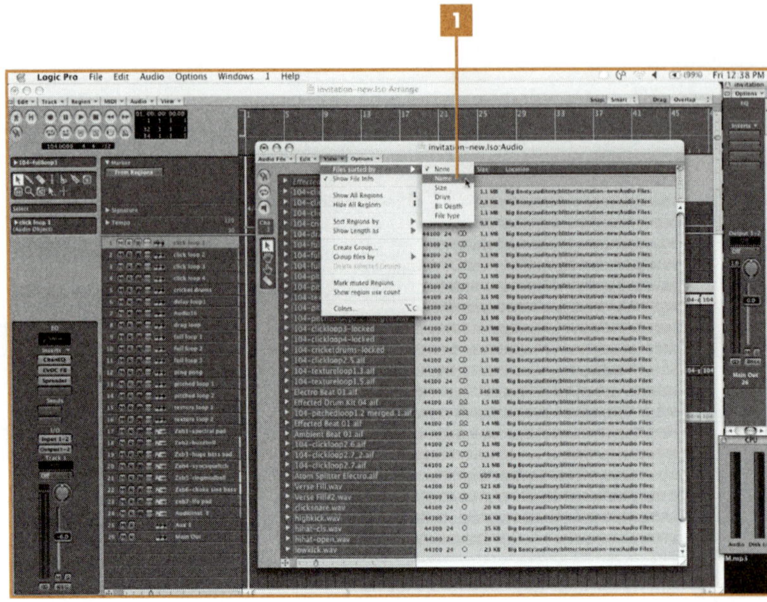

2 Your files are sorted by their name.

1

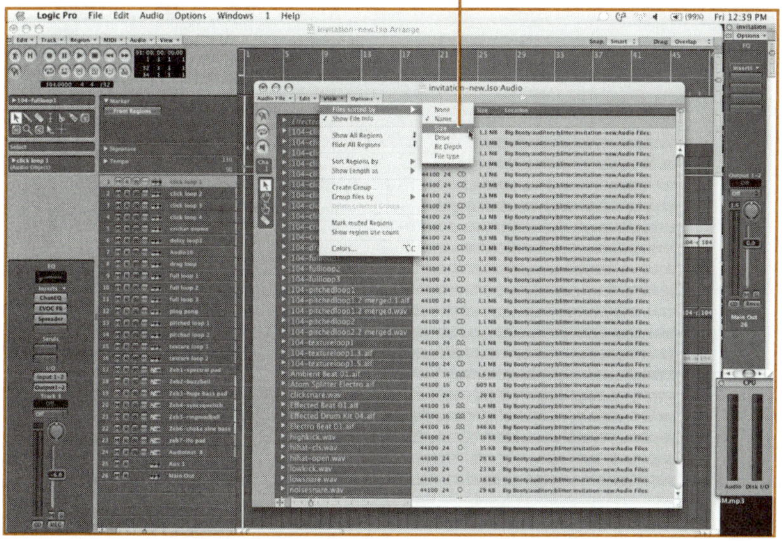

To sort your audio files by size:

1 Select View > Files sorted by > Size.

2

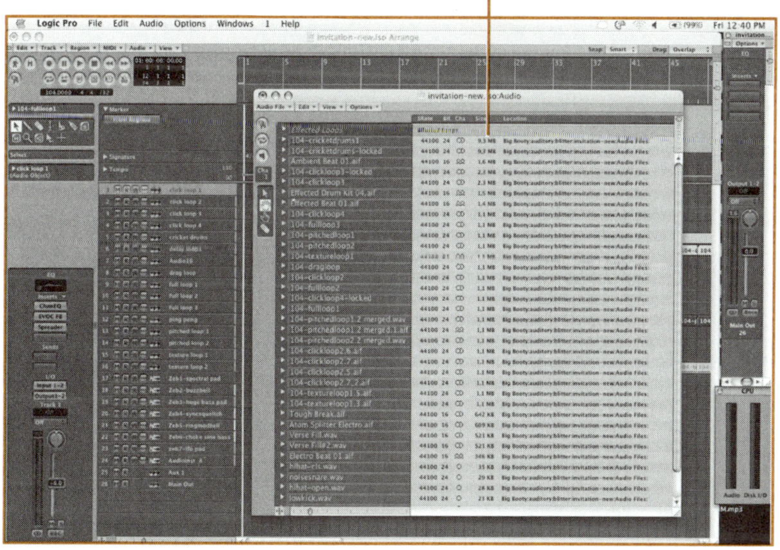

2 Your files are sorted by their size.

To sort your audio files by drive:

1 Select View > Files sorted by > Drive.

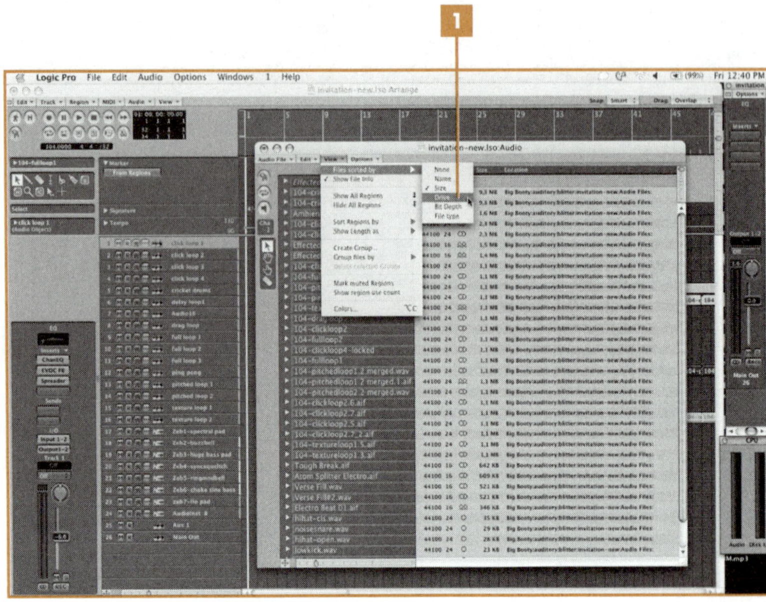

2 Your files are sorted by their drive.

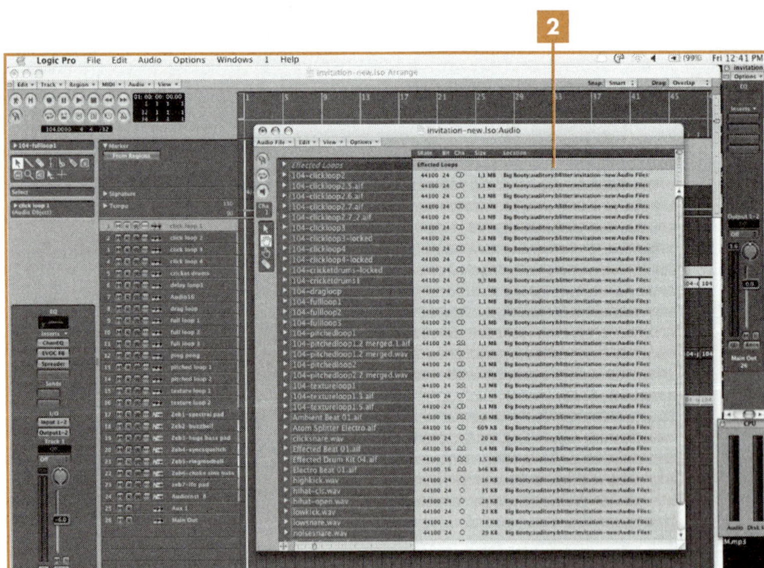

Sorting Audio Regions

Your audio regions are automatically grouped with the audio file that they reference. This cannot be changed. However, when you have many regions referencing the same audio file, you can sort those regions by Start, Length, or Name using the Sort Regions by command.

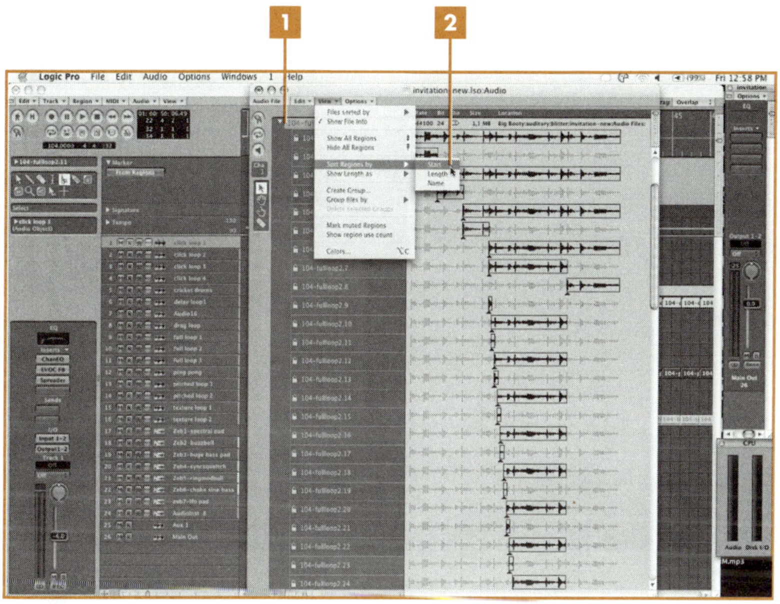

To sort your regions by start time:

1. Choose an audio file and press the triangle to display the regions.
2. Select View > Sort Regions by > Start.

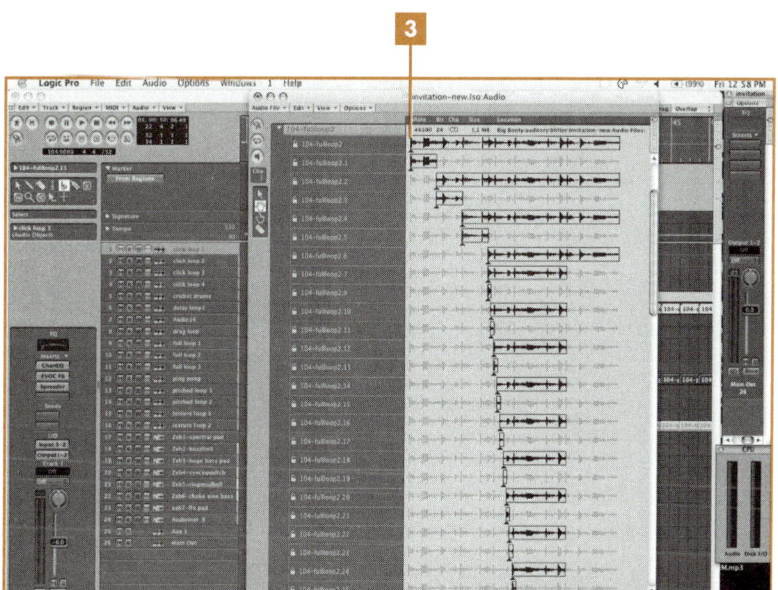

3. Your files are sorted by their start.

To sort your regions by length:

1. Select View > Sort Regions by > Length.

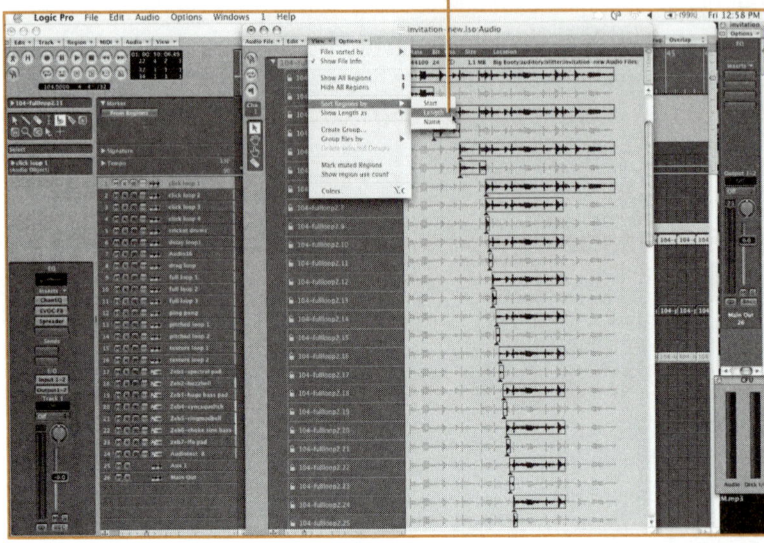

2. Your files are sorted by their length.

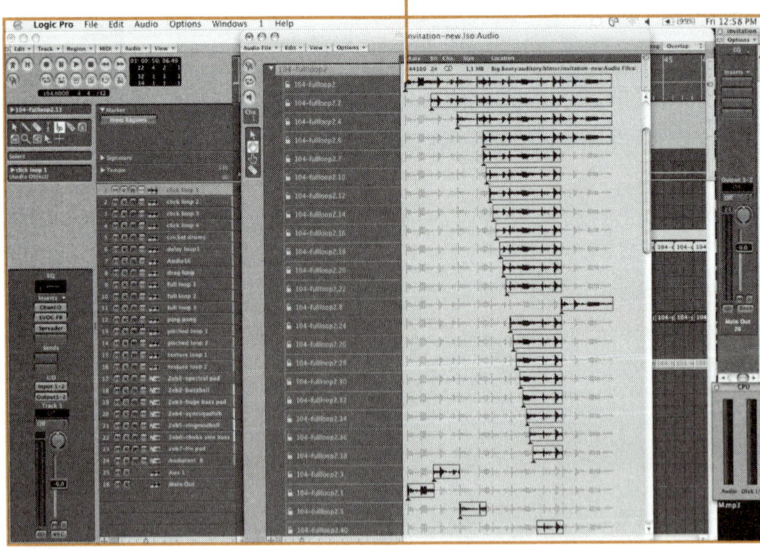

1

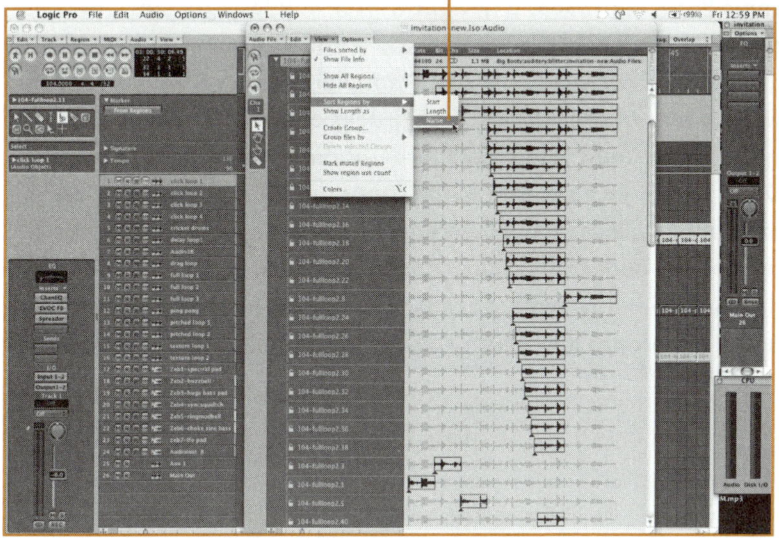

To sort your regions by name:

1. Select View > Sort Regions by > Name.

2

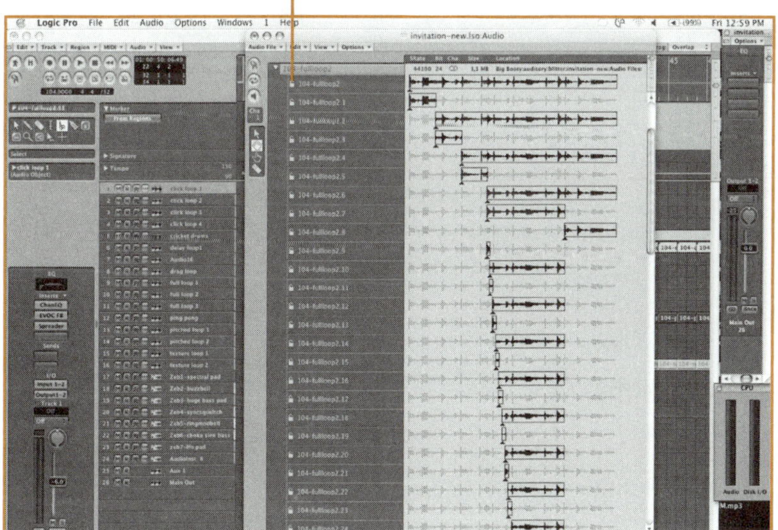

2. Your files are sorted by their name.

Creating Audio Window Groups (Logic Pro Only)

Logic Pro 7 introduces a new, powerful way to organize your audio files in the Audio window: by creating Audio window groups. In other words, let's say that you filled your Audio window with dozens of drum loops, eight tracks of guitar, and half a dozen synth loops. You could create three Audio window groups named Drum Loops, Guitars, and Synth Loops to help you organize all of your files. Your manually created groups have all the same features as audio file groups, and they have a comment area in the Audio window workspace (where the file info would be for an audio file group) into which you can type your personal notes.

Audio Window Groups Only Organize Audio Files

Remember that all audio regions that reference an audio file always move with the parent audio file. So if you put an audio file into an Audio window group, all of its audio regions will also move to the same group.

To create Audio window groups:

1. Select the audio files you want to add to the group.

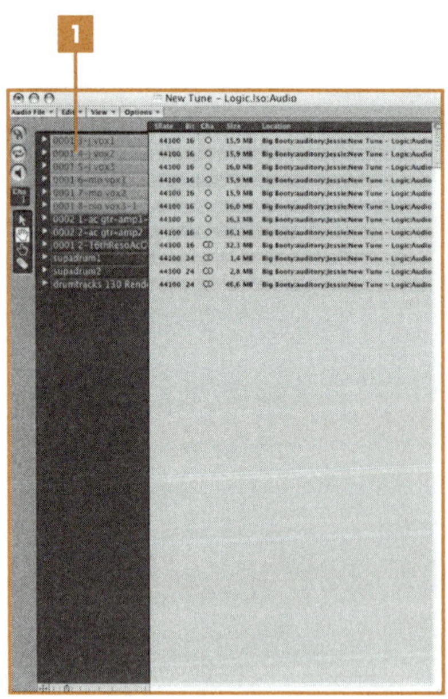

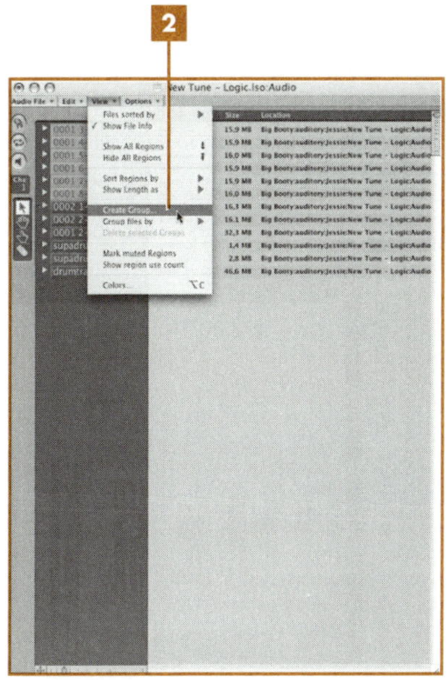

2 Go to View > Create Group.

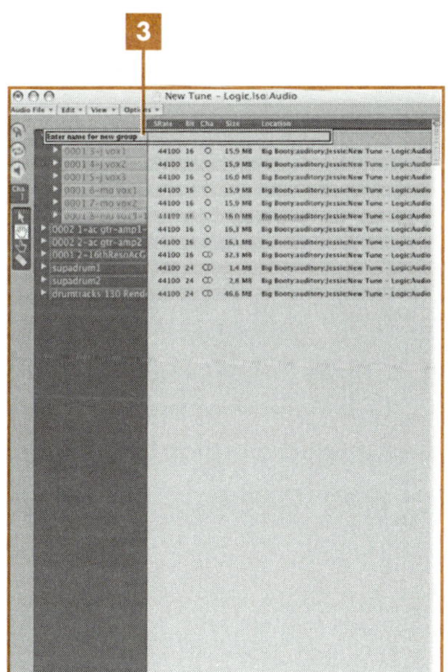

3 Enter the name of the newly created group.

Adding Files to an Audio Window Group

Once your Audio window group is created, you can add additional files to it by simply dragging them onto the group name. When you release the mouse button, the file will be added to the group.

4 Drag an audio file onto the name of the group to add additional files to a group.

Deleting Audio Window Groups

You can delete Audio window groups the same way you would delete an audio file—by hitting the DELETE key. Keep in mind that when you delete an Audio window group, you delete only the group, not the audio files inside the group. The audio files of a deleted group will appear at the top of the Audio window.

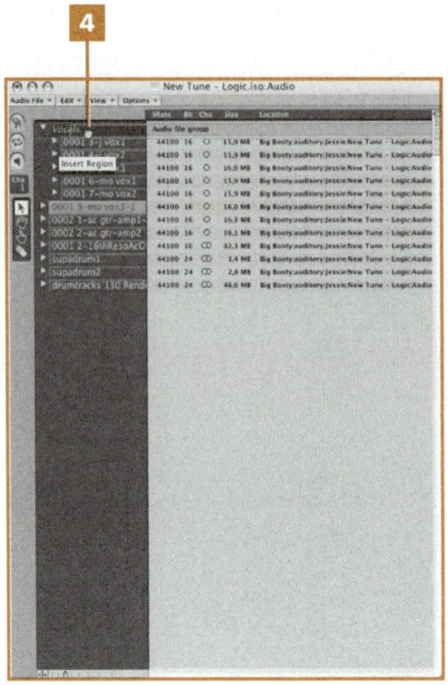

Adjusting Audio Region Boundaries in the Audio Window

You have access to all of the usual Macintosh editing commands in the Audio window (Cut, Copy, Paste, and Clear) but you'll usually want to use the Arrange window for that. One editing function that the Audio window excels at, however, is adjusting the boundaries of an audio region, since it's so convenient to cycle monitor individual regions.

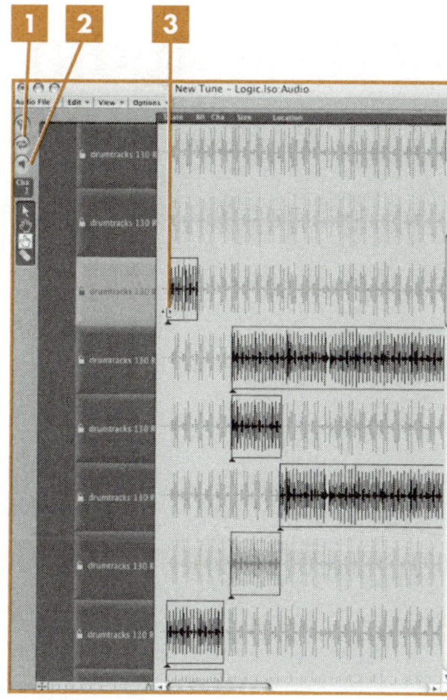

1. **Press** the **Cycle** icon to allow your region to loop as you monitor it.
2. **Press** the **Monitor** button to start playback of the region.
3. **Click** and **hold** the mouse on the left or right edge of a **region**. The pointer will change to a bracket with arrows, and you can now drag it left or right to change the boundary.

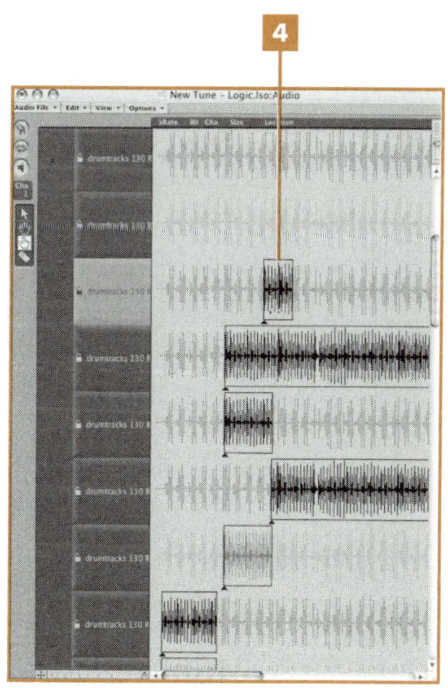

4. You can also click and drag from the center of a region. The cursor will change to the left/right arrows without a bracket. This allows you to move the entire region but maintain its current length.

Adding Audio Files from the Audio Window to the Arrange Window

Since your Audio window is a repository of your Logic project's audio files, it stands to reason that you'll want to add some of those files to the Arrange window. Logic makes this as easy as dragging and dropping!

1 Select the region from the Audio window you would like to add.

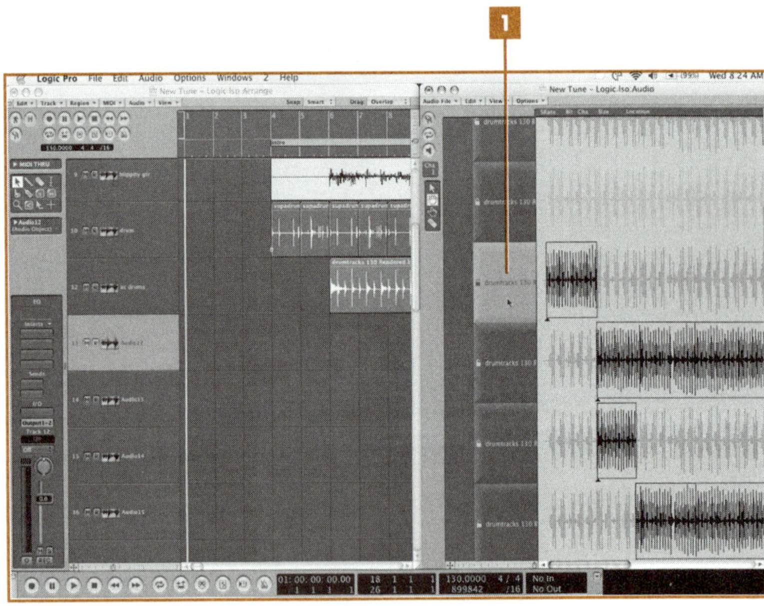

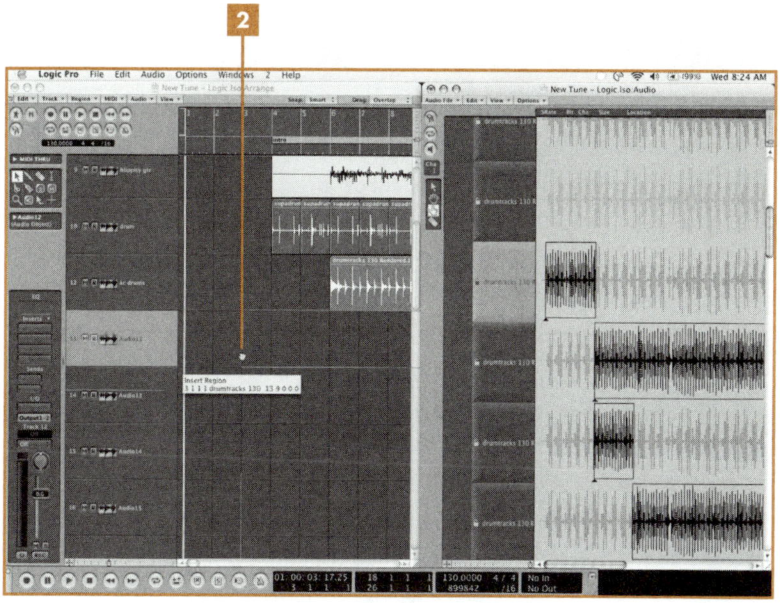

2 Click and drag the region to a track in the Arrange window.

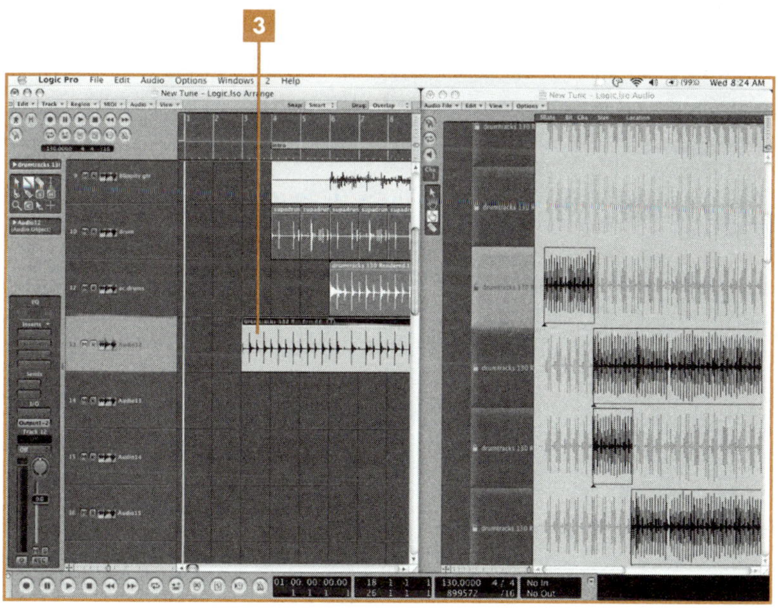

3 The region has been added to the track!

Dragging Multiple Audio Regions into the Arrange Window

You are not limited to dragging a single audio region to the Arrange window. If you drag multiple regions, a dialog box asks you if you want all the regions you are dragging to be placed on a single Audio Track, on multiple Audio Tracks that have already been created in the Arrange window, or if Logic should create a new Audio Track for each region you are dragging.

Using Strip Silence

The Strip Silence function actually appears in three places: the Arrange window, the Audio window, and the Sample Editor. Since this chapter covers two of those three areas of the program, we thought we'd include Strip Silence here. Basically, the Strip Silence function creates a new region for every section of an audio file that is above a user-defined threshold (or "loudness"). The new regions will be separated by all the sections that are below the user-defined threshold. The most obvious use for this is to remove empty areas from your song—where you were in Record mode but nobody was performing, for example. But you can also use Strip Silence more creatively, to do things such as separate out each individual drum hit in a drum loop, for example. Remember—Logic gives you the tools, but how you use them is up to your creativity!

1 Select a region in the Audio window.

2 Go to Options > Strip Silence.

Key Command Alert: Strip Silence

Pressing CONTROL + S with a region selected will open the Strip Silence dialog box.

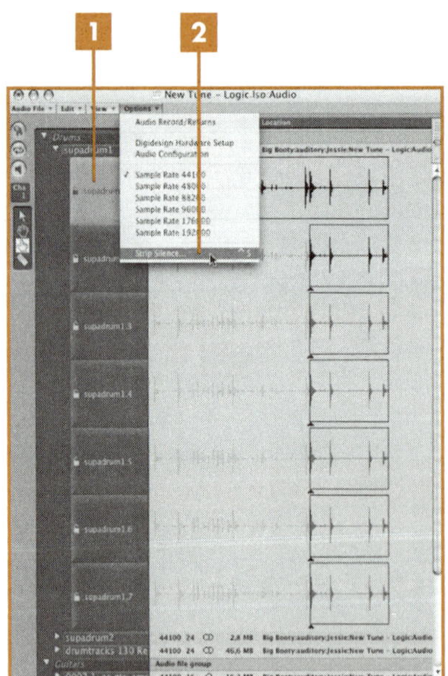

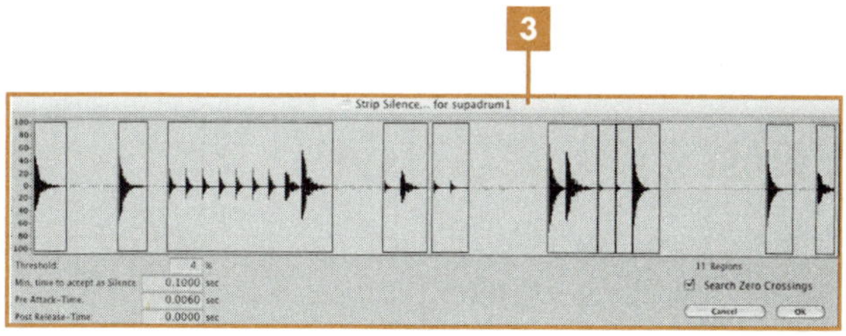

3 The default settings of the Strip Silence window may be perfect for the region you are working on.

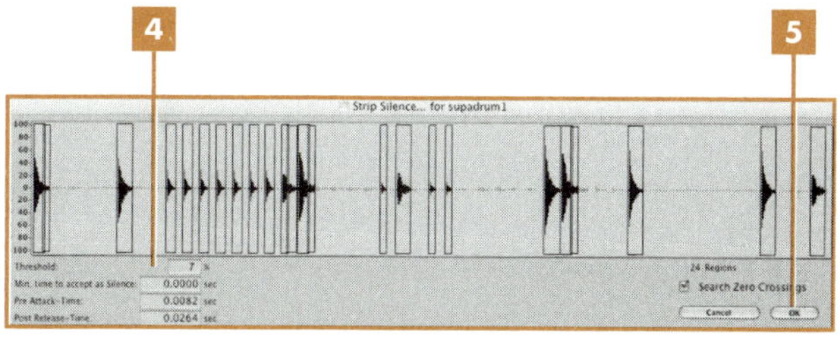

4 Adjust the parameters until you are satisfied with what is being removed and what remains in the region.

5 Press OK

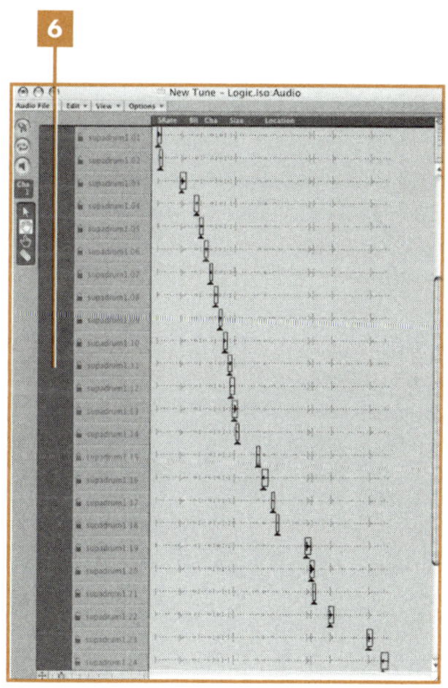

6 The resulting regions are added to the Audio window and can now be added to the Arrange window, saved as individual files, or further manipulated!

A Brief Tour of the Sample Editor

If the idea of "sample editing" sounds complicated to you, don't worry. The Sample Editor features mainly advanced destructive (see "Destructive versus Non-Destructive editing") processing tools that you don't need to worry about right now. We'll just give you a quick tour of the Sample Editor and some example uses.

The Sample Editor opens automatically when you double-click an audio region in either the Arrange or Audio window.

Destructive versus Non-Destructive Editing

You'll often hear the terms "destructive" editing and "non-destructive" editing thrown around when discussing audio editing. The difference is that non-destructive editing doesn't actually touch your audio *file* itself, but rather the audio *regions*. For example, the Strip Silence function is non-destructive—it doesn't remove actual audio data from the file, it just creates new audio regions, which are references to your audio. However, if you actually delete audio in the Sample Editor, that audio is gone from your audio file itself. Be very careful when doing any destructive editing!

Sample Editor Main Area

The main workspace in the Sample Editor window contains:

1. Monitoring options
2. The Toolbox
3. Region overview
4. Region detail

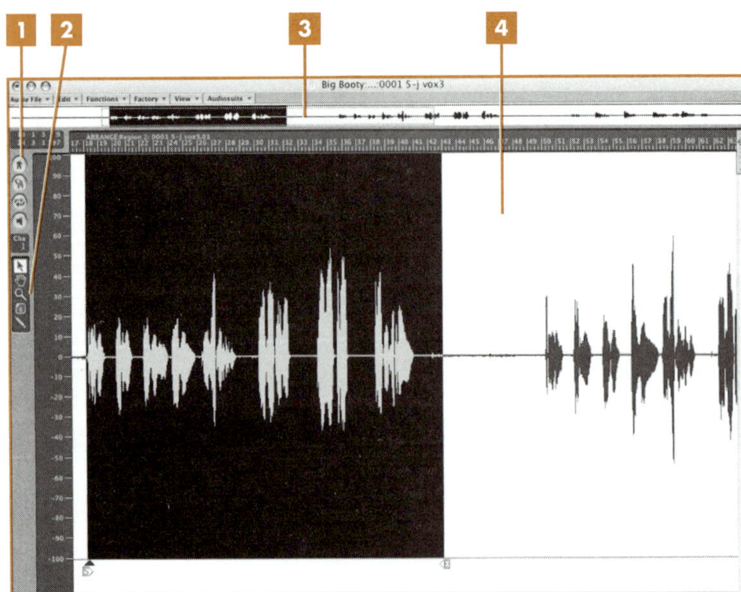

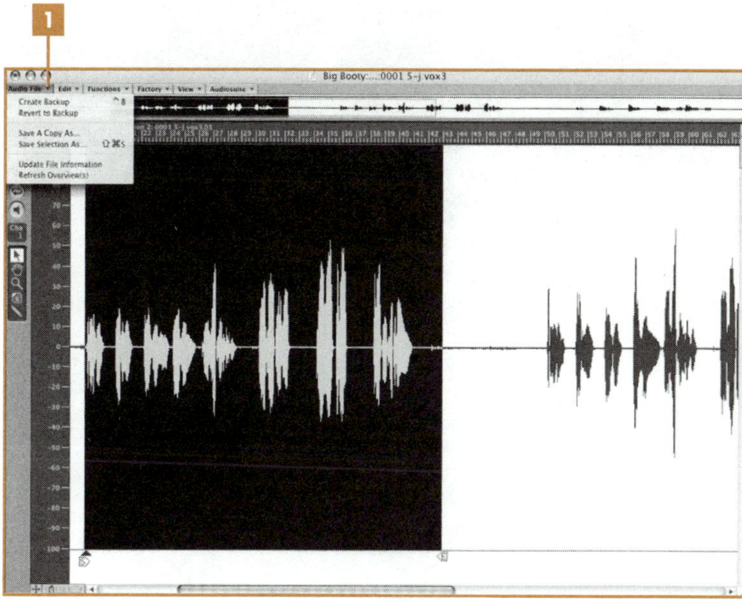

Sample Editor Local Menus

Most of the commands that relate to the Sample Editor window can be found in these local menus. While going into each command is beyond the scope of this book, we do want to familiarize you with the contents and organization of the local menus to help you in your own exploration.

1 **Audio File Menu**: Here you'll find most of the commands relating to adding, exporting, converting, or otherwise manipulating audio files.

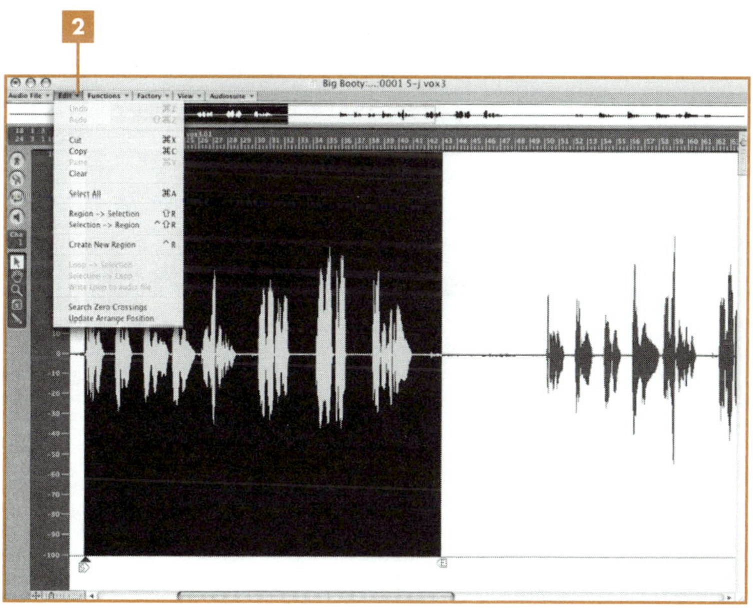

2 **Edit Menu**: This menu contains commands relating to the selection and editing of audio files.

3 Functions Menu: The Functions menu contains many of the common processing functions for which you may wish to use the Sample Editor.

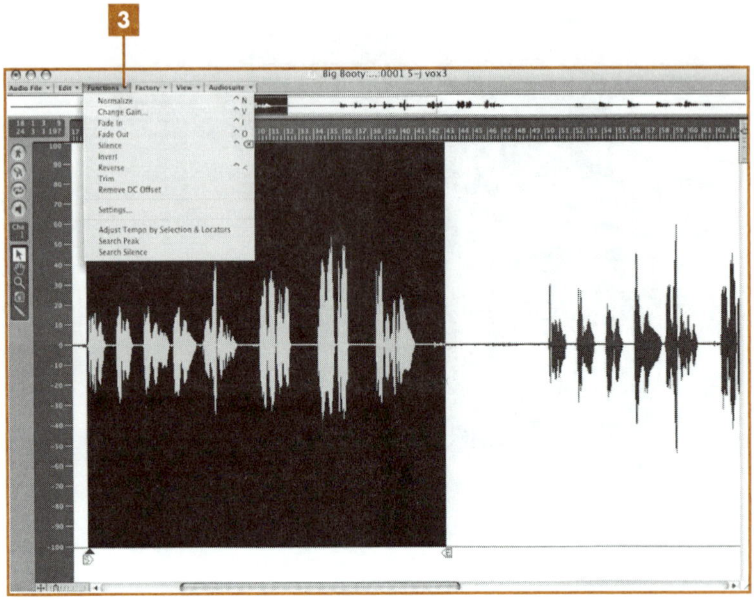

4 Factory Menu: This menu contains the "Digital Factory"—Logic's advanced time- and pitch-related destructive processes.

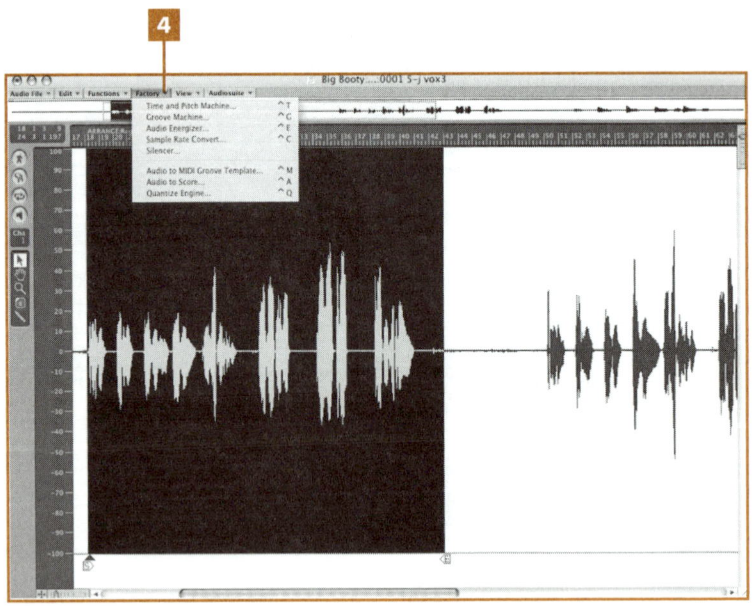

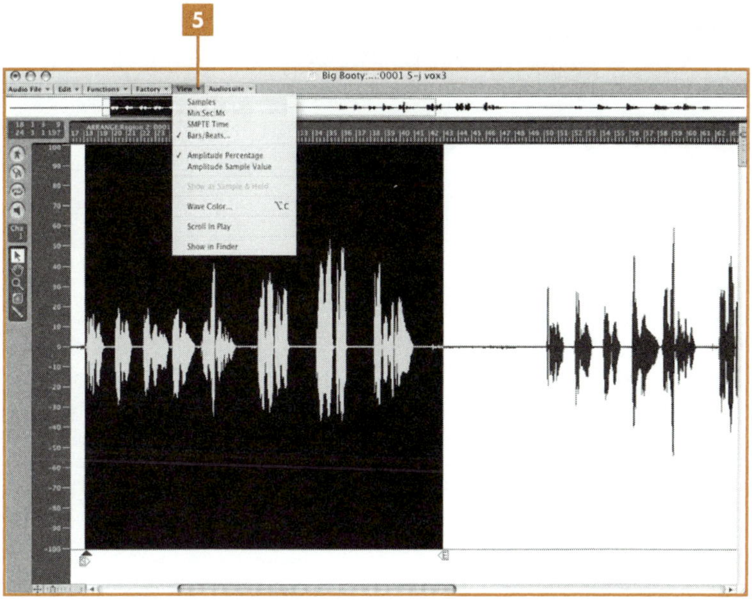

5 View Menu: **The View menu contains options for organizing and viewing your audio files and audio region in the Audio window.**

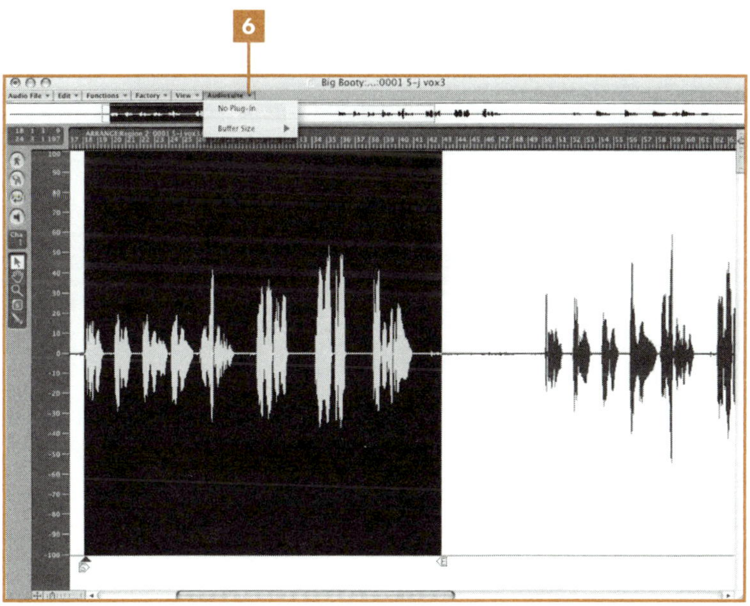

6 Audiosuite Menu: **If you are using a Digidesign Pro Tools TDM system, your Audiosuite plug-ins will appear in this menu.**

Sample Editor Buttons

The Sample Editor contains four buttons:

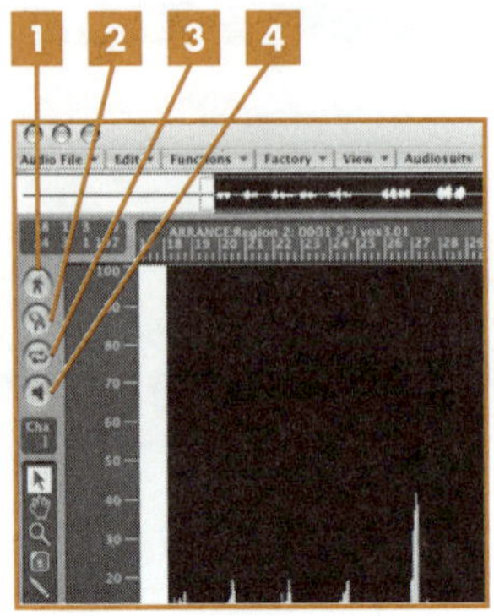

1 Catch Button: When this button is activated, the Sample Edit window will follow playback.

2 Link Button: Clicking the Link button will ensure that the contents of the Audio window will always be linked to any window that is "topped," or in front of all other windows.

3 Region Cycle Button: If this button is clicked, regions being monitored in the Audio window will repeat continuously. See "Auditioning Audio Regions in the Audio Window" earlier in this chapter for more details.

4 Monitor Button: Click this button to monitor regions in the Audio window. See "Auditioning Audio Regions in the Audio Window" earlier in this chapter for more details.

Trimming Audio Files in the Sample Editor

Sample editing is an art unto itself, and it's something that you'll likely never need to do when working on your Logic song. However, if you need to trim some audio from an audio file or the like, here is a very brief overview of the process.

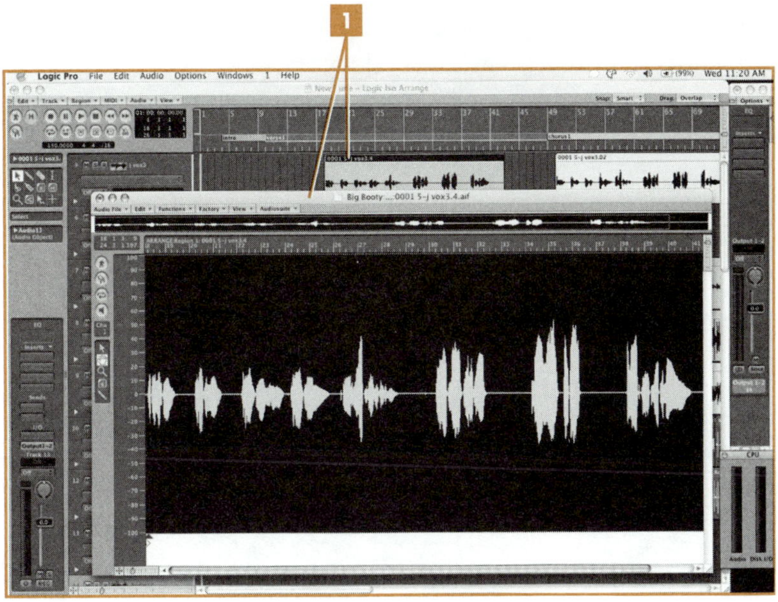

1 Double-click an audio file or region to open it in the Sample Editor.

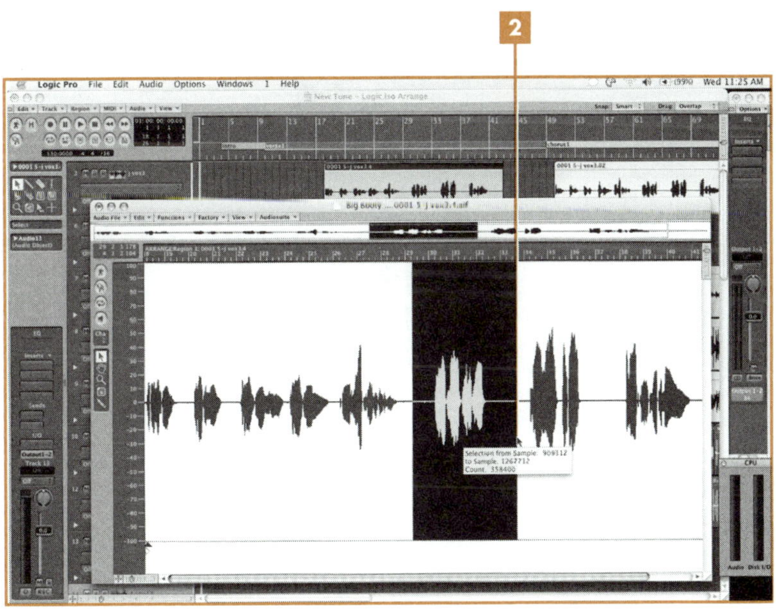

2 Click and drag to select the area of the region you want to delete.

3 Press the DELETE key. Logic will present you with a dialog box warning about the region you are going to delete. Press Delete to complete the operation.

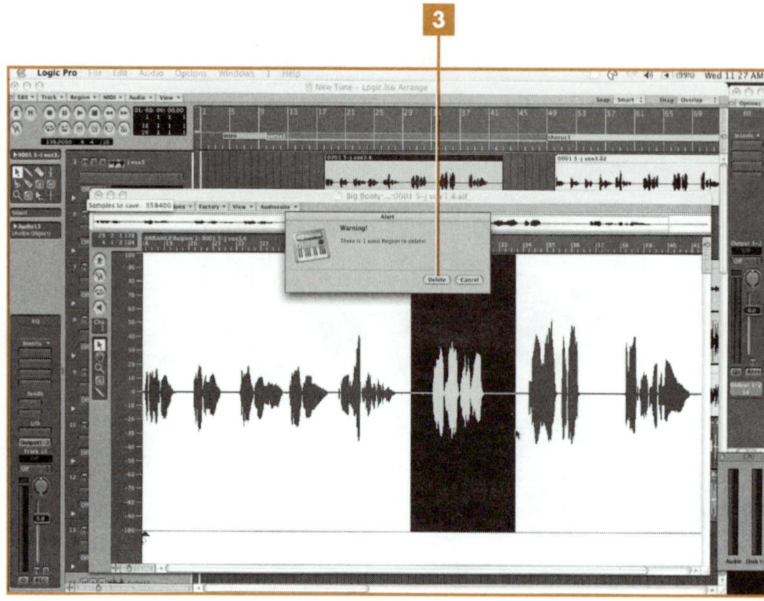

4 The new region is displayed in both the Sample Editor and the Arrange window.

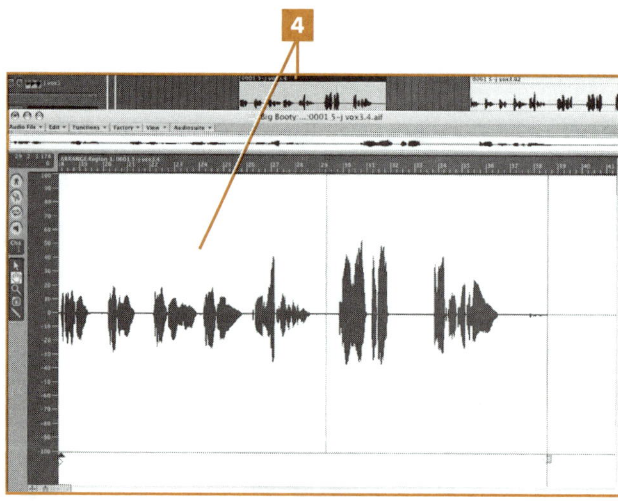

A Quick Look at Some Sample Editor Functions

There are some other generally useful Sample Editor functions we'll take a very brief look at here.

You can use the Sample Editor to Remove DC Offset (the loud "pop" at the beginning of a file recorded on a badly calibrated converter).

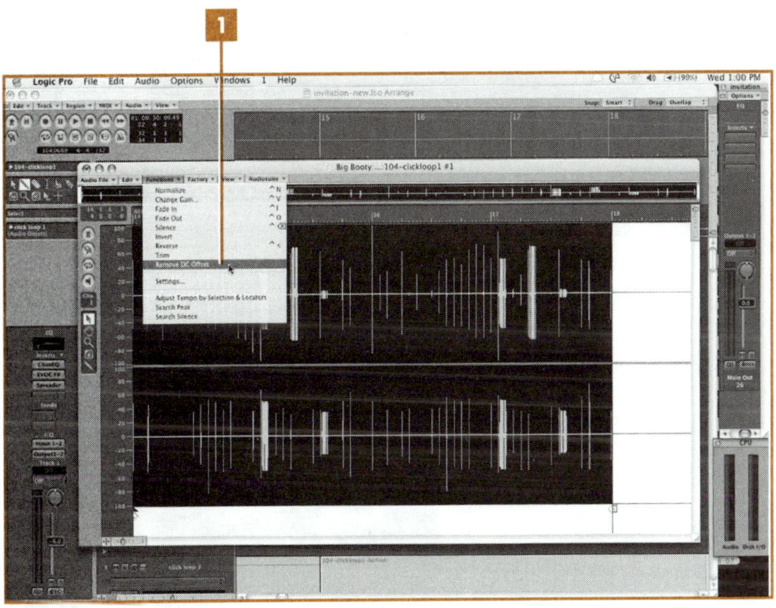

1 With a file open in the Sample Editor, go to Functions > Remove DC Offset.

2 Logic will analyze the file and give you a dialog box with the percentage of found DC offset. Press Remove to process the file.

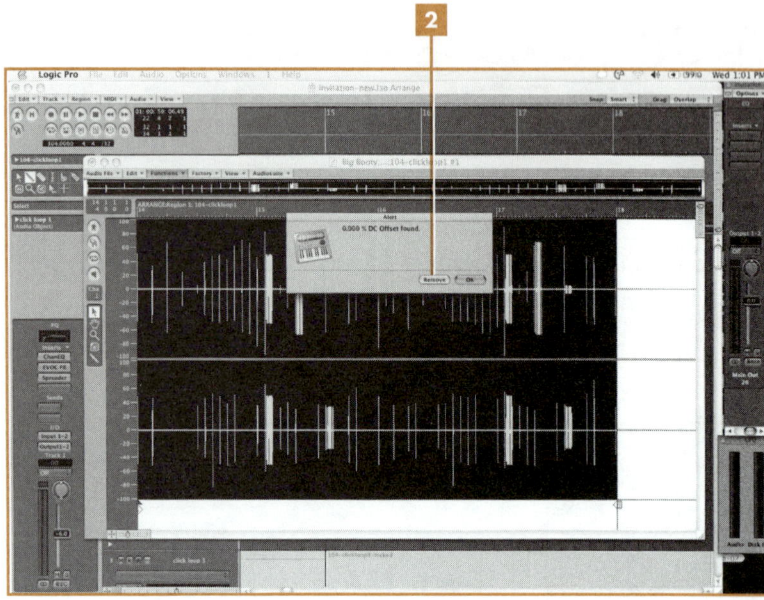

You can use the Time and Pitch Machine to make permanent tempo and pitch changes in your audio file:

1 With a file open in the Sample Editor, go to Factory > Time and Pitch Machine.

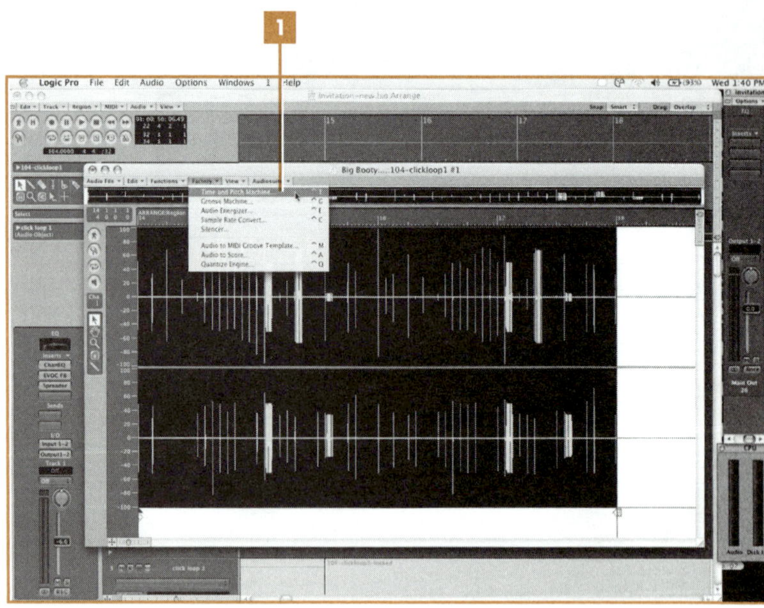

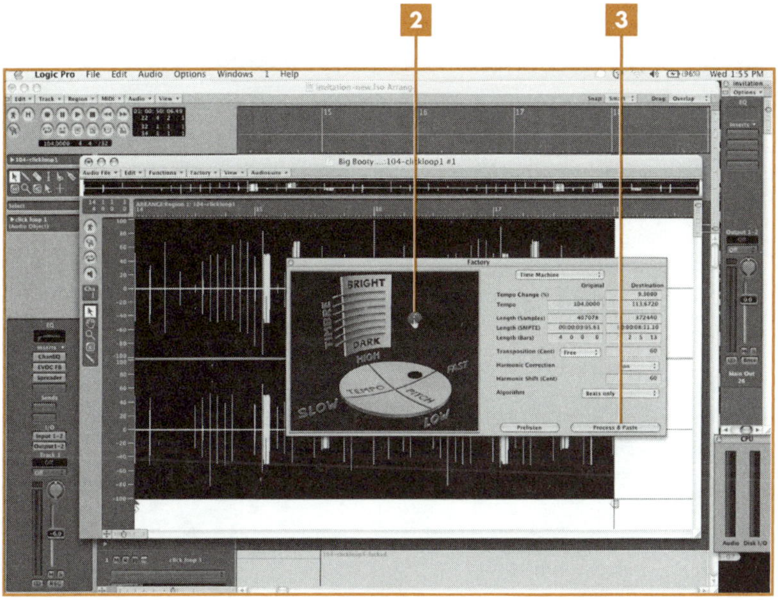

2 **Drag** the **ball** in the left half of the Time Machine to change the parameters or, for more precise changes, enter values numerically in the right half.

3 **Press Process & Paste** to confirm your changes and create a new audio file in place of the original.

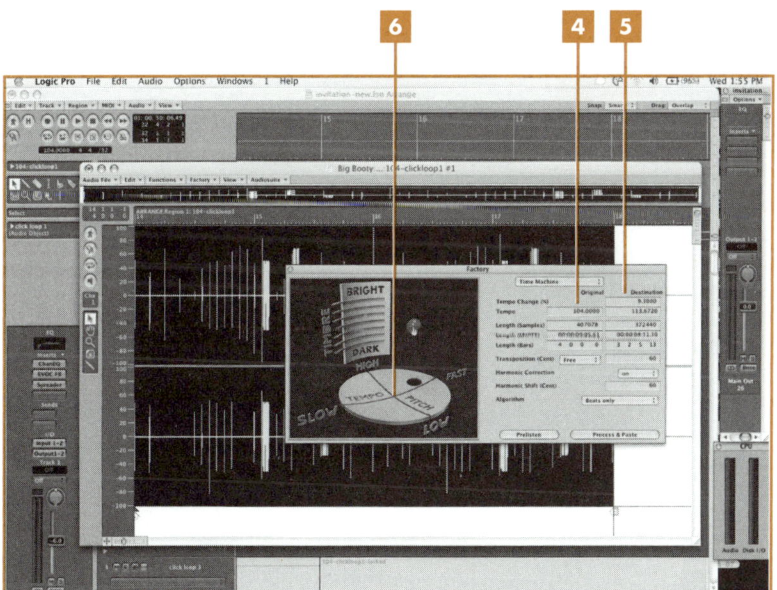

4 This side of the parameter field shows the original values of the region.

5 The Destination side shows the value of the changes to be applied by the Time and Pitch Machine.

6 The left side is a combined display of the parameters from the right side. Here you can see how Pitch, Tempo, and Timbre changes relate to each other.

Finally, you can use the Sample Editor to convert the sample rate of an audio file:

1. With a file open in the Sample Editor, go to Factory > Sample Rate Convert.

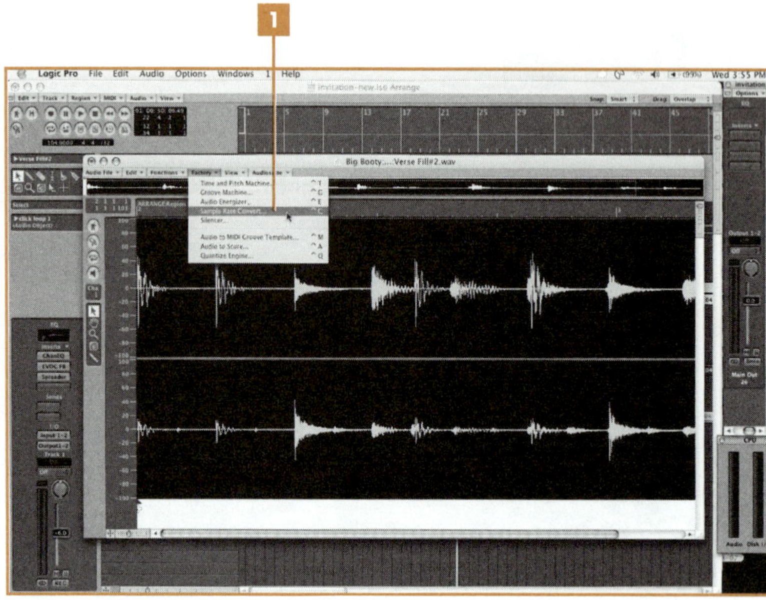

2. Enter the destination sample rate.
3. Press Convert.

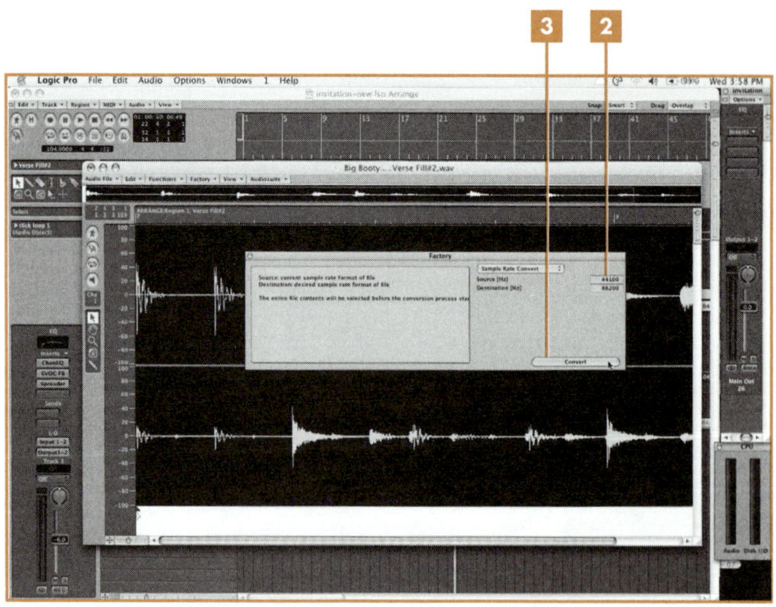

For More Information on the Sample Editor

For a more detailed exploration of the Sample Editor, please see *Logic Pro 7 Power!* (Course Technology, 2004), which explains the more esoteric and advanced functions and how you might want to use them.

8 Working with Audio Instruments

If you're like us, Audio Instruments—or, as they're called in GarageBand, "Software Instruments," or "virtual instruments" in more general terms—are some of the most exciting aspects of making music on your Macintosh. Put simply, an Audio Instrument is a software synthesizer or sampler that generates its sound using Logic's audio engine. In Logic terminology, any of its own software synthesizers and samplers, as well as any third-party Audio Unit synthesizer plug-ins, are considered Audio Instruments.

As you may already know, Logic Pro has a well-earned reputation in the pro audio industry of having the most comprehensive and professional collection of Audio Instruments available in any sequencer package. Even Logic Express comes with a solid collection of professional quality Audio Instruments. We already discussed instantiating Audio Instruments on Audio Instrument Tracks in order to record. We also discussed record-enabling multiple Audio Instrument Tracks in order to layer them. Here, we just want to familiarize you with a few more unique aspects of working with Audio Instruments.

In this chapter, you will learn how to:

- Navigate the Audio Instrument window bar
- Set up Multi-Timbral Audio Instruments
- Set up Multi-Channel Audio Instruments
- Set up Audio Instrument side chains

Navigating the Audio Instrument Window Bar

Every Audio Instrument opens inside Logic's Plug-In window. You'll find a number of pull-down menus that offer access to different features and options available to you on your Audio Instrument. Keep in mind that some menus, such as the Side Chain menu, will be available only on those instruments that offer side chains.

First, you'll want to instantiate an Audio Instrument on an Arrange track and open that Audio Instrument.

1. **Select** an **Audio Instrument Track** in the Arrange window.
2. **Choose** the **Instrument** you would like to open.

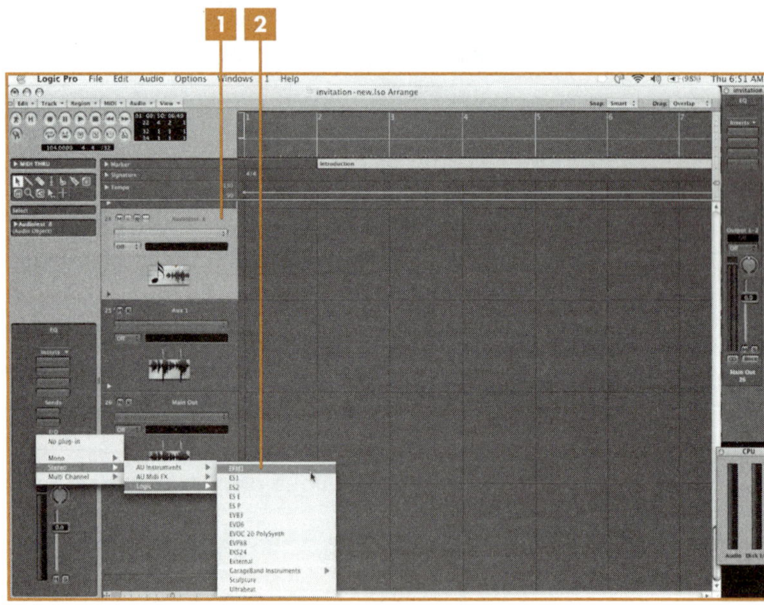

Are Your Audio Instruments Floating or Non-Floating?

When your Audio Instrument window opens, you'll notice that it's always going to be in front of everything else. This is usually what you want. A window that is always on top of every other window like this is called a "floating" window. But sometimes, you may want an Audio Instrument window to be on screen, but in the background until you need it. In those cases, you may want to open your Audio Instrument as a non-floating window. To do this, hold the OPTION key while instantiating or double-clicking the instrument name.

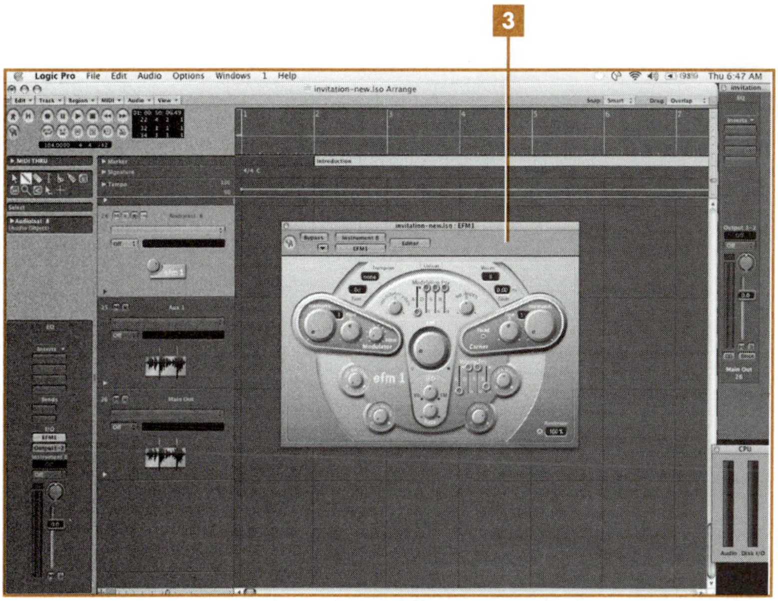

3 Your chosen instrument will open in a floating window after it loads.

All Audio Instruments Are Created Equal

You'll notice that there are two menus for your Audio Instruments: one called Logic and another called Audio Units. That's because when you install third-party Audio Unit plug-in software synthesizers, they are accessed the exact same way you access any other Audio Instrument. It's that easy!

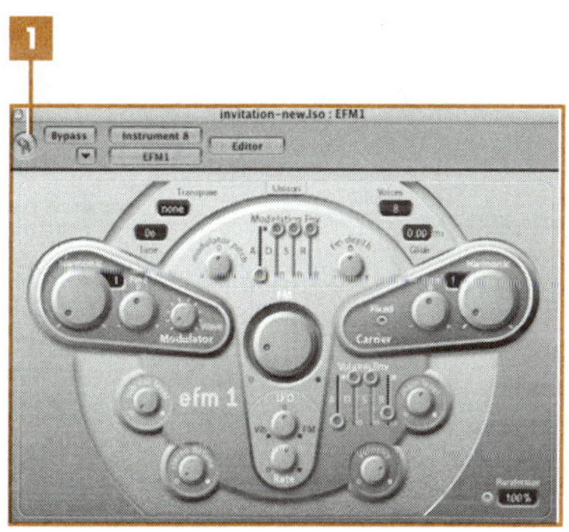

Below is a brief description of each menu.

1 **Link Button**: Pressing this will determine whether subsequently selected Instruments or plug-ins will open in a new window or replace the existing open, floating window.

Reducing Audio Instrument Window Clutter

If you are working with many Audio Instruments, every time you open one of their plug-in windows, it will create another editor window on screen; this can get very cluttered! One way to reduce this clutter is to simply close every unused Audio Instrument window when you are done accessing that window. However, another method is to click the Link button in the corner. Once you click the Link button of a plug-in, any plug-in you open subsequently will replace the currently open plug-in. This way, you don't have to worry about windows piling up on screen. You can also combine methods, having the one Audio Instrument you use all the time always visible, and then having a linked window for other instruments and effects.

2 Bypass Button: This button will effectively turn the Instrument off; not only will the sound be muted, but the Instrument will stop providing a drain on your computer's CPU.

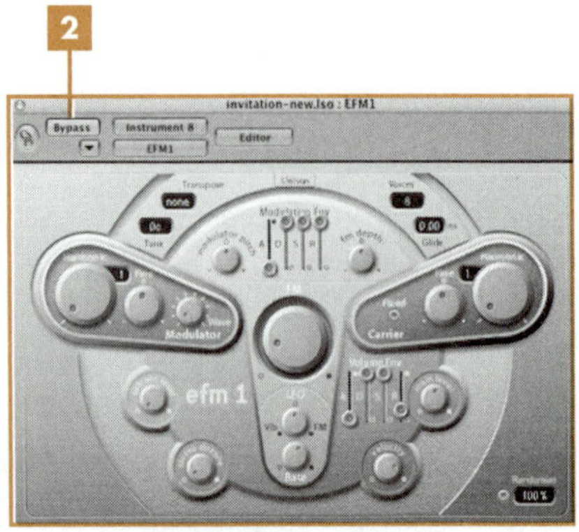

3 Object Menu: Pressing this allows you to change the content of the plug-in window to any other open plug-in on another Arrange track.

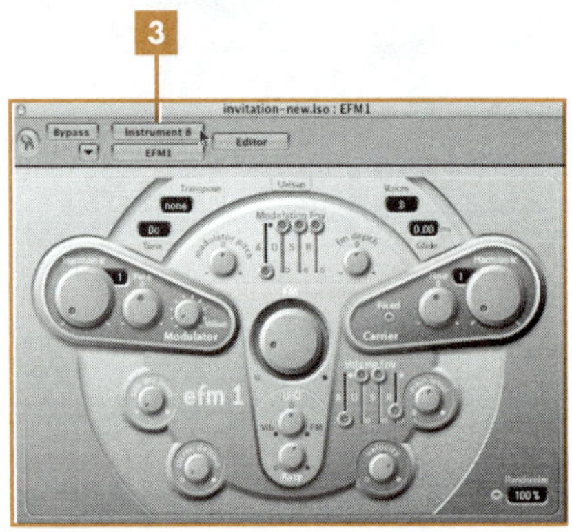

4 Editor Menu: This switches the Instrument display between the graphical interface shown here or the Controls parameter display.

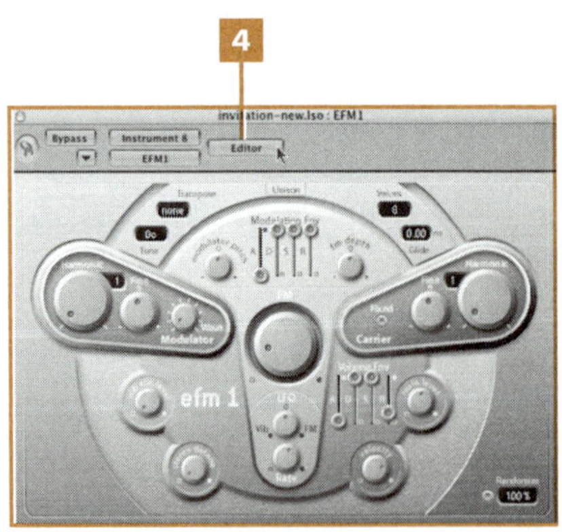

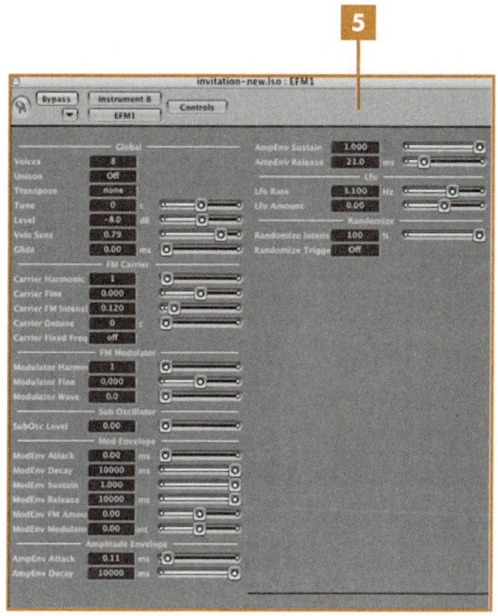

5 Controls Display: This gives you simple access to all the user adjustable controls in your Audio Instrument. When you know exactly the adjustment you want to make, using this no-frills view often saves time.

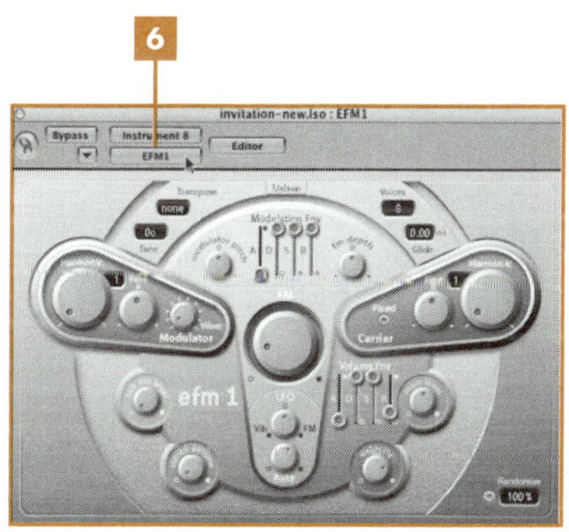

6 Plug-In Menu: Pressing this allows you to switch to any other instantiated plug-in on the same Arrange track.

7 Arrow: This will open a list of saved settings, or presets, available for the Instrument. You can also save and load your own settings from this menu.

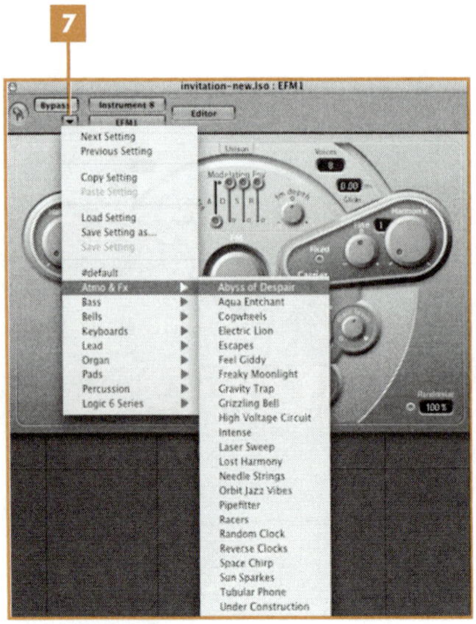

8 AU Preset Menu: With Audio Unit Instruments (such as U-He's Zebra, shown here), there is an additional menu of AU presets providing easy access to settings for the Instrument.

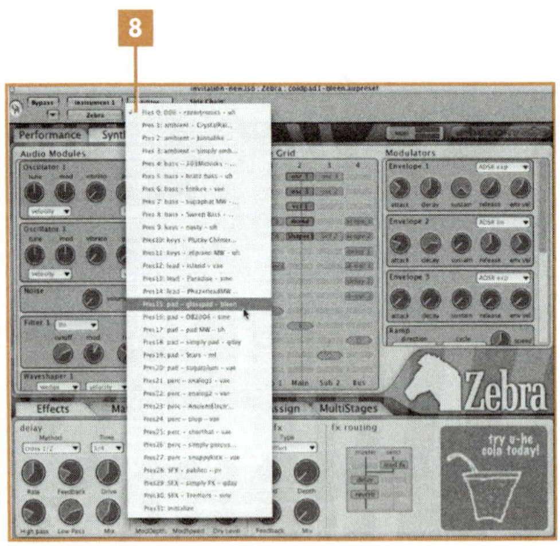

9 Side Chain Menu: Some Instruments (like the EVOC20, shown here) have the ability to receive input or modulation from an external source, such as an Audio Track. This will be explained further a little later.

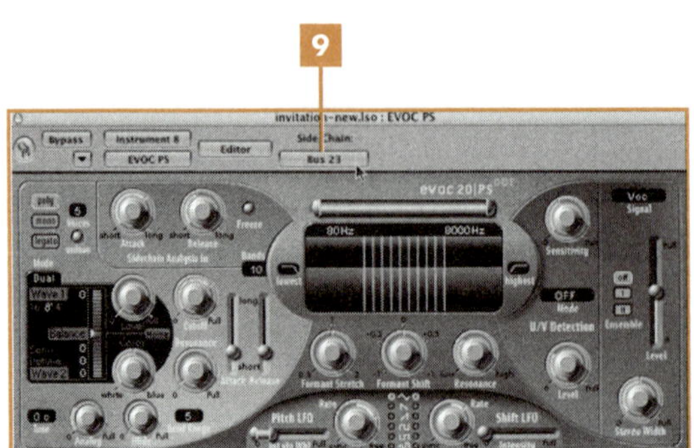

Setting Up Multi-Timbral Audio Instruments

If you're familiar with hardware synthesizers, you already know that a "multi-timbral" synthesizer is one that can play completely different parts, with different patches and settings, on different MIDI channels. Some Audio Instruments are also multi-timbral, allowing multiple Audio Instrument Tracks to play different patches, with different settings, of the same Audio Instrument. Currently, very few of Logic's included instruments are multi-timbral, but a fair number of Audio Unit Instruments are multi-timbral.

Setup is very easy.

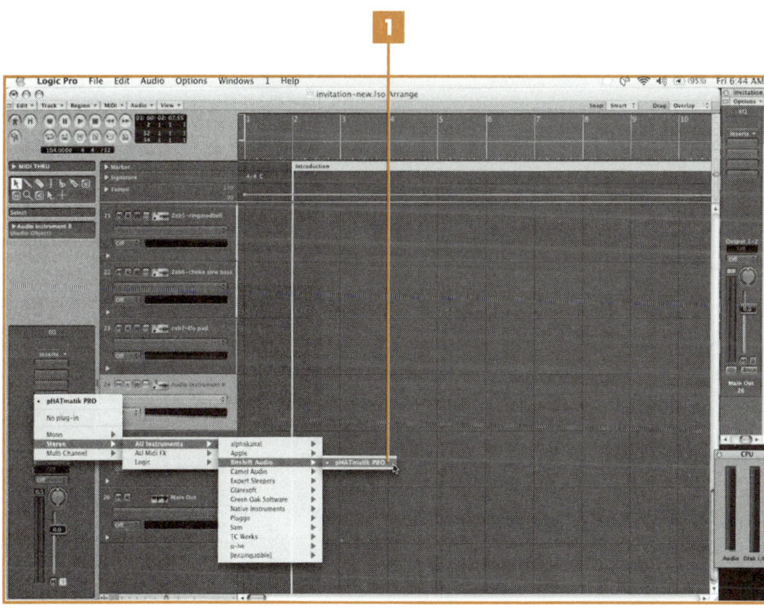

1 With an Audio Instrument Track selected, choose a Multi-Timbral Audio Instrument.

2 In the Audio Instrument's interface, set it to the first MIDI channel you want to use. This one is currently set to Channel 1. Make sure your MIDI keyboard or controller is set to transmit on the same MIDI channel.

3 In the Instrument Settings pane, make sure to set the MIDI channel setting to All. Record your part for the first channel.

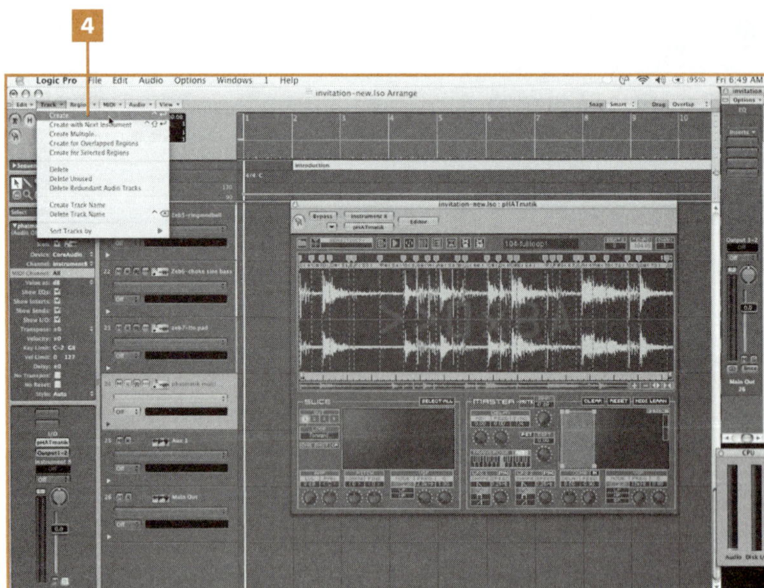

4 Go to Track > Create. This will create a duplicate Audio Object of your current instrument in the Arrange window, with the same instrument and all of its parameters loaded.

Key Command Alert: Create Track

Pressing CONTROL + RETURN will create a duplicate Audio Object of a selected track in the Arrange window.

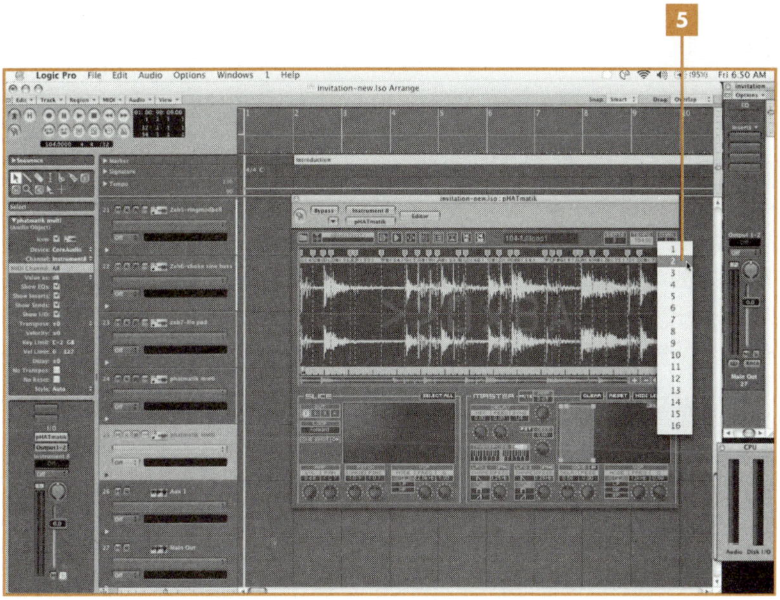

5 Change the MIDI channel on your instrument to the next one you want to use, and load a new setting. Change the MIDI channel on your controller once again to correspond with the new instrument channel.

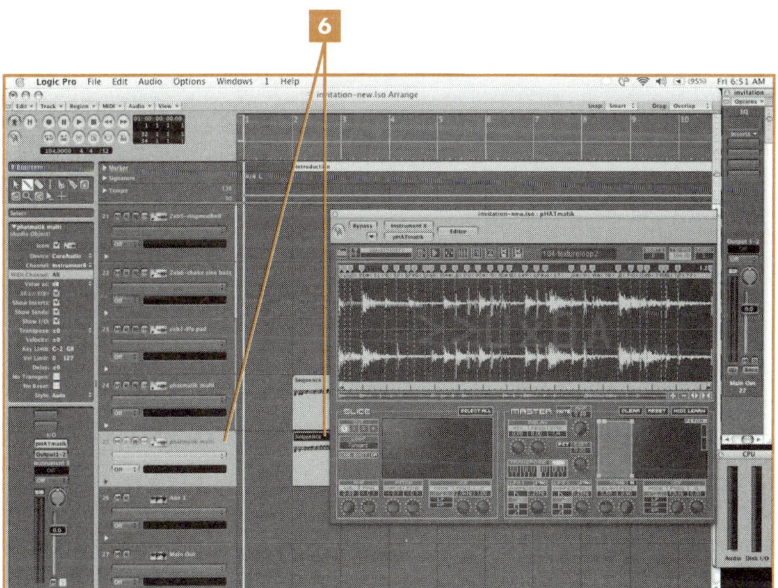

6 Record your second part, and you will now hear both MIDI channels being played from the same instrument!

Setting Up Multi-Channel Audio Instruments

Multi-Channel Audio Instruments—or more descriptively, multiple output channel Audio Instruments— are instruments that offer more than the single stereo output of the Audio Instrument Channel Strip. This feature can be especially useful for drum instruments in which you want each drum to get its own Channel Strip, or multi-timbral instruments in which you can send different voices to different outputs.

Logic's multi-channel support is particularly CPU efficient, making sure that it doesn't create more mixer channels (each of which takes up CPU) than you are actually going to use. This extra efficiency, unfortunately, means that there is a little more user setup required. Luckily, it's conceptually very simple:

1 Select an Audio Instrument track, and insert a Multi-Channel Audio Instrument.

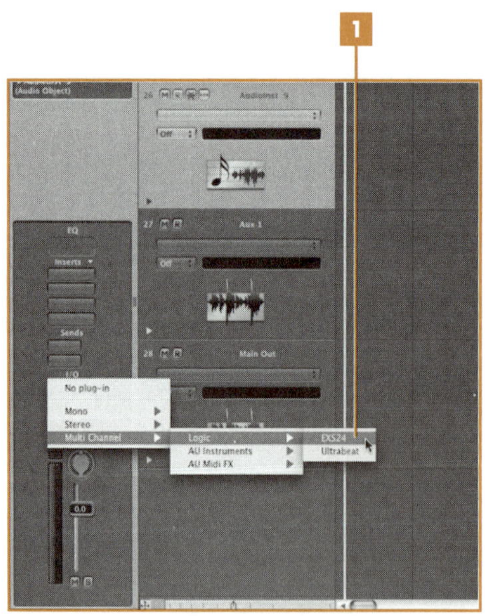

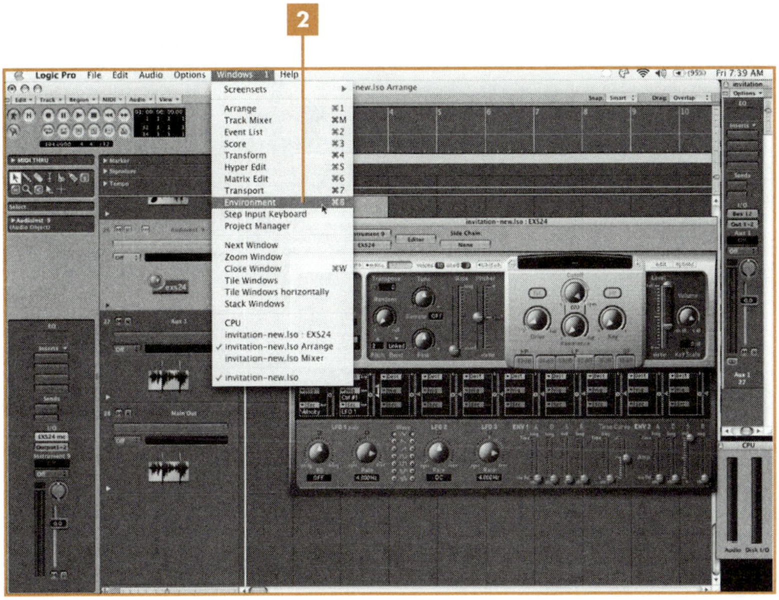

2 You will now venture to the Environment! Go to Windows > Environment, or, if you have a Screenset with an Environment window, press its corresponding Screenset number on your Mac's keyboard.

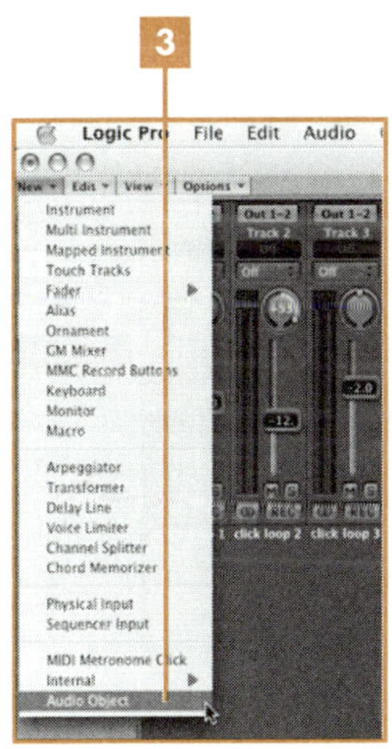

3 Once in the Environment, go to New > Audio Object.

4 In the object's Parameter pane, set the Channel parameter to an unused Aux object.

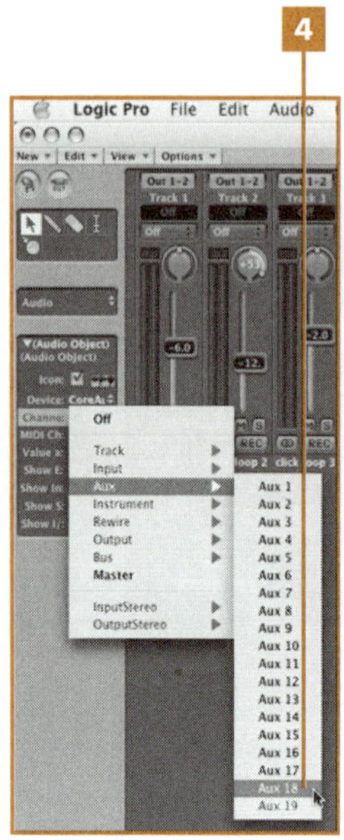

5 Name your new Aux object so that you can easily recognize it.

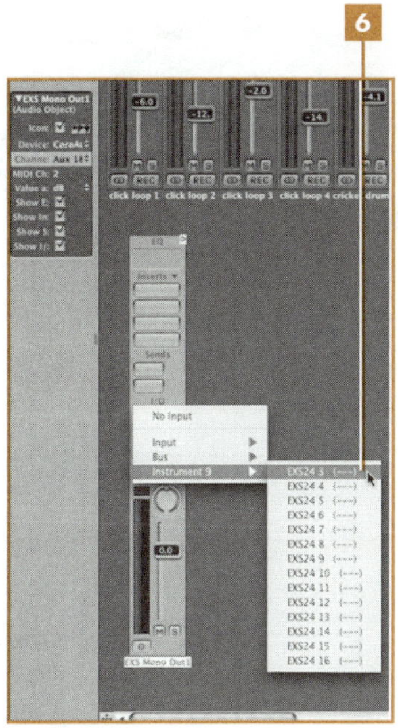

6 Assign the Input of the Aux object to one of the Outputs from the Audio Instrument.

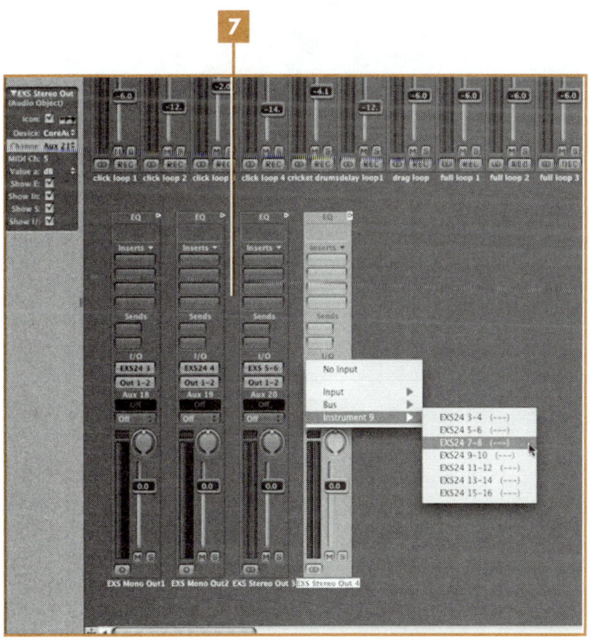

7 Repeat steps 3–6 for as many separate outputs as you need.

8 Return to the Arrange window and create a new track. Click and hold on the name to assign it to one of the newly created Aux objects.

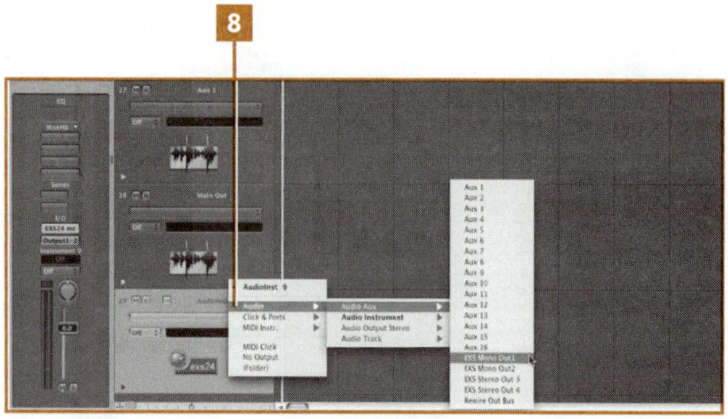

9 Go to Track > Create with Next Instrument, and Logic will add the next sequentially named Environment object, which in this case is the second Aux output track you created.

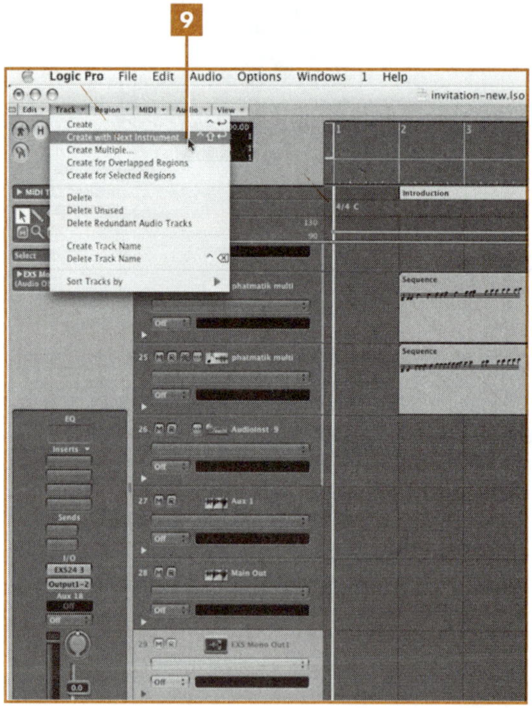

Key Command Alert: Create with Next Instrument

Pressing CONTROL + SHIFT + RETURN will create the next sequentially named Audio Object from the selected track in the Arrange window.

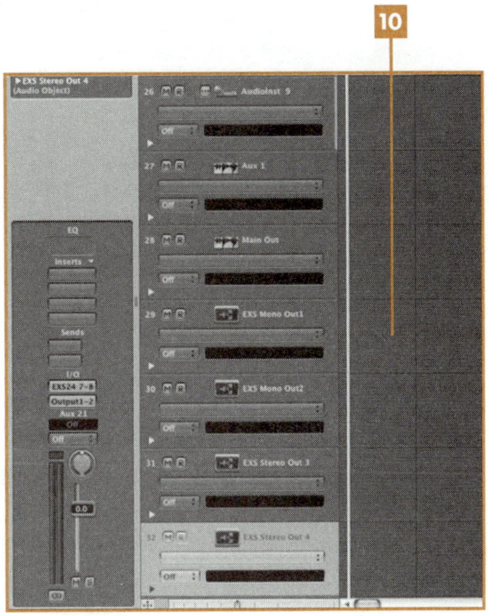

10 Repeat Step 9 as many times as necessary to add the remainder of the Aux outputs.

Setting Up Audio Instrument Side Chains

Some Audio Instruments are able to not only generate sound from MIDI notes, but also process the signal from your Audio tracks. Instruments with this ability will have a special input called a "side chain"—so named because, in hardware, they used to literally daisy chain audio processors from side to side like this!

One example of an Audio Instrument with a side chain would be a vocoder plug-in. A vocoder is used to synthesize an audio signal (typically a vocal); you would instantiate the vocoder Audio Instrument in an Audio Instrument Track, and then choose the Audio Track to vocode in its side chain. Another example is a synthesizer that allows audio signals to pass through its filters; this would be like a hardware synthesizer with audio input jacks on the back panel.

In our example, we'll show you how to route an Audio Track through the side chain of the EVOC20 synthesizer.

1 Insert the EVOC20 on an Audio Instrument Track.

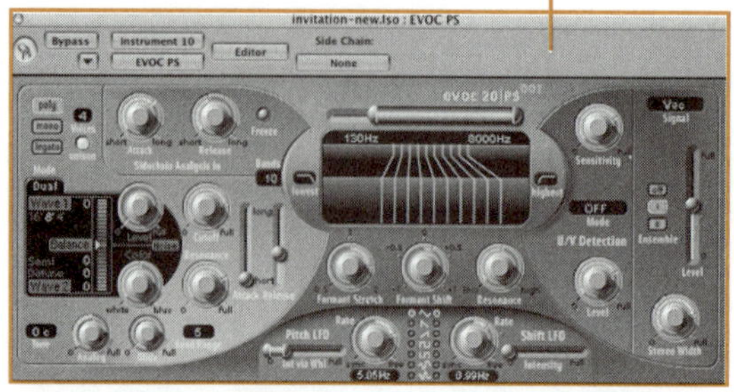

2 Set the Side Chain input to the Track number that you want to use as the source. In this case, it's Track 1.

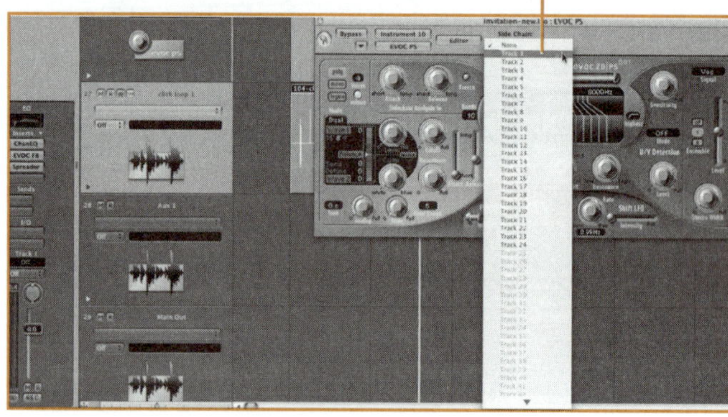

3 If you only want to hear the output of the EVOC20, set the output of the Audio Track to No Output. This will let you hear only the modulated signal from the synthesizer, rather than a blend of the Audio Track and synth.

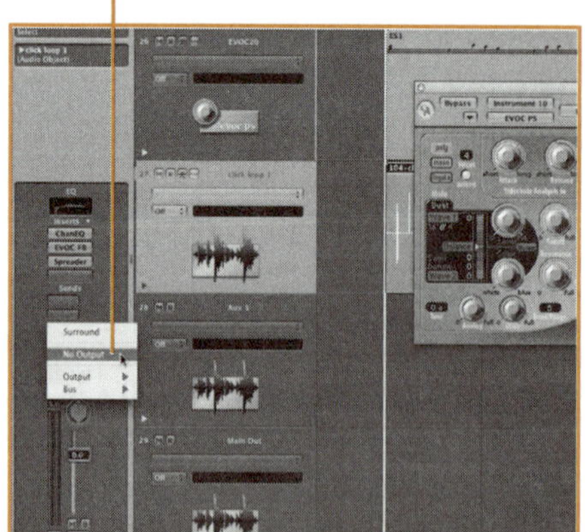

9 Working with MIDI: The Matrix and Hyper Editors

Logic comes from a solid background of innovative and user friendly MIDI sequencing. In fact, Logic's heritage dates back to an early Commodore 64 sequencer called "Supertrack" that was written in the mid-80s! With nearly 20 years of MIDI expertise to draw on, it's no wonder that Logic offers arguably the best MIDI editors and MIDI editing workflow of any available digital audio sequencer.

Obviously, Logic offers far more MIDI editing and processing potential than we can possibly cover here. Nonetheless, the next chapters will cover the basics of MIDI editing in Logic Express and Logic Pro using the most popular MIDI editors in Logic.

In this chapter, you will learn how to:

- Navigate the Matrix Editor
- Program and step-input MIDI into the Matrix Editor
- Resize notes in the Matrix Editor
- Move notes in the Matrix Editor
- Change the velocity of notes in the Matrix Editor
- Quantize notes in the Matrix Editor
- Access Hyper Draw in the Matrix Editor
- Navigate the Hyper Editor
- Configure the Hyper Editor as a MIDI drum editor
- Use the Hyper Editor as a drum editor

Navigating the Matrix Editor

The Matrix Editor is the most popular MIDI editor in Logic, which is why it is the default editor when you double-click a MIDI region in the Arrange window (you can change the default editor in the preferences, however). The Matrix Editor offers you a "piano roll" graphic view of your MIDI notes as bar lines. Each bar line is shown in a graph, or matrix, with the MIDI note as the vertical, or Y, axis, and the bar ruler (the time in your song) as the horizontal, or X, axis. Users of other MIDI software should have no trouble understanding and navigating the elements of Logic's Matrix Editor. For users new to MIDI, the walk-throughs below should get you familiar with the layout of the Matrix Editor in no time!

Here are the main elements of the Matrix Editor.

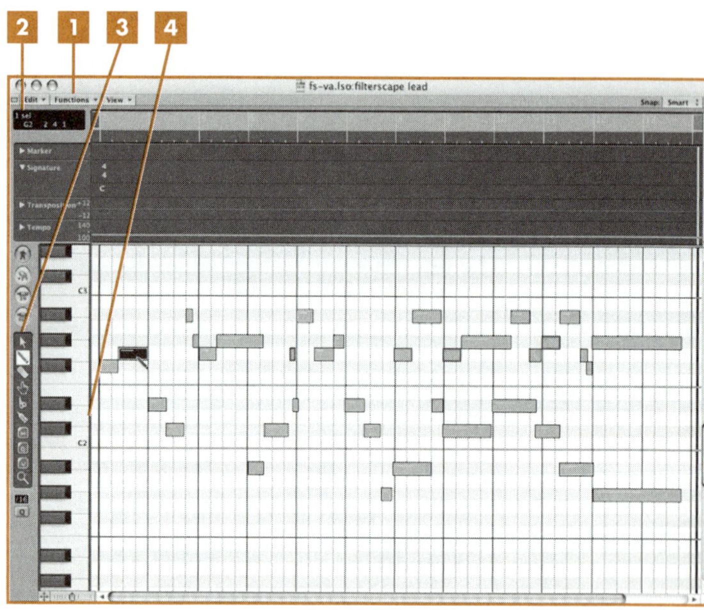

1. Local Menus: The Matrix Editor includes its own local menus, which are described below.
2. Position Display: This window displays the note and position of the currently selected MIDI note or information about your current selection.
3. Matrix Editor Parameter Section: The far left of the Matrix Editor will show the Matrix buttons, Toolbox, and Grid Subdivision window.
4. Matrix Keyboard: This onscreen keyboard indicates the pitch of the notes in the Matrix.

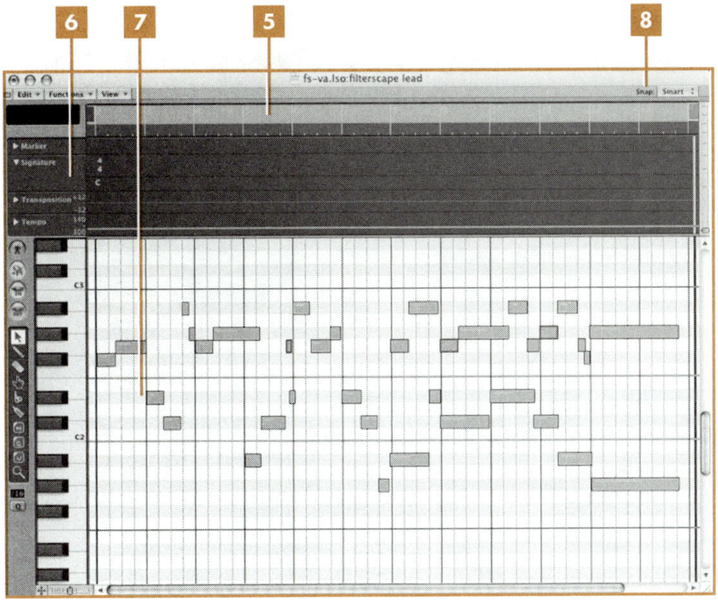

5 Bar Ruler: This ruler displays where you are in your song in measures (bar, beat) and, if you turn it on in the View menu, SMPTE Frames (minutes, seconds).

6 Global Tracks: You can choose to display your Global Tracks in the Matrix Editor.

7 Matrix Area: This is where all the MIDI notes that fill your region are displayed. This is the actual workspace in which you edit the MIDI notes.

8 Snap Menu (Pro Only): This pull-down menu contains a number of different snap values that will automatically snap your notes to specific grid intervals when you move them.

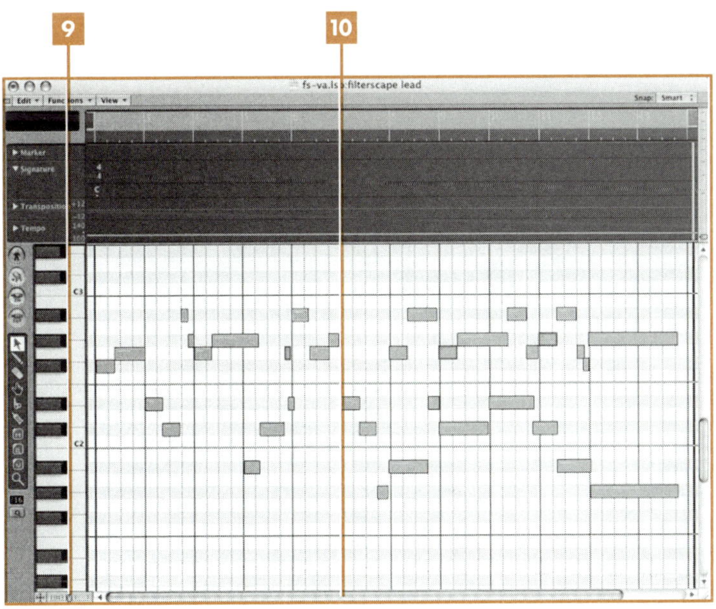

9 Zoom Sliders: These sliders adjust both vertically and horizontally to focus the Matrix Editor workspace tightly on a few notes or to open up the view to a macroscopic view of your MIDI notes. You can hold down the OPTION key while moving a slider to adjust the other slider's dimension.

10 Scroll Bars: These are standard Macintosh scroll bars that allow you to scroll the Arrange window.

Matrix Editor Local Menus

The three local menus of the Matrix Editor include the Edit, Functions, and View menus:

1 Edit Menu: The Edit menu contains the standard Macintosh editing commands, along with MIDI event selection commands and options.

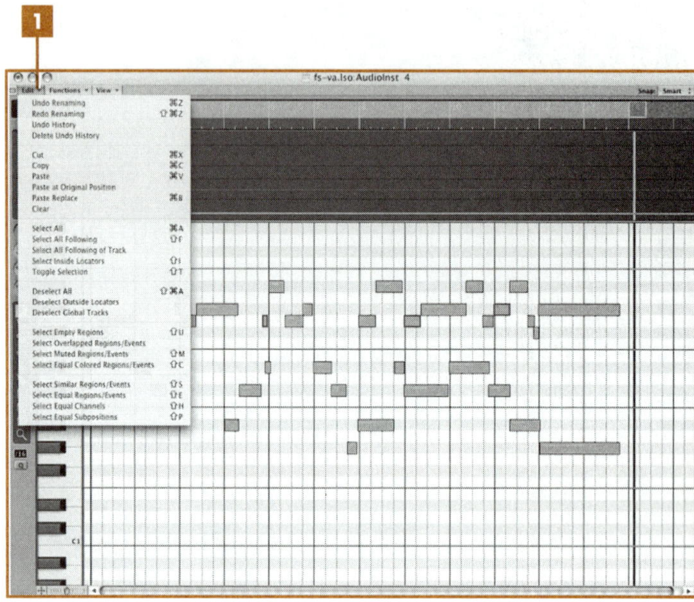

2 Functions Menu: The Functions menu consists of commands that process MIDI events.

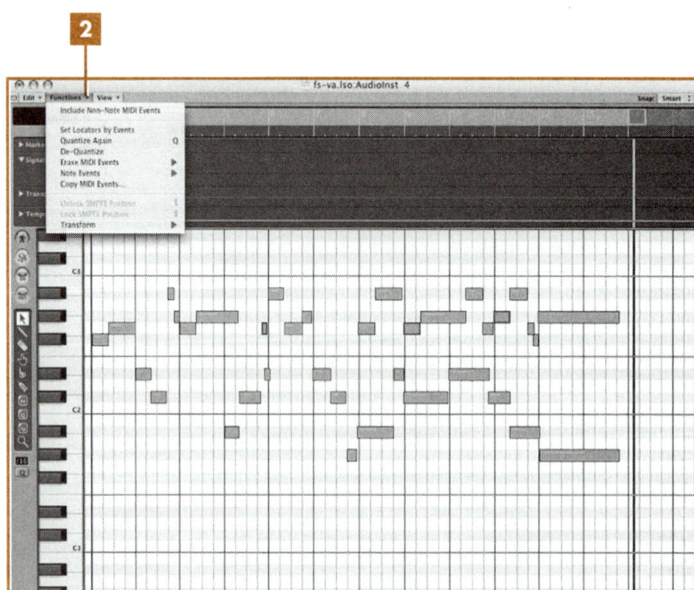

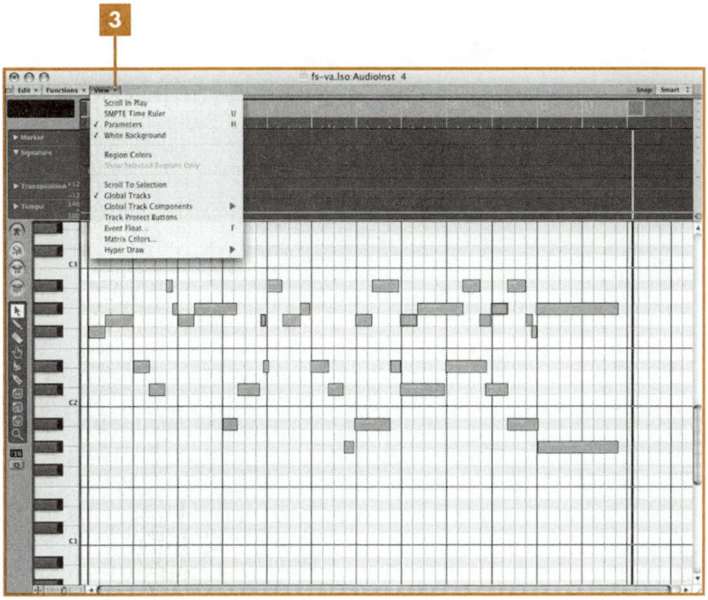

3 View Menu: The View menu contains all the various Global Track and Matrix Editor view options, including the ability to view Hyper Draw (region-based automation).

Matrix Window Buttons

The Matrix Editor offers buttons to allow you to both link it to other windows as well as to record and play back MIDI.

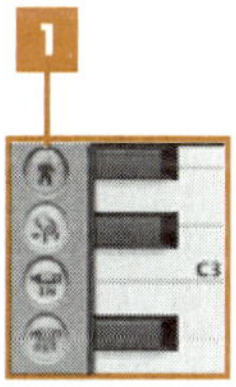

1 Catch Button: Clicking this button will ensure that the visible section of the Matrix Editor will display the current song position. This is especially important when playing back or step-inputting MIDI. If you move the visible section of the Matrix Editor yourself, the Catch button is automatically disengaged so that you don't lose the section you're working on.

2 Link Button: Clicking the Link button will ensure that the contents of the Matrix Editor will always be linked to any window that is "topped," or in front of all other windows. You can double-click this button to engage "Contents Link" mode, in which the Matrix Editor will always show the contents of whatever region is selected in the linked window.

Using the Catch and Link Buttons Together: Contents Catch

If you have both the Catch and Link buttons clicked, Logic will be in "Contents Catch" mode. This acts like Contents Link mode until you start playback. When Logic is playing and the Matrix Editor is in Contents Catch mode, the selected region will change as the Song Position Line moves along the song.

3 MIDI IN Button: If this button is engaged, you can step-input MIDI notes directly into the Matrix Editor. Disengage this button when you are done inputting MIDI to avoid accidentally added notes.

4 MIDI OUT Button: To hear your MIDI notes sounded as you edit, keep this button engaged.

Matrix Editor Toolbox

Since the Matrix Editor is designed for graphic editing, it has a comprehensive set of tools in its toolbox.

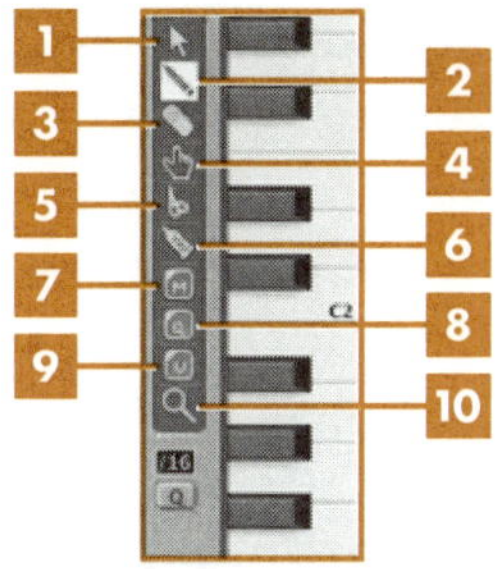

1 Pointer: The Pointer tool is your basic selection tool and move tool. It is also a "smart" tool, meaning, if moved to specific "hot spots" on a region, it can change into the Resize tool, as we'll discuss later in the chapter.

2 Pencil: You can use the Pencil tool to create new notes.

3 Eraser: The Eraser tool deletes notes from the Matrix Editor.

4 Finger: This is the Resize tool in the Matrix Editor—use this to lengthen or shorten MIDI notes.

5 Scissors: You can use the Scissors tool to split notes, as we'll discuss later in the chapter.

6 Glue: You can use the Glue tool to merge one or more notes into a single note.

7 Mute Tool (Pro Only): You can use the Mute tool to mute notes.

8 Quantize Tool: With this tool, you can "quantize" notes, or align them to a grid.

9 Velocity Tool: You can use the Velocity tool to adjust the velocity, or volume, of a MIDI note.

10 Magnifying Glass: You can use the Magnifying Glass tool to zoom into a specific area of the Matrix Editor.

Entering MIDI Notes into the Matrix Editor

Recording MIDI performances from a MIDI controller into the Arrange window is not the only way to get MIDI data into Logic. If you are more comfortable entering notes directly into the Matrix Editor, Logic gives you two ways to do this: programming (or drawing) MIDI notes onto the Matrix Editor with the mouse and step-inputting MIDI.

Programming (or Drawing) MIDI Notes in the Matrix Editor

If you know exactly what you want your MIDI part to be, or if you're more fluid with a mouse than a MIDI keyboard, you'll be happy to hear that you can use the Pencil tool to very easily enter your MIDI parts by hand:

1 Select the Pencil tool from the Matrix Editor Toolbox.

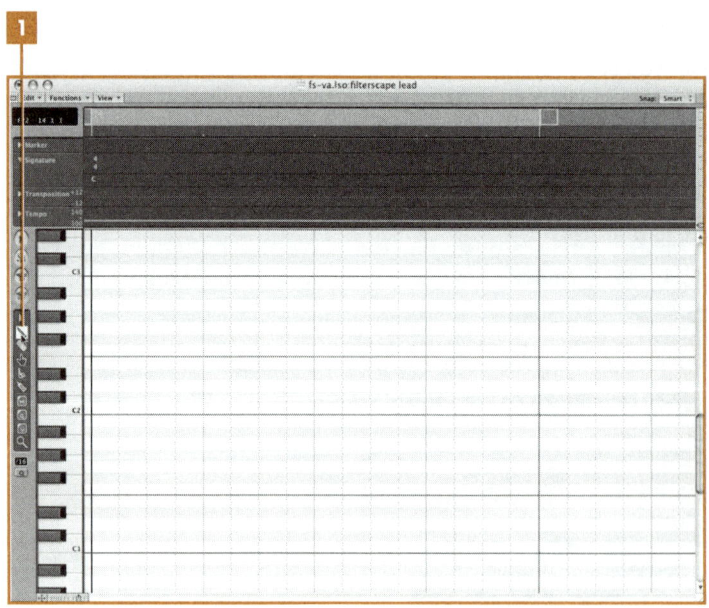

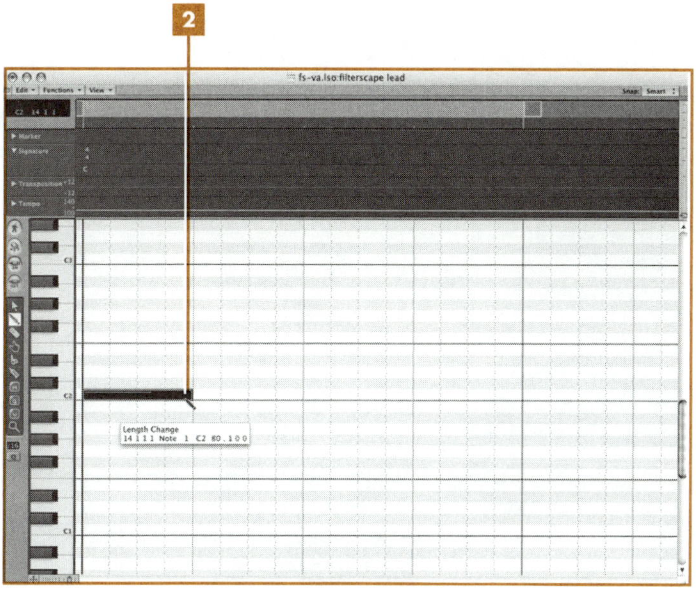

2 Click in the Matrix Area on the notes you want to enter. Clicking and dragging the Pencil will lengthen and shorten the notes as you enter them.

Step-Inputting MIDI Notes into the Matrix Editor

Let's say that you are comfortable entering MIDI notes with a MIDI controller, but you aren't comfortable performing the part you wish to perform in real-time. Or perhaps you want to go for a really tight, "locked to the grid" techno style of MIDI part. It is for cases such as these that you can use the Step Input feature to enter MIDI into the Matrix Editor.

1 Press the MIDI IN button.

2 As you play on your MIDI controller or keyboard, the notes will appear and advance to the next step.

3 The length of each input note is determined by the Grid resolution in the Matrix window.

Step Entry from Your Computer Keyboard or Mouse

While step input lends itself beautifully to using a MIDI controller for note entry, Logic lets you use either your computer keyboard or a mouse. First of all, every note in the Western scale has a key command that you can assign in the Key Command window; this will allow you to type in notes and have them appear in the Matrix Editor. You can also select Windows > Step Input Keyboard to open a special on-screen keyboard specifically for step recording MIDI notes, as shown below.

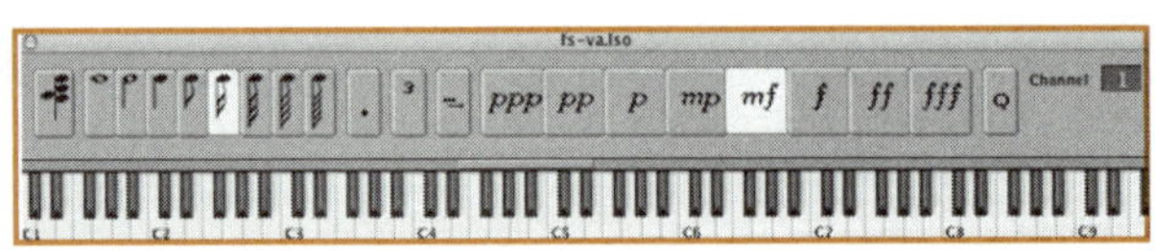

As you can see, Logic's step input features are very flexible, and they offer a way for everyone to input MIDI into the Matrix Editor.

Moving MIDI Notes

One of the most common ways you'll wish to edit notes is to move them. Usually, you'll just want to nudge them a little bit so that they are more "in the pocket" of your groove or performance. However, if you want to drastically change the pitch and location of your notes, that's just as easy!

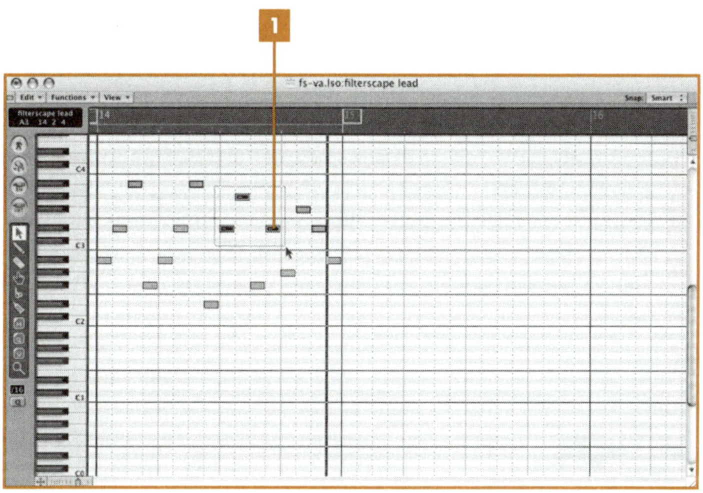

1 Using the Pointer tool, select the note or group of notes you want to move.

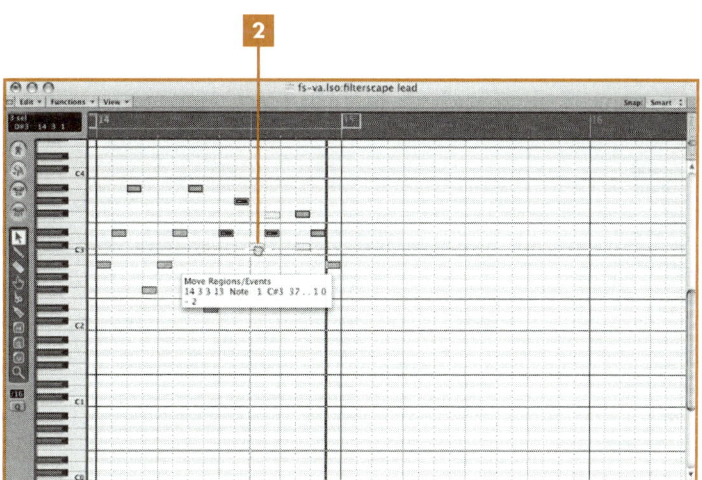

2 Click and drag the note to the new position.

Changing the Velocity of MIDI Notes

Don't worry, we're not going to study the physics of MIDI now! When we talk about the velocity of a MIDI note, what we really mean is its relative volume to the other notes. So if you feel a note is too loud or too soft compared to the other notes, you'll want to change the velocity of that note. Here's how:

MIDI Note Velocity versus MIDI Volume

If you're not familiar with MIDI terminology, you're probably wondering why the volume of a MIDI note is referred to as its velocity, and not simply its volume. The reason is to avoid confusion with another MIDI parameter—MIDI Volume. MIDI Volume controls the output level for an entire MIDI channel. So, in order to differentiate between MIDI Volume and the volume of a MIDI note, note volume is referred to as velocity.

1. **Select** the **Velocity** tool in the Matrix window.

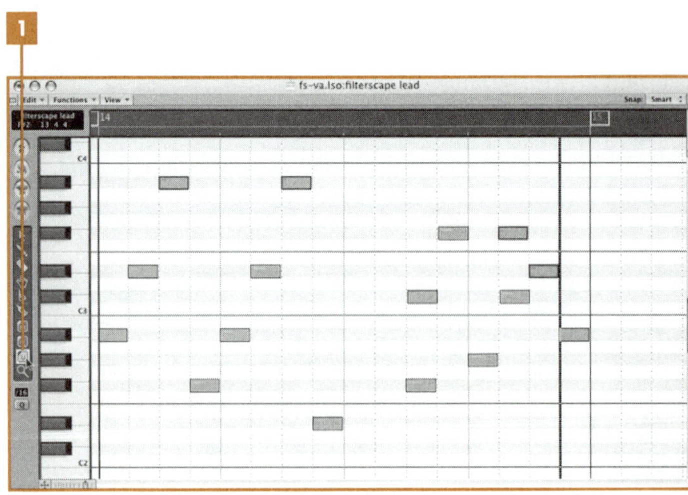

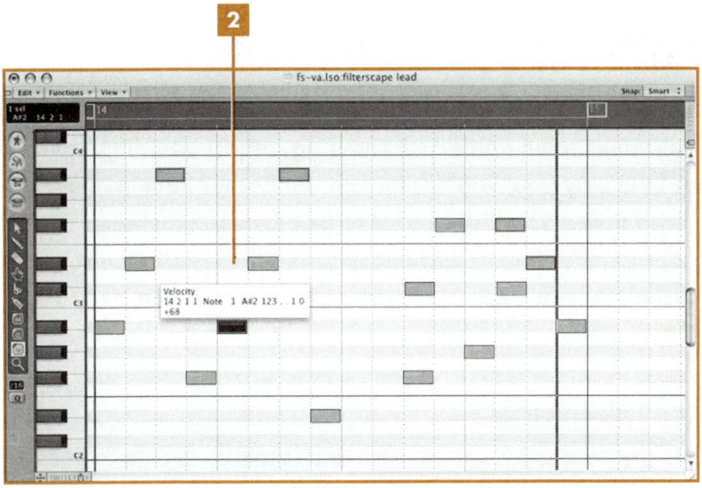

2 Click and drag up or down on a note to raise or lower its velocity.

Changing Pitch and Velocity from Your MIDI Controller

If you select a note in the Matrix Editor, you can actually use your MIDI keyboard controller to change the pitch of the note, or to change its velocity. By double-clicking the MIDI IN button, every time you select a note you will be able to change its velocity and pitch by pressing a note on your MIDI keyboard. The note in the Matrix Editor will change pitch and velocity based on which MIDI note you trigger and its velocity. The note will retain the timing and length it already had.

Resizing MIDI Notes

Very often when you perform a MIDI part live, you'll find that you held onto some notes a bit too long, others you didn't quite let ring out the way you wanted, and so on. Rather than re-perform just those notes, you'll save a lot of time by resizing them. The Matrix Editor makes it incredibly easy to see the length of each note graphically and quickly shorten or lengthen them.

1. Select the Pointer tool.
2. Hover over the end of a note in the Matrix window to change the tool to the Resize tool. Click and drag the note to change the size.

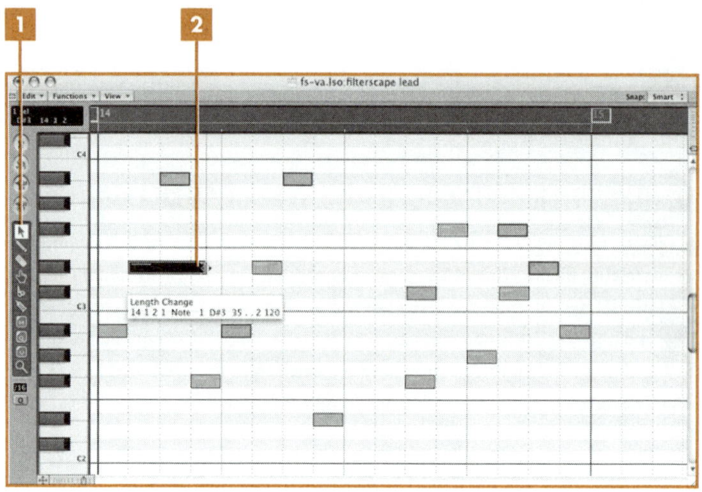

Quantizing MIDI Notes

Quantizing refers to moving all selected MIDI notes to exact positions relative to your chosen grid denominator. For example, if you have your quantize grid set to 1/16th notes, any notes that you select and quantize will be moved to the nearest sixteenth note position. If you find that an entire MIDI part is slightly off beat, or you want to change the feel or groove of a MIDI part, Quantize can be a great tool. Quantize is one of the most powerful editing features at your disposal.

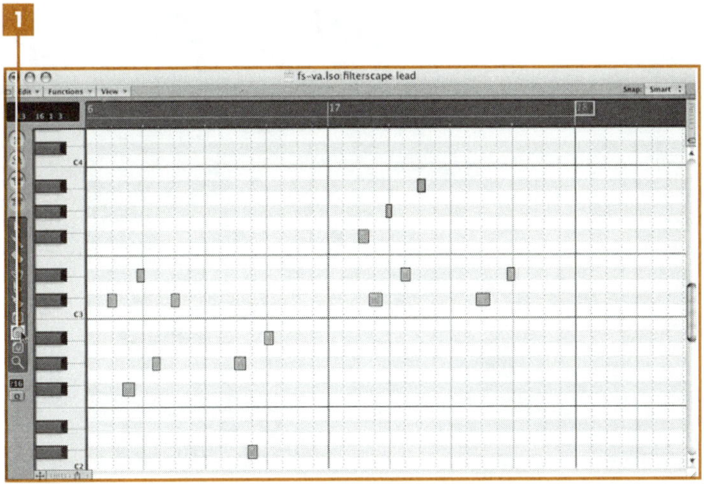

1 Select the Quantize tool in the Matrix window.

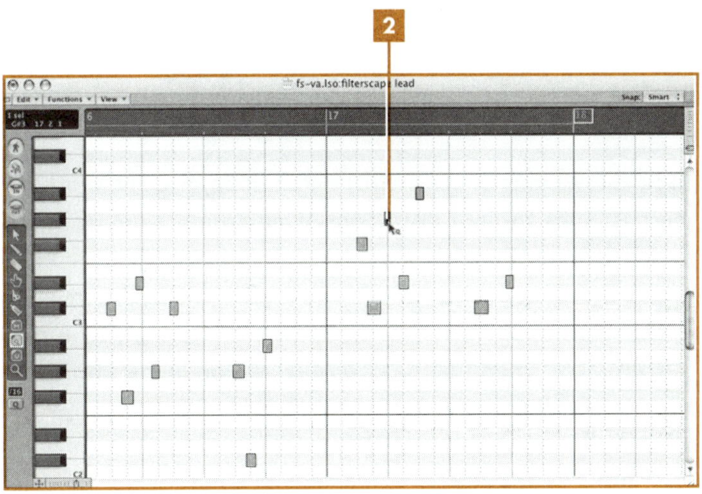

2 Click on a note that you want to move to the grid.

3 The note will now be aligned to the grid according to the selected Quantize value.

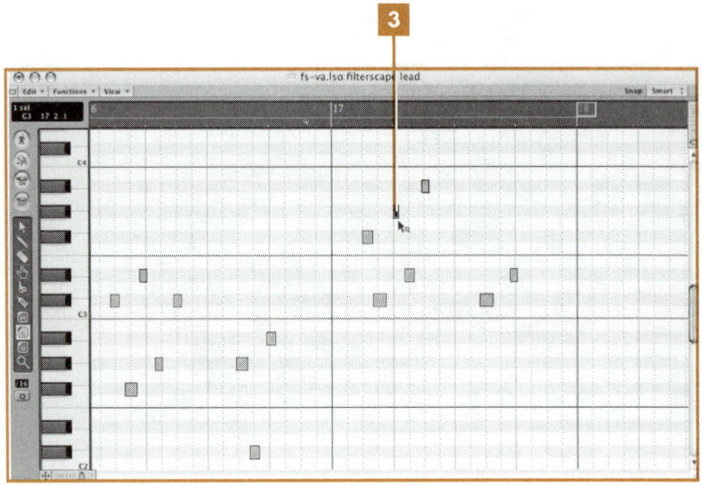

Viewing and Editing Hyper Draw in the Matrix Editor

Logic allows you to write MIDI automation directly into MIDI regions in the form of MIDI control messages. Logic calls this region-based MIDI automation Hyper Draw, since it is drawing events that are placed "over" your MIDI (one of the definitions of hyper is "over"). Since this region-based Hyper Draw is part of the MIDI region, when you open a MIDI region in the Matrix Editor, you can view and edit your Hyper Draw events as you would any other MIDI event, such as MIDI notes.

Viewing Hyper Draw

If you have generated Hyper Draw information with a MIDI controller, or if you want to add Hyper Draw to your region, the first step is to view Hyper Draw data along with your note data.

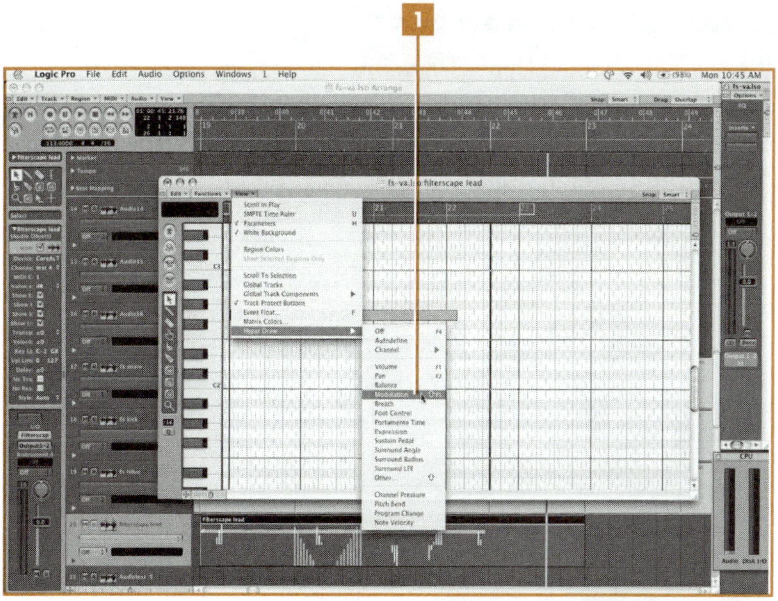

1 In the Matrix window, go to View > Hyper Draw. From here you can select the type of Hyper Draw data you want to see.

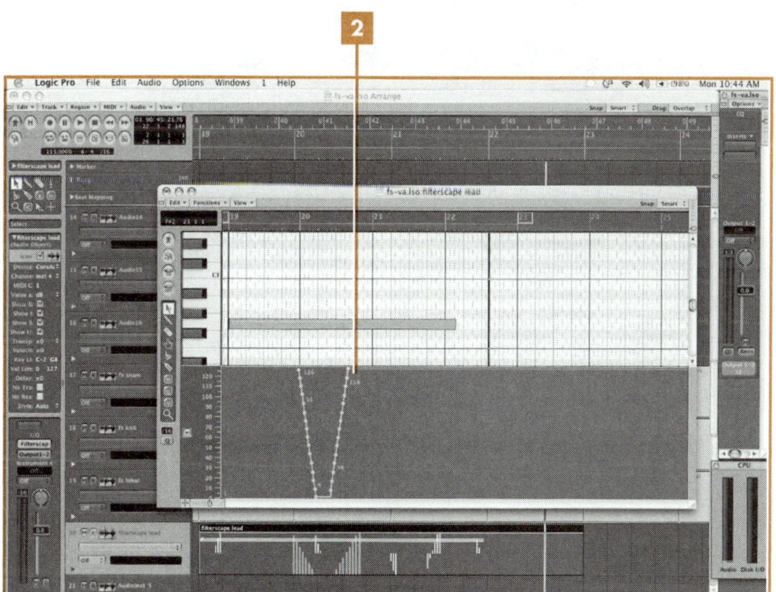

2 The Hyper Draw information is displayed at the bottom of the Matrix window.

Creating Hyper Draw Nodes

If you want to create Hyper Draw information, you can do so similarly to the way you create volume curves in GarageBand, or automation using Logic's Track Automation feature (see Chapter 13, "Advanced Topics In Logic").

1 With the Hyper Draw lane open to the parameter you want to add, choose the Pencil tool in the Matrix window.

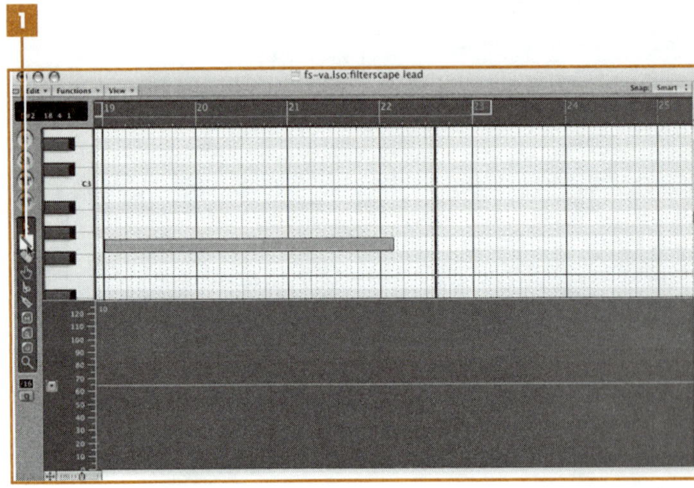

2 Click in the Hyper Draw lane to add a node.

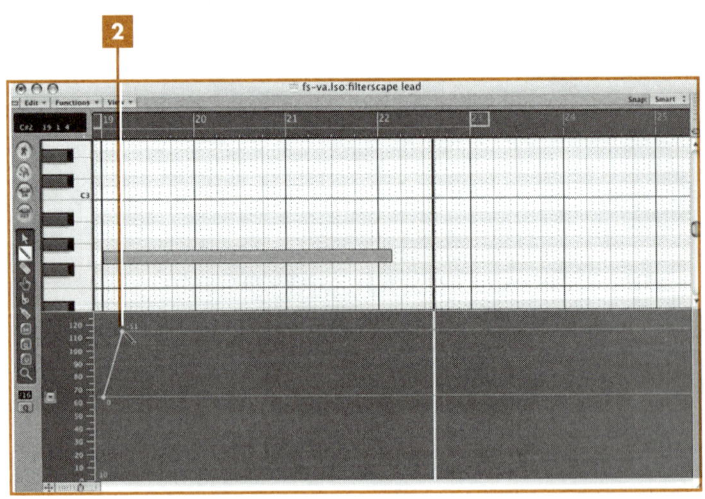

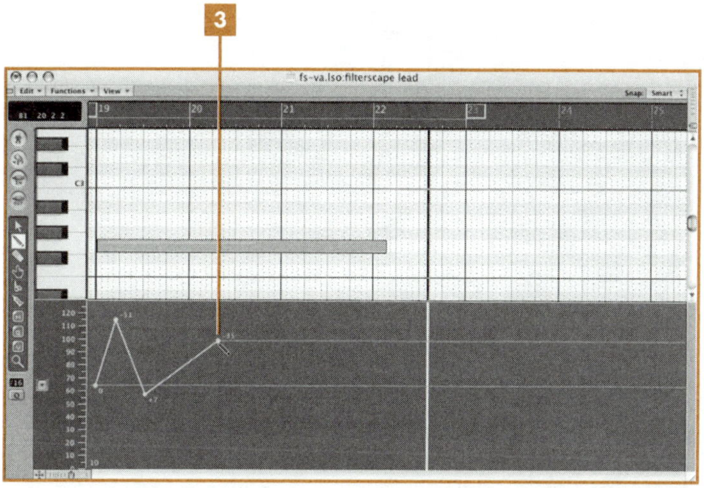

3 **Continue adding nodes** as you wish.

Navigating the Hyper Editor

The Hyper Editor is one of the oldest and most unique MIDI editors in Logic. It looks unusual, so people who are unfamiliar with it often fear that it must be complicated. In truth, it's no more difficult to understand than any other grid-based editor. Basically, the Hyper Editor allows you to edit MIDI events on a grid. Which type of MIDI event, you ask? Why, any type of MIDI event! You can use this to edit MIDI Velocity, Pan, Channel Pressure—and of course note-on events, which are what trigger MIDI notes to play. Because drums lend themselves to being programmed on a grid, one of the main uses of the Hyper Editor is as a drum editor. This section will briefly walk you through that process.

Which Is More Hyper: Hyper Draw or the Hyper Editor?

While the actual concepts within Logic may not be difficult to understand, the fact that separate concepts are often named using the same or similar terms can get confusing. Hyper Draw, the name for the region-based MIDI controller automation in Logic, does not actually have much to do with the Hyper Editor. Both Hyper Draw and Hyper Editor act on MIDI Control events, but that's where the similarity ends. Whereas Hyper Draw is the name for Logic's MIDI region-based automation feature and can be created in Hyper Draw lanes using nodes, the Hyper Editor edits MIDI Control Messages and Events on a grid. Furthermore, you can't actually view the Hyper Draw lane inside the Hyper Editor, although you can access the data itself. So while the word "Hyper" might initially throw you, in practice, the differences between Hyper Draw and the Hyper Editor are obvious.

First, let's get comfortable navigating around the Hyper Editor.

To open the Hyper Edit window:

1. Select a MIDI region in the Arrange window.
2. Go to Windows > Hyper Edit.

Key Command Alert: Hyper Edit

Press COMMAND + 5 to open the Hyper Edit window.

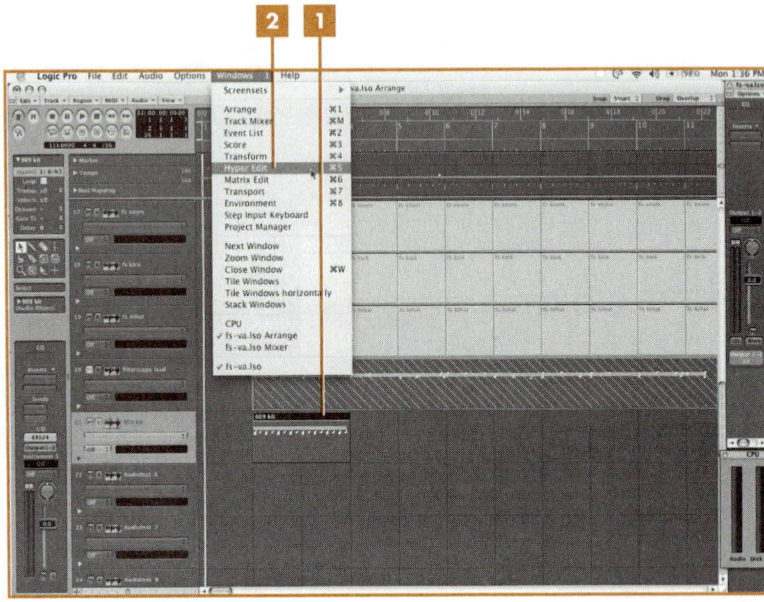

Hyper Editor Local Menus

The Hyper Editor's four local menus share the same Edit and Functions menu as the Matrix Editor, but the rest are unique to the Hyper Editor.

1. Hyper Menu: The Hyper Menu includes commands that let you save "hyper sets"—sets of MIDI event definitions and notes that you can save to use in other songs.

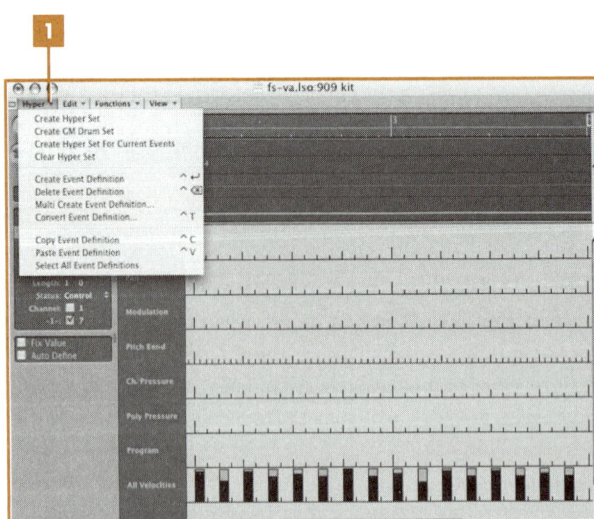

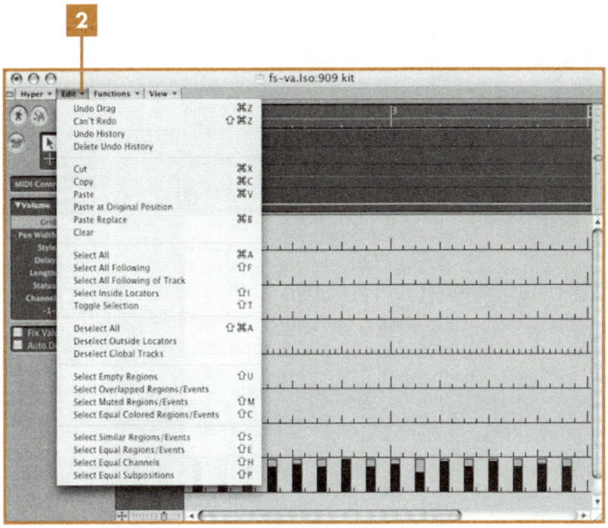

2 **Edit Menu**: The Edit menu contains the standard Macintosh editing commands, along with MIDI event selection commands and options.

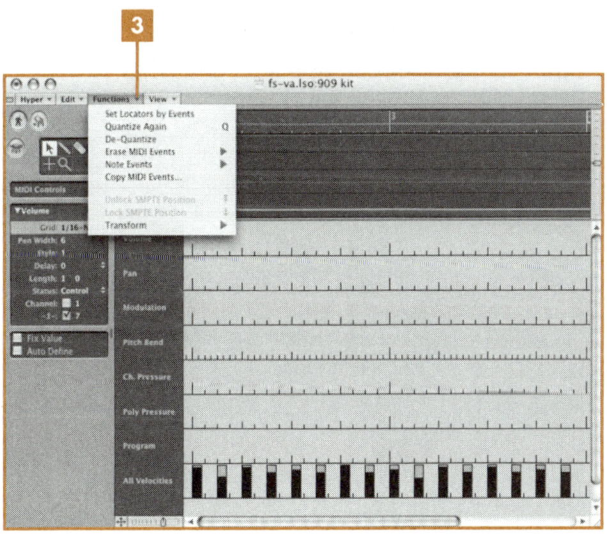

3 **Functions Menu**: The Functions menu consists of commands that process MIDI events.

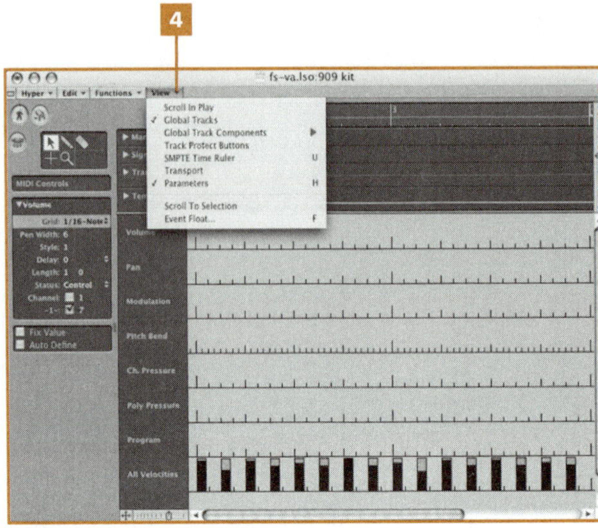

4 View Menu: The View menu contains all the various Global Track and Hyper Editor view options.

Hyper Editor Buttons

There are three buttons in the Hyper Editor:

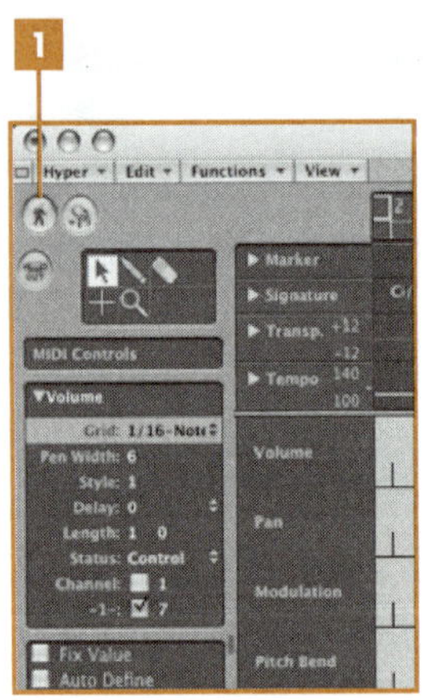

1 Catch Button: Clicking this button will ensure that the visible section of the Hyper Editor will display the current song position. If you move the visible section of the Hyper Editor yourself, the Catch button is automatically disengaged so that you don't lose the section you're working on.

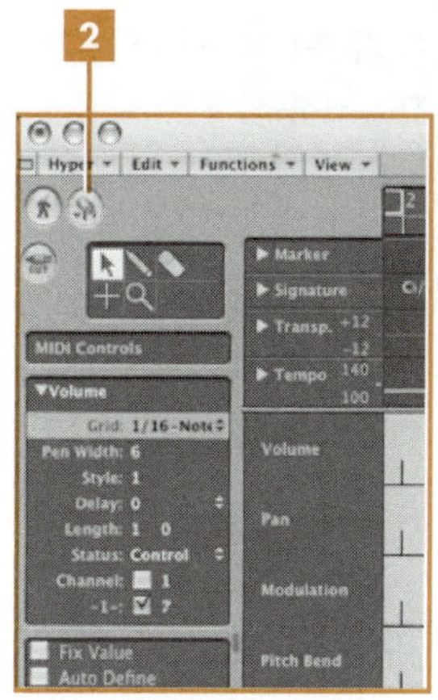

2 Link Button: Clicking the Link button will ensure that the contents of the Hyper Editor will always be linked to any window that is "topped," or in front of all other windows. You can double-click this button to engage "Contents Link" mode, in which the Hyper Editor will always show the data from whatever region is selected in the linked window.

Using the Catch and Link Buttons Together: Contents Catch

If you have both the Catch and Link buttons clicked, Logic will be in "Contents Catch" mode. This acts like Contents Link mode until you start playback. When Logic is playing and the Hyper Editor is in Contents Catch mode, the selected region will change as the Song Position Line moves along the song.

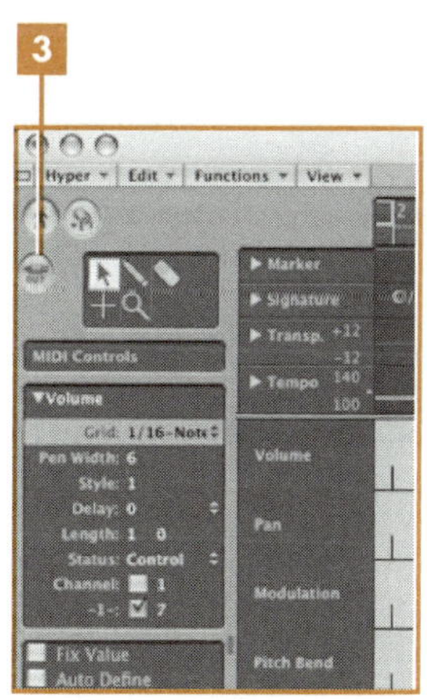

3 MIDI OUT Button: To hear your MIDI notes sound while you are editing, keep this button engaged.

Hyper Editor Toolbox

The Hyper Editor has five tools, one of which (the Crosshair tool) is unique.

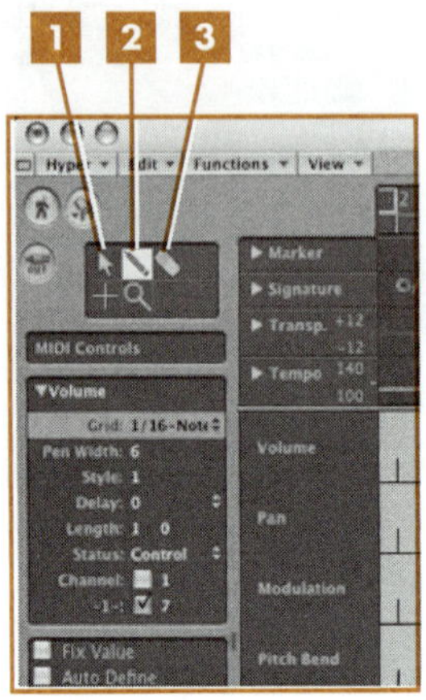

1 Pointer: Use the pointer to select one or more MIDI events.

2 Pencil: You can use the Pencil tool to create new notes.

3 Eraser: The Eraser tool deletes notes from the Hyper Editor.

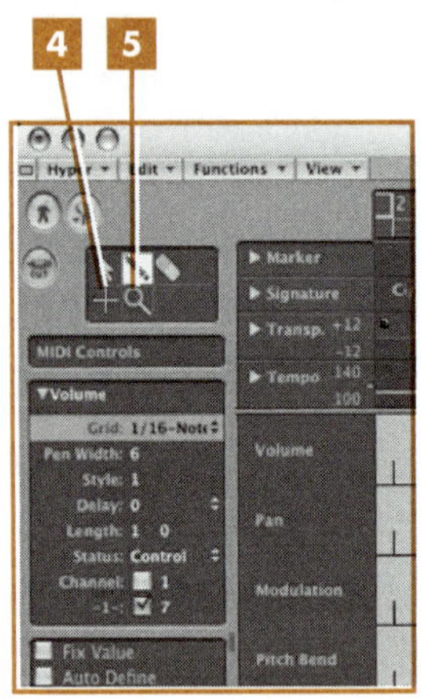

4 Crosshair: The Crosshair tool allows you to draw a straight line over a series of MIDI events. The MIDI events will change values to conform to the line you draw.

5 Magnifying Glass: You can use the Magnifying Glass tool to zoom into a specific area of the Hyper Editor.

Hyper Editor Parameter Boxes

Unlike the Matrix Editor, the Hyper Editor has two parameter boxes.

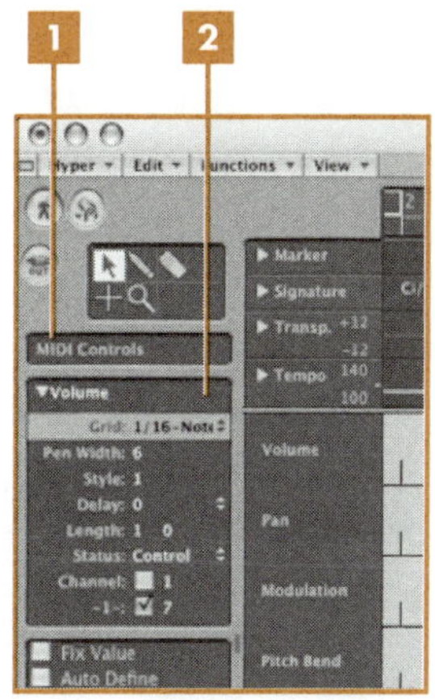

1. Hyper Set Box: Your available Hyper Sets can be selected from this pull-down menu.
2. Event Parameter Box: This parameter box includes the parameters for the MIDI event selected in the Event List

Hyper Editor Editing Area

The actual layout of the Hyper Editor is much like the Arrange window.

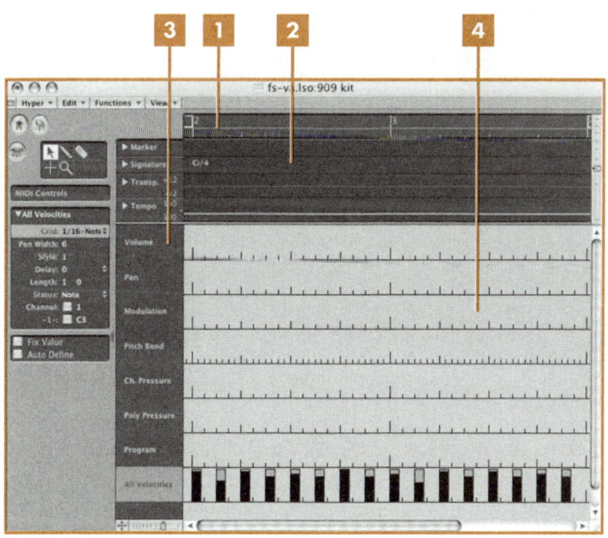

1. Bar Ruler: The Bar Ruler lets you know where you are in your song.
2. Global Tracks: You can choose to view your Global Tracks below the Bar Ruler.
3. Event List: This is where the events assigned to each grid lane are listed
4. Editing Area: This is the actual editing grid in which you can edit MIDI events.

Drum Editing in the Hyper Editor

Ok, now the fun stuff! You can use the Hyper Editor as a very precise drum editor, with a lane for each individual drum and a grid space for each note!

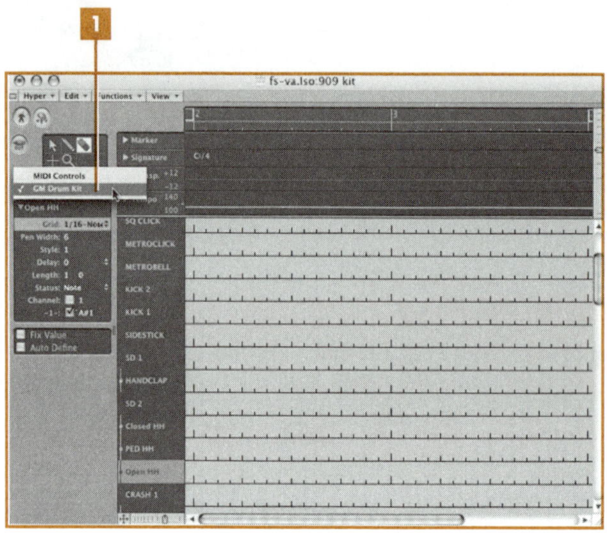

1. Change the Hyperset Box to display GM Drum Kit.

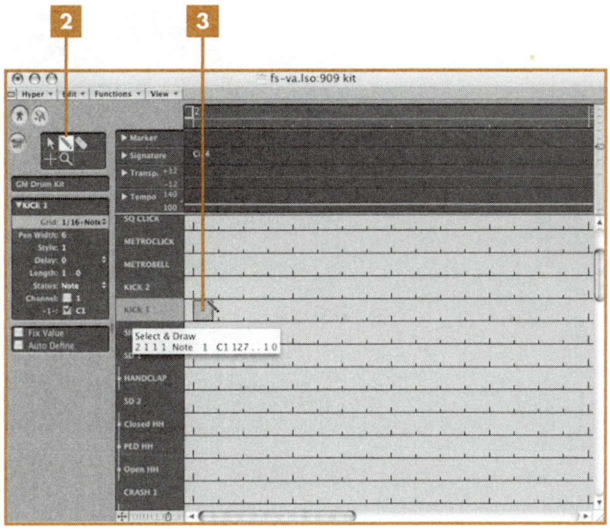

2 Select the Pencil tool in the Hyper Edit window.

3 Click in the editing area next to the drum event. This will add a note on that beat. If you click and drag within the note, the velocity of the note can be adjusted as well.

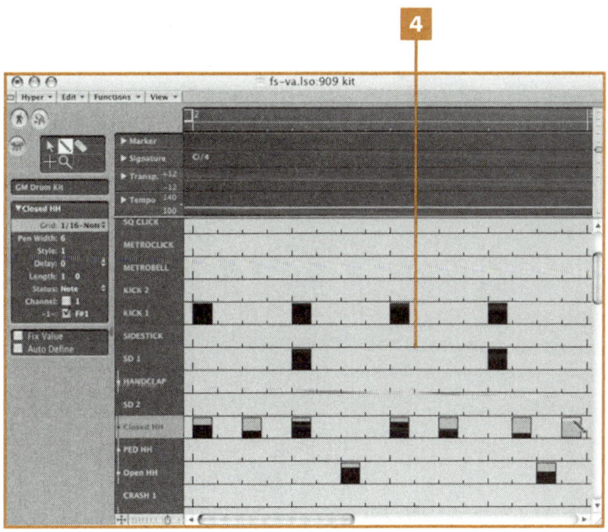

4 Continue adding notes on the various instruments of your drum kit and create some cool beats!

Hyper Editor as A Step Sequencer

Just because the Hyper Editor assumes that if you are programming notes it's for drums doesn't mean it has to be! If you are looking for an "analog step sequencer" style of grid in which to place your arpeggiated synth pulses and techno hits, you just might find that the Hyper Editor suits your needs as well. This will require creating your own Hyper Set, however, and there isn't enough room to explain this concept in this book. You can learn more about creating Hyper Sets in your Logic manual, or get a more thorough walk-through in *Logic Pro 7 Power!* by Orren Merton (Course Technology, 2004).

10 Working with MIDI: The Event List and Score Editor

You didn't think Logic offered only two MIDI editors did you? Of course not—and we've saved arguably the most powerful MIDI editors for this chapter. The Event List and Score Editor offer completely different views of your MIDI data than either the Matrix or Hyper Editor, even though the MIDI information itself is the same regardless of which editor you use. Depending on the type of MIDI data you wish to edit, the type of music you are editing, and your general working methods, you may prefer to edit MIDI in any of these editors or switch between a couple of them. That's one of the greatest things about Logic—it's not only one of the deepest sequencers, but one of the most flexible!

In this chapter, you will learn how to:

- Navigate the Event List
- Program and step-input MIDI into the Event List
- Resize notes in the Event List
- Move notes in the Event List
- Change the velocity of notes in the Event List
- Quantize notes in the Event List
- Edit MIDI Control Messages in the Event List
- Navigate the Score Editor
- Input notes in the Score Editor
- Print out a Score page

Navigating the Event List

The Event List Editor—usually just referred to as the Event List—shows you your MIDI data as one long text list. At first blush, this may seem old fashioned, uninspiring, boring...even downright *unmusical*. But the Event List is also the most precise of all the editors, since you are not editing graphical representations of your MIDI data, but the exact values themselves. In fact, many people use the Event List in tandem with one of the other MIDI editors, using, say, the Matrix Editor for graphic data, and then the Event List for fine tuning their edits. At any rate, the Event List may not be as "sexy" as some of the other editors, but it's certainly one of the most useful!

Here are the main elements of the Event List Editor.

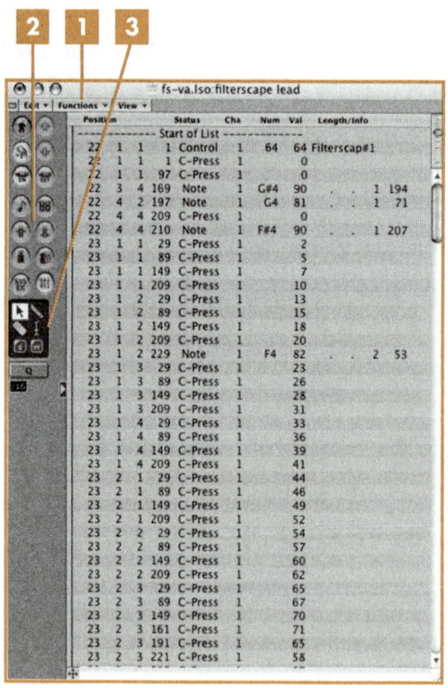

1 **Local Menus**: The Event List includes its own local menus, which are described below.

2 **Event List Buttons**: In addition to the standard MIDI editor Link, Catch, and MIDI IN and MIDI OUT buttons, the Event List offers one button for each type of MIDI event. You can use these buttons to filter out MIDI events you don't need to edit, or to view only one type of MIDI event.

3 **Event List Toolbox**: Here are the Event List tools, which are described below.

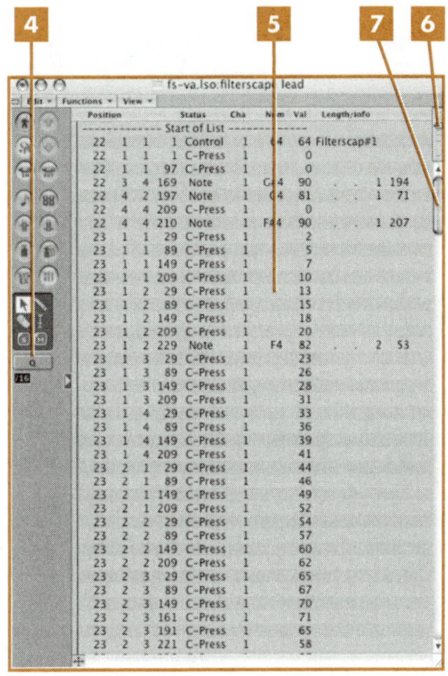

4 Quantize Grid Field and Button: You can select a quantize grid and quantize MIDI using the quantize grid and Quantize button.

5 List Area: This is where all the MIDI events that fill your region are displayed. This is the actual workspace in which you edit the MIDI notes.

6 Zoom Sliders: These sliders adjust vertically to focus the Matrix Editor workspace tightly on a few notes by increasing or decreasing the font size of the text.

7 Scroll Bars: These are standard Macintosh scroll bars that allow you to scroll the Event List window.

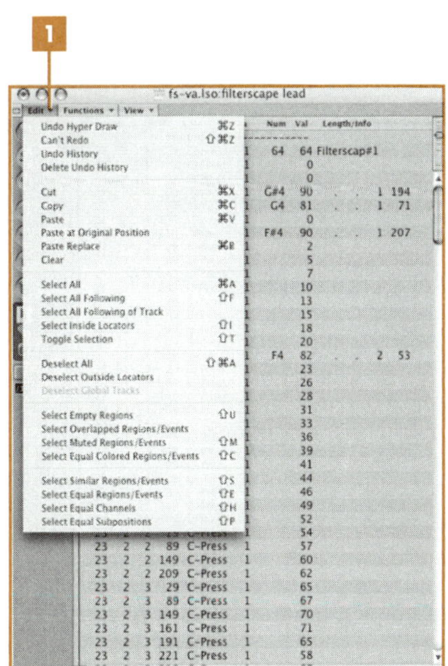

Event List Local Menus

The three local menus of the Matrix Editor include the Edit, Functions, and View menus.

1 Edit Menu: The Edit menu contains the standard Macintosh editing commands, along with MIDI event selection commands and options.

2 **Functions Menu**: The Functions menu consists of commands that process MIDI events.

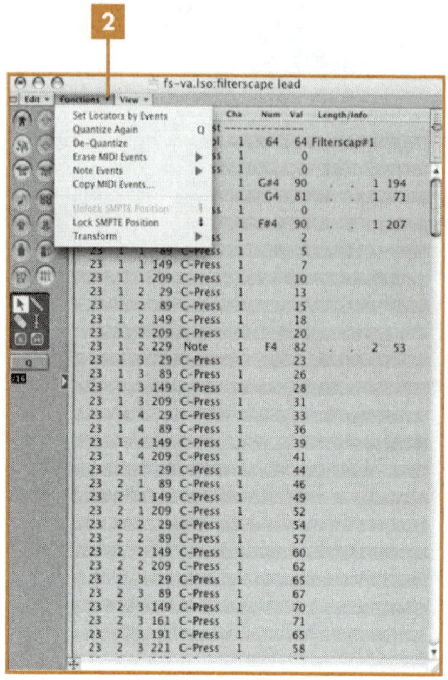

3 **View Menu**: The View menu contains all the various Event List view options.

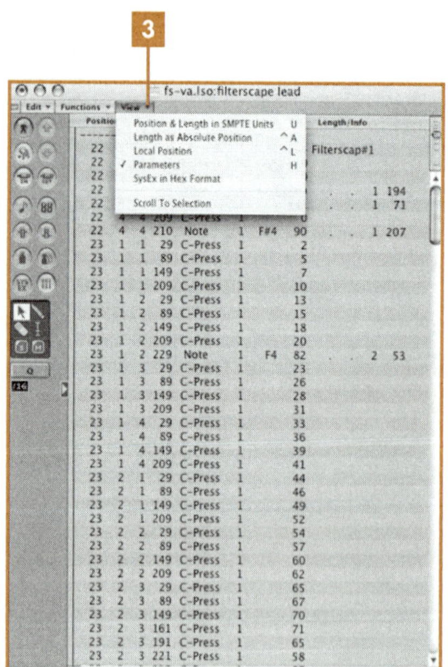

Event List Buttons

The Event List offers buttons to allow you to both link it to other windows and to record and play back MIDI.

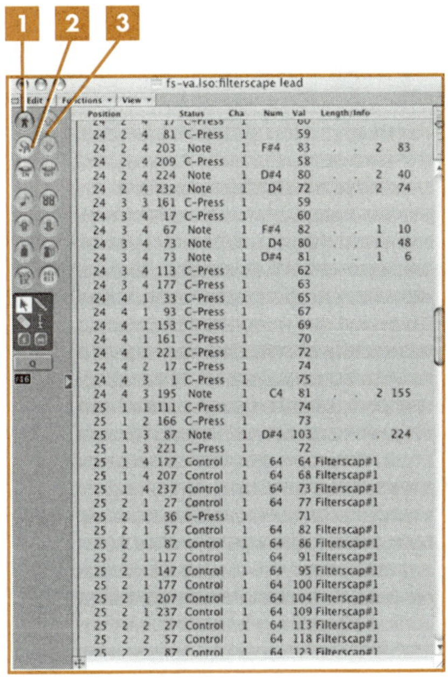

1 Catch Button: Clicking this button will ensure that the arrow at the left of the MIDI events will point to the currently playing or selected MIDI event. This is especially important when playing back or step-inputting MIDI. If you move the visible section of the Event List yourself, the Catch button is automatically disengaged so that you don't lose the section you're working on.

2 Link Button: Clicking the Link button will ensure that the contents of the Event List will always be linked to any window that is "topped," or in front of all other windows. You can double-click this button to engage "Contents Link" mode, in which the Event List will always show the contents of whatever region is selected in the linked window.

Using the Catch and Link Buttons Together: Contents Catch

If you have both the Catch and Link buttons clicked, Logic will be in "Contents Catch" mode. This acts like Contents Link mode until you start playback. When Logic is playing and the Event List is in Contents Catch mode, the selected region will change as the Song Position Line moves along the song.

3 Scroll Buttons: These buttons will move the events displayed in the Event List up or down one event. If an event is selected, that event stays selected.

4 **MIDI IN Button**: If this button is engaged, you can step-input MIDI notes directly into the Matrix Editor.

5 **MIDI OUT Button**: To hear your MIDI notes sound while editing, keep this button engaged.

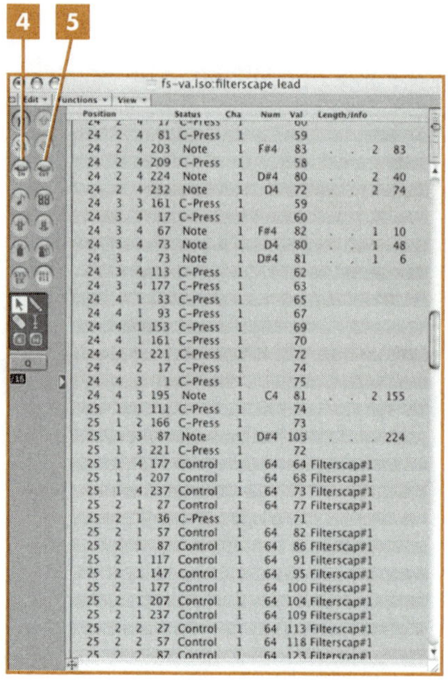

6 **MIDI Event Filter Buttons**: Each of these buttons toggles on or off the view of a specific type of MIDI event. Hovering your mouse over each button will reveal a tool tip that will tell you what each button is. Use these buttons to configure the Event List to display only those events you want to see.

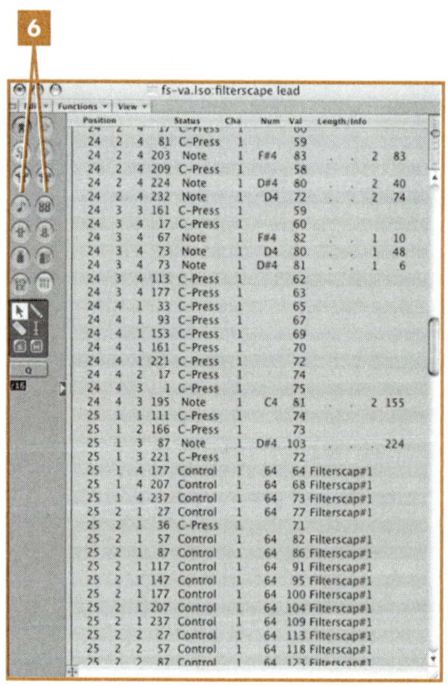

Event List Toolbox

While the Event List isn't primarily known as a graphic editor, it has a number of tools to help you work more efficiently.

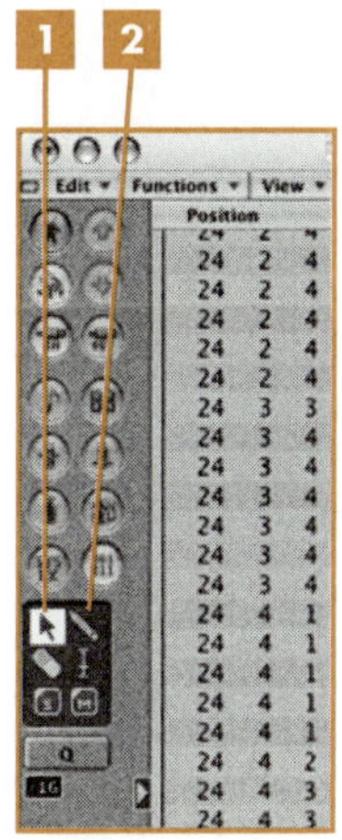

1. Pointer: The Pointer tool is your basic selection and move tool.
2. Pencil: You can use the Pencil tool to create new MIDI events.

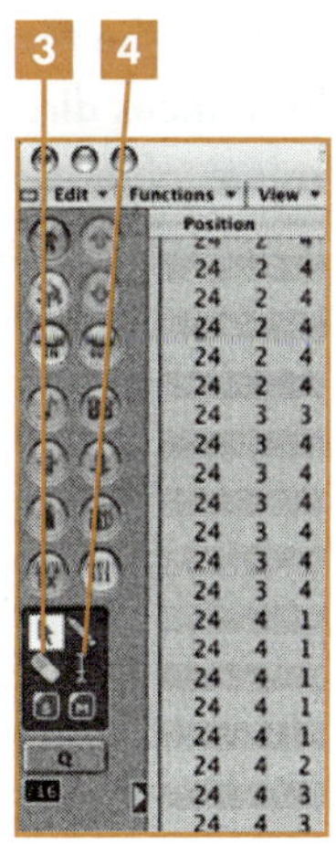

3. Eraser: The Eraser tool deletes MIDI events from the Event List.
4. Text Entry: If your Event List is not showing MIDI events, but the names of regions and folders from the Arrange window, this tool will allow you to rename them.

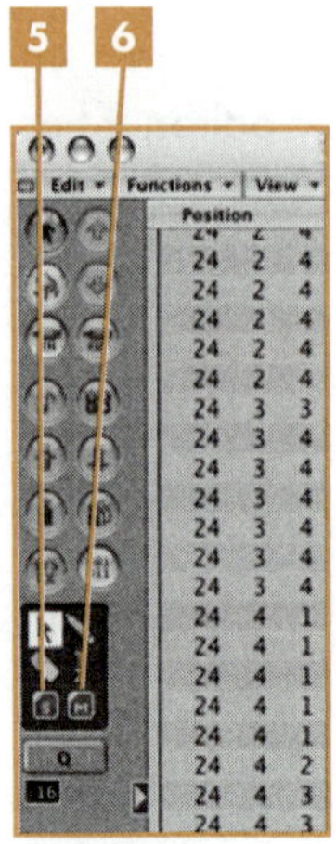

5 Solo: This tool will solo selected MIDI events.

6 Mute: You can use the Mute tool to mute selected MIDI events.

Entering MIDI Notes into the Event List

Just like the Matrix Editor, you can record or program MIDI performances directly into the Event List Editor. If you know the exact values of the MIDI you want to enter, or you like to see the precise results of your step input in list form, entering MIDI into the Event List might be just what you are looking for. Logic gives you two ways to do this: programming MIDI events using the Pencil tool, and step-inputting MIDI.

Programming MIDI Notes in the Event List

If you know exactly what you want your MIDI part to be, or you just want to add a few MIDI events to an existing MIDI region, you can use the Pencil tool to quickly create MIDI events.

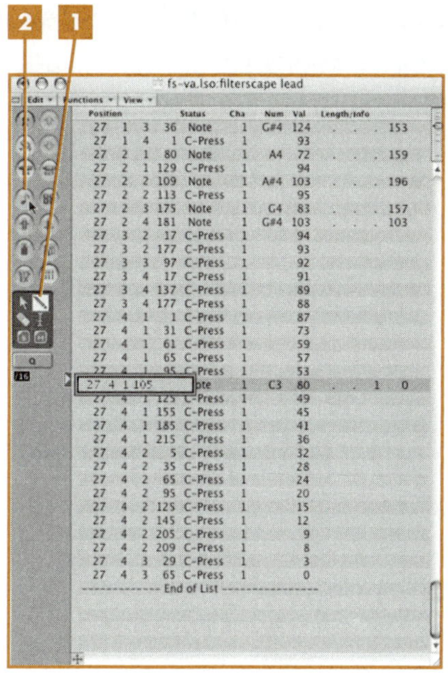

1. **Select** the **Pencil** tool in the Event window.
2. **Click** on the **Toggle Note Events** button to add a note at the Song Position Line. The default is a C3 note with a velocity of 80.

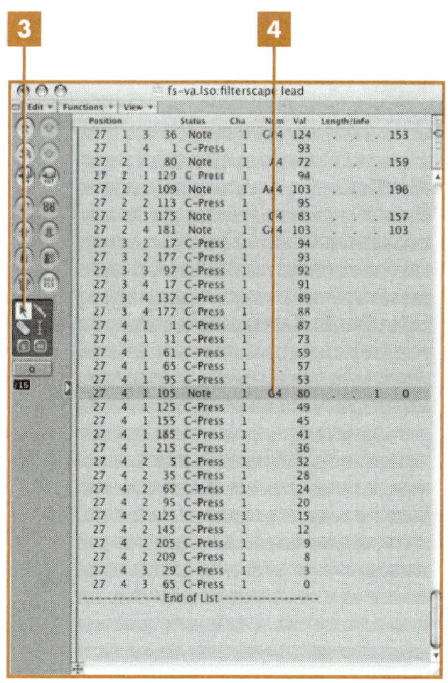

3. **Select** the **Pointer** tool.
4. **Click** and **drag** up or down on the **note value** to change it to the appropriate note for your song.

Step-Inputting MIDI Notes into the Event List

Like the Matrix Editor, you can use Logic's Step Input feature to enter MIDI into the Event List.

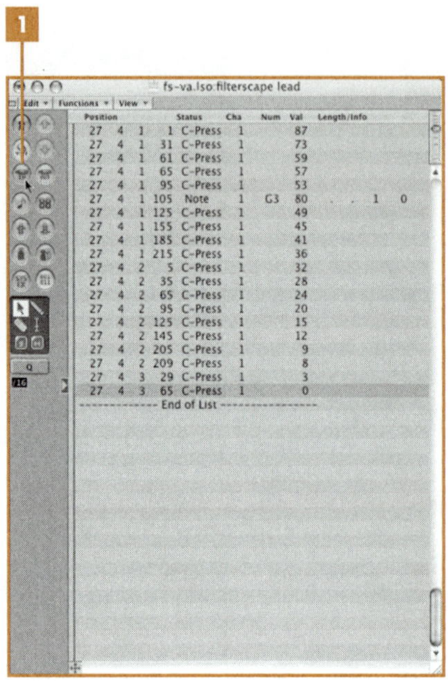

1. **Press** the **MIDI IN** button to turn it on.

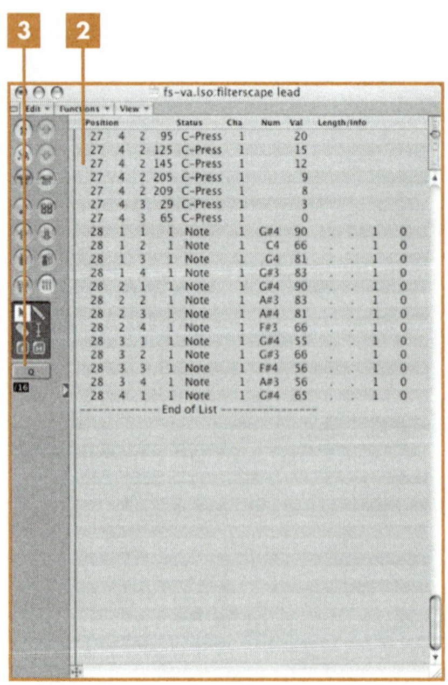

2. **Play** the **notes** on your MIDI controller, and you will see them appear in the Event list.
3. Notes will be added at values determined by the Quantization value.

Step Entry from Your Computer Keyboard or Mouse

While step input lends itself beautifully to using a MIDI controller for note entry, Logic lets you use either your computer keyboard or a mouse. First of all, every note in the Western scale has a key command that you can assign in the Key Command window; this will allow you to type in notes and have them appear in the Event Editor. You can also select Windows > Step Input Keyboard to open a special on-screen keyboard specifically for step recording MIDI notes, as shown below.

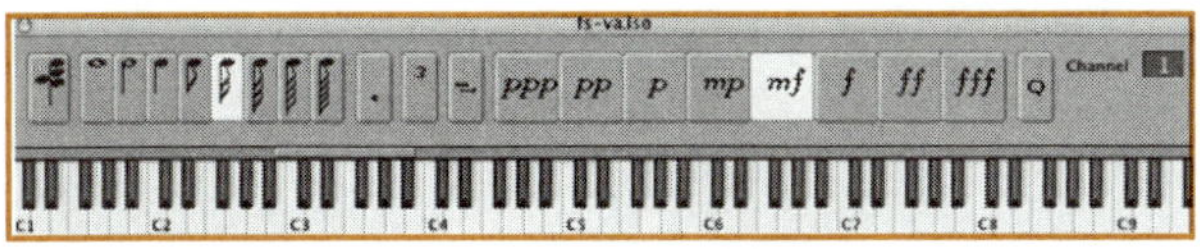

As you can see, Logic's step input features are very flexible, and they offer a way for everyone to input MIDI into the Matrix Editor.

Moving MIDI Notes

You can easily change the pitch and position of notes numerically using the Event List.

To change the position of a note:

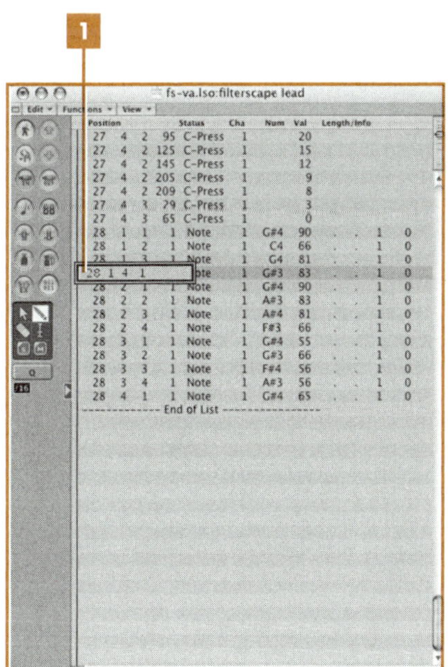

1 Double-click on the position value. This will highlight the current value.

2 **Enter new values** for the position of the note, and **press Return** to commit the change.

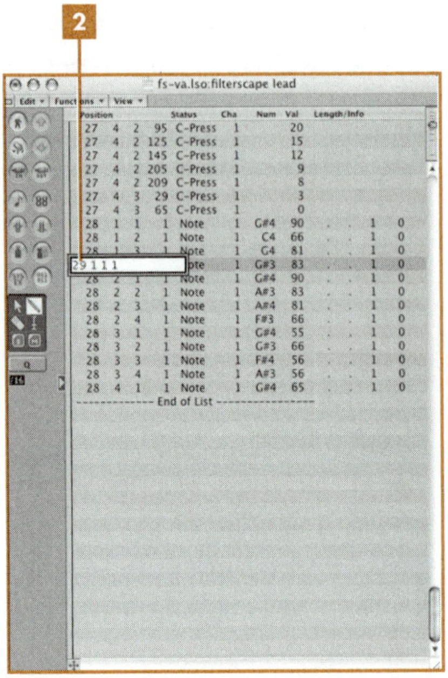

Dragging to Change Values

You can also change a value in the Event Editor by clicking and dragging up or down on the parameter you wish to change.

To change the value of a note:

1 **Double-click** on the **note value**. This will highlight the current value.

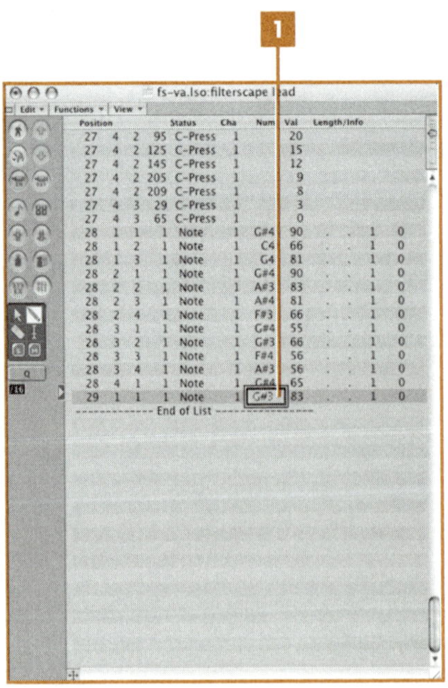

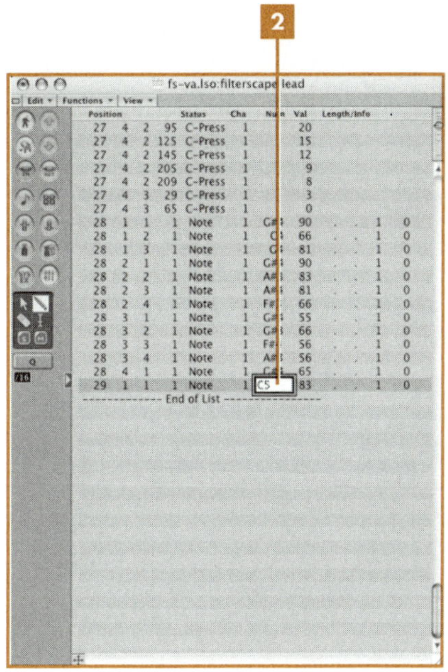

2 Enter the new value of the note, and press Return to commit the change.

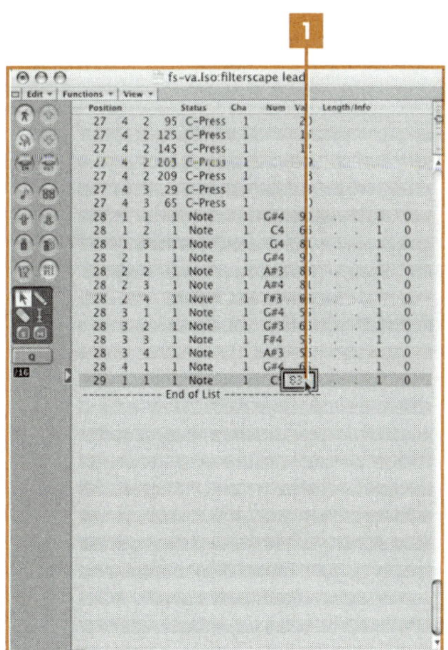

Changing the Velocity of MIDI Notes

Changing the Velocity of MIDI notes in the Event List is very similar to changing the pitch and position:

1 Double-click on the velocity value. This will highlight the current value.

2 **Enter** the **new velocity value** for the note, and **press Return** to commit the change.

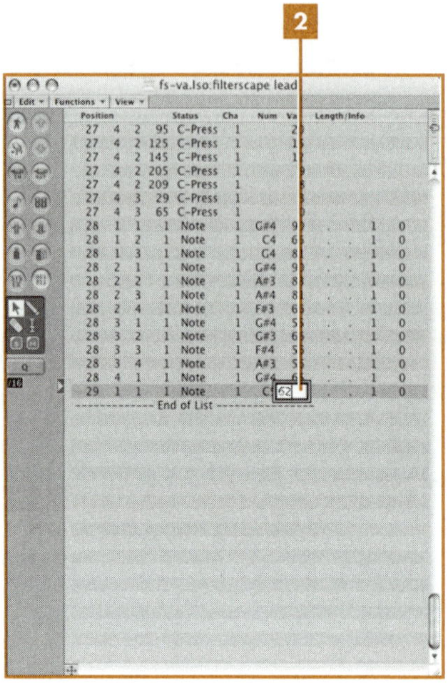

Changing Pitch and Velocity from Your MIDI Controller

If you select a note in the Matrix Editor, you can actually use your MIDI keyboard controller to change the pitch of the note or to change its velocity. By double-clicking the MIDI IN button, every time you select a note you will be able to change its velocity and pitch by pressing a note on your MIDI keyboard. The note in the Matrix Editor will change pitch and velocity based on which MIDI note you trigger and its velocity. The note will retain the timing and length it already had.

Resizing MIDI Notes

Since the Event List offers very precise numeric entries for every MIDI event, it's a great editor to use for resizing MIDI notes to a specific value.

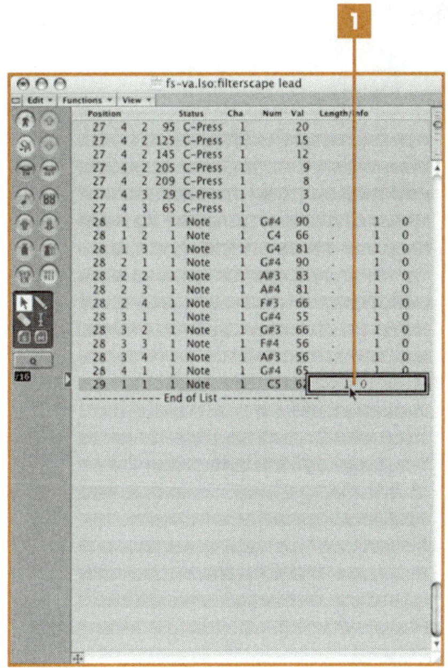

1 Double-click on the note length. This will highlight the current value.

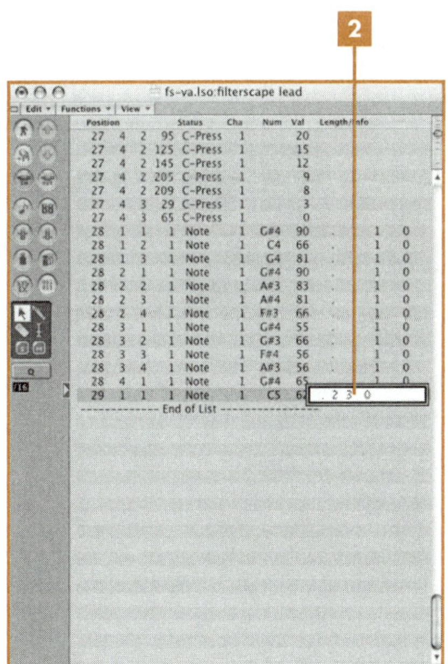

2 Enter the new length for the note and press Return to commit the change.

Quantizing MIDI Notes

Quantizing is explained in the previous chapter. If you are working in the Event List and want to quantize your data, you can easily use the Quantize grid and button for this purpose.

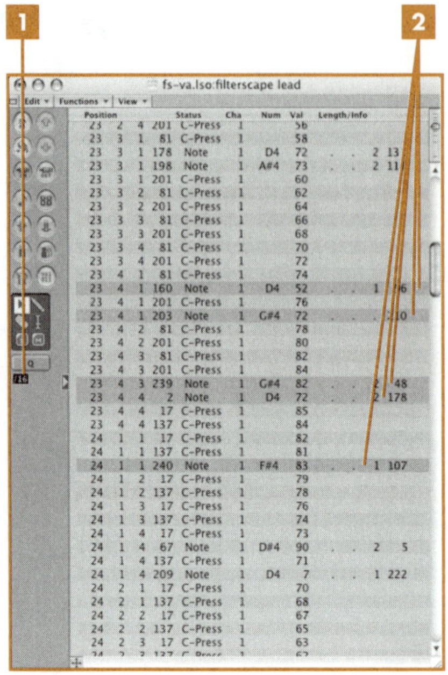

1. **Select** the **Quantization grid** you want your notes to snap to.
2. **Select** the **note** you want to Quantize. (SHIFT + click to select multiple notes.)

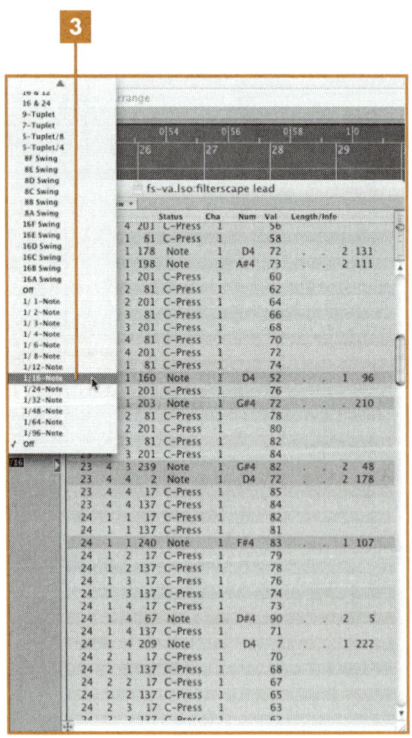

3. **Click** and **hold** the **Quantize** button to turn quantize on, and **select** the **value** you want the notes to snap to.

Navigating the Score Editor

The Score Editor is perhaps the deepest editor in Logic—which makes sense, considering music notation is a language unto itself! Unlike the other editors, its workspace basically resembles a piece of notation paper. In general, for users who write traditional music charts or scores, the Score Editor is the most important editor in Logic; as some film composers say, they practically "live" in the Score Editor. For other users who don't read or write music notation, the Score Editor will not play a major part in their Logic experience.

A complete exploration of the Score Editor is simply not possible in the amount of space we have to discuss MIDI editors. In fact, in Appendix B you'll find a link to a tutorial on the Logic Score Editor that is over 200 pages all by itself! But we wanted to at least bring it to your attention, along with a couple of its most basic uses.

First, let's get comfortable navigating around the Score Editor.

Score Editor Local Menus

The Score Editor's seven local menus share the same Edit and Functions menu as the Matrix Editor, but the rest are unique to the Score Editor.

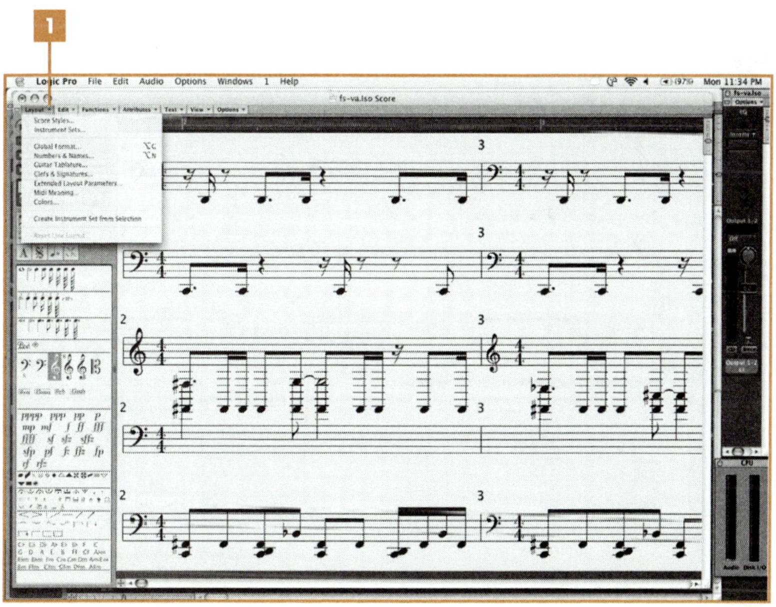

1 Layout Menu: The Layout menu contains options for how to format your score.

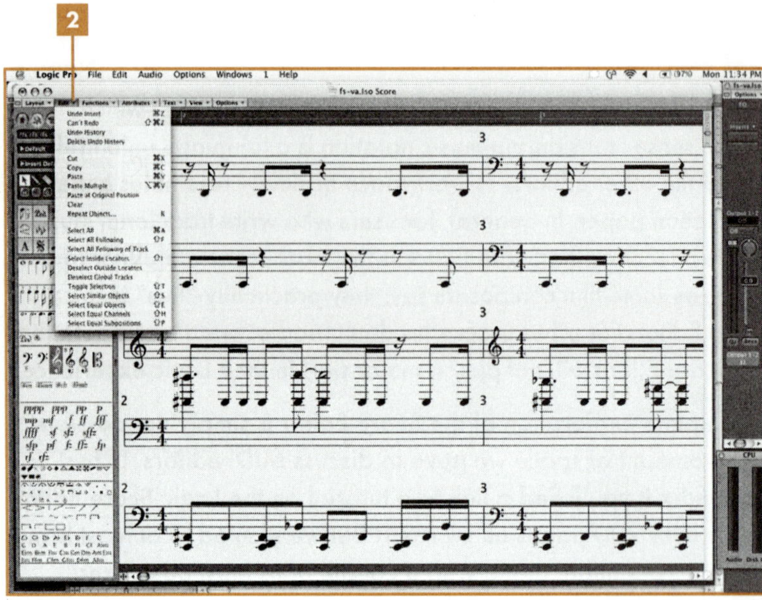

2 Edit Menu: **The Edit menu contains the standard Macintosh editing commands, along with MIDI event selection commands and options.**

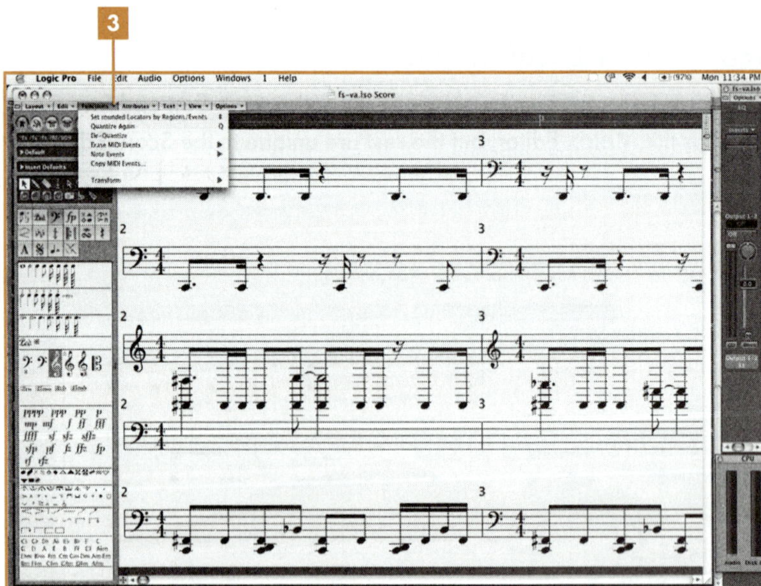

3 Functions Menu: **The Functions menu consists of commands that process MIDI events.**

4 **Attributes Menu**: The Attributes menu contains over 37 different options for altering the attributes of any selected notes.

5 **Text Menu**: The Text menu offers a standard selection of text formatting options.

6 **View Menu**: The View menu contains all the various Global Track and Score Editor view options.

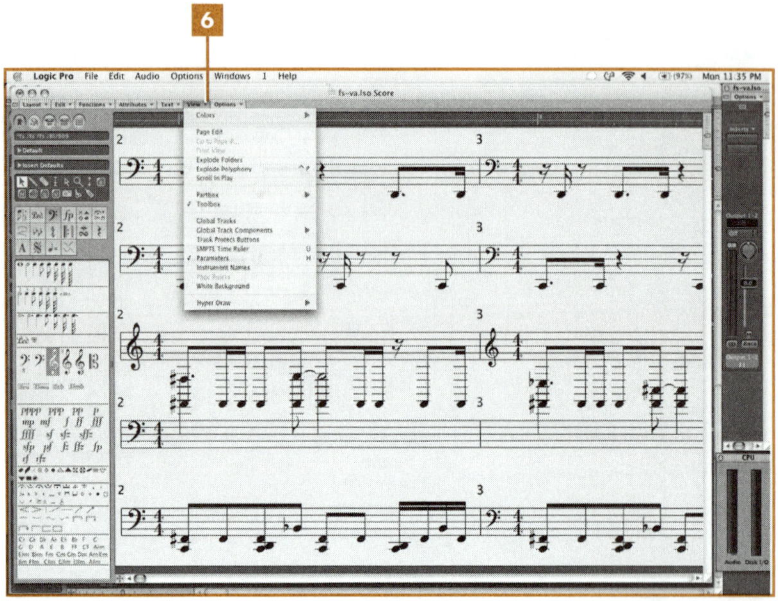

7 **Options Menu**: The Options menu contains a few miscellaneous commands that relate to your score.

Score Editor Parameter Area

The Parameter area of the Score Editor has some elements in common with the other MIDI editors, as well as some that are unique unto itself:

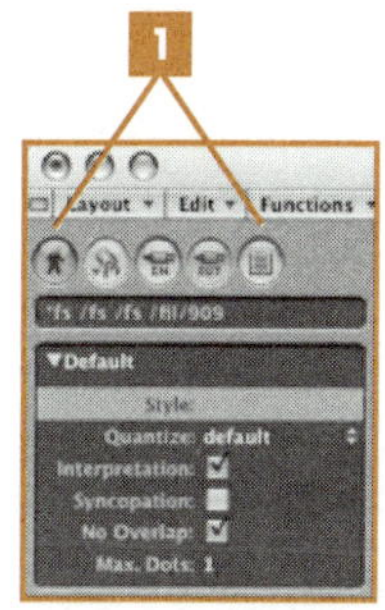

1 Score Editor Buttons: The Score Editor offers the same Link, Catch, MIDI IN, and MIDI OUT buttons as the Matrix Editor and Event List. The one unique button is the Page View button, which toggles a full-page layout view.

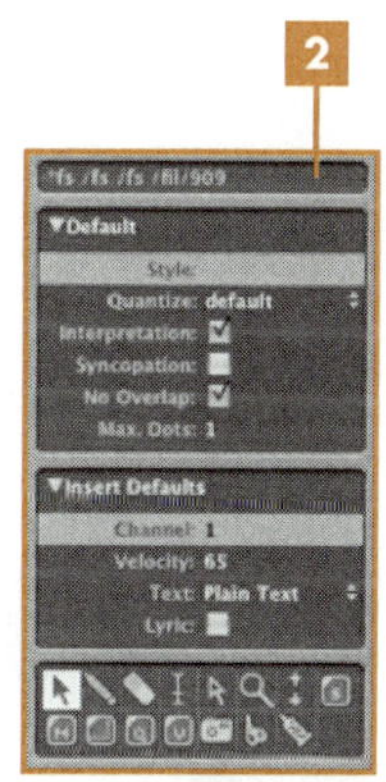

2 Score Editor Parameter Boxes: The Score Editor offers parameter boxes for Instrument Set selection, Region Display parameters, and an Event parameter box.

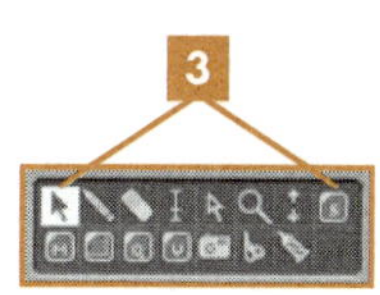

3 Score Editor Toolbox: The Score Editor Toolbox includes standard graphic editing tools, as well as some unique tools to split polyphonic voices and export sections of your score to a graphics application.

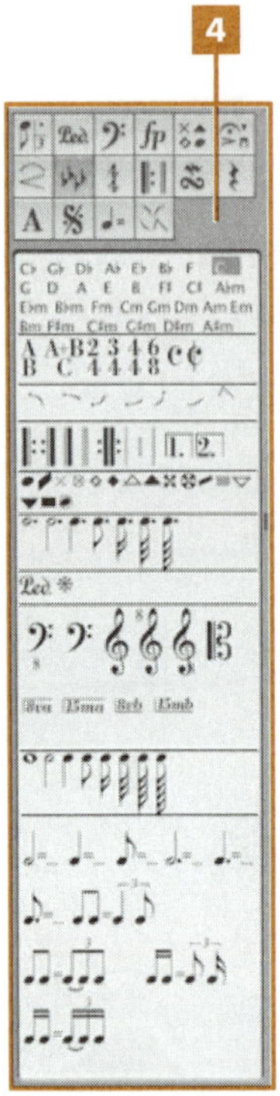

4 **Score Editor Partbox**: The Partbox includes all the various musical notation parts that you might like to you use in your score. Simply select a part and drag it into your score!

Score Editor Editing Area

This is the actual "workspace" of the Score Editor.

1 **Bar Ruler**: The Bar Ruler lets you know where you are in your song.

2 **Global Tracks**: You can choose to view your Global Tracks below the Bar Ruler.

3 **Editing Area**: This is the actual "notation lane" in which you can enter and edit MIDI events.

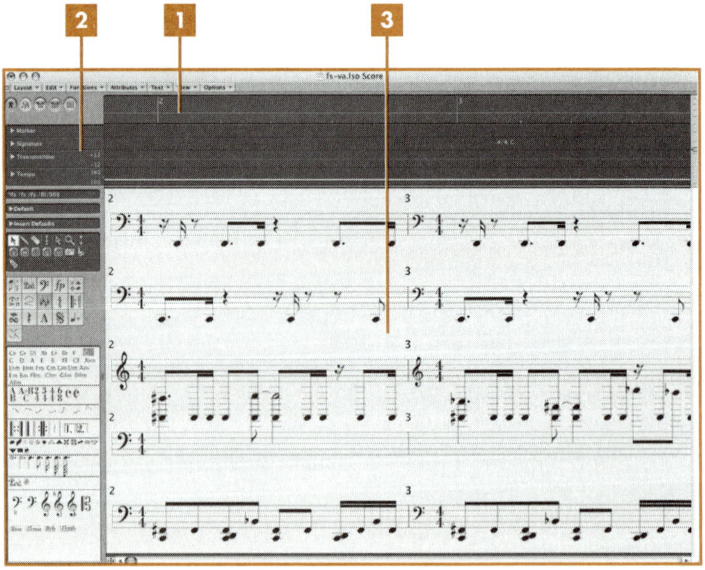

Entering Notes in the Score Editor

There are a number of ways to enter MIDI into the Score Editor. You can drag parts from the Partbox, as mentioned in the "Score Editor Parameter Area" subsection above. You can also record a part in real time, just like you would in the Arrange window. The main way you'd enter MIDI notes in the Score Editor, however, is via step input using your MIDI controller.

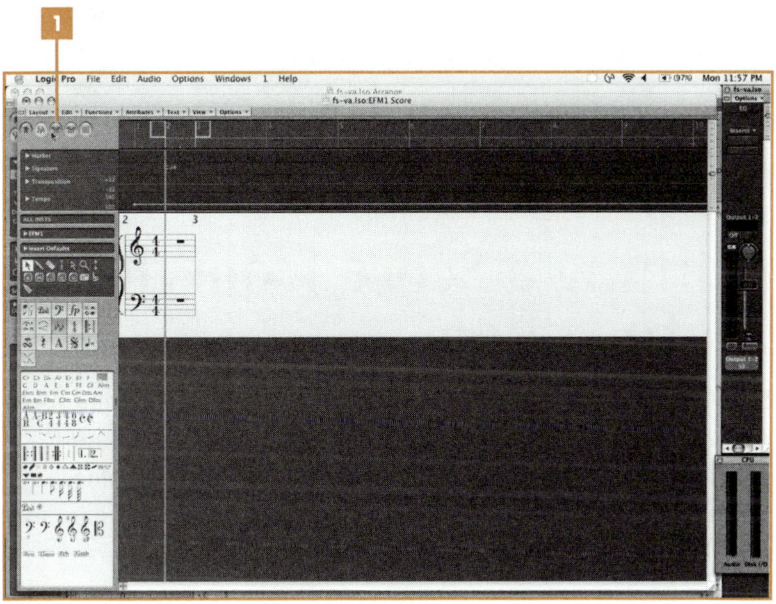

1 Select the MIDI IN button.

2. **Play the notes on your MIDI controller.**
3. **The default length of the notes will be set by the Grid value in the transport.**

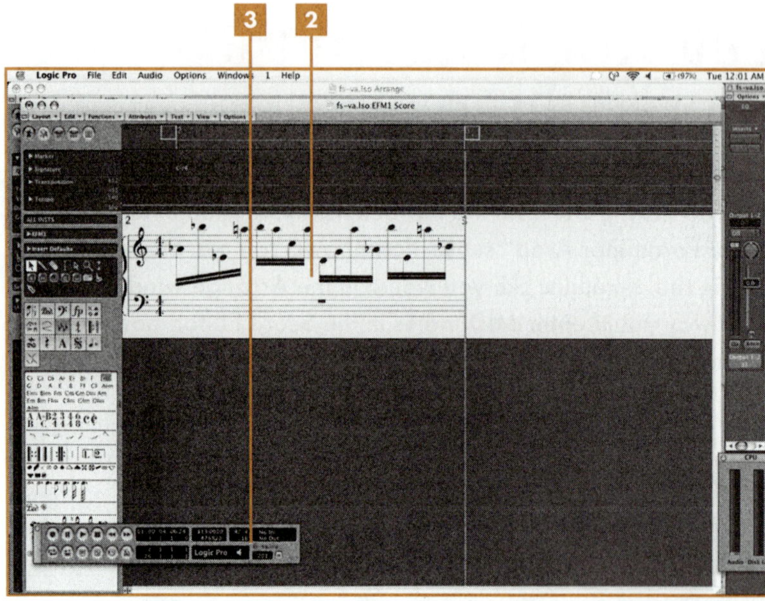

Printing a Score from the Score Editor

Even if you don't enter or edit MIDI inside the Score Editor, if you are working with musicians who work from musical score charts, you can still print out MIDI parts recorded and edited in other areas of Logic. This is perhaps the main use of the Score Editor for people who do not write in musical notation themselves.

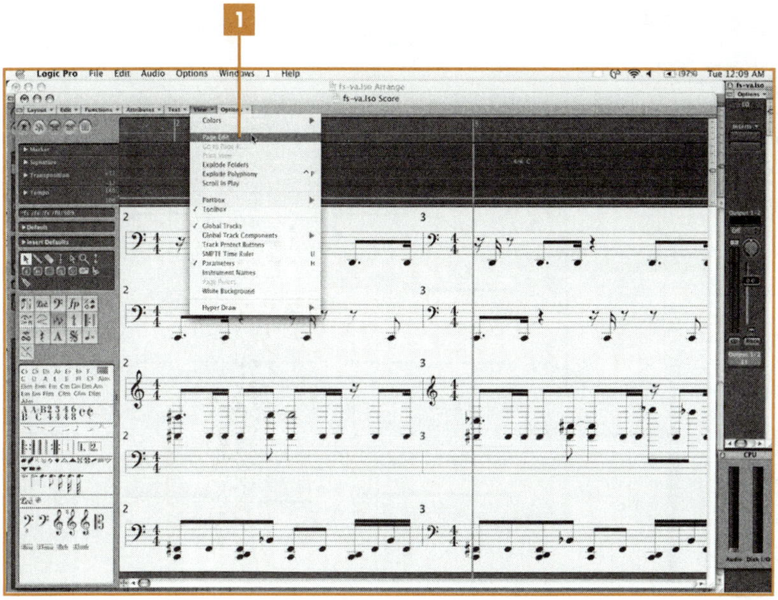

1 Go to View > Page Edit. This will allow you to see all the staves on a page-by-page basis.

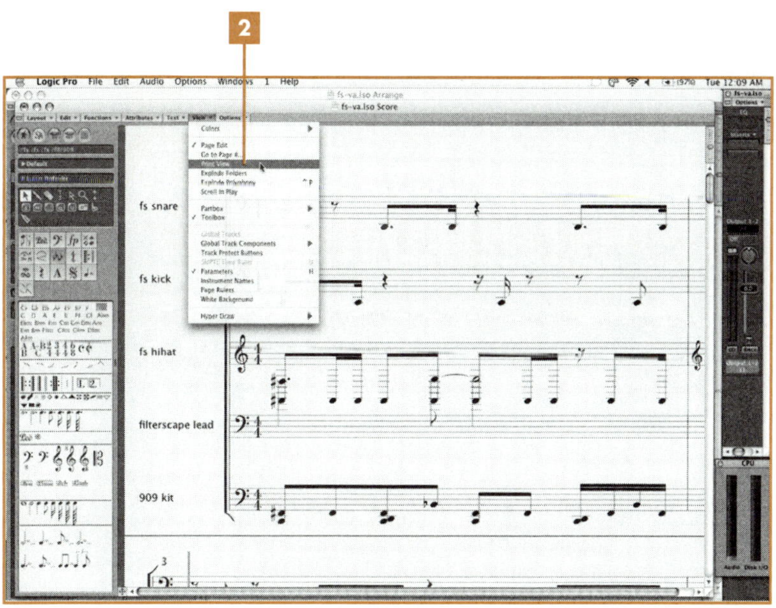

2 Go to View > Print View. This will show the borders and alignment of the pages before printing.

3 **Go to File > Print** as you would normally print a document, and print out your score!

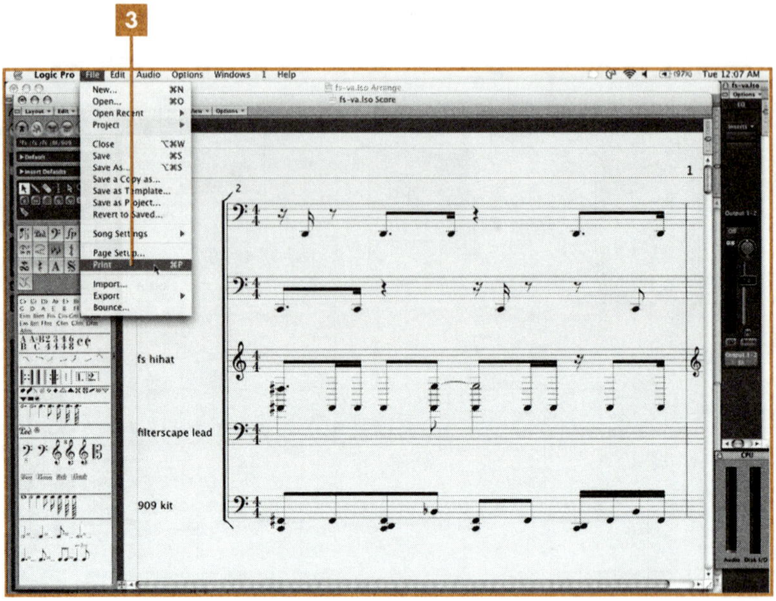

11 Mixing Your Project

It used to be that, if you wanted to mix and process your song, you needed to spend bucket loads of money to go to a professional recording studio that had a huge mixing desk and lots of external processors. Today, you can do all of these things right inside Logic! Many a commercially released song has been mixed using the plug-in processors and mixing capability of Logic, and you will no doubt find that you can use Logic to give your own material a very professional mix.

If you're familiar with how to use a hardware mixer and hardware processors, the concept of Logic's mixer should be easy to grasp. We've already explored the individual channel strip a little in previous chapters; now it's just a matter of learning how to mix them together and using Logic's plug-ins to process your material.

In this chapter, you will learn how to:

- Open the Track Mixer
- Use the Track Mixer view buttons
- Use Insert effects
- Use Send effects
- Use Groups (Logic Pro only)
- Spread your tracks in the stereo panorama
- Adjust the volume of one or more channels
- Use an Aux Object as a master channel strip for a group of channels

Opening the Track Mixer

Logic actually has two mixers: the Track Mixer and the Audio Mixer. The Track Mixer is adaptive, meaning that it consists of each track in your Arrange window; as you add an audio or MIDI track to the Arrange window, it will be automatically added to the Track Mixer. There is also the Audio Mixer, which is part of Logic's Environment window. This mixer contains all the Audio objects you set up in Chapter 2 in the Logic Setup Assistant, but it doesn't adapt to reflect the tracks in your song. Also, it doesn't include channel strips for your MIDI channels. For these reasons, we prefer to use the Track Mixer as our mixer of choice.

The first step, of course, is to open the Track Mixer! There are two ways you can do this. First, you can simply double-click any audio track in the Arrange window.

1 Select a track in the Arrange window and double-click on the track name.

2 The Track Mixer will open in a new window.

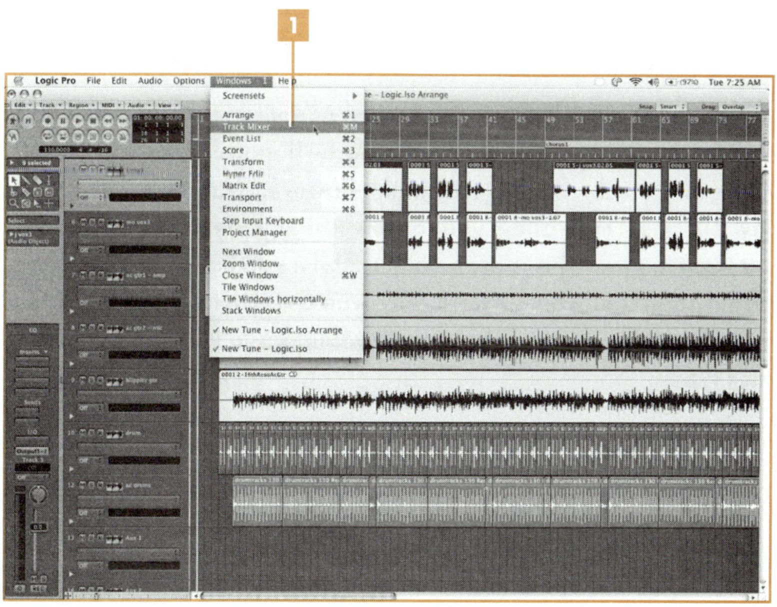

You can also simply open a Track Mixer window from the Windows menu.

1 Go to Windows > Track Mixer.

2 The Track Mixer will open in a new window.

Key Command Alert: Track Mixer

You can also open the Track Mixer by pressing COMMAND + M.

Track Mixer View Buttons

Unlike the other windows in Logic, you're not really going to need to use the Local menus or normal window buttons of the Track Mixer very much, if at all. You might, however, want to use the view buttons. These allow you to view just those types of tracks that you want to view. This is especially useful if you have lots of tracks in your song and want to work only with a single track type at a time. Here's how you can use the view buttons to view only a single track type.

1 Select the type of track you want to limit the view to—in this instance, we've selected Track, which corresponds to the Audio Tracks present in the Arrange window.

2 Only those tracks are displayed.

You can also have more than one view button engaged to limit your view to only certain track types:

1 Hold SHIFT and press a second type of track you want to view.

2 The newly selected type of track will be added to the Track Mixer.

Finally, you can use the Track Mixer to view all the objects you created originally with the Logic Setup Assistant using the Global button:

1 Press the Global button in the Track Mixer.

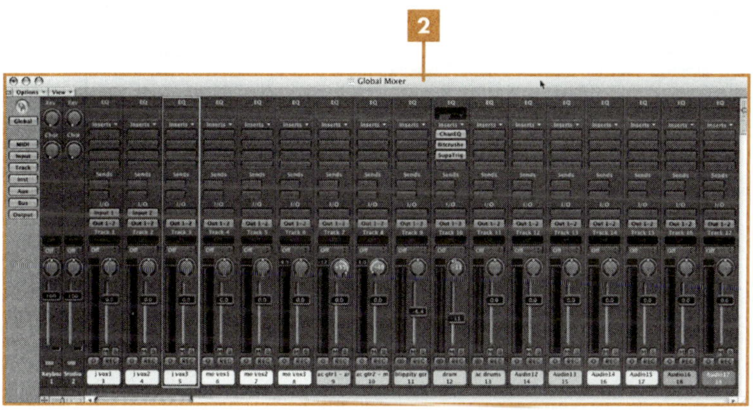

2 All the objects will appear and all the buttons will be selected. If some buttons remain unlit because of a previous Mixer configuration, you can SHIFT + click to add them as you did above.

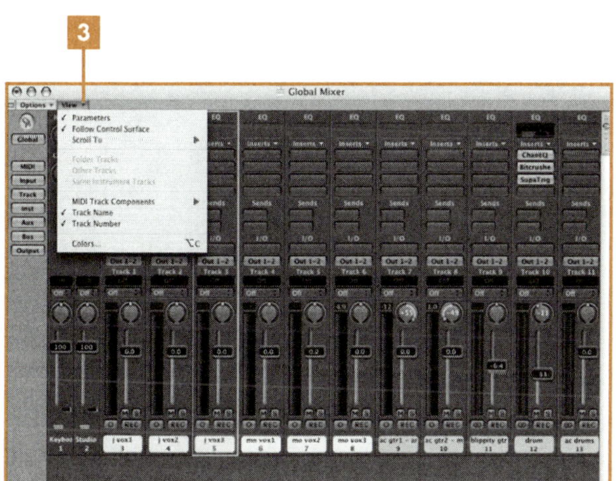

3 View Menu: The View menu contains all the various Event List view options.

Using Insert Effects

Do you wish you could brighten up the sound of your tracks just a little bit? Are the dynamics (difference between loud passages and soft passages) too jarring? Would you like to run your audio through a really creative, sound-mangling processor? These are the kinds of things you can do with Insert effects! Insert effects are so named because you are literally "inserting" a processor into your audio's signal path. Logic Express gives you up to 4 Insert slots per channel strip. Logic Pro gives you up to 15 Insert slots per channel strip.

Logic Express comes with over 38 professional quality effects. Logic Pro comes with over 64 professional quality effects. Not only that, but you can also buy third-party effects that literally "plug-in" to Logic, just as you can buy third-party software synthesizers. These plug-ins must support the Audio Units format. There is no limit to how many plug-ins you can have installed on your computer at one time, but you can never use more effects as Inserts for a single channel strip than the limit of your version of Logic (Express or Pro).

Instantiating a Plug-In on a Channel Strip

The first step in using an effect is to instantiate that effect into an Insert slot of one of your channel strips.

1 Click and hold on the first Insert slot of a track until the plug-in menu appears.

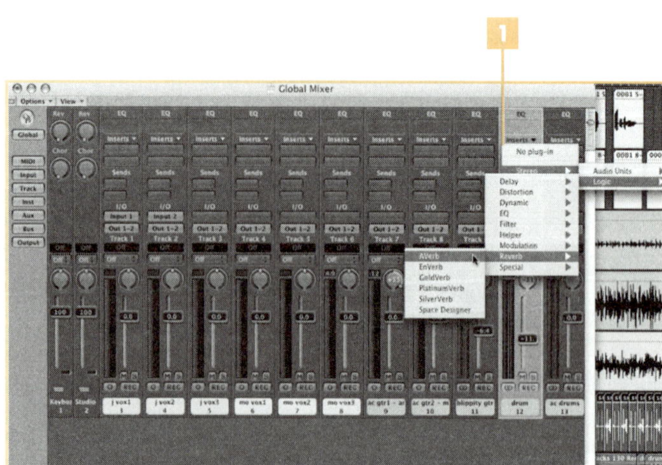

2 **Choose** the kind of **effect** you want to add to the track. The plug-in interface will open and you'll see the name of the plug-in in the Insert slot.

3 **Add** a **second plug-in** to the track. You'll see that Logic automatically adds a third slot for another plug-in when the first two are used!

Loading and Saving Inserts via the Insert Menu

Let's say you have a favorite set of plug-ins that you like to use together. Rather than having to instantiate all of them individually on every channel strip you wish to use them in, Logic lets you load and save sets of Insert effects on each channel strip via the Insert menu on each channel strip. For Audio Instrument tracks, this includes the instrument as well. If you look by the word "Insert" on each channel strip, you'll notice a downward arrow. If you click-hold on this menu, you'll get the Insert menu shown below.

When you select Open, notice that Apple includes a fair amount of preset channel strips of their own for you to try out. Give them a try—some of them are really well done!

Keep in mind that you can only use an Insert strip on the same type of channel strip on which it was originally saved. In other words, if you save an Audio Instrument channel strip, you can only use it with other Audio Instrument channel strips.

Adjusting Effects Parameters

Once you have instantiated your effect, the fun begins! Usually, the default settings of the effect you add to your channel strip will not be exactly what you want. Luckily, just about every effect has a host of parameters you can use to fine tune the effect until it's just right.

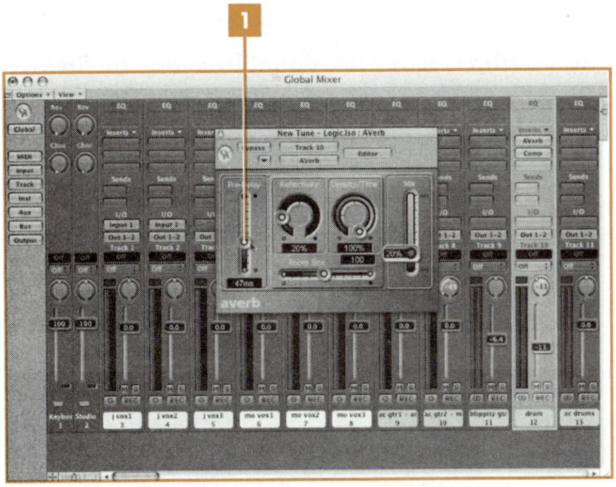

1 Use the mouse to adjust parameters on the plug-in to achieve the effect you like. Logic allows you to listen to the song play as you adjust the parameters.

2 Adjust as many parameters as necessary to achieve your desired result.

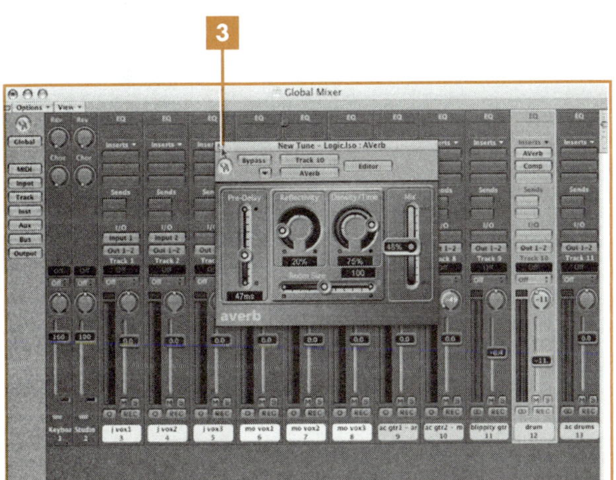

3 Press the Close button on the plug-in window when you are done.

Using Plug-In Side Chains

Some effects allow the signal from one audio track to control various effect parameters. These effects will have a side chain. You already learned how to use side chains with Audio Instruments in Chapter 8, "Working with Audio Instruments." Here is how you use them with Insert effects:

1. In this example, we'll use a vocal on Track 3 to "duck," or reduce, the level of a drum loop using the side chain on the Compressor plug-in. Select Track 3 in the Side Chain menu.

2. By adjusting the parameters of the Compressor while the song plays, we can set how much the vocal track reduces the volume of the drum loop and then how quickly the loop returns to its normal volume when the vocal is silent.

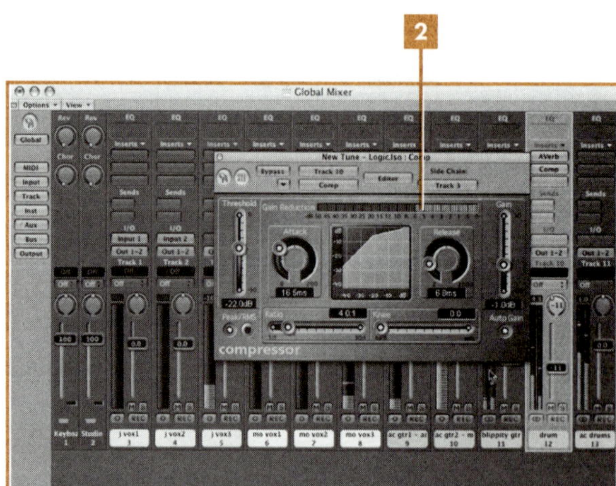

Using Send Effects

Insert effects are great for when you want to process a single channel. But what if you want to use the same effect to process more than one channel? For these situations, instead of wanting to insert an effect into the signal chain of a single channel, you'll want to *send* your audio to an effect that is on a separate channel strip of its own. The way you do this is by using slots on your channel strip named—appropriately enough—Sends! Sends are also useful because you can adjust how much signal from the various channels you want to send. This is advantageous because all the channels that use a given Send can deliver a different amount of signal, instead of all of them delivering the same level of audio.

Setting up Send effects is more complicated than setting up Insert effects, because you not only have to set up the Send on your channel strip, but you need to set up the effect you want to use on that separate channel strip. The special channel strips you'll set up your Send effects on is called a Bus Object, because you can send, or *bus*, any other audio channel to it.

Here we add a chorus effect to a bus and then have two channel strips send signal to that chorus effect.

1 SHIFT + click the Bus button to display your buses in the Track Mixer. If you don't see any when the button is pressed, add a Bus track to the Arrange window first.

2 Add a Chorus plug-in to the Bus track.

3 Click and hold on the first Send slot of an Audio Track and assign it to the bus. In this case, the chorus is on Bus 1.

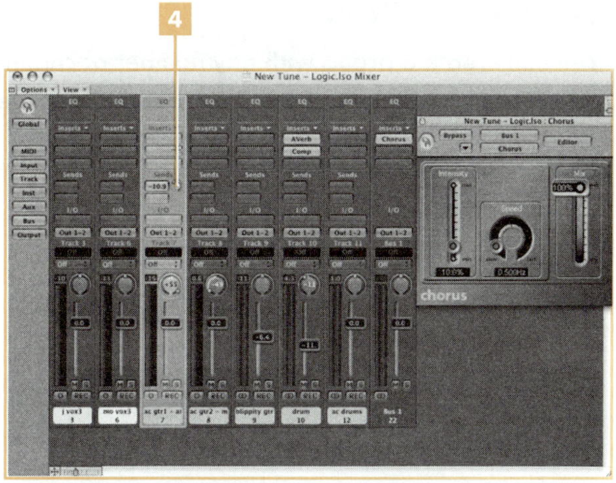

4 Click and drag the mouse on the Send level of the Audio Track—this will control how much of the Audio Track signal is being sent to the bus.

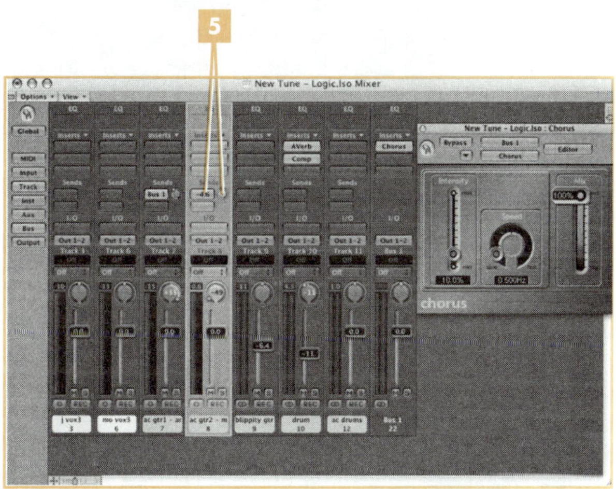

5 Repeat steps 3 and 4 on another Audio Track to send an additional track to the same bus!

Using Groups (Logic Pro Only)

Sometimes, you'll have a group of tracks that you want to always adjust together. For example, let's say that your song has four tracks of background vocals. You may want to keep them in a "background vocal group" so that any changes you make to one channel strip, such as turning down the volume, will be made to all of them. Logic Pro makes this easy by offering the ability to group tracks together for both editing and mixing. Here we'll walk through both setting up and using a group.

Setting Up a Group

You can create a group with any number of channels, and you can add channels to a group that has already been created.

To create a group:

1 Click in the Group field on a track to open the Group menu. Select the group you want to create.

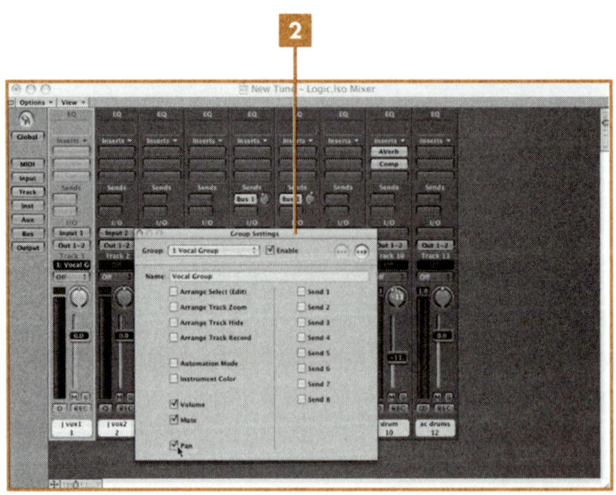

2 The Group Settings dialog box will open once you select a group. Here you can name the group and choose the parameters you want the group to follow.

If you want to add a channel to an already formed group:

1. Add your other tracks to the group by selecting the group you created in each channel strip's individual Group menus.

Adjusting Grouped Parameters

Once you have grouped your tracks and decided which parameters the group will control, a change to one channel in the group will affect every channel. Below, we will adjust the volume of our group:

1. Click and drag on the Volume fader of one of the tracks in your group. You will see all the other grouped tracks move up or down with your mouse movements. Even if your tracks are at different volume levels, they maintain their relative volume as you increase or decrease their gain.

Panning Your Audio

One of the tried and true ways to give each audio signal its own space and depth is to place it in a unique spot in the stereo field, or stereo panorama. Adjusting the stereo position of a channel strip in the stereo panorama is known as panning the track. Panning in Logic couldn't be easier.

1 Click and drag on the panner of a track in the Mixer. You will hear the sound move to the left or right depending on the direction you move the panner.

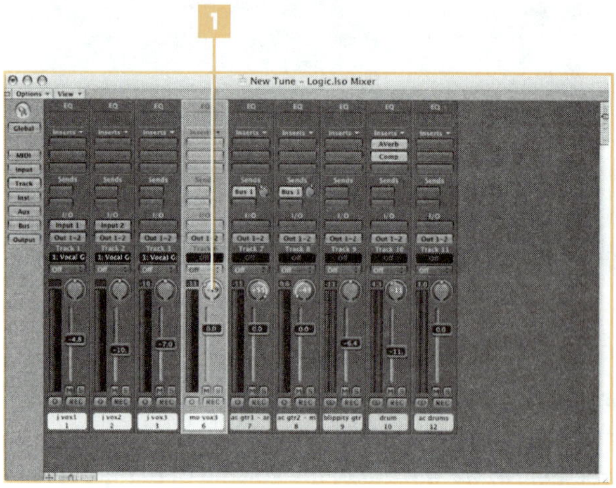

Return to Center

You can quickly return a panned track to the center of the stereo field by OPTION + clicking in the center of the pan knob.

2 Panning a track that competes with another in volume or frequency can help open up a mix. Here a guitar track is moved to the opposite side of the vocal we moved previously.

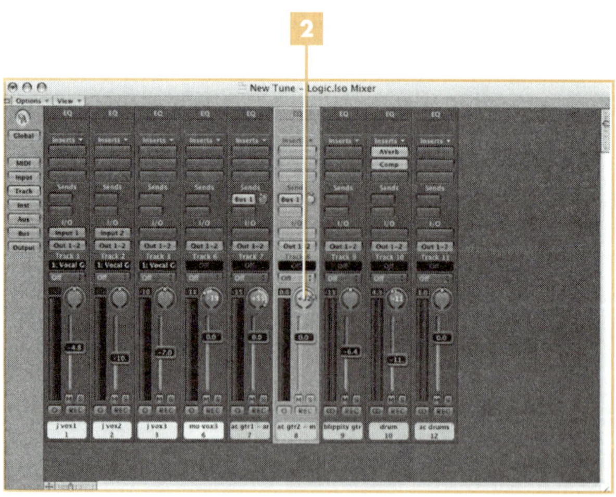

Can I Pan a Stereo Channel?

If a channel strip is a stereo channel, you can still adjust its pan knob. You won't actually be repositioning the signal in the stereo field, but you will be putting more volume emphasis on one side of the signal.

Adjusting the Volume of Your Track

Perhaps the single most common—and important—action in mixing is to adjust the volumes of your tracks so that the sounds you want to stand out are louder than the sounds you want in the background. Anyone familiar with sliding a fader on a mixer will be familiar with how to adjust the volume on a channel strip in Logic.

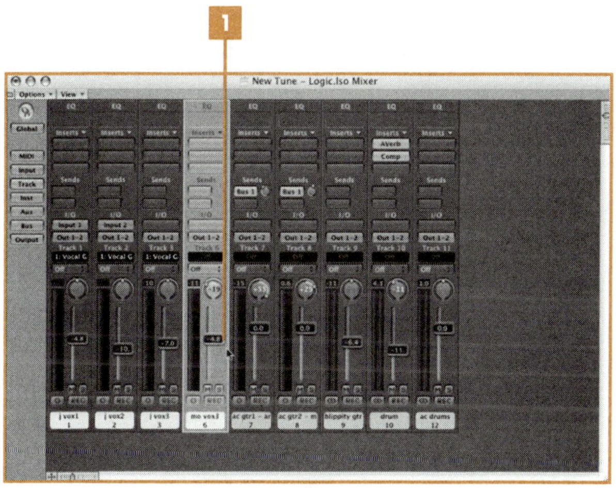

1 Click and drag on the fader of a track in the Mixer. You will hear the sound get louder as you move the fader up or softer as it travels down.

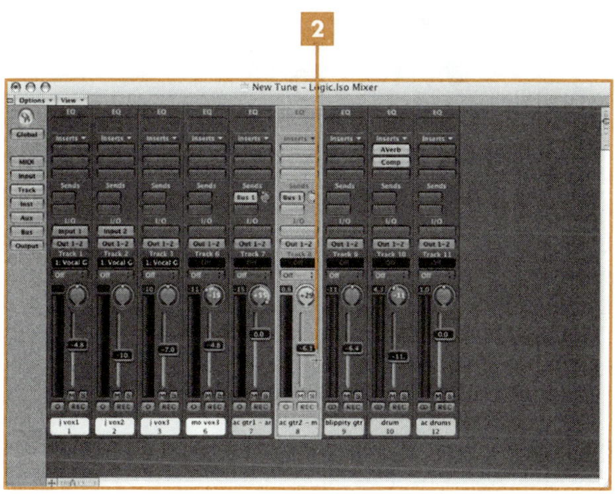

2 Adjusting the volume of other tracks helps place each element of a mix in its own sonic place.

Return to Zero

You can quickly return the volume fader to 0dB by OPTION + clicking anywhere on the volume fader.

Using an Aux Object as a "Master Fader" for a Sub-Group of Channels

We'll end this chapter on using Logic to mix by introducing one of the more advanced, but useful, ways to use Auxiliary Objects (which you've used previously as Multi-Channel Instrument outputs in Chapter 8). Many hardware mixers include things called "sub-groups." Sub-group channels on a mixer act as a "Master Fader," allowing you to "gang" a bunch of tracks together to use the same Inserts, Sends, and so on. This is especially useful for drums and other groups of instruments for which you want the same Insert effect to process every track, and perhaps send the same amount of all the tracks to a Send effect, and so on. In Logic, you can achieve this by creating an Aux Object in your Mixer and then bussing the channels you want in your sub-group to that Aux.

First, you'll need to create an Auxiliary Object and set its input to a bus.

1 **Press** the **Global** button to show all your objects in the mixer. Scroll to the Aux tracks.

2 OPTION + double-click on the background of an Aux track to add it to the Arrange window.

3 Press the Global button to turn off Global view and return to just the tracks and your newly created Aux.

With your Auxiliary Object created and in your Track Mixer, you'll need to send all the channel strips you want to your bus.

4 Set the output of the audio track to the Bus input of the Aux track.

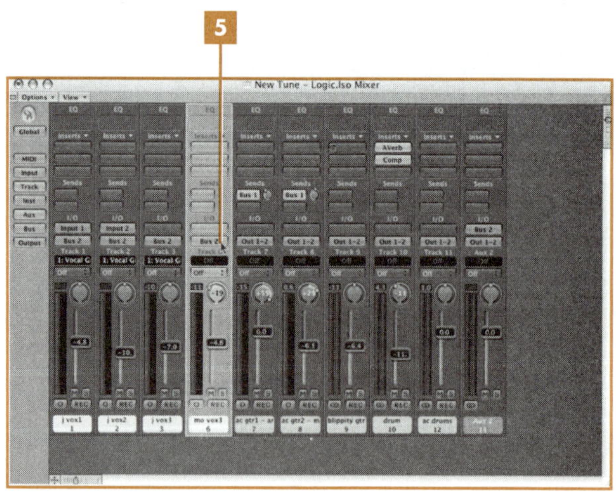

5 Set the outputs of as many tracks as you want to send to the Aux.

Finally, you'll want to set your bus to No Output so it serves only as a patchbay to your Aux and not as an audio destination.

6. Press Global one more time and scroll to the Bus object. Set the output of the bus routed to the Aux object to No Output.

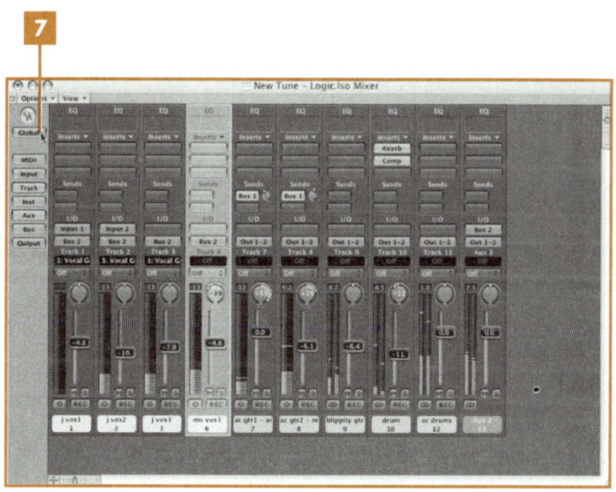

7. Press Global to return to the tracks and Aux view and play your tracks through the Aux object!

12 Finishing Your Project

When your song is recorded, edited, and mixed, there's only one more step—sharing it with the world! Logic lets you do this a number of ways. You can save (or "bounce") a stereo audio file that includes all the elements of your song. You can save a fully uncompressed audio file for later CD mastering, or you can save an MP3 or AAC compressed version of your song. You can even have the song automatically open up in iTunes for listening and transfer to your iPod! You can burn your Logic song directly to CD. Finally, if you intend to take your Logic tracks to a professional recording studio for further mixing and mastering, you can export every audio and Audio Instrument Track into a separate audio file for easy transfer.

In this chapter, you will learn how to:

- Bounce an uncompressed audio file of your song
- Bounce an MP3 file of your song
- Bounce an AAC file of your song
- Burn your song to CD
- Set up iTunes to automatically transfer your song to your iPod
- Export all of your tracks as separate audio files

Bouncing Your Project

In most audio applications, saving a complete mixdown of your entire song is called bouncing. This name harkens back to the days in which a stereo "master tape" was recorded by literally "bouncing" the audio from one tape machine to another. These days, the process is far more automatic, but the term bouncing has stuck.

Logic lets you bounce your song into four different file formats and media: PCM (uncompressed audio), MP3, AAC, or CD. You can choose to bounce to one of these formats or to any combination of them at once. How to configure your bounce varies for each format, however.

Do I Have to Bounce the Whole Song?

No! If you want to bounce just a short section of the song, you can set the Cycle bar to cover the section you want to bounce, and only that portion of your song will be bounced. And you don't have to include absolutely everything in your bounce if you don't want to, either. You can solo only those tracks you want to include, and/or mute those tracks you don't want to include.

Bouncing to PCM Audio

Pulse Code Modulation, or PCM, is the most common method of storing digital audio data. All the standard uncompressed audio file formats you're used to seeing are encoded in PCM format. This is the most common kind of bounce if you want to archive your mix, save it for burning onto a CD later, or ready it for a CD mastering session. Uncompressed audio will always result in the best sound quality.

1 Press the BNCE button on your Output object in the Track Mixer.

Other Methods to Start Your Bounce

Pressing the 'BNCE' button on the Output channel strip isn't the only way to start bouncing your song. You can also use the Bounce menu command by selecting File > Bounce. Another way to bring up the bounce dialog is to press the Rec-Enable button on the Arrange track of your Output object.

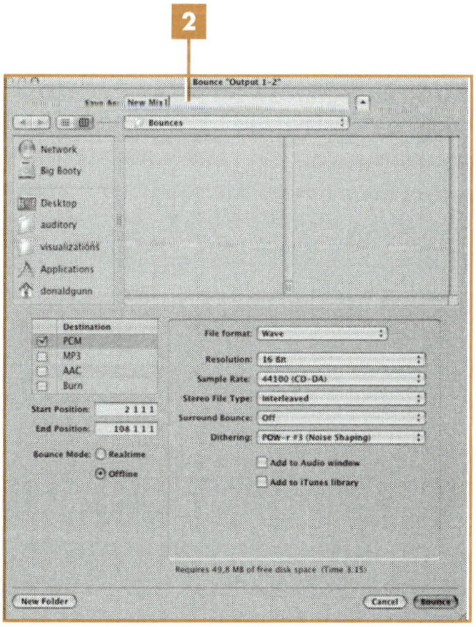

2 The Bounce window gives you a number of options to choose from. First, give your new mix a name.

3 Choose PCM as your destination file type.

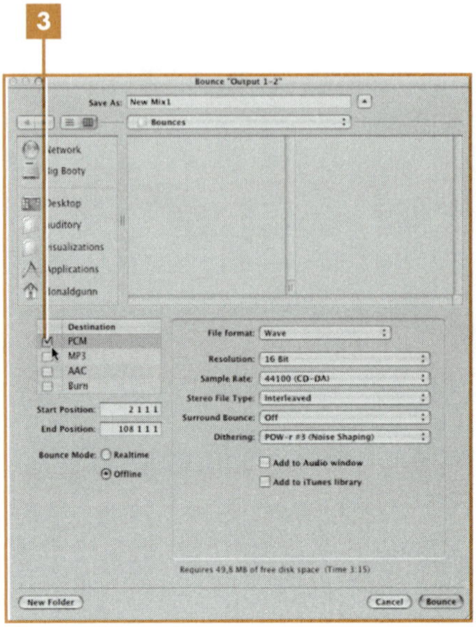

4 Select Realtime or Offline for the Bounce mode. With the Realtime option, you will hear your mix play back as it bounces, while Offline is a faster than real-time bounce with no audio monitoring.

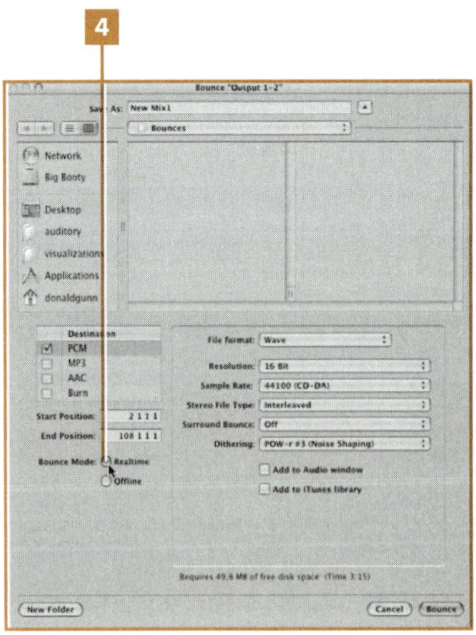

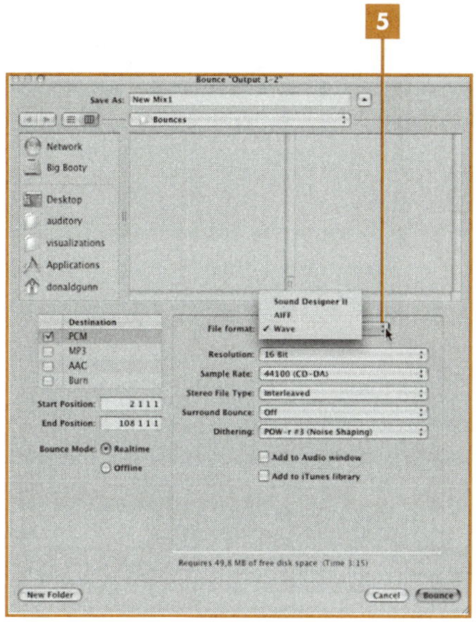

5 **Select the File format for your bounced file.**

Which File Format Should I Choose?

Logic lets you bounce your song in all of the most common file formats: Apple Interchange File Format (AIFF), Broadcast Wave (WAV), and Sound Designer II (SD2). The sound quality of all the formats is identical—the only difference is technical. Which should you choose? Well, that depends on how you intend to use your bounced audio. If you're going to compile a number of songs into a CD, any format will do. If you're going to exchange files with someone who has a specific requirement (such as their application can only accept WAV files), use that format. If you will be importing your audio into a program that can read the time stamps of Broadcast Wave files, such as Pro Tools, use WAV format. If you are going to use your files on a PC, we'd recommend using WAV format, which is the native PC format. And, of course, if in doubt, you can always make multiple bounces in different formats!

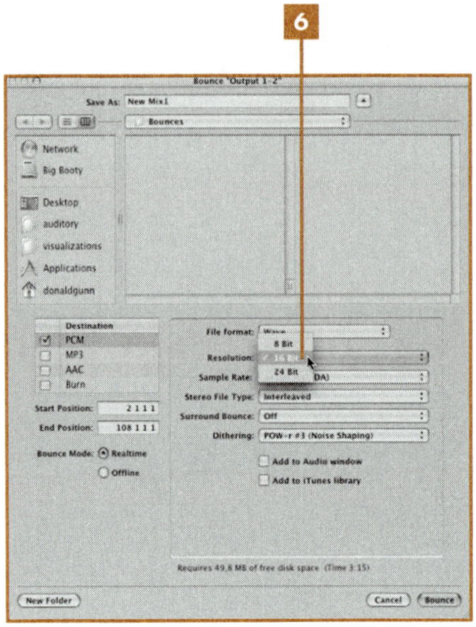

6 Choose the Resolution for your bounced file. 16-bit is the standard for CD-audio, and 24-bit is the standard for files you will deliver to a professional mastering engineer.

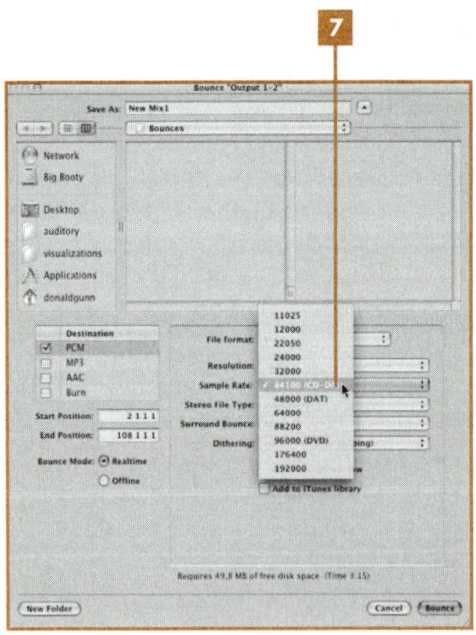

7 Choose the Sample Rate for your bounced file.

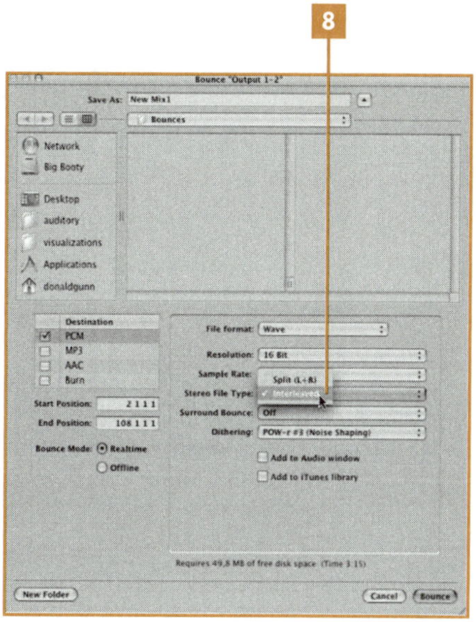

8 Choose the Stereo File Type for your bounced file. The Split (L+R) option creates two files, one for each channel of the stereo file, while Interleaved creates one file with both Left and Right channels in the same file.

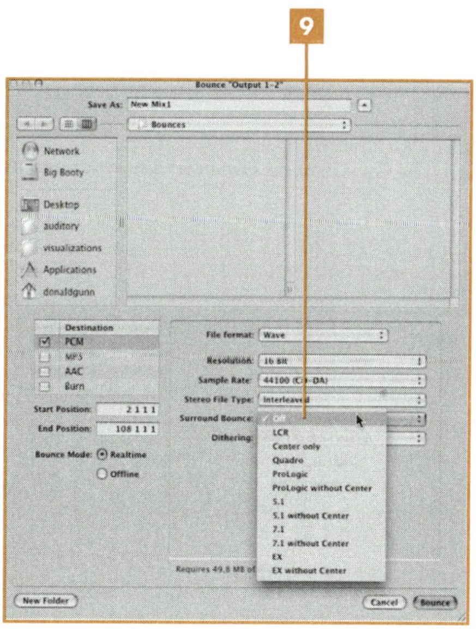

9 If you were mixing a Surround project, this is where you would select the Surround Bounce format.

10 **Choose** the format of **Dithering**. See the "Do I Need to Dither?" sidebar in the **Burn a CD** subsection later in this chapter for more information.

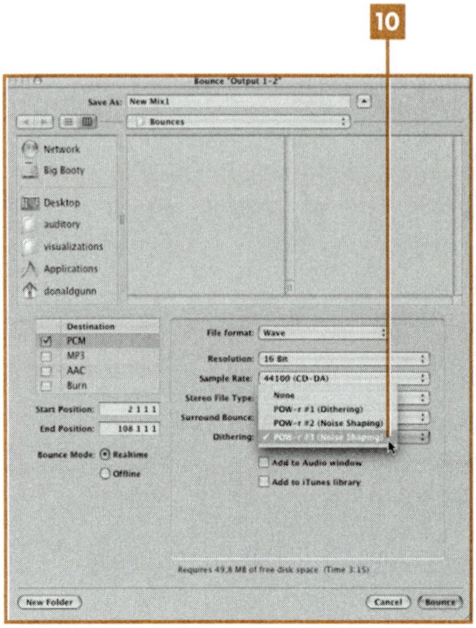

11 You can **choose** to **Add to Audio window** or **Add to iTunes library**.

12 **Press** the **Bounce** button to start the bounce process.

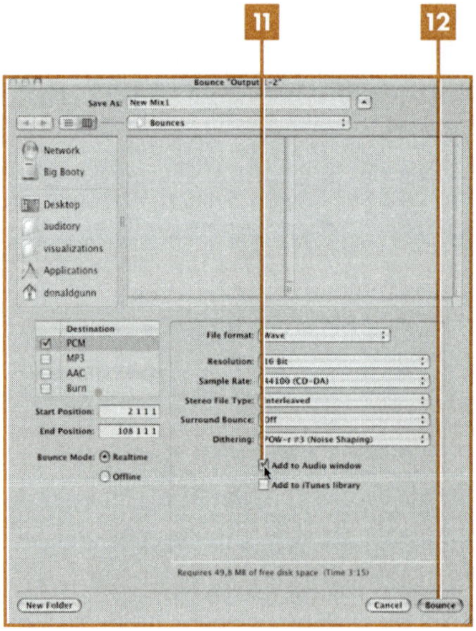

13

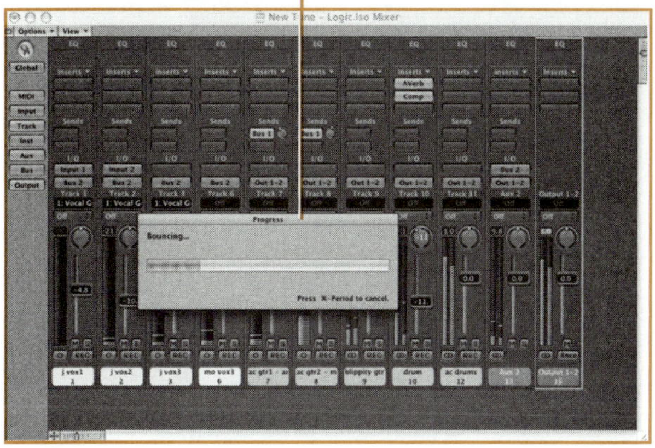

13 The Bouncing progress window will provide feedback on the bounce duration.

Bouncing to MP3

MPEG-3, or MP3, is the most popular compressed audio format. Every media player on both Mac and PC and every handheld media player can play MP3 files. The files are smaller than uncompressed files, so they are far more portable for sharing over the Internet or media players. MP3 is a "lossy" compression format, meaning that in the compression process, some audio information will be thrown away in order to reduce the file size. However, MP3 is definitely "good enough" to share with most people. Logic makes bouncing to MP3 very easy, and it even lets you input ID3 text tags to identify your MP3!

1

1 Press the BNCE button on your Output object in the Track Mixer.

2 Name your bounced file in the Save As field.

3 Choose MP3 as your file Destination.

4 Choose the Bounce Mode.

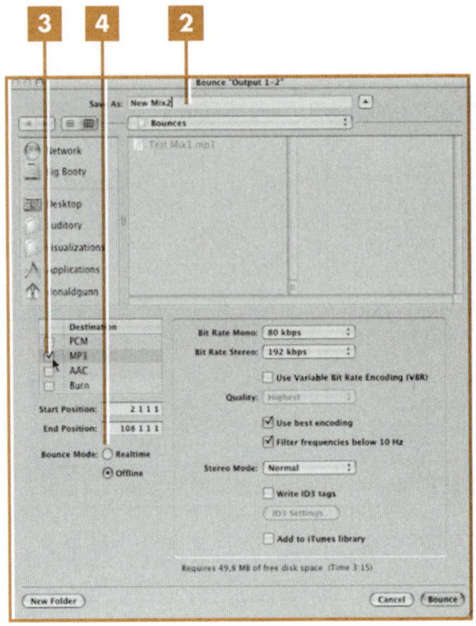

5 Choose the Bit Rate.

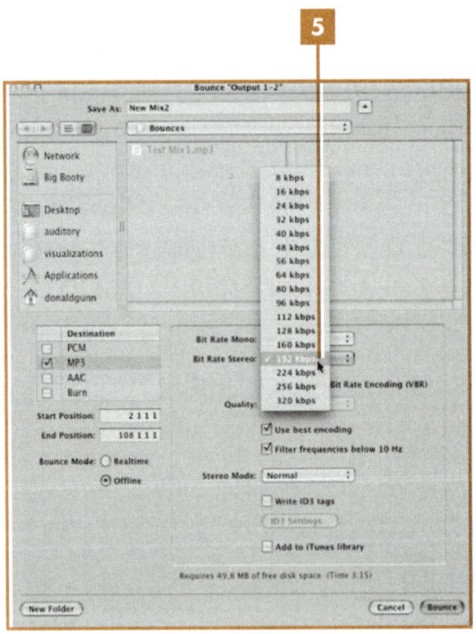

What Bit Rate Should I Choose?

Choosing the right bit rate for your MP3 is a compromise between quality and file size. A low bit rate, such as 128kbps, will result in a smaller file at the expense of sound quality. This is often chosen when the MP3 file is destined to be shared over the Internet, in which case file size is most important. A high bit rate, such as 256kbps, will result in higher quality and a very large file. This is often chosen for MP3 files for personal use, when a small file size isn't as vital. In general, our preferred bit rate is 192kbps. This rate offers good audio quality, and the file size, though significantly larger than 128kbps, is still manageable.

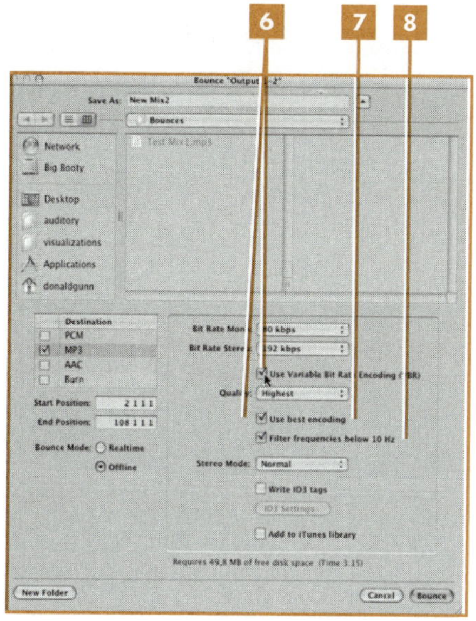

6 You can also choose Use Variable Bit Rate Encoding (VBR). This adjusts the bit rate throughout the mix based on the harmonic complexity of the material.

7 Use Best Encoding will give you the highest possible quality at the chosen bit rate.

8 Filter frequencies below 10Hz allows the MP3 encoder to work more efficiently by eliminating subsonic frequencies.

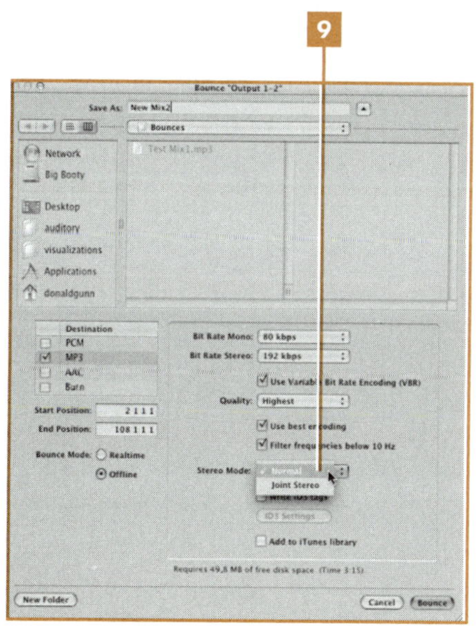

9 Select the Stereo Mode.

10 Check Write ID3 Tags.

11 Press the ID3 Settings button.

12 In the ID3 Settings window, double-click in a Content field to add your settings.

13 Press OK when you are done.

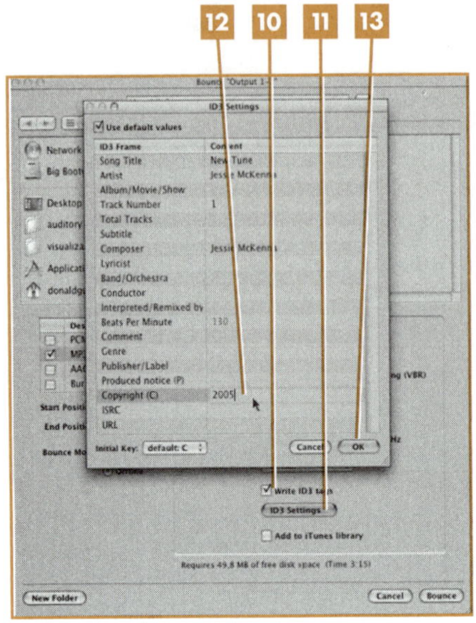

14 Check Add to iTunes library if you want your MP3 added.

15 Press Bounce to start the bouncing process.

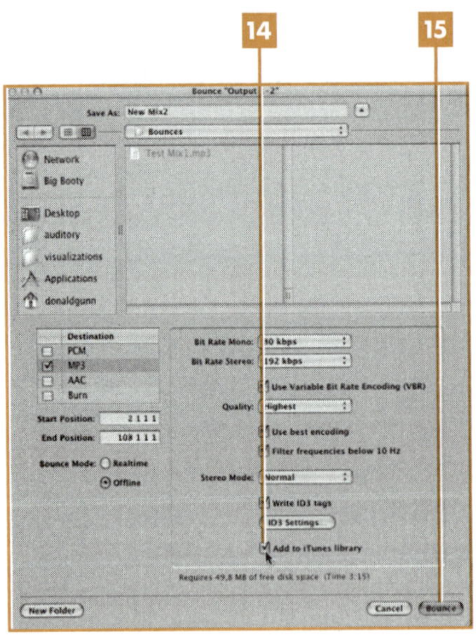

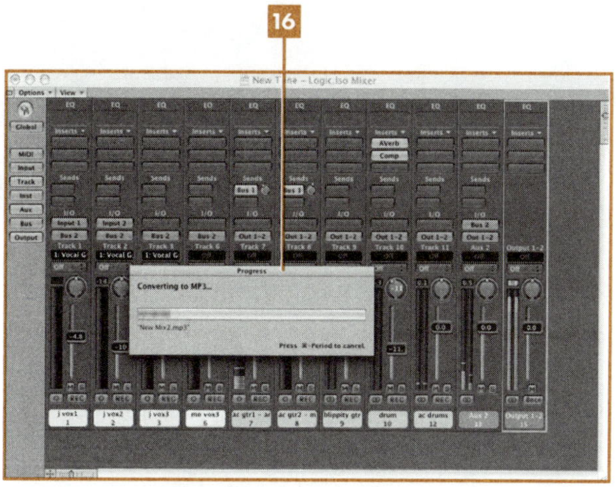

16 Once the bounce has played through, you will see a Progress window as Logic converts to MP3.

Bouncing to AAC

AAC, or Advance Audio Coding, is the next generation of MP3—literally, because AAC is based on the MPEG-4 audio compression codec. This audio format is not quite as universal as MP3, but thanks to Apple's adoption of AAC for the iTunes Music Store, you can play AAC files on most PC- and Mac-based media players... and of course your iPod! If you are sharing your music with people who use iTunes as their main music player, or you want to play it on your iPod, AAC will give you better results than MP3.

1 Press the BNCE button on your Output object in the Track Mixer.

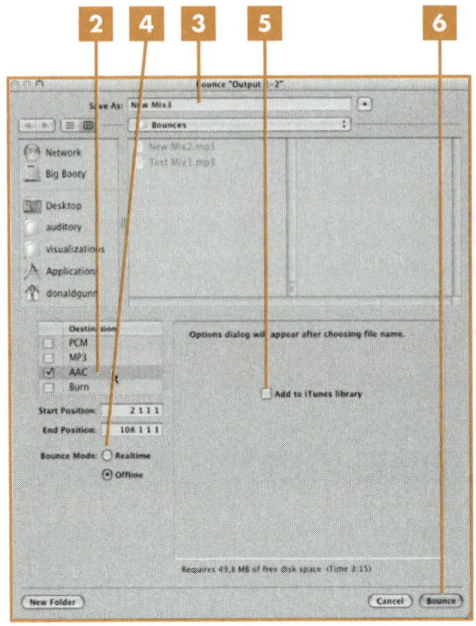

2 Select AAC as your file Destination.

3 Name your bounced file in the Save As field.

4 Select the Bounce Mode.

5 Select Add to iTunes library if you want the new file added.

6 Press Bounce.

ID3 Tags for AAC Files

AAC files can have ID tags just like MP3 files. If you want to add ID tags to your AAC file before you bounce it, you'll need to click into the MP3 Destination section discussed in the previous sub-section, but do not check the selection box for MP3 Bounce (unless of course you want to bounce AAC and MP3 files). Once in the MP3 tab, follow steps 10–13 from the previous sub-section. Then click back into the AAC bounce destination tab.

Note that if you are bouncing both an MP3 and an AAC file, both will have the same ID3 tags.

7 The AAC Sound Settings window will open. Here you can choose the Sample Rate, Size (bit depth), and whether the file will be Mono or Stereo.

8 Press Options for additional parameters.

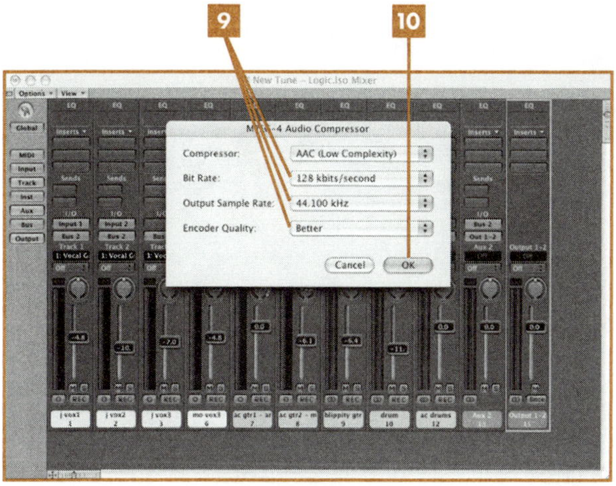

9 Here you can set the parameters of the MPEG-4 Compressor as it writes the AAC file. Choose the Bit Rate, Output Sample Rate, and Encoder Quality.

10 Press OK to return to the Sound Settings window.

What Bit Rate Should I Choose?

As with MP3, choosing the right bit rate for your MP3 is a compromise between quality and file size. As a general rule, we've found that an AAC file sounds similar to an MP3 at the next highest bit rate. In other words, a 128kbps AAC file would sound similar to a 164kbps MP3 file, and so on. We told you our preferred bit rate for MP3 is 192kbps, which you can approximate with a 164kbps AAC file. On the other hand, if file size isn't a problem, you can use a 192kbps AAC file, which will sound even better than an MP3 file at that bit rate.

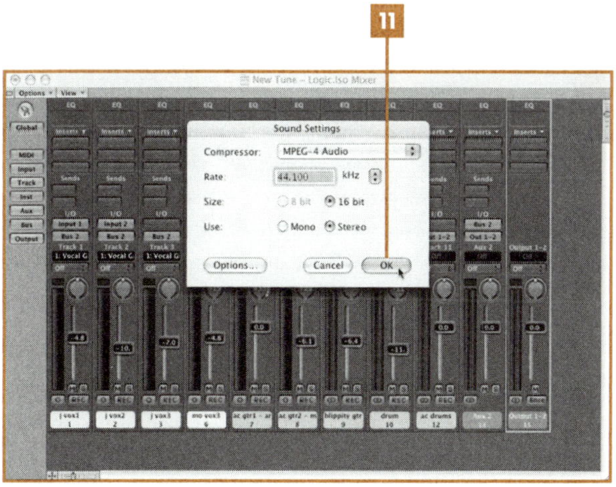

11 Press OK to start the bounce process.

12 Once the bounce has played through, you will see a Progress window as Logic converts to AAC.

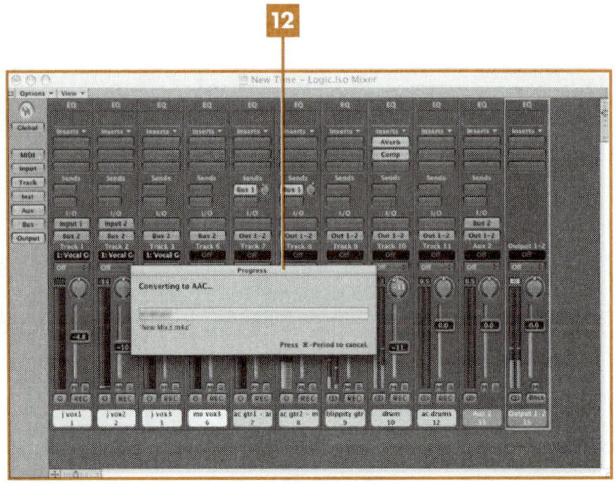

Burn to CD

Finally, Logic will burn your mix onto a CD that will play in any CD player. Obviously, you need to have a drive capable of recording CDs for this to work.

Burn CD in Logic Pro versus Waveburner Pro

If you are a Logic Pro user, another application included in the Logic Pro 7 Install DVD is a professional CD mastering application called Waveburner Pro. Why does Logic Pro 7 come with Waveburner Pro even though Logic can burn CDs itself? Because the CD burning functionality in Logic allows you to burn the current song onto a CD, nothing more. Waveburner Pro is designed for sequencing many songs into a single burnable program, printing out industry standard PQ code for glass mastering of mass manufactured CDs, and so on. In other words, if you're a professional mastering engineer, you'll use Waveburner Pro to deliver CDs to the manufacturing plant, but if you're a musician or running a project studio, you'll use Logic to burn a CD for your friends/bandmates/clients/pets to listen to.

1 Press the BNCE button on your Output object in the Track Mixer.

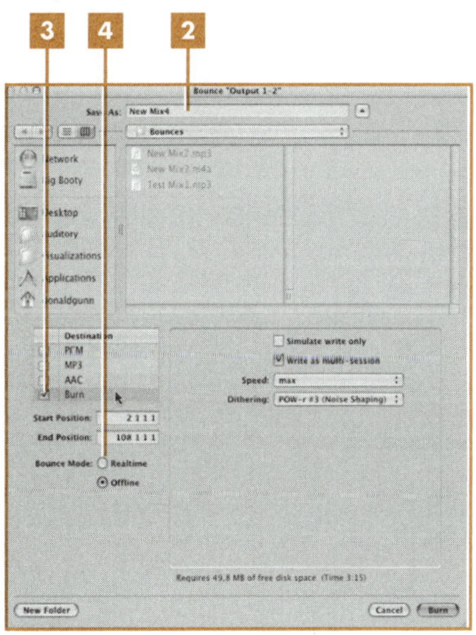

2 Name your bounced file in the Save As field.

3 Choose Burn as your file Destination.

4 Choose the Bounce Mode.

5 Check Simulate write only if you need to check your media or drive. (This is generally not something you need to do.)

6 Check Write as multi-session if you want to leave the CD session open to add more data, like your project files, later. Note that you won't be able to play the CD in an audio CD player until the disc is closed.

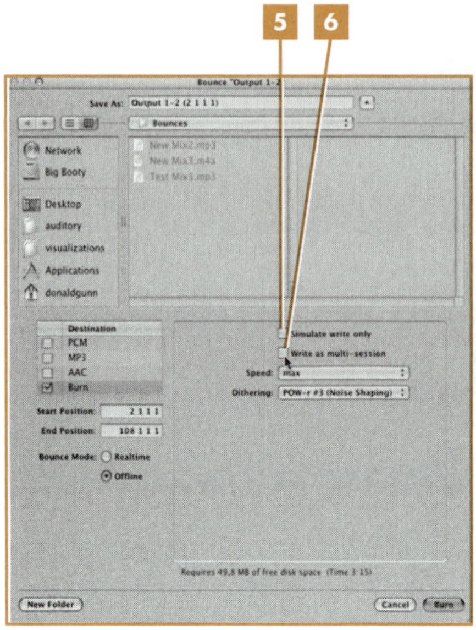

7 Select the Speed at which you want to burn the disc.

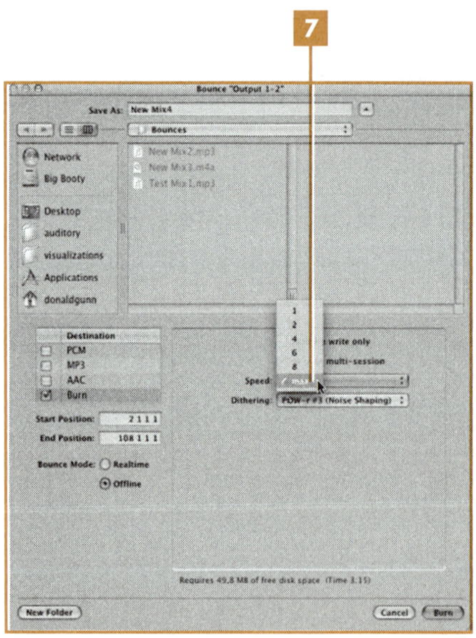

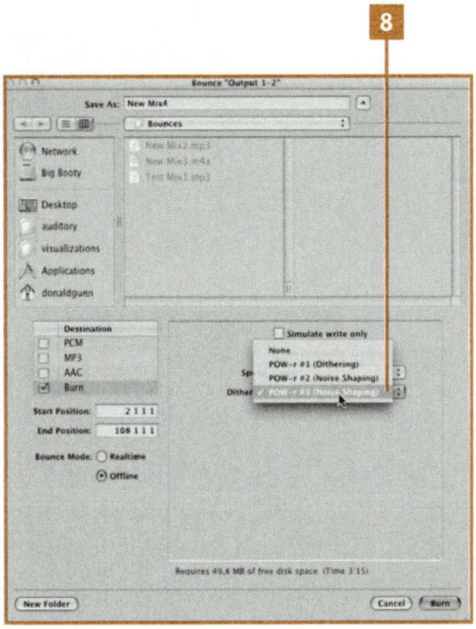

8 Choose the style of Dither to add to the bounce.

Do I Need to Dither?

If you have been recording your audio at 16-bit, you will not need to dither. However, if you have been recording 24-bit files, when you save 24-bit audio into a 16-bit file for CD, the 8 bits that don't make it to the 16-bit file are simply those that happen to be filling the lowest bits of the audio stream; unfortunately, sometimes you have desired audio in those bits. This is called truncating the audio, and this "truncation" can end up sounding harsh. Dithering adds imperceptible amounts and frequencies of noise to your file so that the noise "pushes" all the desired audio into the 16 bits that are saved, and only the noise is eliminated.

As you can imagine, not all dither is created equal. Logic includes the industry standard POW-r dithering algorithms. There are three algorithms—the first is plain, and the second and third have various amounts of "noise shaping" to attempt to tailor the dither even more to your audio material. Use the algorithm that sounds best with your material. In general, you may find that "type 3" is the most appropriate for modern pop and rock music.

9 Press the Burn button.

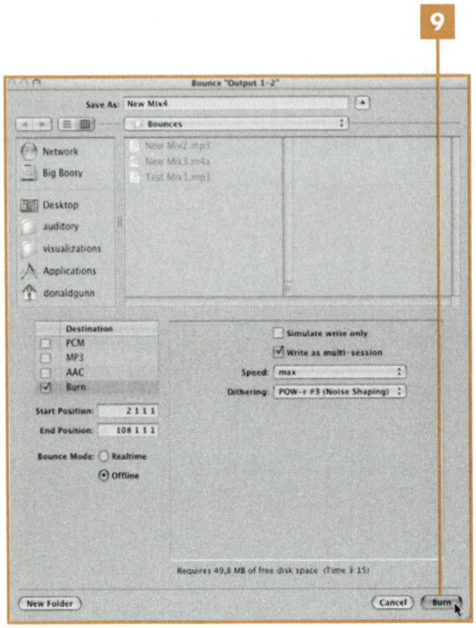

10 Logic will bounce the song and then prompt you to Please insert blank media. Insert a blank CD into your drive and press OK. Logic will then burn your CD!

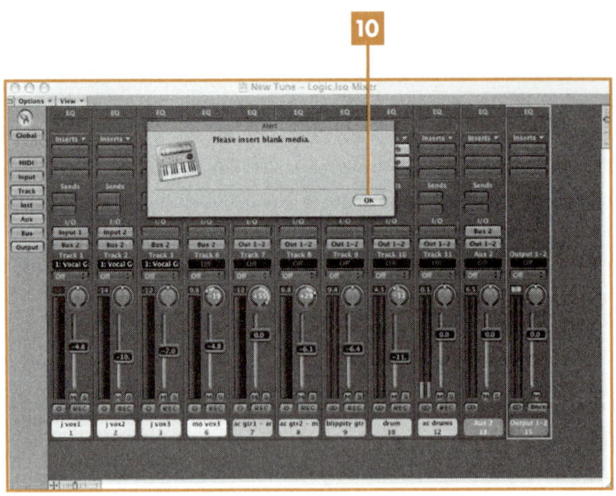

Transfering Your Bounced Song to Your iPod

As you saw in the previous section, from PCM, MP3, and AAC bounces, you can choose to send your bounced file directly to iTunes. Well, you can also configure iTunes to send the bounced song directly to your iPod!

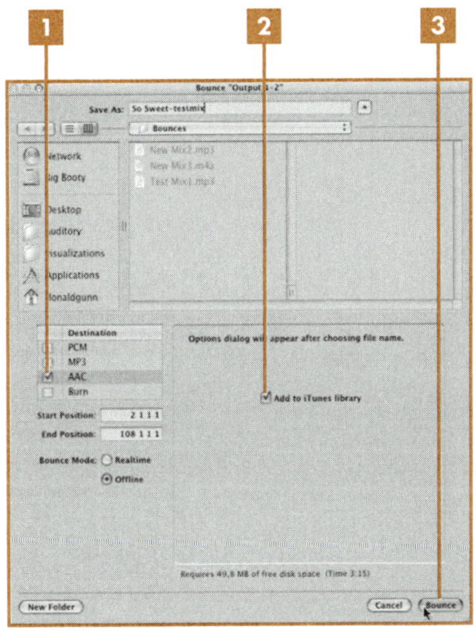

1. Bounce your mix with AAC as the Destination.
2. Check Add to iTunes library.
3. Press the Bounce button.

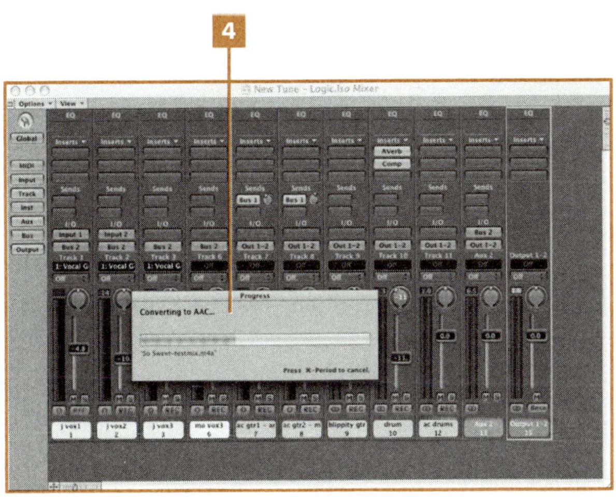

4. Logic will bounce the mix and then convert it to AAC.

5 iTunes will launch and your mix will be in a Logicsongs playlist.

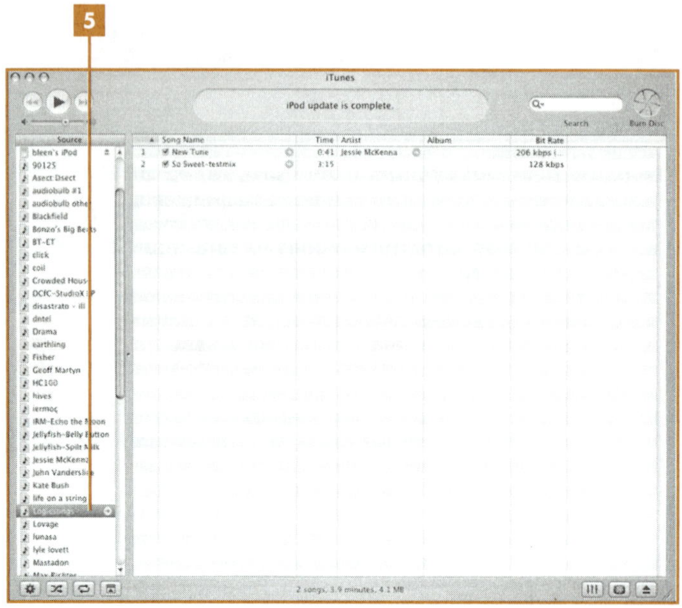

6 Go to iTunes > Preferences.

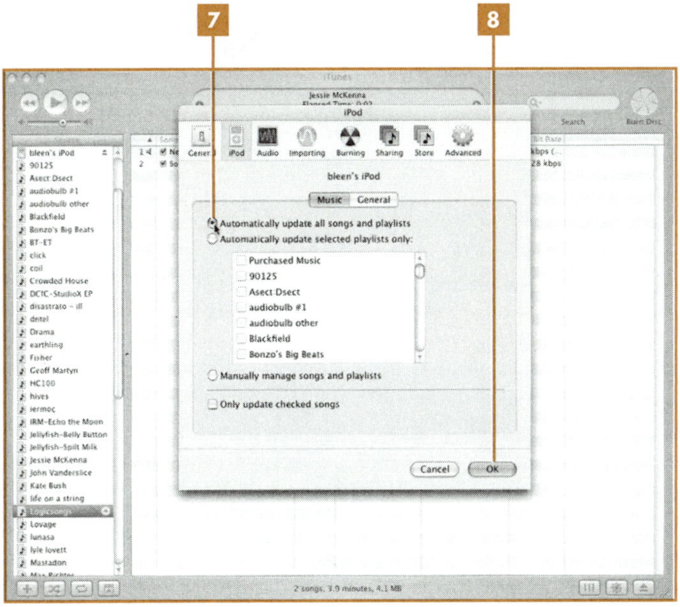

7 In the iPod preferences, select Automatically update all songs and playlists.

8 Click OK.

9 Go to File > Update Songs on (Your iPod's Name).

10 iTunes will now show your iPod being updated with the new files. After doing this the first time, the update should happen automatically.

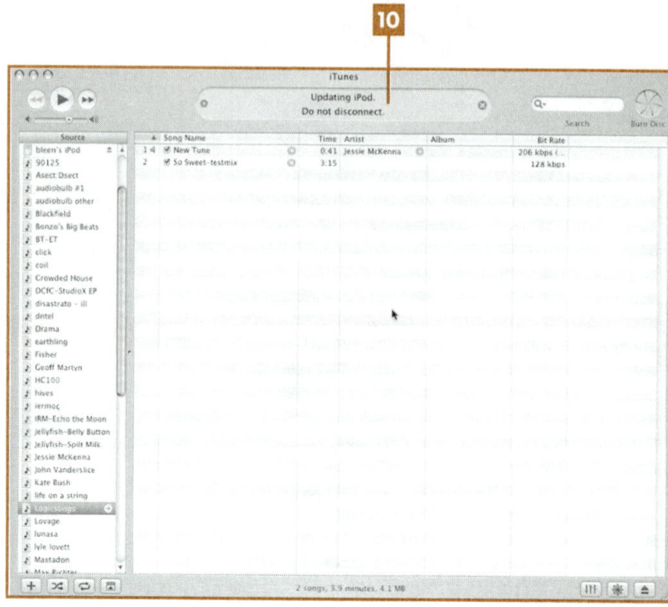

Exporting All Your Tracks

Sometimes when you're finished with your project in Logic, that doesn't mean you're finished with the entire song. You may want to take all your finished audio tracks to combine with other tracks in a professional studio, on your collaborator's system, etc. For these situations, Logic allows you to bounce all your audio and Audio Instrument Tracks into separate files, so you can use them in another system.

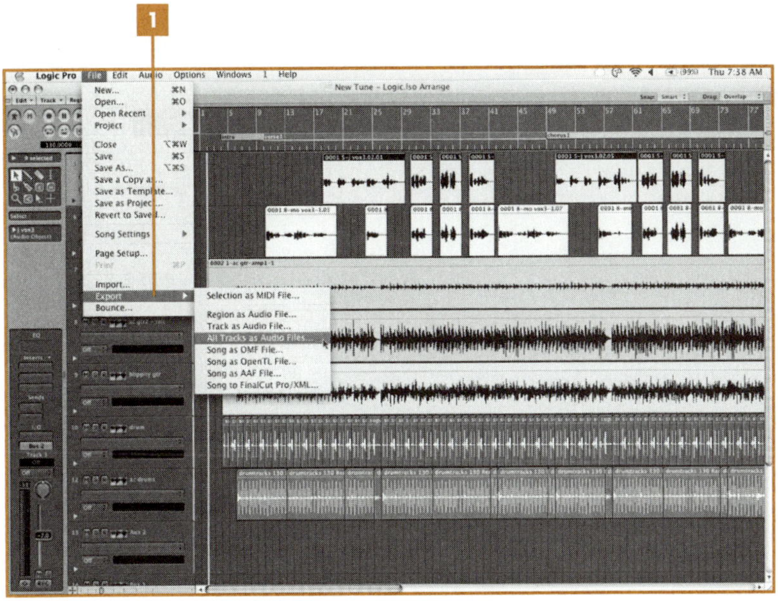

1. Go to File > Export > All Tracks as Audio Files.

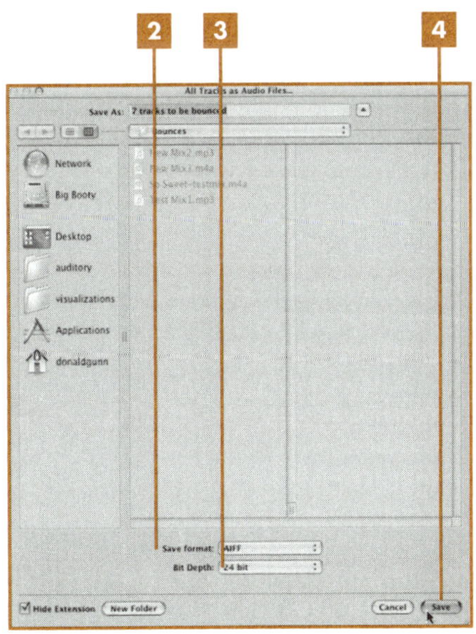

2. Choose the Save format for your files.
3. Choose the Bit Depth for your files.
4. Press Save to export your files.

What If I Don't Need Every Track?

The File > Export > All Tracks as Audio Files command bounces all currently unmuted tracks; in other words, if you want to export all your tracks except a few, you can mute those tracks you don't want. Likewise, if you only want to export a few tracks, you can solo only those tracks you wish to export.

Index

Please Note

For your convenience, you will find references in this index to bonus Chapter 13 and Appendixes A and B, which are on pages 329-366, and those bonus materials can be found on the companion Web site at http://www.courseptr.com/downloads.

B

C

D

E

F

J-K

L

M

P

Q

R

S

U

V

W

X-Z